Technology Manual

Elementary Statistics
Picturing the World

Beverly Dretzke • Kathleen McLaughlin
Dorothy Wakefield

THIRD EDITION

Larson • Farber

PEARSON

Prentice Hall

Upper Saddle River, New Jersey 07458

Editor-in-Chief: Sally Yagan
Aquisitions Editor: Petra Recter
Media Project Manager: Jacquelyn Riotto Zupic
Supplements Editor: Joanne Wendelken
Executive Managing Editor: Kathleen Schiaparelli
Assistant Managing Editor: Becca Richter
Production Editor: Donna Crilly
Manufacturing Buyer: Ilene Kahn
Supplement Cover Manager: TJS Concepts Inc.
Supplement Cover Designer: James Enering

© 2006 Pearson Education, Inc.
Pearson Prentice Hall
Pearson Education, Inc.
Upper Saddle River, NJ 07458

All rights reserved. No part of this book may be reproduced in any form or by any means, without permission in writing from the publisher.

Pearson Prentice Hall™ is a trademark of Pearson Education, Inc.

The author and publisher of this book have used their best efforts in preparing this book. These efforts include the development, research, and testing of the theories and programs to determine their effectiveness. The author and publisher make no warranty of any kind, expressed or implied, with regard to these programs or the documentation contained in this book. The author and publisher shall not be liable in any event for incidental or consequential damages in connection with, or arising out of, the furnishing, performance, or use of these programs.

This work is protected by United States copyright laws and is provided solely for teaching courses and assessing student learning. Dissemination or sale of any part of this work (including on the World Wide Web) will destroy the integrity of the work and is not permitted. The work and materials from it should never be made available except by instructors using the accompanying text in their classes. All recipients of this work are expected to abide by these restrictions and to honor the intended pedagogical purposes and the needs of other instructors who rely on these materials.

Printed in the United States of America

10 9 8 7 6 5 4 3 2

ISBN 0-13-148330-7

Pearson Education Ltd., *London*
Pearson Education Australia Pty. Ltd., *Sydney*
Pearson Education Singapore, Pte. Ltd.
Pearson Education North Asia Ltd., *Hong Kong*
Pearson Education Canada, Inc., *Toronto*
Pearson Educación de Mexico, S.A. de C.V.
Pearson Education—Japan, *Tokyo*
Pearson Education Malaysia, Pte. Ltd.

The Excel Manual

Beverly Dretzke

▼

Elementary Statistics

Picturing the World

Ron Larson
Betsy Farber

▸ Contents:

Getting Started with Microsoft Excel

Overview

This manual is intended as a companion to Larson and Farber's *Elementary Statistics, 3ʳᵈ ed.* It presents instructions on how to use Microsoft Excel to carry out selected examples and exercises from *Elementary Statistics, 3ʳᵈ ed.*

The first section of the manual contains an introduction to Microsoft Excel and how to perform basic operations such as entering data, using formulas, saving worksheets, retrieving worksheets, and printing. All the screens pictured in this manual were obtained using the Office 2003 version of Microsoft Excel on a PC. You may notice slight differences if you are using a different version or a different computer.

Getting Started with the User Interface

GS 1.1	The Mouse

The mouse is a pointer device that allows you to move around the Excel worksheet and to select specific locations and objects. There are four main mouse operations: Select, click, double-click, and right-click.

1. To **select** generally means to move the mouse pointer so that the white arrow is pointing at or is positioned directly over an object. You will often **select** commands in the standard toolbar located near the top of the screen. Some of the more familiar of these commands are open, save, and print.

2. To **click** means to press down on the left button of the mouse. You will frequently select cells of the worksheet and commands by "clicking" the left button.

3. To **double-click** means to press the left mouse button twice in rapid succession.

© 2006 Pearson Education, Inc., Upper Saddle River, NJ. All rights reserved. This material is protected under all copyright laws as they currently exist. No portion of this material may be reproduced, in any form or by any means, without permission in writing from the publisher.

4. To **right-click** means to press down on the right button of the mouse. A right-click is often used to display special shortcut menus.

| GS 1.2 | The Excel Worksheet |

The figure shown below presents a blank Excel worksheet. Important parts of the worksheet are labeled.

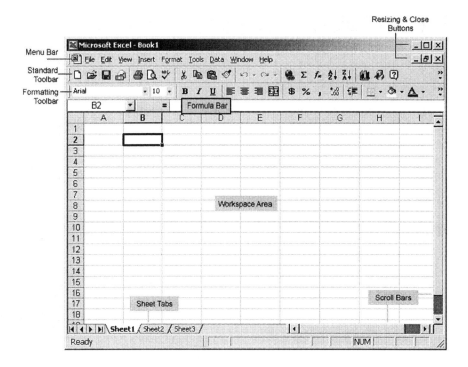

| GS 1.3 | Menu Conventions |

Excel uses standard conventions for all menus. For example, the Menu bar contains the commands File, Edit, View, etc. Selecting one of these commands will "drop down" a menu. The Edit menu is displayed at the top of the next page.

© 2006 Pearson Education, Inc., Upper Saddle River, NJ. All rights reserved. This material is protected under all copyright laws as they currently exist. No portion of this material may be reproduced, in any form or by any means, without permission in writing from the publisher.

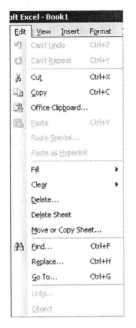

Icons to the left of the Cut, Copy, Paste, and Find commands indicate toolbar buttons that are equivalent to the menu choices.

Keyboard shortcuts are displayed to the right of the commands. For example, Ctrl+X is a keyboard shortcut for Cut.

The triangular markers to the right of Fill and Clear indicate that selection of these commands will result in a second menu of choices.

Selection of commands that are followed by an ellipsis (e.g., Paste Special... and Delete...) will result in the display of a dialog box that usually must be responded to in some way in order for the command to be executed.

The menus found in other locations of the Excel worksheet will operate in the same way.

GS 1.4	Dialog Boxes

Many of the statistical analysis procedures that are presented in this manual are associated with commands that are followed by dialog boxes. Dialog boxes usually require that you select from alternatives that are presented or that you enter your choices.

For example, if you select **Insert→Function**, a dialog box like the one shown at the top of the next page will appear. You make your function category and function name selections by clicking on them. If you want to find out what functions are available, you can type in a brief description of what you would like to do and then click the Go button.

© 2006 Pearson Education, Inc., Upper Saddle River, NJ. All rights reserved. This material is protected under all copyright laws as they currently exist. No portion of this material may be reproduced, in any form or by any means, without permission in writing from the publisher.

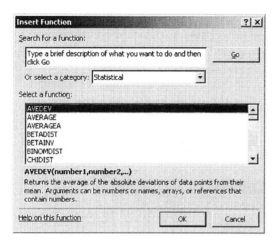

When you click the OK button at the bottom of the dialog box, another dialog box will often be displayed that asks you to provide information regarding location of the data in the Excel worksheet

Getting Started with Opening Files

GS 2.1	Opening a New Workbook

When you start Excel, the screen will open to **Sheet 1** of **Book 1**. Sheet names appear on tabs at the bottom of the screen. The name "Book 1" will appear in the top left corner.

If you are already working in Excel and have finished the analyses for one problem and would like to open a new book for another problem, follow these steps: First, at the top of the screen, click **File→New**. Next, click **New blank workbook** on the right side of the screen. If you were previously working in Book1, the new worksheet will be given the default name Book 2.

The names of books opened during an Excel work session will be displayed at the bottom of the Window menu. To return to one of these books, click **Window** and then click the book name.

© 2006 Pearson Education, Inc., Upper Saddle River, NJ. All rights reserved. This material is protected under all copyright laws as they currently exist. No portion of this material may be reproduced, in any form or by any means, without permission in writing from the publisher.

GS 2.2	Opening a File That Has Already Been Created

To open a file that you or someone else has already created, click on **File→Open**. A list of file locations will appear. Select the location by clicking on it. Many of the data files that are presented in your statistics textbook are available on the CD that accompanies this manual. To open any of these files, you will select **Compact Disc**.

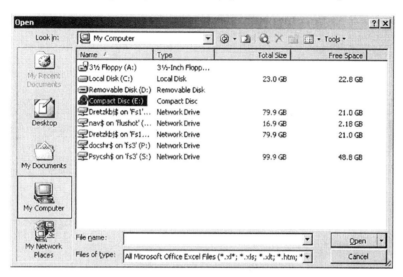

After you click on Compact Disc, a list of folders and files available on the CD will appear. You will need to select the folder or file you want by clicking on it. If you have selected a folder, another screen will appear with a list of files contained in the folder. Click on the name of the file that you would like to open.

Getting Started with Entering Information

GS 3.1	Cell Addresses

Columns of the worksheet are identified by letters of the alphabet and rows are identified by numbers. The cell address A1 refers to the cell located in column A row 1. The dark outline around a cell means that it is "active" and is ready to receive information. In the figure shown at the top of the next page, cell C1 is ready to receive information. You can also see C1 in the **Name Box** to the left of the **Formula Bar**. You can move to different

© 2006 Pearson Education, Inc., Upper Saddle River, NJ. All rights reserved. This material is protected under all copyright laws as they currently exist. No portion of this material may be reproduced, in any form or by any means, without permission in writing from the publisher.

cells of the worksheet by using the mouse pointer and clicking on a cell. You can also press [**Tab**] to move to the right or left, or you can use the arrow keys on the keyboard.

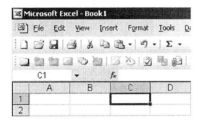

You can also activate a **range** of cells. To activate a range of cells, first click in the top cell and drag down and across (or click in the bottom cell and drag up and across). The range of cells highlighted in the figure below is designated B2:D4.

GS 3.2   Types of Information

Three types of information may be entered into an Excel worksheet.

1. **Text**. The term "text" refers to alphabetic characters or a combination of alphabetic characters and numbers, sometimes called "alphanumeric." The figure provides an example of an entry comprised solely of alphabetic characters (cell A1) and an entry comprised of a combination of alphabetic characters and numbers (cell B1).

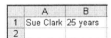

2. **Numeric**. Any cell entry comprised completely of numbers falls into the "numeric" category.

3. **Formulas**. Formulas are a convenient way to perform mathematical operations on numbers already entered into the worksheet. Specific instructions are provided in this manual for problems that require the use of formulas.

© 2006 Pearson Education, Inc., Upper Saddle River, NJ. All rights reserved. This material is protected under all copyright laws as they currently exist.
No portion of this material may be reproduced, in any form or by any means, without permission in writing from the publisher.

GS 3.3	Entering Information

To enter information into a cell of the worksheet, first activate the cell. Then key in the desired information and press [**Enter**]. Pressing the [Enter] key moves you down to the next cell in that column. The information shown below was entered as follows:

1. Click in cell A1. Key in **1**. Press [**Enter**].

2. Key in **2**. Press [**Enter**].

3. Key in **3**. Press [**Enter**].

	A	B
1	1	
2	2	
3	3	
4		
5		

GS 3.4	Using Formulas

When you want to enter a formula, begin the cell entry with an equal sign (=). The arithmetic operators are displayed below.

Arithmetic operator	Meaning	Example
+	Addition	3+2
-	Subtraction	3-2
*	Multiplication	3*2
/	Division	3/2
^	Exponentiation	3^2

Numbers, cell addresses, and functions can be used in formulas. For example, to sum the contents of cells A1 and B1, you can use the formula =A1+B1. To divide this sum by 2, you can use the formula =(A1+B1)/2. Note that Excel carries out expressions in parentheses first and then uses the results to complete the calculations of the formula.

© 2006 Pearson Education, Inc., Upper Saddle River, NJ. All rights reserved. This material is protected under all copyright laws as they currently exist. No portion of this material may be reproduced, in any form or by any means, without permission in writing from the publisher.

Formulas will sometimes not produce the desired results because parentheses were necessary but were not used.

Getting Started with Changing Information

GS 4.1	Editing Information in the Cells

There are several ways that you can edit information that has already been entered into a cell.

1. If you have not completed the entry, you can simply backspace and start over. Clicking on the red X to the left of the Formula Bar will also delete an incomplete cell entry.

2. If you have already completed the entry and another cell is activated, you can click in the cell you want to edit and then press either [**Delete**] or [**Backspace**] to clear the contents of the cell.

3. If you want to edit part of the information in a cell instead of deleting all of it, follow the instructions provided in the example.

    • Let's say that you wanted to enter 1234 in cell A1 but instead entered 124. Return to cell **A1** to make it the active cell by either clicking on it with the mouse or by using the arrow keys.

A1	▾		f_x 124
	A	B	C
1	124		
2			

    • You will see A1 in the Name Box and 124 in the Formula Bar. Click between 2 and 4 in the Formula Bar so that the **I-beam** is positioned there. Enter the number 3 and press [**Enter**].

GS 4.2	Copying Information

To copy the information in one cell to another cell, follow these steps:

© 2006 Pearson Education, Inc., Upper Saddle River, NJ. All rights reserved. This material is protected under all copyright laws as they currently exist. No portion of this material may be reproduced, in any form or by any means, without permission in writing from the publisher.

- First click on the source cell. Then, at the top of the screen, click **Edit→Copy**.

- Click on the target cell where you want the information to be placed. Then, at the top of the screen, click **Edit→Paste**.

To copy a range of cells to another location in the worksheet, follow these steps:

- First click and drag over the range of cells that you want to copy so that they are highlighted. Then, at the top of the screen, click **Edit→Copy**.

- Click in the topmost cell of the target location. Then, at the top of the screen, click **Edit→Paste**.

To copy the contents of one cell to a range of cells follow these steps:

- Let's say that you have entered a formula in cell C1 that adds the contents of cells A1 and B1 and you would like to copy this formula to cells C2 and C3 so that C2 will contain the sum of A2 and B2 and cell C3 will contain the sum of A3 and B3.

- First click in cell C1 to make it the active cell. You will see =A1+B1 in the Formula Bar.

C1	▼	f_x =A1+B1	
	A	B	C	D
1	1	1	2	
2	2	2		
3	3	3		

- At the top of the screen, click **Edit→Copy**.

- Highlight cells C2 and C3 by clicking and dragging over them.

C2	▼	f_x	
	A	B	C	D
1	1	1	2	
2	2	2		
3	3	3		

- At the top of the screen, click **Edit→Paste**. The sums should now be displayed in cells C2 and C3.

C2	▼	f_x =A2+B2	
	A	B	C	D
1	1	1	2	
2	2	2	4	
3	3	3	6	

© 2006 Pearson Education, Inc., Upper Saddle River, NJ. All rights reserved. This material is protected under all copyright laws as they currently exist. No portion of this material may be reproduced, in any form or by any means, without permission in writing from the publisher.

GS 4.3	Moving Information

If you would like to move the contents of one cell from one location to another in the worksheet, follow these steps:

- Click on the cell containing the information that you would like to move.

- At the top of the screen, click **Edit→Cut**.

- Click on the target cell where you want the information to be placed.

- At the top of the screen, click **Edit →Paste**.

If you would like to move the contents of a range of cells to a different location in the worksheet, follow these steps:

- Click and drag over the range of cells that you would like to move so that it is highlighted.

- At the top of the screen, click **Edit→Cut**.

- Click the topmost cell of the new location. (It is not necessary to click and drag over the entire range of the new location.)

- At the top of the screen, click **Edit→Paste**.

*If you make a mistake, just click **Edit→Undo**.*

GS 4.4	Changing the Column Width

There are a couple of different ways that you can use to change the column width. Only one way will be described here. Output from the Descriptive Statistics data analysis tool will be used as an example. As you can see in the output displayed at the top of the next page, many of the labels in column A can only be partially viewed because the default column width is too narrow.

© 2006 Pearson Education, Inc., Upper Saddle River, NJ. All rights reserved. This material is protected under all copyright laws as they currently exist. No portion of this material may be reproduced, in any form or by any means, without permission in writing from the publisher.

	A	B
1		*Test Score*
2		
3	Mean	82.82353
4	Standard E	2.328271
5	Median	85
6	Mode	88
7	Standard D	9.599709

Position the mouse pointer directly on the vertical line between A and B in the letter row at the top of the worksheet — A | B —so that it turns into a black plus sign.

Click and drag to the right until you can read all the output labels. (You can also click and drag to the left to make columns narrower.) After adjusting the column width, your output should appear similar to the output shown below.

	A	B
1		*Test Score*
2		
3	Mean	82.82353
4	Standard Error	2.328271
5	Median	85
6	Mode	88
7	Standard Deviation	9.599709

Getting Started with Sorting Information

GS 5.1	Sorting a Single Column of Information

Let's say that you have entered "Score" in cell A1 and four numbers directly below it and that you would like to sort the numbers in ascending order.

	A
1	Score
2	15
3	79
4	18
5	2

- Click and drag from cell A1 to cell A5 so that the range of cells is highlighted.

You could also click directly on A *in the letter row at the top of the worksheet. This will result in all cells of column A being highlighted.*

© 2006 Pearson Education, Inc., Upper Saddle River, NJ. All rights reserved. This material is protected under all copyright laws as they currently exist. No portion of this material may be reproduced, in any form or by any means, without permission in writing from the publisher.

- At the top of the screen, click **Data→Sort**.

- In the Sort dialog box that appears, you are given the choice of sorting the information in column A in either ascending or descending order. The ascending order has already been selected. Header row has also been selected. This means that the "Score" header will stay in cell A1 and will not be included in the sort. Click **OK** at the bottom of the dialog box.

The cells in column A should now be sorted in ascending order as shown below.

| GS 5.2 | Sorting Multiple Columns of Information |

Your Excel data files will frequently contain multiple columns of information. When you sort multiple columns at the same time, Excel provides a number of options.

© 2006 Pearson Education, Inc., Upper Saddle River, NJ. All rights reserved. This material is protected under all copyright laws as they currently exist. No portion of this material may be reproduced, in any form or by any means, without permission in writing from the publisher.

Let's say that you have a data file that contains the information shown below and that you would like to sort the file by GPA in descending order.

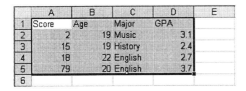

- Click and drag from A1 down and across to D5 so that the entire range of cells is highlighted.

- At the top of the screen, click **Data→Sort**.

- In the Sort dialog box that appears, you are given the option of sorting the data by three different variables. You want to sort only by GPA in descending order. Click the down arrow to the right of the Sort by window until you see GPA and click on **GPA** to select it. Then click the button to the left of **Descending** so that a black dot appears there. You want the variable labels to stay in row 1, so **Header row** should be selected. Click **OK**.

© 2006 Pearson Education, Inc., Upper Saddle River, NJ. All rights reserved. This material is protected under all copyright laws as they currently exist. No portion of this material may be reproduced, in any form or by any means, without permission in writing from the publisher.

The sorted data file is shown below.

	A	B	C	D
1	Score	Age	Major	GPA
2	79	20	English	3.7
3	2	19	Music	3.1
4	18	22	English	2.7
5	15	19	History	2.4

Getting Started with Saving Information

GS 6.1   Saving Files

To save a newly created file for the first time, click **File→Save** at the top of the screen. A Save As dialog box will appear. You will need to select the location for saving the file by clicking on it. In the dialog box shown below, the Local Disk (C:) has been selected.

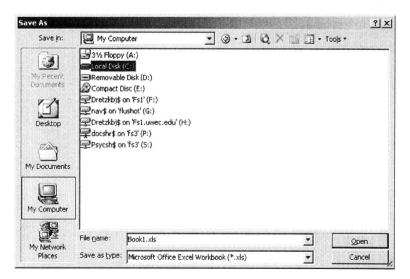

The default file name, displayed in the File name window, is **Book1.xls**. It is highly recommended you replace the default name with a name that is more descriptive. It is also highly recommended that you use the **xls** extension for all your Excel files.

Once you have saved a file, clicking **File→Save** will result in the file being saved in the same location under the same file name. No dialog box will appear. If you would like to save the file in a different location, you will need to click **File→Save As**.

© 2006 Pearson Education, Inc., Upper Saddle River, NJ. All rights reserved. This material is protected under all copyright laws as they currently exist. No portion of this material may be reproduced, in any form or by any means, without permission in writing from the publisher.

GS 6.2	Naming Files

Windows 2003 and Mac versions of Excel will allow file names to have around 200 characters. The extension can have up to three characters. You will find that long, descriptive names will be easier to work with than really short names. For example, if a file contains data that was collected in a survey of Milwaukee residents, you may want to name the file **Milwaukee survey.xls**.

Several symbols cannot be used in file names. These include: forward slash (/), backslash (\), greater-than sign (>), less-than sign (<), asterisk (*), question mark (?), quotation mark ("), pipe symbol (|), color (:), and semicolon (;).

Getting Started with Printing Information

GS 7.1	Printing Worksheets

To print a worksheet, click **File→Print**. The Print dialog box will appear.

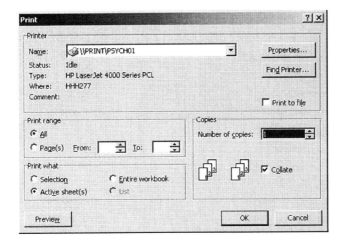

Under Print range, you will usually select **All**, and under Print what, you will usually select **Active sheet(s)**. The default number of copies is 1, but you can increase this if you need more copies. When the Print dialog box has been completed as you would like, click **OK**.

© 2006 Pearson Education, Inc., Upper Saddle River, NJ. All rights reserved. This material is protected under all copyright laws as they currently exist. No portion of this material may be reproduced, in any form or by any means, without permission in writing from the publisher.

GS 7.2	Page Setup

Excel provides a number of page setup options for printing worksheets. To access these options, click **File→Page Setup**. Under **Page**, you may want to select the Landscape orientation for worksheets that have several columns of data. Under **Sheet**, you may want to select Gridlines.

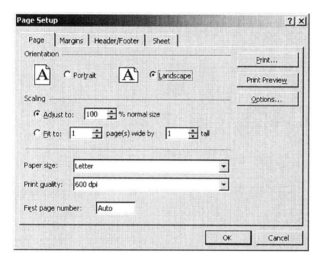

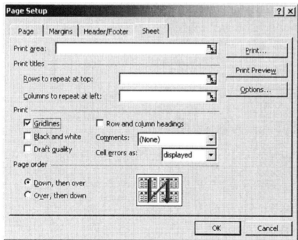

© 2006 Pearson Education, Inc., Upper Saddle River, NJ. All rights reserved. This material is protected under all copyright laws as they currently exist. No portion of this material may be reproduced, in any form or by any means, without permission in writing from the publisher.

Getting Started with Add-ins

GS 8.1	Loading Excel's Analysis Toolpak

The Analysis Tookpak is an Excel Add-In that may not necessarily be loaded. If it does not appear at the bottom of the Tools menu, then click on **Add-Ins** in the Tools menu to get the dialog box shown below.

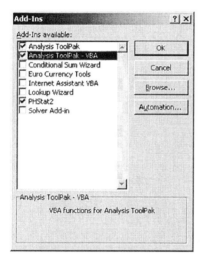

Click in the box to the left of **Analysis ToolPak** to place a checkmark there. Then click **OK**. The ToolPak will load and will be listed at the bottom of the Tools menu as shown at the top of the next page.

© 2006 Pearson Education, Inc., Upper Saddle River, NJ. All rights reserved. This material is protected under all copyright laws as they currently exist. No portion of this material may be reproduced, in any form or by any means, without permission in writing from the publisher.

GS 8.2

Loading the PHStat2 Add-In

PHStat2 is a Prentice Hall statistical add-in that is included on the CD-ROM that accompanies this Excel manual. The instructions that are given here also appear in the PHStat readme file.

To use the Prentice Hall PHStat2 Microsoft Excel add-in, you first need to run the setup program (Setup.exe) located in the PHStat2 folder on the CD-ROM. The setup program will install the PHStat2 program files to your system and add icons on your Desktop and Start Menu for PHStat2. Depending on the age of your Windows system files, some Windows system files may be updated during the setup process as well. Note that PHStat2 is compatible with Microsoft Excel 97, Microsoft Excel 2000, and Microsoft Excel 2003. PHStat2 is not compatible with Microsoft Excel 95.

During the Setup program you will have the opportunity to specify:

a. The directory into which to copy the PHStat2 files (default is \Program Files\Prentice Hall\PHStat2).

b. The name of the Start Programs folder to contain the PHStat2 icon.

© 2006 Pearson Education, Inc., Upper Saddle River, NJ. All rights reserved. This material is protected under all copyright laws as they currently exist. No portion of this material may be reproduced, in any form or by any means, without permission in writing from the publisher.

To begin using the Prentice Hall PHStat2 Microsoft Excel add-in, click the appropriate Start Menu or Desktop icon for PHStat2 that was added to your system during the setup process.

When a new, blank Excel worksheet appears, check the Tools menu to make sure that both the **Analysis ToolPak** and **Analysis ToolPak–VBA** have been checked.

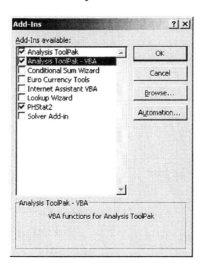

© 2006 Pearson Education, Inc., Upper Saddle River, NJ. All rights reserved. This material is protected under all copyright laws as they currently exist. No portion of this material may be reproduced, in any form or by any means, without permission in writing from the publisher.

Introduction to Statistics

CHAPTER

1

Technology

| ► Example (pg. 30) | Generating a List of Random Numbers |

You will be generating a list of 15 random numbers between 1 and 167 to use in selecting a random sample of 15 cars assembled at an auto plant.

If the PHStat2 add-in has not been loaded, you will need to load it before continuing. Follow the instructions in Section GS 8.2.

---

1. Open a new, blank Excel worksheet.

2. At the top of the screen, select **PHStat→Sampling→Random Sample Generation**.

3. Complete the Random Sample Generator dialog box as shown below. A sample of 15 cars will be randomly selected from a population of 167. The topmost cell in the output will contain the title "Car #." Click **OK**.

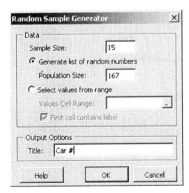

© 2006 Pearson Education, Inc., Upper Saddle River, NJ. All rights reserved. This material is protected under all copyright laws as they currently exist. No portion of this material may be reproduced, in any form or by any means, without permission in writing from the publisher.

The output is displayed in a new worksheet named "RandomNumbers." Because the numbers were generated randomly, it is not likely that your output will be exactly the same.

	A
1	Car #
2	121
3	67
4	35
5	115
6	29
7	134
8	138
9	45
10	20
11	34
12	43
13	84
14	18
15	33
16	90

◄

► Exercise 1 (pg. 31)	Generating a List of Random Numbers for a CPA

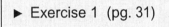

You will be generating a list of 8 random numbers between 1 and 74 to use in selecting a random sample of accounts. You will also be ordering the generated list from lowest to highest.

If the PHStat2 add-in has not been loaded, you will need to load it before continuing. Follow the instructions in Section GS 8.2.

1. Open a new, blank Excel worksheet.

2. At the top of the screen, select **PHStat→Sampling→Random Sample Generation**.

© 2006 Pearson Education, Inc., Upper Saddle River, NJ. All rights reserved. This material is protected under all copyright laws as they currently exist. No portion of this material may be reproduced, in any form or by any means, without permission in writing from the publisher.

3. Complete the Random Sample Generator dialog box as shown below. A sample of eight accounts will be randomly selected from a population of 74. "Account #" will appear in the top cell of the output. Click **OK**.

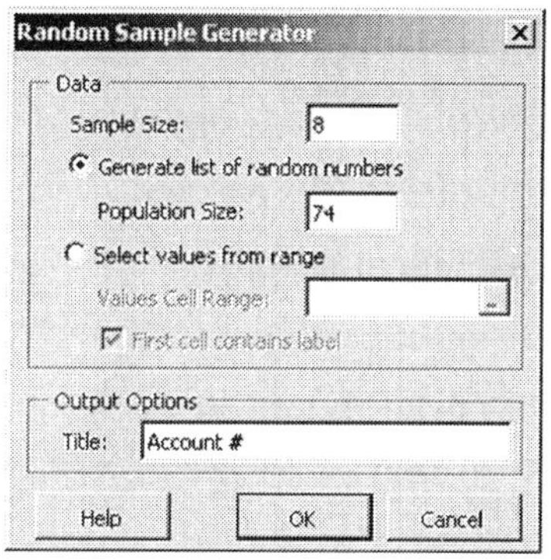

Random Sample Generator	✕
Data	
Sample Size:	8
⦿ Generate list of random numbers	
Population Size:	74
⦿ Select values from range	
Values Cell Range:	[ ] ...
☑ First cell contains label	
Output Options	
Title:	Account #
Help	OK Cancel

4. Sort the numbers in ascending order.

For instructions on how to sort, refer to Sections GS 5.1 and GS 5.2.

	A
1	Account #
2	19
3	52
4	45
5	35
6	53
7	16
8	15
9	32

The sorted set of eight random numbers is displayed below. Because the numbers were generated randomly, it is not likely that your output will be exactly the same.

	A
1	Account #
2	15
3	16
4	19
5	32
6	35
7	45
8	52
9	53

◀

© 2006 Pearson Education, Inc., Upper Saddle River, NJ. All rights reserved. This material is protected under all copyright laws as they currently exist. No portion of this material may be reproduced, in any form or by any means, without permission in writing from the publisher.

▶ Exercise 2 (pg. 31) | Generating a List of Random Numbers for a Quality Control Department

---

If the PHStat2 add-in has not been loaded, you will need to load it before continuing. Follow the instructions in Section GS 8.2.

---

1. Open a new Excel worksheet.

2. At the top of the screen, select **PHStat→Sampling→Random Sample Generation**.

3. Complete the Random Sample Generator dialog box as shown below. A sample of 20 batteries will be randomly selected from a population of 200. "Battery #" will appear in the top cell of the generated output. Click **OK**.

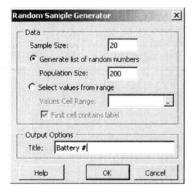

4. Sort the numbers in ascending order.

For instructions on how to sort, see Sections GS 5.1 and GS 5.2.

The sorted set of 20 random numbers is displayed at the top of the next page. Because the numbers were generated randomly, it is unlike that your output will be exactly the same.

© 2006 Pearson Education, Inc., Upper Saddle River, NJ. All rights reserved. This material is protected under all copyright laws as they currently exist. No portion of this material may be reproduced, in any form or by any means, without permission in writing from the publisher.

	A
1	Battery #
2	10
3	38
4	52
5	56
6	64
7	65
8	76
9	81
10	83
11	102
12	105
13	107
14	108
15	118
16	121
17	130
18	154
19	189
20	198
21	199

◄

► Exercise 3 (pg. 31)	Generating Three Random Samples from a Population of Ten Digits

You will be generating three random samples of five digits each from the population: 0, 1, 2, 3, 4, 5, 6, 7, 8, 9. You will also compute the average of each sample.

If the PHStat2 add-in has not been loaded, you will need to load it before continuing. Follow the instructions in Section GS 8.2.

1. Open a new Excel worksheet. Enter the numbers 0 through 9 in column A.

	A
1	0
2	1
3	2
4	3
5	4
6	5
7	6
8	7
9	8
10	9

2. Compute the average using the AVERAGE function. To do this, first click in the cell immediately below the last number in the population, cell **A11**, where you will place the average. Then, at the top of the screen click **Insert→Function**.

© 2006 Pearson Education, Inc., Upper Saddle River, NJ. All rights reserved. This material is protected under all copyright laws as they currently exist. No portion of this material may be reproduced, in any form or by any means, without permission in writing from the publisher.

3. Select the **Statistical** category. Select the **AVERAGE** function. Click **OK**.

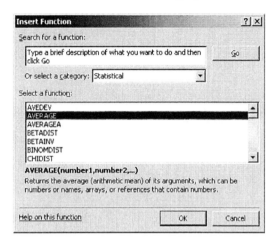

4. Complete the AVERAGE dialog box as shown below. Click **OK**.

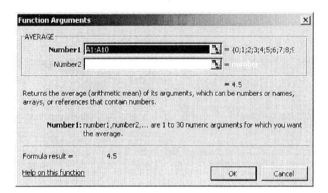

The average, 4.5, is displayed in cell A11 of the worksheet.

	A
1	0
2	1
3	2
4	3
5	4
6	5
7	6
8	7
9	8
10	9
11	4.5

5. You will now select the first random sample of five digits. At the top of the screen, select **PHStat→Sampling→Random Sample Generation**.

© 2006 Pearson Education, Inc., Upper Saddle River, NJ. All rights reserved. This material is protected under all copyright laws as they currently exist. No portion of this material may be reproduced, in any form or by any means, without permission in writing from the publisher.

6. Complete the Random Sample Generator dialog box as shown below. Five numbers will be randomly selected from the numbers displayed in cells A1 through A10 in the worksheet. Cell A1 does not contain a label. "Sample 1" will appear in the top cell of the generated output. Click **OK**.

A quick way to enter the range is to first click in the Values Cell Range field of the dialog box. Then click on cell A1 in the worksheet and drag down to cell A10. Be careful that you do not include cell A11 in the range.

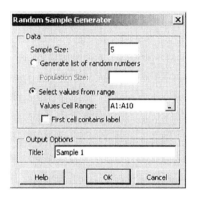

The random sample of five digits is placed in a sheet named "RandomNumbers." Because the numbers were generated randomly, it is not likely that your output will be exactly the same.

	A
1	Sample 1
2	4
3	8
4	3
5	2
6	6

7. Use the AVERAGE function to find the average. To do this, first click in the cell immediately below the last number in the sample—cell **A7**. Then, at the top of the screen, click **Insert→Function**.

8. Select the **Statistical** category. Select the **AVERAGE** function. Click **OK**.

9. Complete AVERAGE dialog box as shown at the top of the next page. Click **OK**.

© 2006 Pearson Education, Inc., Upper Saddle River, NJ. All rights reserved. This material is protected under all copyright laws as they currently exist. No portion of this material may be reproduced, in any form or by any means, without permission in writing from the publisher.

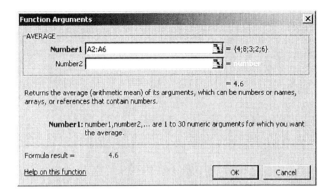

10. The average of the sample, 4.6, is now displayed in cell A7 of the worksheet. Repeat steps 5-9 to generate two more samples and compute the averages.

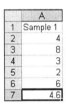

	A
1	Sample 1
2	4
3	8
4	3
5	2
6	6
7	4.6

To return to the sheet that contains the population values, click on the Sheet1 tab located near the bottom of your screen.

► **Exercise 5 (pg. 31)**   Simulating Rolling a Six-Sided Die 60 Times

---

You will be simulating rolling a six-sided die 60 times and making a tally of the results.

If the PHStat2 add-in has not been loaded, you will need to load it before continuing. Follow the instructions in Section GS 8.2.

---

1. Open a new Excel worksheet and enter the digits 1 through 6 in column A. These digits represent the possible outcomes of rolling a die.

© 2006 Pearson Education, Inc., Upper Saddle River, NJ. All rights reserved. This material is protected under all copyright laws as they currently exist. No portion of this material may be reproduced, in any form or by any means, without permission in writing from the publisher.

	A
1	1
2	2
3	3
4	4
5	5
6	6

2. At the top of the screen, click **Tools→Data Analysis**. Select **Sampling** and click **OK**.

If Data Analysis does not appear as a choice in the Tools menu, you will need to load the Microsoft Excel Analysis ToolPak add-in. Follow the procedure in Section GS 8.1 before continuing.

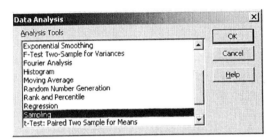

3. Complete the Sampling dialog box as shown below. Click **OK**.

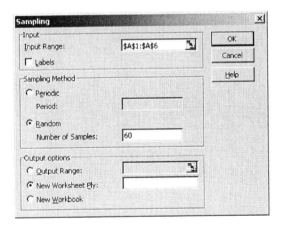

The output will be displayed in a new worksheet. The first 7 entries are shown at the top of the next page. Because the numbers were generated randomly, it is not likely that your output will be exactly the same.

© 2006 Pearson Education, Inc., Upper Saddle River, NJ. All rights reserved. This material is protected under all copyright laws as they currently exist. No portion of this material may be reproduced, in any form or by any means, without permission in writing from the publisher.

	A
1	6
2	1
3	2
4	2
5	2
6	6
7	4

4. To make a tally of the results, first select **PHStat→Descriptive Statistics→One-Way Tables & Charts**. Then complete the One-Way Tables & Charts dialog box as shown below. The Type of Data is "Raw Categorical Data." The data are located in cells A1 through A60. There is no label in the first cell (A1). The output will be given the title "Rolling a Die." A bar chart will be part of the output. Click **OK**.

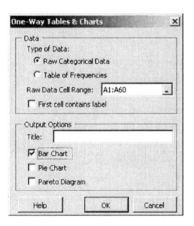

© 2006 Pearson Education, Inc., Upper Saddle River, NJ. All rights reserved. This material is protected under all copyright laws as they currently exist. No portion of this material may be reproduced, in any form or by any means, without permission in writing from the publisher.

The bar chart is displayed in a sheet named "Bar Chart."

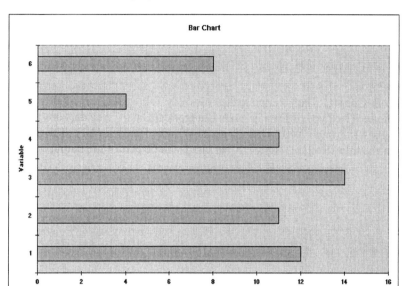

5. Click on the **OneWay Table** sheet tab at the bottom of the screen. This sheet contains a frequency distribution of the outcomes.

	A	B	C
1	One-Way Summary Table		
2			
3	Count of Variable		
4	Variable ▼	Total	
5	1	12	
6	2	11	
7	3	14	
8	4	11	
9	5	4	
10	6	8	
11	Grand Total	60	

6. Click on the **DataCopy** sheet tab at the bottom of the screen. This sheet contains a copy of the generated data set with the word "Variable" inserted in cell A1.

◀

© 2006 Pearson Education, Inc., Upper Saddle River, NJ. All rights reserved. This material is protected under all copyright laws as they currently exist. No portion of this material may be reproduced, in any form or by any means, without permission in writing from the publisher.

Descriptive Statistics

Section 2.1 Frequency Distributions and Their Graphs

► Example 7 (pg. 42)	Constructing Histograms

You will be constructing a histogram for the frequency distribution of the Internet data in Example 2 on page 37.

1. Open worksheet "Internet" in the Chapter 2 folder. These data represent the number of minutes 50 Internet subscribers spent during their most recent Internet session. You will use Data Analysis located in the Tools menu to construct a histogram for these data.

    If Data Analysis does not appear as a choice in the Tools menu, you will need to load the Microsoft Excel Analysis ToolPak add-in. Follow the procedure in Section GS 8.1 before continuing.

2. Excel's histogram procedure uses grouped data to generate a frequency distribution and a frequency histogram. The procedure requires that you indicate a "bin" for each class. The number that you specify for each bin is actually the upper limit of the class. The upper limits for the Internet data are given on page 35 of your text and are based on a class width of 12. You see that 18 is the upper limit for the first class, 30 is the upper limit for the second class, and so on. The bin for the first class will contain a count of all observations less than or equal to 18, the bin for the second class will contain a count of all observations between 19 and 30, and so on. Enter **Bin** in cell C1 and key in the upper limits in column C as shown at the top of the next page.

© 2006 Pearson Education, Inc., Upper Saddle River, NJ. All rights reserved. This material is protected under all copyright laws as they currently exist. No portion of this material may be reproduced, in any form or by any means, without permission in writing from the publisher.

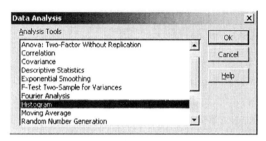

	A	B	C
1	Internet subscribers	Bin	
2	50		18
3	40		30
4	41		42
5	17		54
6	11		66
7	7		78
8	22		90

3. Click **Tools**→**Data Analysis**. Select **Histogram**, and click **OK**.

4. Complete the Histogram dialog box as shown below and click **OK**.

To enter the input and bin ranges quickly, follow these steps. First click in the Input Range field of the dialog box. Then, in the worksheet, click and drag from cell A1 to cell A51. You will then see $A$1:$A$51 displayed in the Input Range field. Next click in the Bin Range field. Then click and drag from cell C1 through cell C8 in the worksheet. You will see $C$1:$C$8 displayed in the Bin Range field.

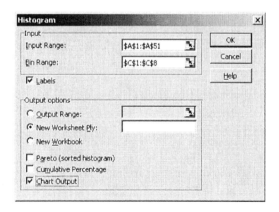

© 2006 Pearson Education, Inc., Upper Saddle River, NJ. All rights reserved. This material is protected under all copyright laws as they currently exist. No portion of this material may be reproduced, in any form or by any means, without permission in writing from the publisher.

Note the checkmark in the box to the left of Labels. In your worksheet, "Internet subscribers" appears in cell A1, and "Bin" appears in cell C1. Because you included these cells in the Input Range and Bin Range, respectively, you need to let Excel know that these cells contain labels rather than data. Otherwise Excel will attempt to use the information in these cells when constructing the frequency distribution and histogram.

You should see output similar to the output displayed below.

	A	B	C	D E F G H I J
1	Bin	Frequency		
2	18	6		
3	30	10		
4	42	13		
5	54	8		
6	66	5		
7	78	6		
8	90	2		
9	More	0		
10				
11				

If you want to change the height and width of the chart, begin by clicking anywhere within the figure. Handles appear along the perimeter. You can change the shape of the figure by clicking on a handle and dragging it. You can make the figure small and short or you can make it tall and wide. You can also click within the figure and drag it to move it to a different location on the worksheet.

---

5. You will now follow steps to modify the histogram so that it is displayed in a more informative and attractive manner. First, make the chart taller so that it is easier to read. To do this, first click within the figure near a border. Black square handles appear. Click on the center handle on the bottom border of the figure and drag it down a few rows.

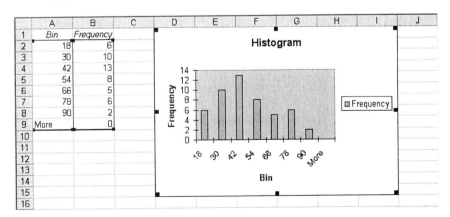

© 2006 Pearson Education, Inc., Upper Saddle River, NJ. All rights reserved. This material is protected under all copyright laws as they currently exist.
No portion of this material may be reproduced, in any form or by any means, without permission in writing from the publisher.

6. Next remove the space between the vertical bars. **Right click** on one of the vertical bars. Select **Format Data Series** from the shortcut menu that appears.

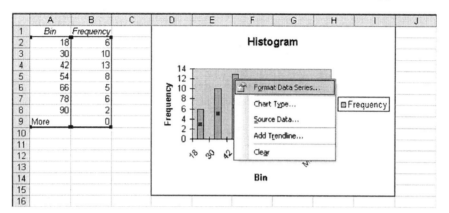

7. Click on the **Options** tab at the top of the Format Data Series dialog box. Change the value in the Gap width box to 0. Click **OK**.

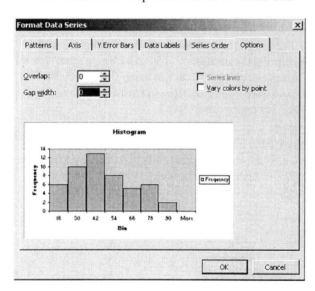

8. Change the X-axis values from upper limits to midpoints. The midpoints are displayed in a table on page 37 of your textbook. Enter these midpoints in column C of the Excel worksheet as shown at the top of the next page.

© 2006 Pearson Education, Inc., Upper Saddle River, NJ. All rights reserved. This material is protected under all copyright laws as they currently exist. No portion of this material may be reproduced, in any form or by any means, without permission in writing from the publisher.

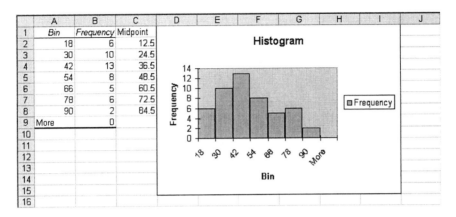

9. **Right click** on a vertical bar. Select **Source Data** from the shortcut menu that appears.

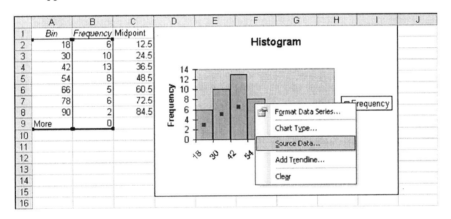

10. Click on the **Series** tab at the top of the Source Data dialog box. The ranges displayed in the Values field and the Category (X) axis labels field refer to the frequency distribution table in the top left of the worksheet. You do not want to include row 9, because that is the row containing information related to the "More" category. You also want the midpoint values in column C to be displayed on the X axis rather than the column A bin values. First, change the 9 to 8 in the **Values** field so that the entry reads **=Sheet1!$B$2:$B$8**. Next, edit the **Category (X) axis labels** field so that the entry reads **=Sheet1!$C$2:$C$8**. Click **OK**.

© 2006 Pearson Education, Inc., Upper Saddle River, NJ. All rights reserved. This material is protected under all copyright laws as they currently exist.
No portion of this material may be reproduced, in any form or by any means, without permission in writing from the publisher.

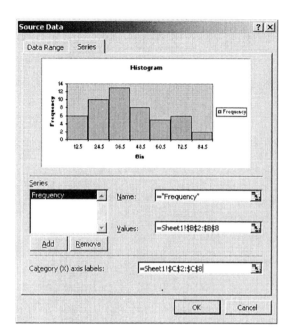

11. You will use Chart Options to modify three aspects of the histogram: Titles, gridlines, and legend. **Right click** in the gray plot area of the chart and select **Chart Options** from the shortcut menu that appears.

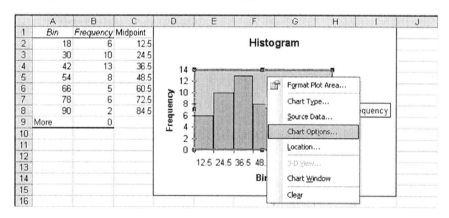

12. Click on the **Titles** tab at the top of the Chart Options dialog box. Change the Chart title from "Histogram" to **Internet Usage**. Change the Category (X) axis label from "Bin" to **Time online (in minutes)**.

© 2006 Pearson Education, Inc., Upper Saddle River, NJ. All rights reserved. This material is protected under all copyright laws as they currently exist. No portion of this material may be reproduced, in any form or by any means, without permission in writing from the publisher.

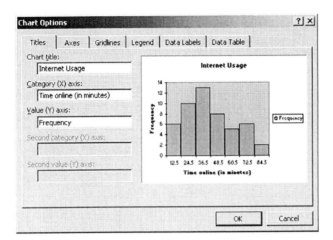

13. Click on the **Gridlines** tab at the top of the Chart Options dialog box. Under Value (Y) axis, click in the **Major gridlines** box so that a checkmark appears there.

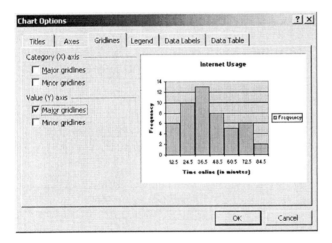

14. Click on the **Legend** tab. To remove the frequency legend displayed at the right of the histogram chart, click in the **Show legend** box to remove the checkmark. Click **OK**. Your histogram chart should now appear similar to the one displayed at the top of the next page.

© 2006 Pearson Education, Inc., Upper Saddle River, NJ. All rights reserved. This material is protected under all copyright laws as they currently exist. No portion of this material may be reproduced, in any form or by any means, without permission in writing from the publisher.

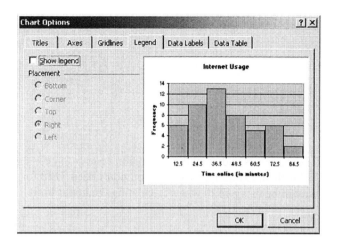

> ▶ Exercise 25 (pg. 46)

Constructing a Frequency Distribution and
Frequency Histogram for the July Sales Data

1. Open worksheet "Ex2_1-25" in the Chapter 2 folder.

2. Sort the data so that it is easy to identify the minimum and maximum data entries. In the sorted data set, you see that the minimum sales value is 1000 and that the maximum is 7119.

For instructions on how to sort, see Sections GS 5.1 and GS 5.2.

---

3. Calculate class width using the formula given in your textbook:

$$\text{Class width} = \frac{\text{Maximum data entry} - \text{Minimum data entry}}{\text{Number of classes}}$$

The exercise instructs you to use 6 for the number of classes.

$$\text{Class width} = \frac{7119 - 1000}{6} = 1019.83 . \text{ Round up to 1020.}$$

4. The textbook instructs you to use the minimum data entry as the lower limit of the first class. To find the remaining lower limits, add the class width of 1020 to the lower limit of each previous class. Enter **Lower Limit** in cell B1 of the worksheet,

© 2006 Pearson Education, Inc., Upper Saddle River, NJ. All rights reserved. This material is protected under all copyright laws as they currently exist. No portion of this material may be reproduced, in any form or by any means, without permission in writing from the publisher.

and enter **1000** in cell B2. You will now use a formula to compute the remaining lower limits, and you will have Excel do these calculations for you. In cell B3, enter the formula **=B2+1020** as shown below. Press **[Enter]**.

	A	B	C
1	July Sales	Lower Limit	
2	2114	1000	
3	2468	=B2+1020	
4	7119		

5. Click in cell **B3** where 2020 now appears and copy the formula in cell B3 to cells B4 through B8. Because 7119 is the maximum data entry, you don't need 7120 for the histogram. However, you will be using 7120 when calculating the upper limit for the last class interval.

	A	B	C
1	July Sales	Lower Limit	
2	2114	1000	
3	2468	2020	
4	7119	3040	
5	1876	4060	
6	4105	5080	
7	3183	6100	
8	1932	7120	

6. Enter **Upper Limit** in cell C1 of the worksheet. The textbook says that the upper limit is equal to one less than the lower limit of the next higher class. You will use a formula to compute the upper limits, and you will have Excel do the computations for you. Click in cell C2 and enter the formula **=B3-1** as shown below. Press **[Enter]**.

	A	B	C	D
1	July Sales	Lower Limit	Upper Limit	
2	2114	1000	=B3-1	
3	2468	2020		

7. Copy the formula in cell C2 (where 2019 now appears) to cells C3 through C7. These are the upper limits that you will use as bins for constructing the histogram chart.

	A	B	C	D
1	July Sales	Lower Limit	Upper Limit	
2	2114	1000	2019	
3	2468	2020	3039	
4	7119	3040	4059	
5	1876	4060	5079	
6	4105	5080	6099	
7	3183	6100	7119	

© 2006 Pearson Education, Inc., Upper Saddle River, NJ. All rights reserved. This material is protected under all copyright laws as they currently exist.
No portion of this material may be reproduced, in any form or by any means, without permission in writing from the publisher.

8.   Click **Tools→Data Analysis**. Select **Histogram** and click **OK**.

If Data Analysis does not appear as a choice in the Tools menu, you will need to load the Microsoft Excel Analysis ToolPak add-in. Follow the procedure in Section GS 8.1 before continuing

---

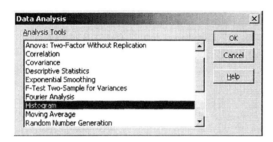

9.   Complete the fields in the Histogram dialog box as shown below. The July sales data are located in cells A1 through A23 of the worksheet. The bins (upper limits) are located in cells C1 through C7. The top cells in these ranges are labels—"July Sales" and "Upper Limit," so click in the Labels box to place a checkmark there. The output will be placed in a new Excel workbook. The output will include a chart. Click **OK**.

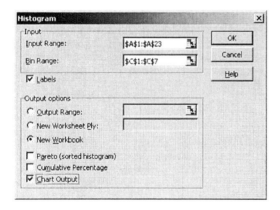

© 2006 Pearson Education, Inc., Upper Saddle River, NJ. All rights reserved. This material is protected under all copyright laws as they currently exist. No portion of this material may be reproduced, in any form or by any means, without permission in writing from the publisher.

You should see output similar to the output displayed below.

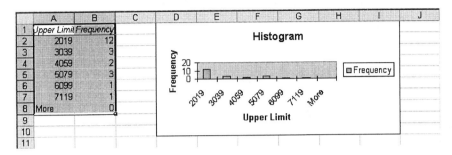

10. You will now follow steps to modify the histogram so that it is displayed in a more accurate and informative manner. First, make the chart taller so that it is easier to read. To do this, first click within the figure near a border. Black square handles appear. Click on the center handle on the bottom border of the figure and drag it down a few rows.

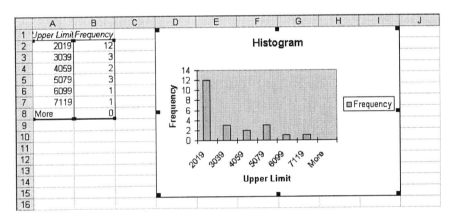

© 2006 Pearson Education, Inc., Upper Saddle River, NJ. All rights reserved. This material is protected under all copyright laws as they currently exist. No portion of this material may be reproduced, in any form or by any means, without permission in writing from the publisher.

11. Remove the space between the vertical bars. **Right click** on one of the vertical bars. Select **Format Data Series** from the shortcut menu that appears.

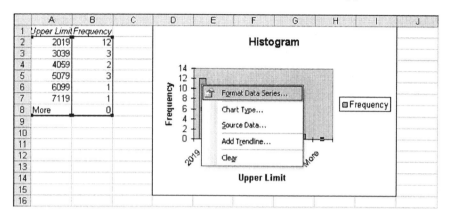

12. Click on the **Options** tab at the top of the Format Data Series dialog box. Change the value in the Gap width box to 0. Click **OK**.

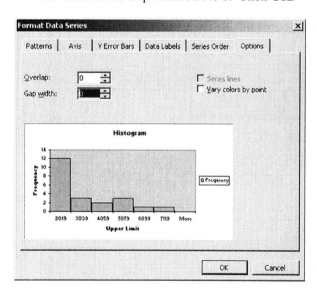

© 2006 Pearson Education, Inc., Upper Saddle River, NJ. All rights reserved. This material is protected under all copyright laws as they currently exist.
No portion of this material may be reproduced, in any form or by any means, without permission in writing from the publisher.

13. Delete the word "More" from the X axis. **Right click** on a vertical bar. Select **Source Data** from the shortcut menu that appears.

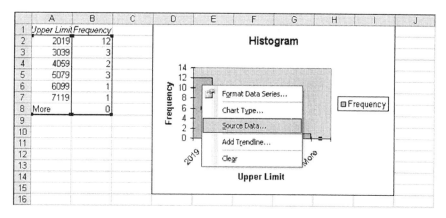

14. Click on the **Series** tab at the top of the Source Data dialog box. You do not want to include row 8 of the frequency distribution because that is the row containing information related to the "More" category. Change the 8 to 7 in the **Values** field so that it reads **=Sheet1!$B$2:$B$7**. Change the 8 to 7 in the **Category (X) axis labels** field so that it reads **=Sheet1!$A$2:$A$7**. Click **OK**.

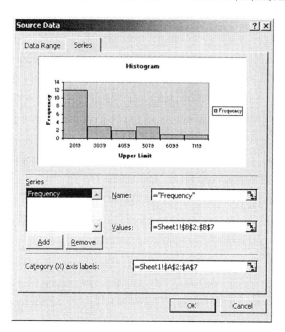

© 2006 Pearson Education, Inc., Upper Saddle River, NJ. All rights reserved. This material is protected under all copyright laws as they currently exist. No portion of this material may be reproduced, in any form or by any means, without permission in writing from the publisher.

15. You will use Chart Options to modify three aspects of the histogram: Titles, gridlines, and legend. **Right click** in the gray plot area of the chart and select **Chart Options** from the shortcut menu that appears.

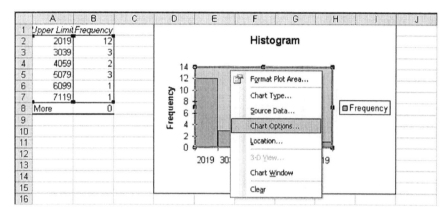

16. Click on the **Titles** tab at the top of the Chart Options dialog box. Change the Chart title from "Histogram" to **July Sales**. Change the Category (X) label from "Upper Limit" to **Dollars**.

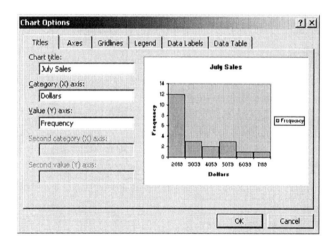

© 2006 Pearson Education, Inc., Upper Saddle River, NJ. All rights reserved. This material is protected under all copyright laws as they currently exist. No portion of this material may be reproduced, in any form or by any means, without permission in writing from the publisher.

17. Click on the **Gridlines** tab at the top of the Chart Options dialog box. Under Value (Y) axis, click in the **Major gridlines** box.

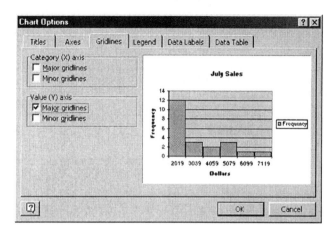

18. Click on the **Legend** tab. To remove the frequency legend displayed at the right of the histogram chart, click in the **Show legend** box to remove the checkmark. Click **OK**. Your histogram chart should now appear similar to the one displayed below.

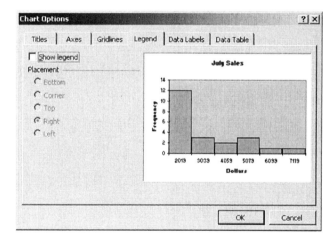

© 2006 Pearson Education, Inc., Upper Saddle River, NJ. All rights reserved. This material is protected under all copyright laws as they currently exist.
No portion of this material may be reproduced, in any form or by any means, without permission in writing from the publisher.

Section 2.2 More Graphs and Displays

► Example 1 (pg. 49)	Constructing a Stem-and-Leaf Plot

If the PHStat2 add-in has not been loaded, you will need to load it before continuing. Follow the instructions in Section GS 8.2.

1. Open worksheet "RBIs" in the Chapter 2 folder.

2. At the top of the screen, click **PHStat→Descriptive Statistics→Stem-and-Leaf Display**.

3. Complete the entries in the Stem-and-Leaf Display dialog box as shown below. Click **OK**.

© 2006 Pearson Education, Inc., Upper Saddle River, NJ. All rights reserved. This material is protected under all copyright laws as they currently exist. No portion of this material may be reproduced, in any form or by any means, without permission in writing from the publisher.

The output is displayed in a new sheet named "StemLeafPlot."

	A	B	C	D	E
1				Stem-and-Leaf Display	
2					
3				Stem unit 10	
4					
5	Statistics			7	8
6	Sample Size	50		8	
7	Mean	125.14		9	
8	Median	123.5		10	5 8 9 9 9
9	Std. Deviation	14.53919		11	2 2 2 3 4 6 7 8 8 8 9 9 9
10	Minimum	78		12	1 1 2 2 2 3 4 4 6 6 6 6 6 9 9
11	Maximum	159		13	0 2 3 3 4 9 9
12				14	0 2 4 5 5 7 8
13				15	5 9

◄

► Example 4 (pg. 52)	Constructing a Pie Chart

1. Open a new, blank Excel worksheet and enter the motor vehicle frequency table as shown below.

	A	B
1	Vehicle type	Killed
2	Cars	22385
3	Trucks	8457
4	Motorcycles	2806
5	Other	497

2. Click in any cell within the table. Then click **Insert→Chart**.

If a cell within the table is activated when you select Chart, the data range will automatically be entered into the Chart dialog box.

3. Under Chart type, in the Chart Type dialog box, select **Pie**. Under Chart sub-type, select the first one in the top row by clicking on it. Click **Next** at the bottom of the dialog box.

© 2006 Pearson Education, Inc., Upper Saddle River, NJ. All rights reserved. This material is protected under all copyright laws as they currently exist. No portion of this material may be reproduced, in any form or by any means, without permission in writing from the publisher.

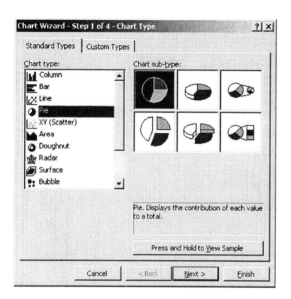

4. Check the accuracy of the data range in the Chart Source Data dialog box. It should read =**Sheet1!$A$1:$B$5**. Make any necessary corrections. Then click **Next**.

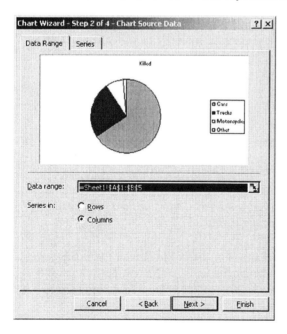

© 2006 Pearson Education, Inc., Upper Saddle River, NJ. All rights reserved. This material is protected under all copyright laws as they currently exist. No portion of this material may be reproduced, in any form or by any means, without permission in writing from the publisher.

5. Click the **Titles** tab at the top of the Chart Options dialog box. Change the title from "Killed" to **Motor Vehicle Occupants Killed in 1991**.

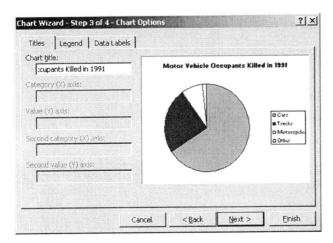

6. Click the **Data Labels** tab at the top of the Chart Options dialog box. Click the boxes to the left of **Category name** and **Percentage** so that checkmarks appear in the boxes. Also click the **Show leader lines** box. Click **Next**.

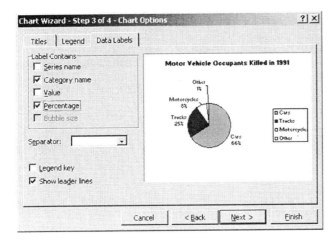

© 2006 Pearson Education, Inc., Upper Saddle River, NJ. All rights reserved. This material is protected under all copyright laws as they currently exist. No portion of this material may be reproduced, in any form or by any means, without permission in writing from the publisher.

7. The Chart Location dialog box presents two options for placing your chart output. For this example, select **As object in**. Click **Finish**.

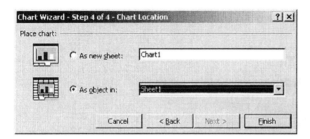

8. In the chart shown below, the final letter of "Motorcycles" is shown below the rest of the word.

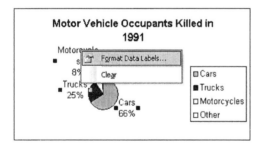

To fix this, first **right click** directly on the Motorcycle label. Then click on **Format Data Labels** in the shortcut menu that appears.

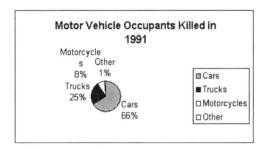

© 2006 Pearson Education, Inc., Upper Saddle River, NJ. All rights reserved. This material is protected under all copyright laws as they currently exist. No portion of this material may be reproduced, in any form or by any means, without permission in writing from the publisher.

9. Click the **Font** tab at the top of the Format Data Labels dialog box. In the Size: window, change the size from 10 to **9**. Click **OK**.

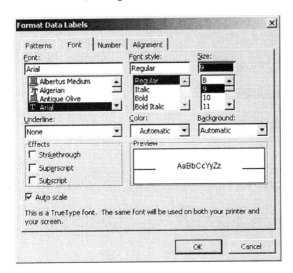

10. The chart title is now on top of a data label. To provide more space at the top of the chart, first click within the figure near a border. Black square handles appear. Click on the center handle on the top border of the figure and drag it up a few rows.

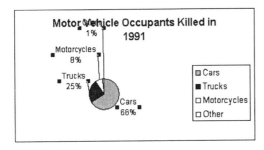

© 2006 Pearson Education, Inc., Upper Saddle River, NJ. All rights reserved. This material is protected under all copyright laws as they currently exist. No portion of this material may be reproduced, in any form or by any means, without permission in writing from the publisher.

Your pie chart for the motor vehicle data should look similar to the one shown below.

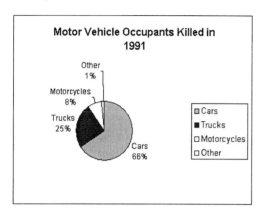

▶ Example 5 (pg. 53)	Constructing a Pareto Chart

1. Open a new, blank Excel worksheet, and enter the customer complaint information as shown below.

	A	B
1	Source	Frequency
2	Home furnishing	7792
3	Computer sales & service	5733
4	Auto dealers	14668
5	Auto repair	9728
6	Dry cleaning	4649

2. In a Pareto chart, the vertical bars are placed in order of decreasing height. Excel's Chart function will display the information in the order in which it appears in the worksheet. So, you need to sort the information in descending order by Frequency.

For instructions on how to sort, see Sections GS 5.1 and GS 5.2.

	A	B
1	Source	Frequency
2	Auto dealers	14668
3	Auto repair	9728
4	Home furnishing	7792
5	Computer sales & service	5733
6	Dry cleaning	4649

© 2006 Pearson Education, Inc., Upper Saddle River, NJ. All rights reserved. This material is protected under all copyright laws as they currently exist. No portion of this material may be reproduced, in any form or by any means, without permission in writing from the publisher.

3. After sorting the data, click on any cell within the data table. Then click
    Insert→Chart.

4. In the Chart Type dialog box, select a **Column** chart type. Click on the top left
    chart sub-type to select it. Click **Next**.

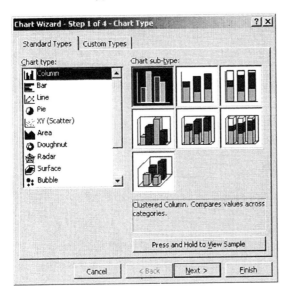

© 2006 Pearson Education, Inc., Upper Saddle River, NJ. All rights reserved. This material is protected under all copyright laws as they currently exist.
No portion of this material may be reproduced, in any form or by any means, without permission in writing from the publisher.

5. Check the range displayed in the Chart Source Data dialog box to make sure it is accurate. It should read =Sheet1!$A1:$B$6. Make any necessary corrections. Then click **Next**.

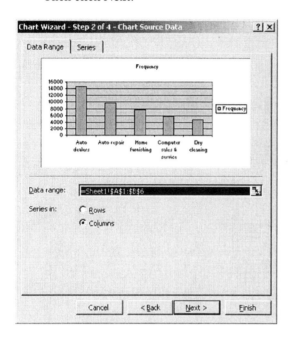

6. Click the **Titles** tab at the top of the Chart Options dialog box. In the Chart title field, enter **Customer Complaints Received by the Better Business Bureau**. In the Category (X) axis field, enter **Type of Business**. In the Value (Y) axis field, enter **Frequency**.

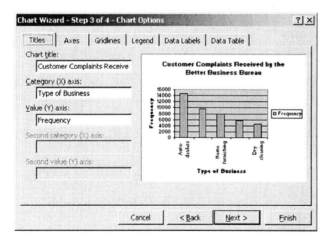

© 2006 Pearson Education, Inc., Upper Saddle River, NJ. All rights reserved. This material is protected under all copyright laws as they currently exist. No portion of this material may be reproduced, in any form or by any means, without permission in writing from the publisher.

7. Click the **Legend** tab at the top of the Chart Options dialog box. Click in the box to the left of **Show legend** so that no checkmark appears there. This will remove the Frequency legend on the right side of the chart. Click **Next**.

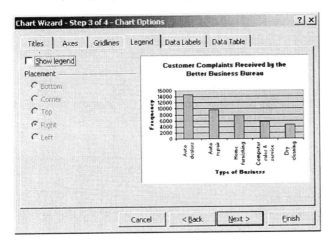

8. The Chart Location dialog box presents two options for placement of the chart. For this example, select **As new sheet**. Click **Finish**.

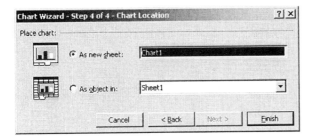

© 2006 Pearson Education, Inc., Upper Saddle River, NJ. All rights reserved. This material is protected under all copyright laws as they currently exist. No portion of this material may be reproduced, in any form or by any means, without permission in writing from the publisher.

Your chart should look similar to the one shown below.

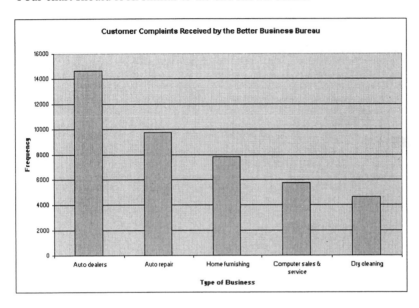

◄

> ► Example 7 (pg. 55)   Constructing a Time Series Chart

1. Open worksheet "Cellphone" in the Chapter 2 folder.

2. Click in any cell within the table. At the top of the screen, click **Insert** and select **Chart** from the menu that appears.

© 2006 Pearson Education, Inc., Upper Saddle River, NJ. All rights reserved. This material is protected under all copyright laws as they currently exist. No portion of this material may be reproduced, in any form or by any means, without permission in writing from the publisher.

3. In the Chart Type dialog box, select the **XY (Scatter)** chart type by clicking on it. Then click on the topmost chart sub-type. Click **Next**.

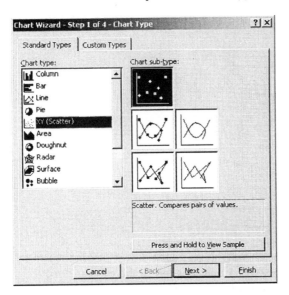

4. In the Chart Source Data dialog box, edit the data range so that it does not include the average bill data in column C of the worksheet. The entry in the data range field should be **=Sheet1!$A$3:$B$13**. Click **Next**.

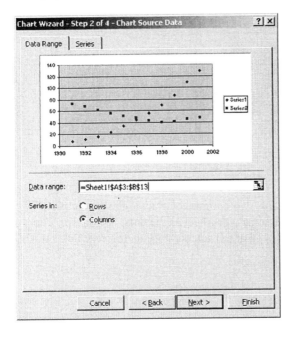

© 2006 Pearson Education, Inc., Upper Saddle River, NJ. All rights reserved. This material is protected under all copyright laws as they currently exist. No portion of this material may be reproduced, in any form or by any means, without permission in writing from the publisher.

5. Click the **Titles** tab at the top of the Chart Options dialog box. In the Chart title field, enter **Cellular Telephone Subscribers by Year**. In the Value (X) Axis field, enter **Year**. In the Value (Y) axis field, enter **Subscribers (in millions)**.

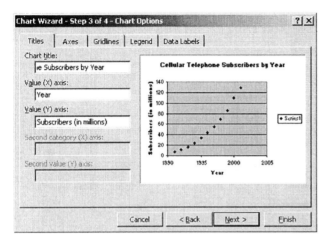

6. Click the **Legend** tab at the top of the Chart Options dialog box. Click in the box to the left of **Show Legend** so that a checkmark does not appear there. This removes the Subscribers legend from the right side of the scatter plot. Click **Next**.

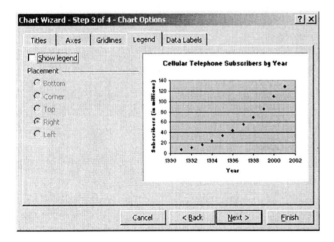

7. The Chart Location dialog box presents two options for placing the scatter plot. For this example, select **As object in** the same worksheet as the data. To do this, click the button to the left of **As object in** so that a black dot appears there. Click **Finish**.

© 2006 Pearson Education, Inc., Upper Saddle River, NJ. All rights reserved. This material is protected under all copyright laws as they currently exist. No portion of this material may be reproduced, in any form or by any means, without permission in writing from the publisher.

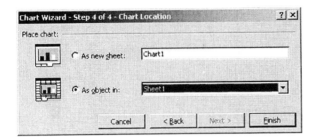

8. The scatter plot that you will obtain is quite compressed. Make it taller so that it is easier to read. To do this, first click within the figure near a border. Black square handles appear. Then click on the center handle on the bottom border of the figure and drag it down a few rows.

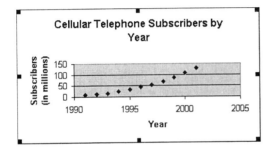

Your scatter plot should now look similar to the one shown below.

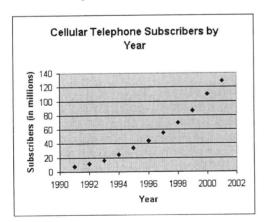

© 2006 Pearson Education, Inc., Upper Saddle River, NJ. All rights reserved. This material is protected under all copyright laws as they currently exist. No portion of this material may be reproduced, in any form or by any means, without permission in writing from the publisher.

Section 2.3 Measures of Central Tendency

▶ Example 6 (pg. 63)	Comparing the Mean, Median, and Mode

If the PHStat2 add-in has not been loaded, you will need to load it before continuing. Follow the instructions in Section GS 8.2.

1. Open worksheet "ages" in the Chapter 2 folder. The instructions for Try It Yourself 6 at the bottom of page 63 tell you to remove the data entry of 65 years. Because 65 is the bottom entry in the data set, you do not need to delete it. Instead, you will not include it in the input range.

2. At the top of the screen, click **Tools→Data Analysis**. Select **Descriptive Statistics** and click **OK**.

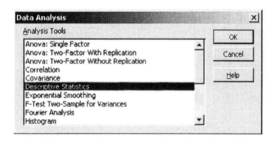

3. Complete the Descriptive Statistics dialog box as shown at the top of the next page. The entry in the **Input Range** field presents the worksheet location of the age data. The checkmark to the left of **Labels in First Row** lets Excel know that the entry in cell A1 is a label and is not to be included in the computations. The output will be placed in a **New Worksheet**. The checkmark to the left of **Summary statistics** requests that the output include summary statistics for the specified set of data. Click **OK**.

© 2006 Pearson Education, Inc., Upper Saddle River, NJ. All rights reserved. This material is protected under all copyright laws as they currently exist. No portion of this material may be reproduced, in any form or by any means, without permission in writing from the publisher.

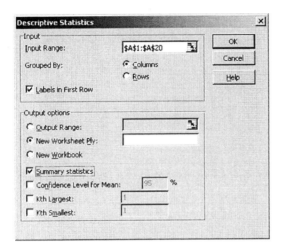

4. You will want to increase the width of column A of the output so that you can read the labels. Your output should be similar to the output shown below. The mean of the sample is 21.58, the median is 21, and the mode is 20.

Be careful when using the value of the mode reported in the Descriptive Statistics output. If there is a tie for the mode, Excel reports only the first modal value that occurs in the data set. Therefore, it is always a good idea to construct a frequency distribution table to go along with the Descriptive Statistics output.

	A	B
1	Ages of students in Class	
2		
3	Mean	21.57895
4	Standard Error	0.327276
5	Median	21
6	Mode	20
7	Standard Deviation	1.426565
8	Sample Variance	2.035088
9	Kurtosis	-1.27106
10	Skewness	0.335563
11	Range	4
12	Minimum	20
13	Maximum	24
14	Sum	410
15	Count	19

5. Construct a frequency distribution table to see if the data set is unimodal or multimodal. Go back to the worksheet containing the age data. To do this, click on the **Sheet1** tab near the bottom of the screen. Then select **PHStat→Descriptive Statistics→One-Way Tables & Charts**.

© 2006 Pearson Education, Inc., Upper Saddle River, NJ. All rights reserved. This material is protected under all copyright laws as they currently exist. No portion of this material may be reproduced, in any form or by any means, without permission in writing from the publisher.

6. Complete the One-Way Tables & Charts dialog box as shown below. Click **OK**.

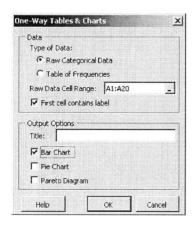

The bar chart is displayed in a worksheet named "Bar Chart."

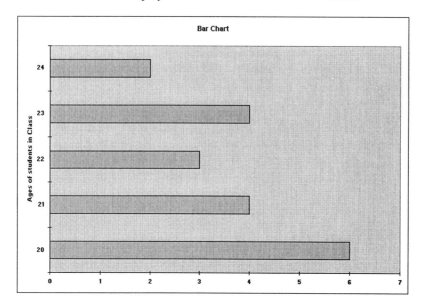

7. Click on the **OneWay Table** sheet tab at the bottom of the screen. This sheet contains a frequency distribution of the ages. You can see by looking at the bar chart and the frequency distribution that the age distribution is unimodal. The modal value of 20 has a frequency of six.

© 2006 Pearson Education, Inc., Upper Saddle River, NJ. All rights reserved. This material is protected under all copyright laws as they currently exist. No portion of this material may be reproduced, in any form or by any means, without permission in writing from the publisher.

	A	B
1	One-Way Summary Table	
2		
3	Count of Ages of students in Class	
4	Ages of students in Class ▼	Total
5	20	6
6	21	4
7	22	3
8	23	4
9	24	2
10	Grand Total	19

Section 2.4 Measures of Variation

▶ Example 5 (pg. 78)	Using Technology to Find the Standard Deviation

1. Open worksheet "Rentrates" in the Chapter 2 folder.

2. Click **Tools→Data Analysis**. Select **Descriptive Statistics** and click **OK**.

> *If Data Analysis does not appear as a choice in the Tools menu, you will need to load the Microsoft Excel Analysis ToolPak add-in. Follow the procedure in Section GS 8.1 before continuing.*

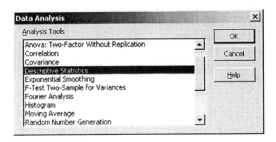

© 2006 Pearson Education, Inc., Upper Saddle River, NJ. All rights reserved. This material is protected under all copyright laws as they currently exist.
No portion of this material may be reproduced, in any form or by any means, without permission in writing from the publisher.

3. Complete the Descriptive Statistics dialog box as shown below. Click **OK**.

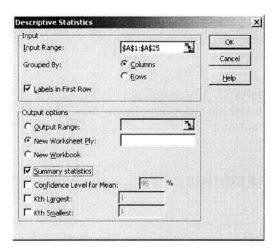

You will want to make Column A of the output wider so that you can read the labels. Your Descriptive Statistics output should be similar to the output shown below. The mean is 33.73 and the standard deviation is 5.09.

	A	B
1	Rental rates	
2		
3	Mean	33.72917
4	Standard Error	1.038864
5	Median	35.375
6	Mode	37
7	Standard Deviation	5.089373
8	Sample Variance	25.90172
9	Kurtosis	-0.74282
10	Skewness	-0.70345
11	Range	16.75
12	Minimum	23.75
13	Maximum	40.5
14	Sum	809.5
15	Count	24

© 2006 Pearson Education, Inc., Upper Saddle River, NJ. All rights reserved. This material is protected under all copyright laws as they currently exist. No portion of this material may be reproduced, in any form or by any means, without permission in writing from the publisher.

Section 2.5 Measures of Position

▶ Example 2 (pg. 94) | Using Technology to Find Quartiles

1. Open worksheet "Tuition" in the Chapter 2 folder. Key in labels for the quartiles as shown below. Then click in cell **C2** to place the first quartile there.

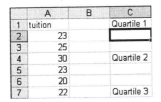

	A	B	C
1	tuition		Quartile 1
2	23		
3	25		
4	30		Quartile 2
5	23		
6	20		
7	22		Quartile 3

2. You will be using the QUARTILE function to obtain the first, second, and third quartiles for the tuition data. At the top of the screen, click **Insert→Function**.

3. Select the **Statistical** category. Select the **QUARTILE** function. Click **OK**.

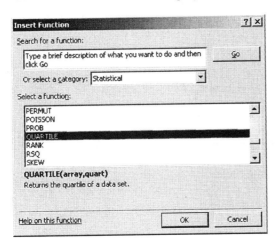

4. Complete the QUARTILE dialog box as shown at the top of the next page. Click **OK**.

© 2006 Pearson Education, Inc., Upper Saddle River, NJ. All rights reserved. This material is protected under all copyright laws as they currently exist. No portion of this material may be reproduced, in any form or by any means, without permission in writing from the publisher.

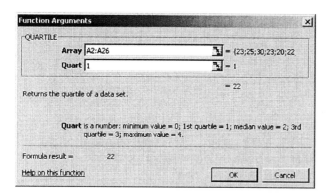

5. Click in cell **C5** to place the second quartile there.

6. At the top of the screen, click **Insert→Function**.

7. Select the **Statistical** category and the **QUARTILE** function. Click **OK**.

8. Complete the QUARTILE dialog box as shown below. Click **OK**.

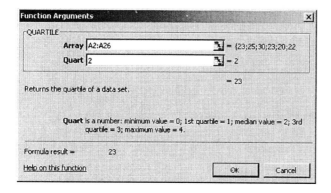

9. Click in cell **C8** to place the third quartile there.

10. At the top of the screen, click **Insert→Function**.

11. Select the **Statistical** category and the **QUARTILE** function. Click **OK**.

12. Complete the QUARTILE dialog box as shown at the top of the next page. Click **OK**.

© 2006 Pearson Education, Inc., Upper Saddle River, NJ. All rights reserved. This material is protected under all copyright laws as they currently exist. No portion of this material may be reproduced, in any form or by any means, without permission in writing from the publisher.

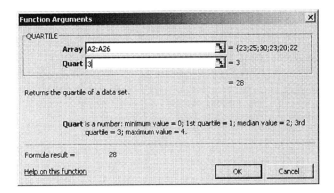

Your output should look similar to the output displayed below.

	A	B	C
1	tuition		Quartile 1
2	23		22
3	25		
4	30		Quartile 2
5	23		23
6	20		
7	22		Quartile 3
8	21		28

▶ **Example 4 (pg. 96)**   Drawing a Box-and-Whisker Plot

If the PHStat2 add-in has not been loaded, you will need to load it before continuing. Follow the instructions in Section GS 8.2.

1. Open a new Excel worksheet and enter the test scores of 15 employees enrolled in a CPR training course as shown at the top of the next page.

© 2006 Pearson Education, Inc., Upper Saddle River, NJ. All rights reserved. This material is protected under all copyright laws as they currently exist. No portion of this material may be reproduced, in any form or by any means, without permission in writing from the publisher.

	A
1	Test Score
2	13
3	9
4	18
5	15
6	14
7	21
8	7
9	10
10	11
11	20
12	5
13	18
14	37
15	16
16	17

2.   At the top of the screen, select **PHStat→Descriptive Statistics→Box-and-Whisker Plot**.

3.   Complete the Box-and-Whisker Plot dialog box as shown below. Click **OK**.

The Five-Number Summary is displayed in a worksheet named "FiveNumbers."

	A	B	C
1	CPR Training Test Scores		
2			
3	Five-number Summary		
4	Minimum	5	
5	First Quartile	10	
6	Median	15	
7	Third Quartile	18	
8	Maximum	37	

© 2006 Pearson Education, Inc., Upper Saddle River, NJ. All rights reserved. This material is protected under all copyright laws as they currently exist.
No portion of this material may be reproduced, in any form or by any means, without permission in writing from the publisher.

The box-and-whisker plot is displayed in a worksheet named "BoxWhiskerPlot."

CPR Training Test Scores

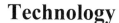

Technology

► Exercises 1 & 2 (pg. 113)	Finding the Sample Mean and the Sample Standard Deviation

1. Open worksheet "Tech2" in the Chapter 2 folder.

2. Click **Tools→Data Analysis**. Select **Descriptive Statistics** and click OK.

If Data Analysis does not appear as a choice in the Tools menu, you will need to load the Microsoft Excel Analysis ToolPak add-in. Follow the procedure in Section GS 8.1 before continuing.

© 2006 Pearson Education, Inc., Upper Saddle River, NJ. All rights reserved. This material is protected under all copyright laws as they currently exist.
No portion of this material may be reproduced, in any form or by any means, without permission in writing from the publisher.

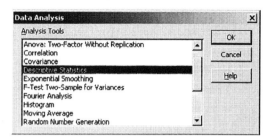

3. Complete the Descriptive Statistics dialog box as shown below. Click **OK**.

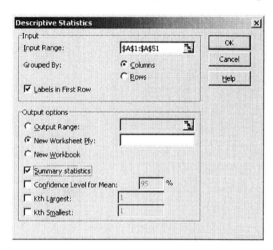

You will want to adjust the width of column A of the output so that you can read the labels. Your Descriptive Statistics output should be similar to the output shown below. The sample mean is 2270.54 and the sample standard deviation is 653.1822.

	A	B
1	Monthly Milk Production	
2		
3	Mean	2270.54
4	Standard Error	92.37391
5	Median	2207
6	Mode	2207
7	Standard Deviation	653.1822
8	Sample Variance	426647
9	Kurtosis	0.567664
10	Skewness	0.549267
11	Range	3138
12	Minimum	1147
13	Maximum	4285
14	Sum	113527
15	Count	50

© 2006 Pearson Education, Inc., Upper Saddle River, NJ. All rights reserved. This material is protected under all copyright laws as they currently exist. No portion of this material may be reproduced, in any form or by any means, without permission in writing from the publisher.

► Exercises 3 & 4 (pg. 113)	Constructing a Frequency Distribution and a Frequency Histogram

1. Open worksheet "Tech2" in the Chapter 2 folder.

2. Sort the data in ascending order. In the sorted data set you can see that the minimum production is 1147 pounds. Scroll down to find the maximum production. The maximum production, displayed in cell A51, is 4285 pounds.

For instructions on how to sort, refer to Sections GS 5.1 and GS 5.2.

	A	B	C
1	Monthly Milk Production		
2	1147		
3	1230		

50	3512		
51	4285		

3. Enter **Lower Limit** in cell D1 of the worksheet. The textbook tells you to use the minimum value as the lower limit of the first class. Enter **1147** in cell D2. You will calculate the remaining lower limits by adding the class width of 500 to the lower limit of each previous class. You will use a formula to do these computations in the Excel worksheet. Click in cell **D3** and key in **=D2+500** as shown below. Press [**Enter**].

	A	B	C	D
1	Monthly Milk Production			Lower Limit
2	1147			1147
3	1230			=D2+500

4. Click in cell **D3** (where 1647 now appears) and copy the contents of cell D3 to cells D4 through D9. Because the maximum milk production is 4285 pounds, you have calculated one more lower limit than is needed for the histogram. The value of 4647, however, will be used when calculating the upper limit of the last class.

	A	B	C	D
1	Monthly Milk Production			Lower Limit
2	1147			1147
3	1230			1647
4	1258			2147
5	1294			2647
6	1319			3147
7	1449			3647
8	1619			4147
9	1647			4647

© 2006 Pearson Education, Inc., Upper Saddle River, NJ. All rights reserved. This material is protected under all copyright laws as they currently exist. No portion of this material may be reproduced, in any form or by any means, without permission in writing from the publisher.

5. Enter **Upper Limit** in cell E1. The upper limit is equal to one less than the lower limit of the next higher class. To do these calculations, you will enter a formula in the Excel worksheet. Click in cell E2 and enter the formula **=D3-1** as shown in the worksheet below. Press [**Enter**].

	A	B	C	D	E
1	Monthly Milk Production			Lower Limit	Upper Limit
2	1147			1147	=D3-1
3	1230			1647	
4	1258			2147	
5	1294			2647	
6	1319			3147	
7	1449			3647	
8	1619			4147	
9	1647			4647	

6. Copy the formula in E2 (where 1646 now appears) to cells E3 through E8. You will use these upper limits for the bins when you construct the histogram chart.

	A	B	C	D	E
1	Monthly Milk Production			Lower Limit	Upper Limit
2	1147			1147	1646
3	1230			1647	2146
4	1258			2147	2646
5	1294			2647	3146
6	1319			3147	3646
7	1449			3647	4146
8	1619			4147	4646
9	1647			4647	

7. At the top of the screen, click **Tools→Data Analysis**. Select **Histogram** and click **OK**.

If Data Analysis does not appear as a choice in the Tools menu, you will need to load the Microsoft Excel Analysis ToolPak add-in. Follow the procedure in Section GS 8.1 before continuing.

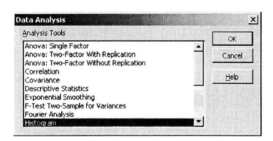

© 2006 Pearson Education, Inc., Upper Saddle River, NJ. All rights reserved. This material is protected under all copyright laws as they currently exist. No portion of this material may be reproduced, in any form or by any means, without permission in writing from the publisher.

8. Complete the fields in the histogram dialog box as shown below. Click **OK**.

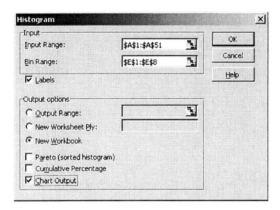

9. You will now follow steps to modify the histogram so that it is presented in a more informative manner. Begin by making the chart taller so that it is easier to read. To do this, first click within the figure near a border. Black square handles appear. Click on the center handle at the bottom border of the figure and drag it down a few rows.

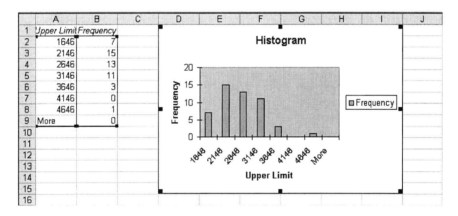

© 2006 Pearson Education, Inc., Upper Saddle River, NJ. All rights reserved. This material is protected under all copyright laws as they currently exist.
No portion of this material may be reproduced, in any form or by any means, without permission in writing from the publisher.

12. Remove the "More" category from the X axis. **Right click** in the gray plot area of the histogram and select **Source Data** from the shortcut menu that appears.

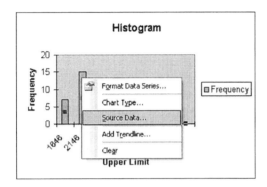

13. Click the **Series** tab at the top of the Source Data dialog box. "More" appears in cell A9 of the worksheet and its zero frequency appears in cell B9. To exclude the information in row 9 from the chart, edit the entry in the Values window and the entry in the Category (X) axis labels window. The entry in the Values window should read **=Sheet1!$B$2:$B$8**. The entry in the Category (X) axis labels window should read **=Sheet1!$A$2:$A$8**. Click **OK**.

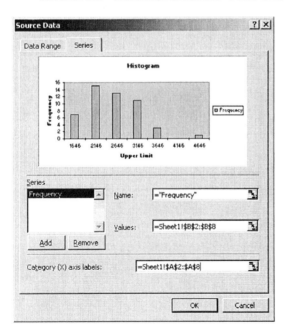

© 2006 Pearson Education, Inc., Upper Saddle River, NJ. All rights reserved. This material is protected under all copyright laws as they currently exist. No portion of this material may be reproduced, in any form or by any means, without permission in writing from the publisher.

14. **Right click** in the gray plot area of the histogram and select **Chart Options** from the menu that appears.

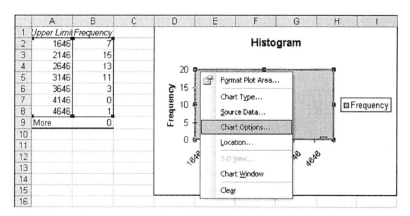

15. Click the **Titles** tab at the top of the Chart Options dialog box. In the Chart title field, replace "Histogram" with **Monthly Milk Production of 50 Holstein Dairy Cows**. In the Category (X) axis field, enter **Pounds**.

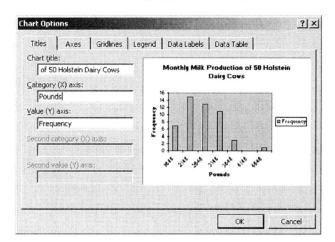

© 2006 Pearson Education, Inc., Upper Saddle River, NJ. All rights reserved. This material is protected under all copyright laws as they currently exist. No portion of this material may be reproduced, in any form or by any means, without permission in writing from the publisher.

16. Click the **Gridlines** tab at the top of the Chart Options dialog box. Click in the box next to **Major gridlines** under Value (Y) axis so that a checkmark appears there.

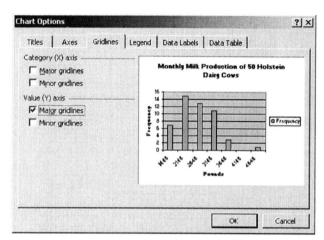

17. Click the **Legend** tab at the top of the Chart Options dialog box. Click in the box to the left of **Show Legend** to remove the checkmark. The removal of the checkmark will delete the frequency legend from the right side of the histogram chart. Click **OK**.

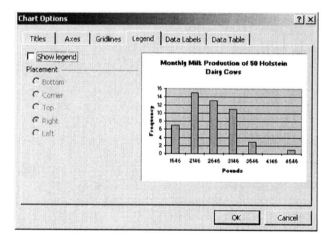

© 2006 Pearson Education, Inc., Upper Saddle River, NJ. All rights reserved. This material is protected under all copyright laws as they currently exist.
No portion of this material may be reproduced, in any form or by any means, without permission in writing from the publisher.

18. Remove the space between the vertical bars. **Right click** on one of the vertical bars. Select **Format Data Series** from the shortcut menu that appears.

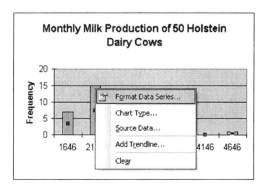

19. Click on the **Options** tab at the top of the Format Data Series dialog box. Change the value in the Gap width box to 0. Click **OK**.

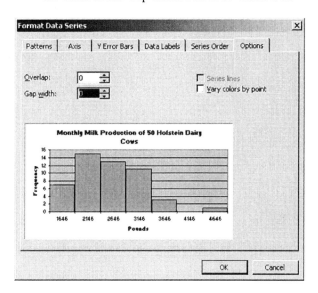

© 2006 Pearson Education, Inc., Upper Saddle River, NJ. All rights reserved. This material is protected under all copyright laws as they currently exist. No portion of this material may be reproduced, in any form or by any means, without permission in writing from the publisher.

Your completed histogram should look similar to the one displayed below.

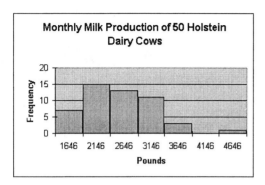

© 2006 Pearson Education, Inc., Upper Saddle River, NJ. All rights reserved. This material is protected under all copyright laws as they currently exist. No portion of this material may be reproduced, in any form or by any means, without permission in writing from the publisher.

Probability

Section 3.2 Conditional Probability and the Multiplication Rule

▶ Exercise 32 (pg. 139)   Simulating the "Birthday Problem"

You will be generating 24 random numbers between 1 and 365.

> *If the PHStat2add-in has not been loaded, you will need to load it before continuing. Follow the instructions in Section GS 8.2.*

1. Open a new Excel worksheet.

2. You will be entering the numbers 1 through 365 in the worksheet. To do this, you will fill column A with a number series. Begin by entering the numbers 1 and 2 in column A as shown below. You are starting a number series that will increase in increments of one.

3. You will now complete the series all the way to 365. Begin by clicking in cell A1 and dragging down to cell A2 so that both cells are highlighted as shown below.

4. Move the mouse pointer in cell A2 to the bottom right corner of that cell so that the white plus sign turns into a black plus sign. This black plus sign is called the "fill handle." While the fill handle is displayed, hold down on the left mouse button and drag down column A until you reach cell A365. Release the mouse button. You should see the numbers from 1 to 365 in column A.

© 2006 Pearson Education, Inc., Upper Saddle River, NJ. All rights reserved. This material is protected under all copyright laws as they currently exist.
No portion of this material may be reproduced, in any form or by any means, without permission in writing from the publisher.

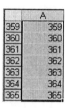

5. At the top of the screen, click **Tools→Data Analysis**. Select **Sampling** and click **OK**.

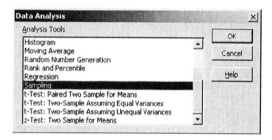

6. Complete the Sampling dialog box as shown below. Click **OK**.

You will be generating 10 different samples of 24 numbers. The first set of 24 numbers will be placed in column B, the second in column C, etc.

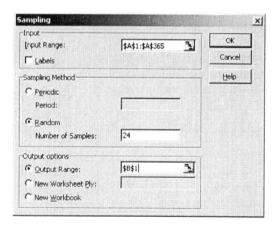

© 2006 Pearson Education, Inc., Upper Saddle River, NJ. All rights reserved. This material is protected under all copyright laws as they currently exist. No portion of this material may be reproduced, in any form or by any means, without permission in writing from the publisher.

7. The 24 numbers, generated randomly with replacement, are displayed in column B. (Because the numbers were generated randomly, it is not likely that your output will be exactly the same.) Construct a frequency distribution to see if there are any repetitions. Select **PHStat→Descriptive Statistics→One-Way Tables & Charts**.

	A	B
1	1	160
2	2	190
3	3	55
4	4	313
5	5	242
6	6	250
7	7	190
8	8	52
9	9	66
10	10	100
11	11	294
12	12	126
13	13	40
14	14	320
15	15	25
16	16	299
17	17	93
18	18	8
19	19	25
20	20	356
21	21	349
22	22	324
23	23	25
24	24	27

8. Complete the One-Way Tables & Charts dialog box as shown below. Click **OK**.

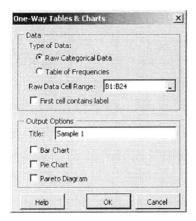

© 2006 Pearson Education, Inc., Upper Saddle River, NJ. All rights reserved. This material is protected under all copyright laws as they currently exist. No portion of this material may be reproduced, in any form or by any means, without permission in writing from the publisher.

9. The frequency distribution table is displayed in a worksheet named "OneWayTable." In this example, you can see that the value of 25 has a frequency of 3 and the value of 190 has a frequency of 2.

	A	B
1	Sample 1	
2		
3	Count of Variable	
4	Variable ▼	Total
5	8	1
6	25	3
7	27	1
8	40	1
9	52	1
10	55	1
11	66	1
12	93	1
13	100	1
14	126	1
15	160	1
16	190	2
17	242	1
18	250	1
19	294	1
20	299	1
21	313	1
22	320	1

Scrolling down, you can see no more repetitions in this example.

23	324	1
24	349	1
25	356	1
26	Grand Total	24

© 2006 Pearson Education, Inc., Upper Saddle River, NJ. All rights reserved. This material is protected under all copyright laws as they currently exist. No portion of this material may be reproduced, in any form or by any means, without permission in writing from the publisher.

10. Generate the second sample. Go back to the sheet containing the numbers 1 through 365 by clicking on the **Sheet1** tab near the bottom of the screen. Then click **Tools→Data Analysis**. Select **Sampling** and click **OK**. Complete the Sampling dialog box as shown below. The second set of randomly generated numbers will be placed in column C. Click **OK**.

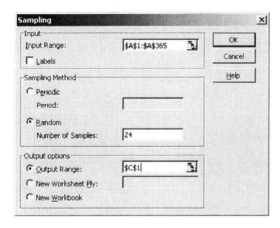

11. Construct a frequency distribution to see if there are any repetitions. Select **PHStat→Descriptive Statistics→One-Way Tables & Charts**. Complete the One-Way Tables & Charts dialog box as shown below. Click **OK**.

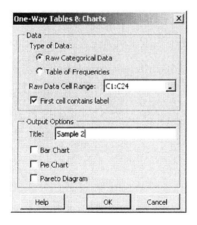

© 2006 Pearson Education, Inc., Upper Saddle River, NJ. All rights reserved. This material is protected under all copyright laws as they currently exist. No portion of this material may be reproduced, in any form or by any means, without permission in writing from the publisher.

12. The frequency distribution table is displayed in a worksheet named "OneWayTable2." In this example, you can see that the value of 94 and 133 have a frequency of 2.

	A	B
1	Sample 2	
2		
3	Count of 167	
4	167 ▼	Total
5	1	1
6	23	1
7	31	1
8	60	1
9	70	1
10	72	1
11	94	2
12	105	1
13	110	1
14	111	1
15	123	1
16	133	2
17	167	1
18	169	1
19	224	1
20	263	1
21	286	1
22	301	1

Scrolling down, you see no more repetitions in this example.

23	324	1
24	329	1
25	345	1
26	Grand Total	23

13. Repeat the appropriate steps until you have generated 10 different samples of 24 numbers.

◀

© 2006 Pearson Education, Inc., Upper Saddle River, NJ. All rights reserved. This material is protected under all copyright laws as they currently exist.
No portion of this material may be reproduced, in any form or by any means, without permission in writing from the publisher.

Section 3.4 Counting Principles

► Example 3 (pg. 152)	Finding the Number of Permutations of n Objects

1. You are asked to determine how many different final standings are possible in the Central Division. Open a new Excel worksheet and click in cell **A1** to place the output there. You will be using the PERMUT function to calculate the number of permutations.

2. Click **Insert→Function**.

3. Select the **Statistical** category. Select the **PERMUT** function. Click **OK**.

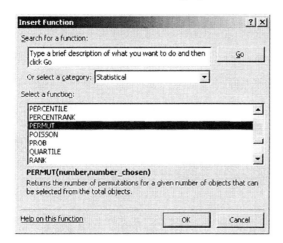

© 2006 Pearson Education, Inc., Upper Saddle River, NJ. All rights reserved. This material is protected under all copyright laws as they currently exist.
No portion of this material may be reproduced, in any form or by any means, without permission in writing from the publisher.

4.   Complete the PERMUT dialog box as shown below. There are six teams in the
     National League Central Division. The number of different final standings is equal
     to 6! Click **OK**.

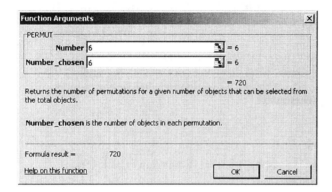

The output is shown below. There are 720 possible different final standings.

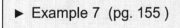

► Example 7 (pg. 155)   Finding the Number of Combinations

1.   You are asked to calculate how many ways the manager can form a three-person
     advisory committee from 16 employees. You will be using the COMBIN function
     to calculate the number of combinations. Open a new Excel worksheet and click in
     cell **A1** to place the output there.

2.   Click **Insert→Function**.

© 2006 Pearson Education, Inc., Upper Saddle River, NJ. All rights reserved. This material is protected under all copyright laws as they currently exist.
No portion of this material may be reproduced, in any form or by any means, without permission in writing from the publisher.

3. Select the **Math & Trig** category. Select the **COMBIN** function. Click **OK**.

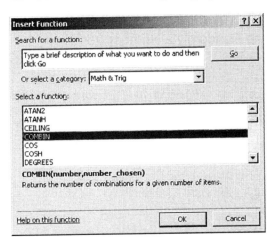

4. Complete the COMBIN dialog box as shown below. Click **OK**.

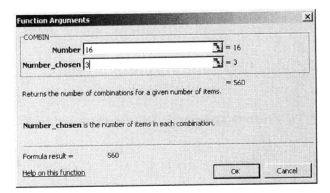

The output is shown below. There are 1,820 different combinations.

© 2006 Pearson Education, Inc., Upper Saddle River, NJ. All rights reserved. This material is protected under all copyright laws as they currently exist. No portion of this material may be reproduced, in any form or by any means, without permission in writing from the publisher.

Technology

▶ Exercise 3 (pg. 169)	Selecting Randomly a Number from 1 to 11

If the PHStat2 add-in has not been loaded, you will need to load it before continuing. Follow the instructions in Section GS 8.2.

You will be given the steps to follow to complete Exercise 3 and Exercise 3B.

1. You will first select randomly a number between 1 and 11. Open a new Excel worksheet. Enter the numbers 1 through 11 in cells A1 through A11 as shown below.

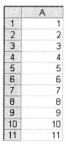

2. At the top of the screen, click **Tools→Data Analysis**. Select **Sampling**, and click **OK**.

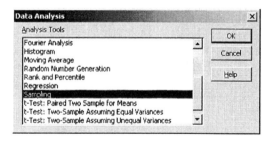

© 2006 Pearson Education, Inc., Upper Saddle River, NJ. All rights reserved. This material is protected under all copyright laws as they currently exist. No portion of this material may be reproduced, in any form or by any means, without permission in writing from the publisher.

3. Complete the Sampling dialog box as shown below. Click **OK**.

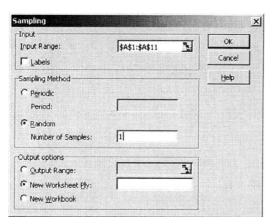

4. The output is displayed in a new sheet. The number 6 was selected. Because the
    number was selected randomly, your output may not be the same. You will now
    select randomly 100 integers from 1 to 11. Click the **Sheet1** tab near the bottom of
    the screen to go back to the worksheet displaying the numbers from 1 to 11.

5. Click **Tools→Data Analysis**. Select **Sampling** and click **OK**.

6. Complete the Sampling dialog box as shown below. Click **OK**.

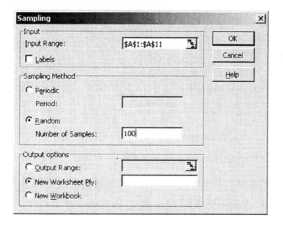

© 2006 Pearson Education, Inc., Upper Saddle River, NJ. All rights reserved. This material is protected under all copyright laws as they currently exist.
No portion of this material may be reproduced, in any form or by any means, without permission in writing from the publisher.

7. The output is displayed in a new sheet. You will need to scroll down to see the entire listing of the 100 randomly generated integers. You will now tally the results. Select **PHStat→Descriptive Statistics→One-Way Tables & Charts**.

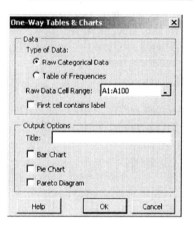

8. Complete the One-Way Tables & Charts dialog box as shown below. Click **OK**.

Be sure to remove the checkmark next to First cell contains label. Otherwise, your summary table will include only 99 observations.

The output for Exercise 3B is displayed below. Your output should have the same format. Because the numbers were generated randomly, however, it is not likely that your numbers will be exactly the same.

	A	B	C
1	One-Way Summary Table		
2			
3	Count of Variable		
4	Variable ▼	Total	
5	1	10	
6	2	7	
7	3	17	
8	4	12	
9	5	8	
10	6	13	
11	7	5	
12	8	6	
13	9	11	
14	10	8	
15	11	3	
16	Grand Total	100	

◀

▶ Exercise 5 (pg. 169)	Composing Mozart Variations with Dice

If the PHStat2 add-in has not been loaded, you will need to load it before continuing. Follow the instructions in Section GS 8.2.

You will first be given the steps to follow to complete Exercise 5 and then the steps to follow to complete Exercise 5B. In Exercise 5, you will select randomly two integers from 1, 2, 3, 4, 5, and 6. This simulates tossing two six-sided dice one time. You will then sum the two integers and subtract 1 from the sum. This is Mozart's procedure (described at the top of page 169) for selecting a musical phrase from 11 different choices.

1. To select randomly two integers between 1 and 6, begin by opening a new Excel worksheet and entering the numbers 1 through 6 in column A as shown below.

	A
1	1
2	2
3	3
4	4
5	5
6	6

© 2006 Pearson Education, Inc., Upper Saddle River, NJ. All rights reserved. This material is protected under all copyright laws as they currently exist. No portion of this material may be reproduced, in any form or by any means, without permission in writing from the publisher.

2.   At the top of the screen, click **Tools→Data Analysis**. Select **Sampling** and click
     OK.

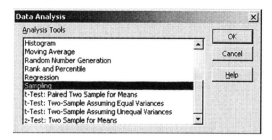

3.   Complete the Sampling dialog box as shown below. Click **OK**.

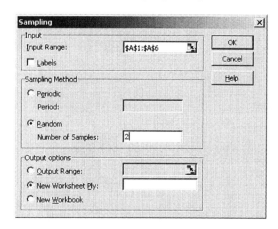

4.   The output is displayed in a new worksheet. The numbers 6 and 4 were selected.
     Mozart's instructions are to sum the numbers and subtract 1. The result is 9.
     Therefore, musical phrase number 9 would be selected for the first bar of Mozart's
     minuet.

© 2006 Pearson Education, Inc., Upper Saddle River, NJ. All rights reserved. This material is protected under all copyright laws as they currently exist.
No portion of this material may be reproduced, in any form or by any means, without permission in writing from the publisher.

5. Exercise 5B asks you to select 100 integers between 1 and 11. This simulates, 100
    times, Mozart's procedure of tossing two die, finding the sum, and subtracting 1.
    You are also asked to tally the results. Begin by entering the numbers 1 through 11
    in a new worksheet as shown below.

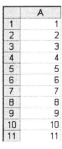

6. Click **Tools→Data Analysis**. Select **Sampling** and click **OK**.

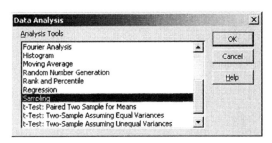

7. Complete the Sampling dialog box as shown below. Click **OK**.

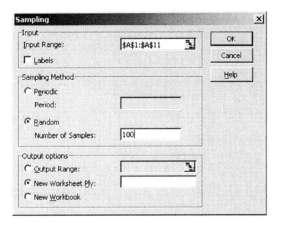

© 2006 Pearson Education, Inc., Upper Saddle River, NJ. All rights reserved. This material is protected under all copyright laws as they currently exist.
No portion of this material may be reproduced, in any form or by any means, without permission in writing from the publisher.

8. The output is displayed in a new sheet. You need to scroll down to see the entire listing of the 100 randomly generated integers. You will now tally the results. Select **PHStat→Descriptive Statistics→One-Way Tables & Charts**.

	A
1	9
2	10
3	10
4	11
5	10
6	5
7	4

9. Complete the One-Way Tables and Charts dialog box as shown below. Click **OK**.

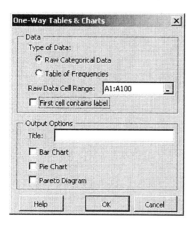

10. The output from Exercise 5B is displayed below. Because the numbers were generated randomly, it unlikely that your numbers will be exactly the same.

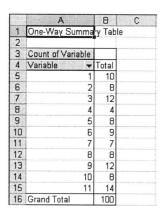

	A	B	C
1	One-Way Summary Table		
2			
3	Count of Variable		
4	Variable	Total	
5	1	10	
6	2	8	
7	3	12	
8	4	4	
9	5	8	
10	6	9	
11	7	7	
12	8	8	
13	9	12	
14	10	8	
15	11	14	
16	Grand Total	100	

© 2006 Pearson Education, Inc., Upper Saddle River, NJ. All rights reserved. This material is protected under all copyright laws as they currently exist. No portion of this material may be reproduced, in any form or by any means, without permission in writing from the publisher.

Discrete Probability Distributions

Section 4.2 Binomial Distributions

| ▶ Example 4 (pg. 188) | Finding a Binomial Probability Using Technology |

1. In Try It Yourself 4, you are asked to find the probability that exactly 178 people will use more than one topping on their hot dogs. Open a new Excel worksheet and click in cell **A1** to place the output there.

2. Click **Insert→Function**.

3. Select the **Statistical** category. Select the **BINOMDIST** function. Click **OK**.

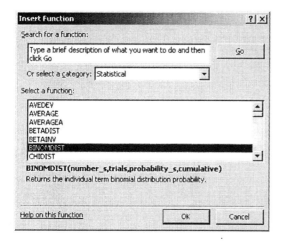

© 2006 Pearson Education, Inc., Upper Saddle River, NJ. All rights reserved. This material is protected under all copyright laws as they currently exist. No portion of this material may be reproduced, in any form or by any means, without permission in writing from the publisher.

4. Complete the BINOMDIST dialog box as shown below. Click **OK**.

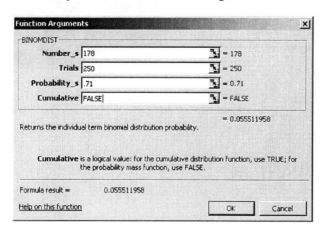

The BINOMDIST function returns a result of 0.055512.

▶ Example 7 (pg. 191)   Constructing and Graphing a Binomial Distribution

1. Open a new, blank Excel worksheet and enter the information shown below. You will be using the BINOMDIST function to calculate binomial probabilities for 0, 1, 2, 3, 4, 5, and 6 households.

	A	B	C
1	Households	Relative frequency	
2	0		
3	1		
4	2		
5	3		
6	4		
7	5		
8	6		

2. Click in cell **B2** below "Relative frequency." Click **Insert→Function**.

© 2006 Pearson Education, Inc., Upper Saddle River, NJ. All rights reserved. This material is protected under all copyright laws as they currently exist. No portion of this material may be reproduced, in any form or by any means, without permission in writing from the publisher.

3. Under Function category, select **Statistical**. Under Function name, select
   BINOMDIST. Click **OK**.

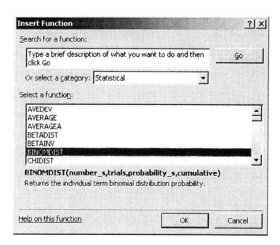

4. Complete the BINOMDIST dialog box as shown below. Click **OK**.

*You are entering a relative cell address without dollar signs (i.e., A2) in the
Number_s field because you will be copying the contents of cell B2 to cells B3
through B8. You want the column A cell address to change from A2 to A3, A4, A5,
..., A8 when the formula is copied from cell B2 to cells B3 through B8.*

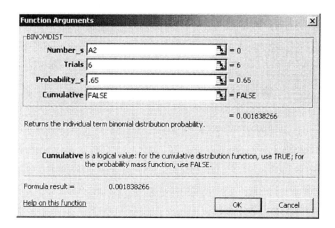

© 2006 Pearson Education, Inc., Upper Saddle River, NJ. All rights reserved. This material is protected under all copyright laws as they currently exist.
No portion of this material may be reproduced, in any form or by any means, without permission in writing from the publisher.

5. Copy the contents of cell B2 to cells B3 through B8.

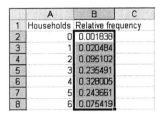

	A	B	C
1	Households	Relative frequency	
2	0	0.001838	
3	1	0.020484	
4	2	0.095102	
5	3	0.235491	
6	4	0.328005	
7	5	0.243661	
8	6	0.075419	

6. Click in any cell in the data table. Then click **Insert→Chart**.

7. Under Chart type, in the Chart Type dialog box, select **Column**. Under Chart sub-type, select the first one in the top row by clicking on it. Click **Next**.

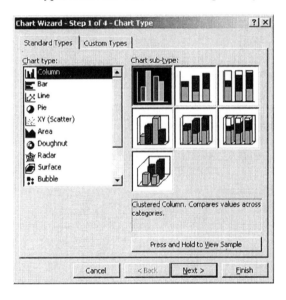

© 2006 Pearson Education, Inc., Upper Saddle River, NJ. All rights reserved. This material is protected under all copyright laws as they currently exist.
No portion of this material may be reproduced, in any form or by any means, without permission in writing from the publisher.

8. Check the accuracy of the data range in the Chart Source Data dialog box. It should read **=Sheet1!$A$1:$B$8**. Make any necessary corrections. Then click **Next**.

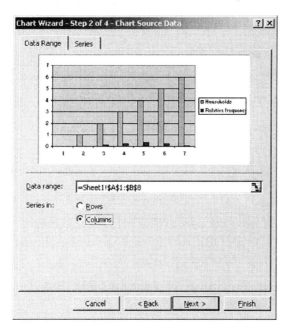

9. Click the **Titles** tab at the top of the Chart Options dialog box. In the Chart title window, enter **Subscribing to Cable TV**. In the Category (X) axis window, enter **Households**. In the Value (Y) axis window, enter **Relative Frequency**.

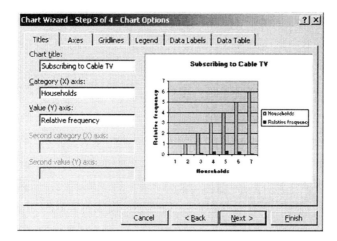

© 2006 Pearson Education, Inc., Upper Saddle River, NJ. All rights reserved. This material is protected under all copyright laws as they currently exist. No portion of this material may be reproduced, in any form or by any means, without permission in writing from the publisher.

10.   Click the **Legend** tab at the top of the Chart Options dialog box. Click in the box to the left of **Show legend** so that no checkmark appears there. This will remove the Households and Relative frequency legends on the right side of the chart. Click **Next**.

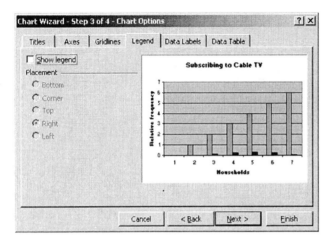

11.   The Chart Location dialog box presents two options for placement of the chart. For this example, select **As object in**. Click **Finish**.

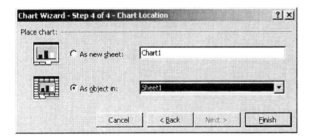

© 2006 Pearson Education, Inc., Upper Saddle River, NJ. All rights reserved. This material is protected under all copyright laws as they currently exist.
No portion of this material may be reproduced, in any form or by any means, without permission in writing from the publisher.

12. Make the chart taller so that it is easier to read. To do this, first click within the figure near a border so that black square handles appear. Click on the center handle on the bottom border of the figure and drag it down a few rows. Your chart should look similar to the one shown below.

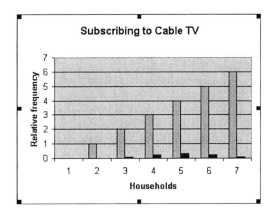

13. Correct the number scales displayed on the Y-axis and the X-axis. **Right click** on one of the vertical bars. Select **Source Data** from the shortcut menu that appears.

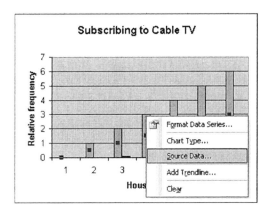

© 2006 Pearson Education, Inc., Upper Saddle River, NJ. All rights reserved. This material is protected under all copyright laws as they currently exist. No portion of this material may be reproduced, in any form or by any means, without permission in writing from the publisher.

14. Click the **Series** tab at the top of the Source Data dialog box. In the Series window, select **Relative Frequency** by clicking on it. Then click the **Remove** button below the Series window.

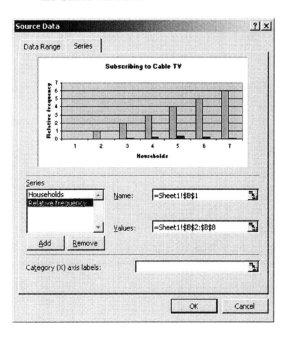

© 2006 Pearson Education, Inc., Upper Saddle River, NJ. All rights reserved. This material is protected under all copyright laws as they currently exist. No portion of this material may be reproduced, in any form or by any means, without permission in writing from the publisher.

15. The Y-axis values are displayed in column B, so the entry in the **Values** window should be =**Sheet1!$B$2:$B$8**. First delete the information in the Values window. Next, click in the Values window, click on cell B2 of the worksheet, and drag down to cell B8. In the Values window, you should now see =**Sheet1!$B$2:$B$8**.

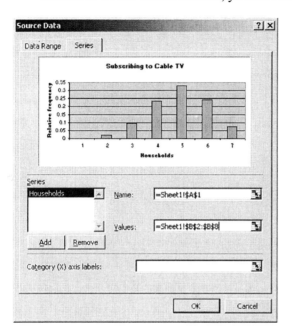

© 2006 Pearson Education, Inc., Upper Saddle River, NJ. All rights reserved. This material is protected under all copyright laws as they currently exist. No portion of this material may be reproduced, in any form or by any means, without permission in writing from the publisher.

16. Column A contains the numbers you want displayed on the X-axis. Click in the Category (X) axis labels window. Then click on cell A2 of the worksheet and drag down to cell A8. The entry in the Category (X) axis labels field should now read **=Sheet1!$A$2:$A$8**. Click **OK**.

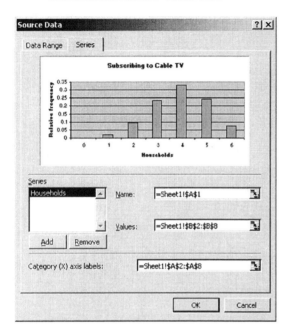

17. Remove the space between the vertical bars. **Right click** on one of the vertical bars. Select **Format Data Series** from the shortcut menu that appears.

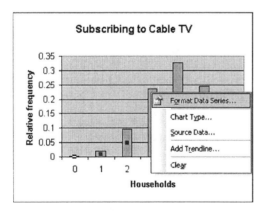

© 2006 Pearson Education, Inc., Upper Saddle River, NJ. All rights reserved. This material is protected under all copyright laws as they currently exist. No portion of this material may be reproduced, in any form or by any means, without permission in writing from the publisher.

18. Click the **Options** tab at the top of the Format Data Series dialog box. Change the value in the Gap width box to 0. Click **OK**. Your relative frequency histogram should look similar to the one shown below.

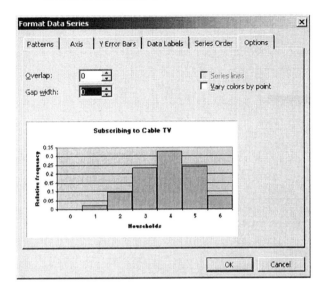

Section 4.3 More Discrete Probability Distributions

▶ Example 3 (pg. 200)	Finding a Poisson Probability

You will be using the POISSON function to find the probability that 2 rabbits are found on any given acre of a field when a population count shows that there is an average of 3.6 rabbits per acre living in the field.

1. Open a new Excel worksheet and click in cell **A1** to place the output there.

2. At the top of the screen, click **Insert→Function**.

© 2006 Pearson Education, Inc., Upper Saddle River, NJ. All rights reserved. This material is protected under all copyright laws as they currently exist.
No portion of this material may be reproduced, in any form or by any means, without permission in writing from the publisher.

3.   Select the **Statistical** category. Select the **POISSON** function. Click **OK**.

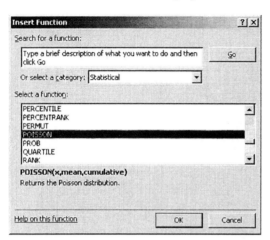

4.   Complete the POISSON dialog box as shown below. Click **OK**.

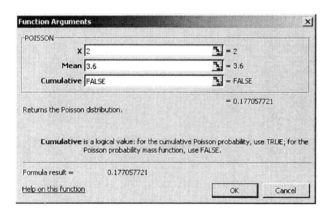

The POISSON function returns a result of 0.177058.

© 2006 Pearson Education, Inc., Upper Saddle River, NJ. All rights reserved. This material is protected under all copyright laws as they currently exist.
No portion of this material may be reproduced, in any form or by any means, without permission in writing from the publisher.

Technology

▶ Exercise 1 (pg. 213) Creating a Poisson Distribution with μ = 4 for x = 0 to 20

1. Open a new Excel worksheet and enter the numbers 0 through 20 in column A as shown below. Then click in cell **B1** of the worksheet to place the output from the POISSON function there.

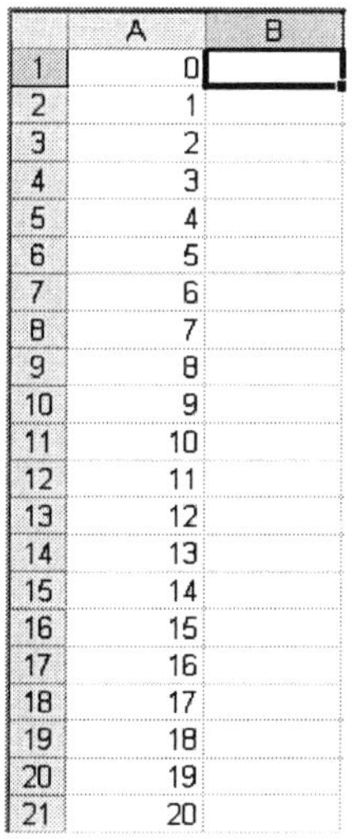

	A	B
1	0	
2	1	
3	2	
4	3	
5	4	
6	5	
7	6	
8	7	
9	8	
10	9	
11	10	
12	11	
13	12	
14	13	
15	14	
16	15	
17	16	
18	17	
19	18	
20	19	
21	20	

2. At the top of the screen, click **Insert→Function**.

© 2006 Pearson Education, Inc., Upper Saddle River, NJ. All rights reserved. This material is protected under all copyright laws as they currently exist. No portion of this material may be reproduced, in any form or by any means, without permission in writing from the publisher.

3. Select the **Statistical** category. Select the **POISSON** function. Click **OK**.

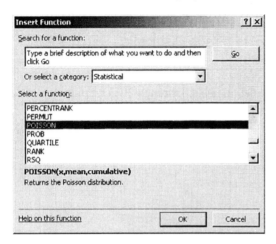

4. Complete the POISSON dialog box as shown below. Click **OK**.

You are entering a relative cell address without dollar signs (i.e., A1) in the X field because you will be copying the contents of cell B1 to cells B2 through B11. You want the column A cell address to change from A1 to A2, A3, A4, ..., A21 when the formula is copied from cell B1 to cells B2 through B21.

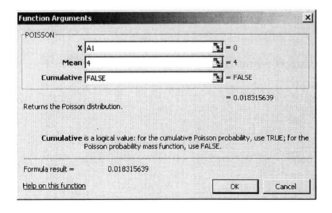

© 2006 Pearson Education, Inc., Upper Saddle River, NJ. All rights reserved. This material is protected under all copyright laws as they currently exist. No portion of this material may be reproduced, in any form or by any means, without permission in writing from the publisher.

5. Copy the contents of cell B1 to cells B2 through B11.

	A	B
1	0	0.018316
2	1	0.073263
3	2	0.146525
4	3	0.195367
5	4	0.195367
6	5	0.156293
7	6	0.104196
8	7	0.05954
9	8	0.02977
10	9	0.013231
11	10	0.005292
12	11	0.001925
13	12	0.000642
14	13	0.000197
15	14	5.64E-05
16	15	1.5E-05
17	16	3.76E-06
18	17	8.85E-07
19	18	1.97E-07
20	19	4.14E-08
21	20	8.28E-09

6. Construct a histogram of the Poisson distribution. First click in any cell of the table in the worksheet. Then, at the top of the screen, click **Insert→Chart**.

7. Under Chart type, in the Chart Type dialog box, select **Column**. Under Chart sub-type, select the first one in the top row by clicking on it. Click **Next**.

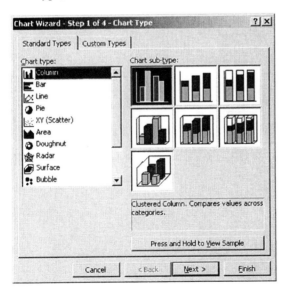

© 2006 Pearson Education, Inc., Upper Saddle River, NJ. All rights reserved. This material is protected under all copyright laws as they currently exist. No portion of this material may be reproduced, in any form or by any means, without permission in writing from the publisher.

8. Check the accuracy of the data range in the Chart Source Data dialog box. It should read **=Sheet1!$A$1:$B$21**. Make any necessary corrections. Then click **Next**.

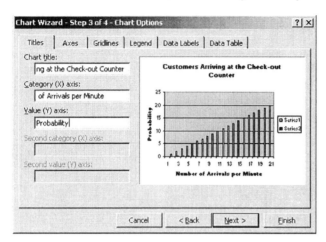

9. Click the **Titles** tab at the top of the Chart Options dialog box. In the Chart title window, enter **Customers Arriving at the Check-out Counter**. In the Category (X) axis window, enter **Number of Arrivals per Minute**. In the Value (Y) axis window, enter **Probability**.

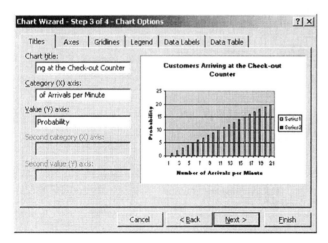

© 2006 Pearson Education, Inc., Upper Saddle River, NJ. All rights reserved. This material is protected under all copyright laws as they currently exist. No portion of this material may be reproduced, in any form or by any means, without permission in writing from the publisher.

10. Click the **Legend** tab at the top of the Chart Options dialog box. Click in the box to the left of **Show Legend** to remove the checkmark. The removal of the checkmark will delete the Series 1 and Series 2 legends from the right side of the histogram chart. Click **Next**.

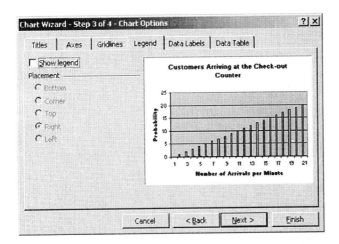

11. The Chart Location dialog box presents two options for placement of the chart. For this exercise, select **As object in**. Click **Finish**.

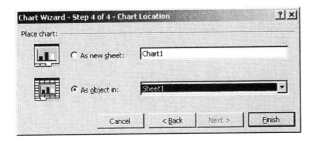

© 2006 Pearson Education, Inc., Upper Saddle River, NJ. All rights reserved. This material is protected under all copyright laws as they currently exist. No portion of this material may be reproduced, in any form or by any means, without permission in writing from the publisher.

12. Make the chart taller so that it is easier to read. To do this, first click within the figure near a border so that black square handles appear. Click on the center handle on the bottom border of the figure and drag it down a few rows. Your chart should look similar to the one shown below.

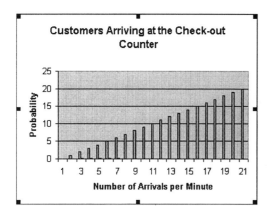

13. Correct the number scales displayed on the Y-axis and the X-axis. **Right click** on one of the vertical bars. Select **Source Data** from the shortcut menu that appears.

© 2006 Pearson Education, Inc., Upper Saddle River, NJ. All rights reserved. This material is protected under all copyright laws as they currently exist. No portion of this material may be reproduced, in any form or by any means, without permission in writing from the publisher.

14. Click the **Series** tab at the top of the Source Data dialog box. In the Series window, select Series1 by clicking on it. Then click the **Remove** button below the Series window.

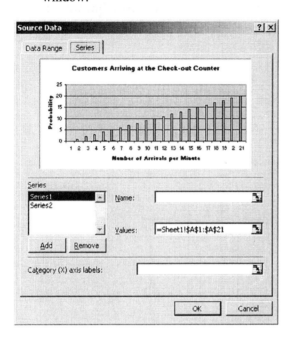

© 2006 Pearson Education, Inc., Upper Saddle River, NJ. All rights reserved. This material is protected under all copyright laws as they currently exist. No portion of this material may be reproduced, in any form or by any means, without permission in writing from the publisher.

15. The probabilities that should be displayed on the Y-axis are located in column B of
     the worksheet. The entry in the Values window should be **=Sheet1!$B$1:$B$21**.
     Revise the entry if necessary. To do this, first delete the information in the Values
     window. Then click in the Values window. Next click in cell B1 of the worksheet
     and drag down to cell B21. In the Values window you should now see
     =Sheet1!$B$1:$B$21.

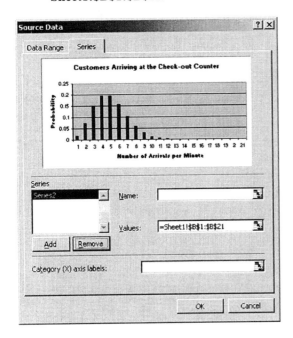

© 2006 Pearson Education, Inc., Upper Saddle River, NJ. All rights reserved. This material is protected under all copyright laws as they currently exist.
No portion of this material may be reproduced, in any form or by any means, without permission in writing from the publisher.

16. The numbers you want displayed on the X-axis are in column A of the worksheet. Click in the Category (X) axis labels window. Then click on cell A1 of the worksheet and drag down to cell A21. The entry in the Category (X) axis labels field should now read **=Sheet1!$A$1:$A$21**. Click **OK**.

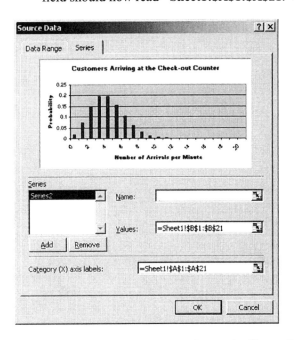

17. Remove the space between the vertical bars. **Right click** on one of the vertical bars. Select **Format Data Series** from the shortcut menu that appears.

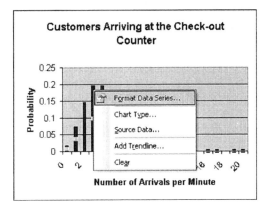

© 2006 Pearson Education, Inc., Upper Saddle River, NJ. All rights reserved. This material is protected under all copyright laws as they currently exist. No portion of this material may be reproduced, in any form or by any means, without permission in writing from the publisher.

18. Click the **Options** tab at the top of the Format Data Series dialog box. Change the value in the Gap width box to 0. Click **OK**. Your histogram should look similar to the one shown below.

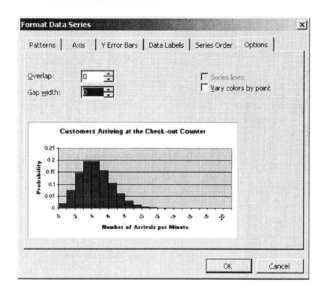

| ► Exercise 3 (pg. 213) | Generating a List of 20 Random Numbers with a Poisson Distribution for μ = 4 |

1. Open a new, blank Excel worksheet. At the top of the screen, click **Tools→Data Analysis**. Select **Random Number Generation** and click **OK**.

If Data Analysis does not appear as a choice in the Tools menu, you will need to load the Microsoft Excel Analysis ToolPak add-in. Follow the procedure in Section GS 8.1 before continuing.

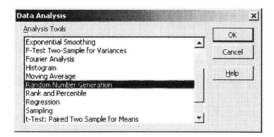

© 2006 Pearson Education, Inc., Upper Saddle River, NJ. All rights reserved. This material is protected under all copyright laws as they currently exist.
No portion of this material may be reproduced, in any form or by any means, without permission in writing from the publisher.

2. Complete the Random Number Generation dialog box as shown below. The
    Number of Variables indicates the number of columns of values that you want in
    the output table. **Number of Random Numbers** to be generated is 20. Select the
    Poisson distribution. **Lambda** is the expected value (μ), which is equal to 4. The
    output will be placed in the current worksheet with A1 as the left topmost cell.
    Click **OK**.

The 20 numbers generated for this example are shown below. Because the numbers were
generated randomly, it is not likely that your numbers will be exactly the same.

	A
1	4
2	6
3	3
4	3
5	2
6	4
7	4
8	4
9	4
10	0
11	3
12	5
13	1
14	5
15	4
16	2
17	6
18	3
19	2
20	5

© 2006 Pearson Education, Inc., Upper Saddle River, NJ. All rights reserved. This material is protected under all copyright laws as they currently exist.
No portion of this material may be reproduced, in any form or by any means, without permission in writing from the publisher.

Normal Probability Distributions

Section 5.1 Introduction to Normal Distributions and the Standard Normal Distribution

▶ Example 4 (pg. 222)   Finding Area Under the Standard Normal Curve

1. Open a new Excel worksheet and click in cell **A1** to place the output there.

2. At the top of the screen, click **Insert→Function**.

3. Select the **Statistical** category. Select the **NORMSDIST** function. Click **OK**.

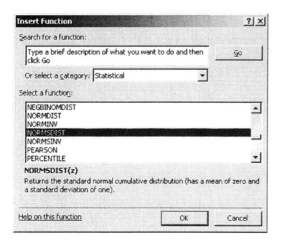

© 2006 Pearson Education, Inc., Upper Saddle River, NJ. All rights reserved. This material is protected under all copyright laws as they currently exist. No portion of this material may be reproduced, in any form or by any means, without permission in writing from the publisher.

4. Complete the NORMSDIST dialog box as shown below. Click **OK**.

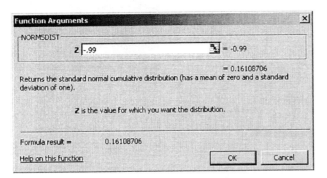

The output is displayed in cell A1 of the worksheet. The area under the standard normal curve to the left of z = –0.99 is 0.161087.

► Example 5 (pg. 222)	Finding Area Under the Standard Normal Curve

1. Open a new Excel worksheet. The area to the right of z = 1.06 is equal to 1 minus the area to the left of z = 1.06. In cell A1, enter **=1-** as shown below.

2. At the top of the screen, click **Insert→Function**.

© 2006 Pearson Education, Inc., Upper Saddle River, NJ. All rights reserved. This material is protected under all copyright laws as they currently exist. No portion of this material may be reproduced, in any form or by any means, without permission in writing from the publisher.

3. Select the **Statistical** category. Select the **NORMSDIST** function. Click **OK**.

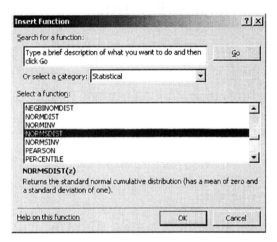

4. Complete the NORMSDIST dialog box as shown below. Click **OK**.

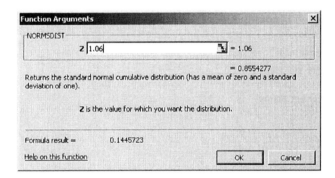

The output is displayed in cell A1 of the worksheet. The area under the standard normal curve to the right of z = 1.06 is 0.144572. In the formula bar, you should see f_x =1-NORMSDIST(1.06).

© 2006 Pearson Education, Inc., Upper Saddle River, NJ. All rights reserved. This material is protected under all copyright laws as they currently exist. No portion of this material may be reproduced, in any form or by any means, without permission in writing from the publisher.

Section 5.2 Normal Distributions: Finding Probabilities

▶ Example 3 (pg. 231)	Using Technology to Find Normal Probabilities

1.   Open a new Excel worksheet and click in cell **A1** to place the output there.

2.   At the top of the screen, click **Insert→Function**.

3.   Select the **Statistical** category. Select the **NORMDIST** function. Click **OK**.

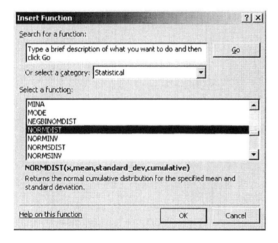

© 2006 Pearson Education, Inc., Upper Saddle River, NJ. All rights reserved. This material is protected under all copyright laws as they currently exist.
No portion of this material may be reproduced, in any form or by any means, without permission in writing from the publisher.

4.   Complete the NORMDIST dialog box as shown below. Click **OK**.

The output is displayed in cell A1 of the worksheet. The probability is equal to 0.054799.

	A
1	0.054799

◀

5.3 Normal Distributions: Finding Values

▶ Example 2 (pg. 238)	Finding a z-Score Given a Percentile

1.   We will start with finding the z-score that corresponds to P_5. Open a new Excel worksheet and click in cell **A1** to place the output there.

2.   At the top of the screen, click **Insert→Function**.

© 2006 Pearson Education, Inc., Upper Saddle River, NJ. All rights reserved. This material is protected under all copyright laws as they currently exist. No portion of this material may be reproduced, in any form or by any means, without permission in writing from the publisher.

3. Select the Statistical category. Select the **NORMSINV** function. Click **OK**.

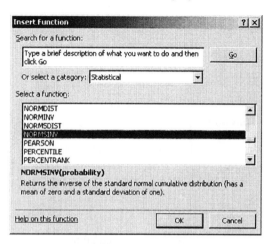

4. Complete the NORMSINV dialog box as shown below. Click **OK**.

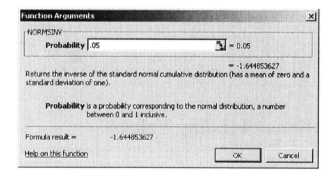

5. The function returns a z-score of -1.64485. To find the z-scores for P50 and P90, repeat these steps using probabilities of .50 and .90, respectively.

◀

© 2006 Pearson Education, Inc., Upper Saddle River, NJ. All rights reserved. This material is protected under all copyright laws as they currently exist. No portion of this material may be reproduced, in any form or by any means, without permission in writing from the publisher.

▶ Example 4 (pg. 240)   Finding a Specific Data Value

1. You will find the lowest civil service exam score you can earn and still be eligible for employment. Open a new Excel worksheet and click in cell **A1** to place the output there.

2. At the top of the screen, click **Insert→Function**.

3. Select the **Statistical** category. Select the **NORMINV** function. Click **OK**.

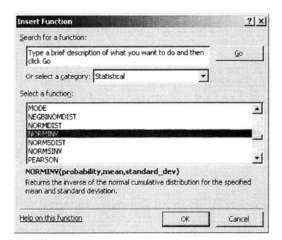

4. Complete the NORMINV dialog box as shown below. Click **OK**.

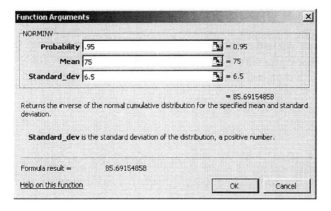

© 2006 Pearson Education, Inc., Upper Saddle River, NJ. All rights reserved. This material is protected under all copyright laws as they currently exist.
No portion of this material may be reproduced, in any form or by any means, without permission in writing from the publisher.

5. The NORMINV function returns a value of 85.69155.

	A
1	85.69155

◀

Technology

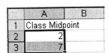

▶ Exercise 1 (pg. 277)   Finding the Mean Age in the United States

1. Open a new, blank Excel worksheet. Enter **Class Midpoint** in cell A1. You will be entering the numbers displayed in the table on page 277 of your text. Begin by entering the first two midpoints, **2** and **7**, as shown below.

	A	B
1	Class Midpoint	
2	2	
3	7	

2. You will now fill column A with a series. Click in cell A2 and drag down to cell A3 so that both cells are highlighted.

	A	B
1	Class Midpoint	
2	2	
3	7	

3. Move the mouse pointer in cell A3 to the right lower corner of the cell so that the white plus sign turns into a black plus sign. The black plus sign is called the "fill handle." Click the left mouse button and drag the fill handle down to cell A21.

© 2006 Pearson Education, Inc., Upper Saddle River, NJ. All rights reserved. This material is protected under all copyright laws as they currently exist.
No portion of this material may be reproduced, in any form or by any means, without permission in writing from the publisher.

	A	B
1	Class Midpoint	
2	2	
3	7	
4	12	
5	17	
6	22	
7	27	
8	32	
9	37	
10	42	
11	47	
12	52	
13	57	
14	62	
15	67	
16	72	
17	77	
18	82	
19	87	
20	92	
21	97	

4. Enter **Relative Frequency** in cell B1. Then enter the proportion equivalents of the percentages in column B as shown below.

	A	B	C
1	Class Midpoint	Relative Frequency	
2	2	0.067	
3	7	0.068	
4	12	0.074	
5	17	0.072	
6	22	0.07	
7	27	0.062	
8	32	0.068	
9	37	0.073	
10	42	0.081	
11	47	0.076	
12	52	0.066	
13	57	0.055	
14	62	0.042	
15	67	0.034	
16	72	0.03	
17	77	0.026	
18	82	0.019	
19	87	0.01	
20	92	0.005	
21	97	0.002	

5. Click in cell C2 and enter a formula to multiply the midpoint by the relative frequency. The formula is **=A2*B2**. Press [**Enter**].

	A	B	C
1	Class Midpoint	Relative Frequency	
2	2	0.067	=A2*B2
3	7	0.068	

6. Copy the contents of cell C2 to cells C3 through C21.

© 2006 Pearson Education, Inc., Upper Saddle River, NJ. All rights reserved. This material is protected under all copyright laws as they currently exist.
No portion of this material may be reproduced, in any form or by any means, without permission in writing from the publisher.

	A	B	C
1	Class Midpoint	Relative Frequency	
2	2	0.067	0.134
3	7	0.068	0.476
4	12	0.074	0.888
5	17	0.072	1.224
6	22	0.07	1.54
7	27	0.062	1.674
8	32	0.068	2.176
9	37	0.073	2.701
10	42	0.081	3.402
11	47	0.076	3.572
12	52	0.066	3.432
13	57	0.055	3.135
14	62	0.042	2.604
15	67	0.034	2.278
16	72	0.03	2.16
17	77	0.026	2.002
18	82	0.019	1.558
19	87	0.01	0.87
20	92	0.005	0.46
21	97	0.002	0.194

7. The weighted mean is equal to the sum of the products in column C. (Refer to
    Section 2.3 in your text.) Click in cell **C22** of the worksheet to place the sum there.
    Click the AutoSum button near the top of the screen. It looks like this: . The
    range of numbers to be included in the sum is displayed in cell C22. You should see
    =SUM(C2:C21). Make any necessary corrections. Then press [**Enter**].

20	92	0.005	0.46
21	97	0.002	0.194
22			=SUM(C2:C21)

8. The mean, displayed in cell C22, is 36.48 years. Save this worksheet so that you
    can use it again for Exercise 5, page 277.

20	92	0.005	0.46
21	97	0.002	0.194
22			36.48

◀

► **Exercise 2 (pg. 277)**   Finding the Mean of the Set of Sample
                            Means

1. Open worksheet "Tech5" in the Chapter 5 folder.

© 2006 Pearson Education, Inc., Upper Saddle River, NJ. All rights reserved. This material is protected under all copyright laws as they currently exist.
No portion of this material may be reproduced, in any form or by any means, without permission in writing from the publisher.

2. Click in cell **A38** at the bottom of the column of numbers to place the mean in that cell.

3. At the top of the screen, click **Insert→Function**.

4. Select the **Statistical** category. Select the **AVERAGE** function. Click **OK**.

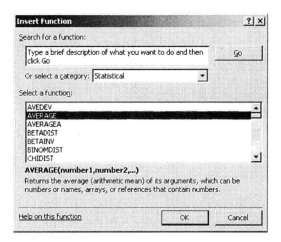

5. The range that will be included in the average is shown in the Number 1 window. Check to be sure that it is accurate. It should read **A2:A37**. Make any necessary corrections. Then click **OK**.

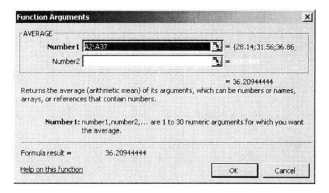

© 2006 Pearson Education, Inc., Upper Saddle River, NJ. All rights reserved. This material is protected under all copyright laws as they currently exist.
No portion of this material may be reproduced, in any form or by any means, without permission in writing from the publisher.

The mean of the sample means is displayed in cell A38 of the worksheet. The mean is equal to 36.20944.

36	31.27
37	35.8
38	36.20944

| ► Exercise 5 (pg. 277) | Finding the Standard Deviation of Ages in the United States |

1. Open the worksheet that you prepared for Exercise 1, page 277.

	A	B	C
1	Class Midpoint	Relative Frequency	
2	2	0.067	0.134
3	7	0.068	0.476
4	12	0.074	0.888
5	17	0.072	1.224

2. To find the standard deviation of the population of ages, you will first calculate squared deviation scores. Click in cell **D1** and enter the label, **Sqd Dev Score**.

	A	B	C	D	E
1	Class Midpoint	Relative Frequency		Sqd Dev Score	
2		2	0.067	0.134	

3. Click in cell **D2** and enter the formula =(A2-36.48)^2 and press [**Enter**].

	A	B	C	D	E
1	Class Midpoint	Relative Frequency		Sqd Dev Score	
2	2	0.067	0.134	=(A2-36.48)^2	

4. Copy the formula in cell D2 to cells D3 through D21.

© 2006 Pearson Education, Inc., Upper Saddle River, NJ. All rights reserved. This material is protected under all copyright laws as they currently exist. No portion of this material may be reproduced, in any form or by any means, without permission in writing from the publisher.

	A	B	C	D	E
1	Class Midpoint	Relative Frequency		Sqd Dev Score	
2	2	0.067	0.134	1188.87	
3	7	0.068	0.476	869.0704	
4	12	0.074	0.888	599.2704	
5	17	0.072	1.224	379.4704	
6	22	0.07	1.54	209.6704	
7	27	0.062	1.674	89.8704	
8	32	0.068	2.176	20.0704	
9	37	0.073	2.701	0.2704	
10	42	0.081	3.402	30.4704	
11	47	0.076	3.572	110.6704	
12	52	0.066	3.432	240.8704	
13	57	0.055	3.135	421.0704	
14	62	0.042	2.604	651.2704	
15	67	0.034	2.278	931.4704	
16	72	0.03	2.16	1261.67	
17	77	0.026	2.002	1641.87	
18	82	0.019	1.558	2072.07	
19	87	0.01	0.87	2552.27	
20	92	0.005	0.46	3082.47	
21	97	0.002	0.194	3662.67	

5. Each of the squared deviations will be weighted by its relative frequency. Click in cell E2. Enter the formula =D2*B2 and press [Enter].

	A	B	C	D	E
1	Class Midpoint	Relative Frequency		Sqd Dev Score	
2	2	0.067	0.134	1188.87	=D2*B2

6. Copy the formula in cell E2 to cells E3 through E21.

	A	B	C	D	E
1	Class Midpoint	Relative Frequency		Sqd Dev Score	
2	2	0.067	0.134	1188.87	79.65432
3	7	0.068	0.476	869.0704	59.09679
4	12	0.074	0.888	599.2704	44.34601
5	17	0.072	1.224	379.4704	27.32187
6	22	0.07	1.54	209.6704	14.67693
7	27	0.062	1.674	89.8704	5.571965
8	32	0.068	2.176	20.0704	1.364787
9	37	0.073	2.701	0.2704	0.019739
10	42	0.081	3.402	30.4704	2.468102
11	47	0.076	3.572	110.6704	8.41095
12	52	0.066	3.432	240.8704	15.89745
13	57	0.055	3.135	421.0704	23.15887
14	62	0.042	2.604	651.2704	27.35336
15	67	0.034	2.278	931.4704	31.66999
16	72	0.03	2.16	1261.67	37.86011
17	77	0.026	2.002	1641.87	42.68863
18	82	0.019	1.558	2072.07	39.36934
19	87	0.01	0.87	2552.27	25.5227
20	92	0.005	0.46	3082.47	15.41235
21	97	0.002	0.194	3662.67	7.325341

7. You are working with a relative frequency distribution of midpoints. For this type of distribution, the variance is equal to the sum of the squared deviation scores. Click in cell **E22** to place the sum of the squared deviation scores there. Click the AutoSum button near the top of the screen. It looks like this: **Σ**. The range of

© 2006 Pearson Education, Inc., Upper Saddle River, NJ. All rights reserved. This material is protected under all copyright laws as they currently exist. No portion of this material may be reproduced, in any form or by any means, without permission in writing from the publisher.

numbers to be included in the sum is displayed in cell E22. You should see =**SUM(E2:E21)**. Make any necessary corrections. Then press [**Enter**].

20	92	0.005	0.46	3082.47	15.41235
21	97	0.002	0.194	3662.67	7.325341
22			36.48		=SUM(E2:E21)

8. Click in cell **E23** to place the standard deviation there. The standard deviation is the square root of the variance. In cell E23, enter the formula =**sqrt(E22)** and press [**Enter**].

20	92	0.005	0.46	3082.47	15.41235
21	97	0.002	0.194	3662.67	7.325341
22			36.48		509.1796
23					=sqrt(E22)

9. The standard deviation of ages in the United States is approximately equal to 22.42. For future reference purposes, you may want to add labels for the mean, variance, and standard deviation as shown below.

20	92	0.005	0.46	3082.47	15.41235
21	97	0.002	0.194	3662.67	7.325341
22		Mean =	36.48	Var =	509.1796
23				St Dev =	22.56501

▶ Exercise 6 (pg. 277)	Finding the Standard Deviation of the Set of Sample Means

1. Open worksheet "Tech5" in the Chapter 5 folder. This is the same data set that you used for Exercise 2, page 277. If you placed the mean (36.20944) in cell A38 for Exercise 2, page 277, you should delete it now.

	A	B
1	mean ages	
2	28.14	
3	31.56	
4	36.86	

2. At the top of the screen, click **Tools→Data Analysis**.

If Data Analysis does not appear as a choice in the Tools menu, you will need to load the Microsoft Excel Analysis ToolPak add-in. Follow the procedure in Section GS 8.1 before continuing.

© 2006 Pearson Education, Inc., Upper Saddle River, NJ. All rights reserved. This material is protected under all copyright laws as they currently exist. No portion of this material may be reproduced, in any form or by any means, without permission in writing from the publisher.

3. Select **Descriptive Statistics** and click **OK**.

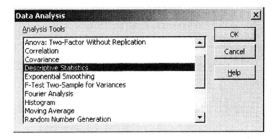

4. Complete the Descriptive Statistics dialog box as shown below. Click **OK**.

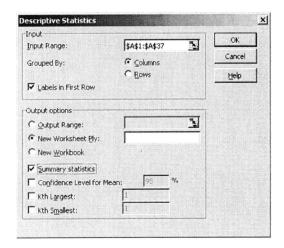

© 2006 Pearson Education, Inc., Upper Saddle River, NJ. All rights reserved. This material is protected under all copyright laws as they currently exist.
No portion of this material may be reproduced, in any form or by any means, without permission in writing from the publisher.

You will want to make column A wider so that you can read all the labels in the output table. The standard deviation is equal to 3.551804.

	A	B
1	*mean ages*	
2		
3	Mean	36.20944
4	Standard Error	0.591967
5	Median	36.155
6	Mode	#N/A
7	Standard Deviation	3.551804
8	Sample Variance	12.61531
9	Kurtosis	0.343186
10	Skewness	0.207283
11	Range	16.58
12	Minimum	28.14
13	Maximum	44.72
14	Sum	1303.54
15	Count	36

◀

© 2006 Pearson Education, Inc., Upper Saddle River, NJ. All rights reserved. This material is protected under all copyright laws as they currently exist. No portion of this material may be reproduced, in any form or by any means, without permission in writing from the publisher.

Confidence Intervals

CHAPTER

6

Section 6.1 Confidence Intervals for the Mean (Large Samples)

▶ Example 4 (pg. 284)	Constructing a Confidence Interval Using Technology

If the PHStat2 add-in has not been loaded, you will need to load it before continuing. Follow the instructions in Section GS 8.2.

1. Open the "Sentence" worksheet in the Chapter 6 folder.

2. At the top of the screen, select **PHStat → Confidence Intervals → Estimate for the Mean, sigma known**.

3. Complete the Estimate for the Mean dialog box as shown at the top of the next page. Click **OK**.

© 2006 Pearson Education, Inc., Upper Saddle River, NJ. All rights reserved. This material is protected under all copyright laws as they currently exist. No portion of this material may be reproduced, in any form or by any means, without permission in writing from the publisher.

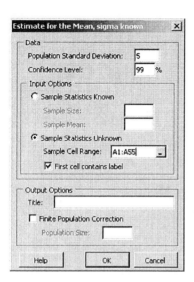

The output is displayed in a new worksheet. The lower limit of the confidence interval is 10.7 and the upper limit is 14.2.

	A	B
1	Confidence Interval Estimate for the Mean	
2		
3	Data	
4	Population Standard Deviation	5
5	Sample Mean	12.42592593
6	Sample Size	54
7	Confidence Level	99%
8		
9	Intermediate Calculations	
10	Standard Error of the Mean	0.680413817
11	Z Value	-2.5758293
12	Interval Half Width	1.75262985
13		
14	Confidence Interval	
15	Interval Lower Limit	10.67329608
16	Interval Upper Limit	14.17855578

© 2006 Pearson Education, Inc., Upper Saddle River, NJ. All rights reserved. This material is protected under all copyright laws as they currently exist. No portion of this material may be reproduced, in any form or by any means, without permission in writing from the publisher.

▶ Example 5 (pg. 285)	Constructing a Confidence Interval, σ Known

If the PHStat2 add-in has not been loaded, you will need to load it before continuing. Follow the instructions in Section GS 8.2.

1. Open a new, blank Excel worksheet. At the top of the screen, select **PHStat →
Confidence Intervals → Estimate for the Mean, sigma known**.

2. Complete the Estimate for the Mean dialog box as shown below. Click **OK**.

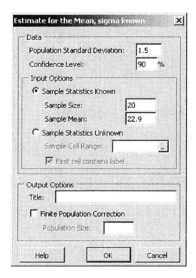

Your output should look the same as the output displayed at the top of the next page. The lower limit of the 90% confidence interval is 22.3 and the upper limit is 23.5.

© 2006 Pearson Education, Inc., Upper Saddle River, NJ. All rights reserved. This material is protected under all copyright laws as they currently exist. No portion of this material may be reproduced, in any form or by any means, without permission in writing from the publisher.

	A	B
1	Confidence Interval Estimate for the Mean	
2		
3	Data	
4	Population Standard Deviation	1.5
5	Sample Mean	22.9
6	Sample Size	20
7	Confidence Level	90%
8		
9	Intermediate Calculations	
10	Standard Error of the Mean	0.335410197
11	Z Value	-1.64485363
12	Interval Half Width	0.551700678
13		
14	Confidence Interval	
15	Interval Lower Limit	22.34829932
16	Interval Upper Limit	23.45170068

◀

Section 6.2 Confidence Intervals for the Mean (Small Samples)

▶ Example 2 (pg. 297)	Constructing a Confidence Interval

If the PHStat2 add-in has not been loaded, you will need to load it before continuing. Follow the instructions in Section GS 8.2.

1. Open a new, blank Excel worksheet. At the top of the screen, select **PHStat →
    Confidence Intervals → Estimate for the Mean, sigma unknown**.

2. Complete the Estimate for the Mean dialog box as shown at the top of the next page.
    Click **OK**.

© 2006 Pearson Education, Inc., Upper Saddle River, NJ. All rights reserved. This material is protected under all copyright laws as they currently exist.
No portion of this material may be reproduced, in any form or by any means, without permission in writing from the publisher.

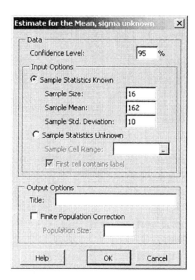

The output is displayed in a new worksheet. The lower limit of the 95% confidence interval is 156.7 and the upper limit is 167.3.

	A	B
1	**Confidence Interval Estimate for the Mean**	
2		
3	**Data**	
4	**Sample Standard Deviation**	10
5	**Sample Mean**	162
6	**Sample Size**	16
7	**Confidence Level**	95%
8		
9	Intermediate Calculations	
10	Standard Error of the Mean	2.5
11	Degrees of Freedom	15
12	t Value	2.131449536
13	Interval Half Width	5.328623839
14		
15	**Confidence Interval**	
16	**Interval Lower Limit**	156.67
17	**Interval Upper Limit**	167.33

© 2006 Pearson Education, Inc., Upper Saddle River, NJ. All rights reserved. This material is protected under all copyright laws as they currently exist. No portion of this material may be reproduced, in any form or by any means, without permission in writing from the publisher.

Section 6.3 Confidence Intervals for Population Proportions

▶ Example 2 (pg. 305) | Constructing a Confidence Interval for p

If the PHStat2 add-in has not been loaded, you will need to load it before continuing. Follow the instructions in Section GS 8.2.

1. Open a new, blank Excel worksheet. At the top of the screen, select **PHStat** → **Confidence Intervals** → **Estimate for the Proportion**.

2. Complete the Estimate for the Proportion dialog box as shown below. Click **OK**.

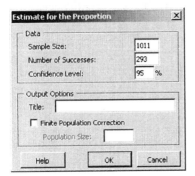

Your output should look like the output displayed at the top of the next page. The lower limit of the 95% confidence interval is 0.262 and the upper limit is 0.318.

© 2006 Pearson Education, Inc., Upper Saddle River, NJ. All rights reserved. This material is protected under all copyright laws as they currently exist. No portion of this material may be reproduced, in any form or by any means, without permission in writing from the publisher.

	A	B
1	**Confidence Interval Estimate for the Mean**	
2		
3	**Data**	
4	**Sample Size**	1011
5	**Number of Successes**	293
6	**Confidence Level**	95%
7		
8	Intermediate Calculations	
9	Sample Proportion	0.289812067
10	Z Value	-1.95996398
11	Standard Error of the Proportion	0.014268204
12	Interval Half Width	0.027965165
13		
14	**Confidence Interval**	
15	**Interval Lower Limit**	0.261846902
16	**Interval Upper Limit**	0.317777233

◀

6.4 Confidence Intervals for Variance and Standard Deviation

▶ Example 2 (pg. 315)	Constructing a Confidence Interval

If the PHStat2 add-in has not been loaded, you will need to load it before continuing. Follow the instructions in Section GS 8.2.

1. Open a new, blank Excel worksheet. At the top of the screen, select **PHStat** → **Confidence Intervals** → **Estimate for the Population Variance**.

2. Complete the Estimate for the Population Variance dialog box as shown at the top of the next page. Click **OK**.

© 2006 Pearson Education, Inc., Upper Saddle River, NJ. All rights reserved. This material is protected under all copyright laws as they currently exist. No portion of this material may be reproduced, in any form or by any means, without permission in writing from the publisher.

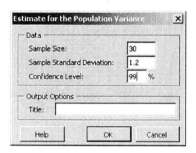

Your output should look the same as the output displayed below. The left and right endpoints of the confidence interval for σ^2 are 0.80 and 3.18, respectively.   The left and right endpoints of the confidence interval for σ are 0.89 and 1.78, respectively.

	A	B	C	D	E
1	Confidence Interval Estimate for the Population Variance				
2					
3	Data				
4	Sample Size	30			
5	Sample Standard Deviation	1.2			
6	Confidence Level	99%			
7					
8	Intermediate Calculations				
9	Degrees of Freedom	29			
10	Sum of Squares	41.76			
11	Single Tail Area	0.005			
12	Lower Chi-Square Value	13.12115			
13	Upper Chi-Square Value	52.33562			
14					
15	Results				
16	Interval Lower Limit for Variance	0.797927			
17	Interval Upper Limit for Variance	3.182648			
18					
19	Interval Lower Limit for Standard Deviation	0.893268			
20	Interval Upper Limit for Standard Deviation	1.783998			
21					
22	Assumption:				
23	Population from which sample was drawn has an approximate normal distribution.				

◄

Technology

► Exercise 1 (pg. 327)	Finding a 95% Confidence Interval for p

If the PHStat2 add-in has not been loaded, you will need to load it before continuing. Follow the instructions in Section GS 8.2.

© 2006 Pearson Education, Inc., Upper Saddle River, NJ. All rights reserved. This material is protected under all copyright laws as they currently exist. No portion of this material may be reproduced, in any form or by any means, without permission in writing from the publisher.

3. Open a new, blank Excel worksheet. At the top of the screen, select **PHStat** →
    Confidence Intervals → **Estimate for the Proportion**.

4. Complete the Estimate for the Proportion dialog box as shown below. Click **OK**.

Your output should look the same as the output displayed below. The lower limit of the
95% confidence interval is 0.028 and the upper limit is 0.052.

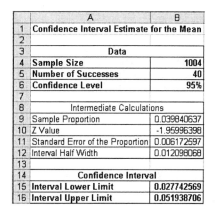

	A	B
1	Confidence Interval Estimate for the Mean	
2		
3	Data	
4	Sample Size	1004
5	Number of Successes	40
6	Confidence Level	95%
7		
8	Intermediate Calculations	
9	Sample Proportion	0.039840637
10	Z Value	-1.95996398
11	Standard Error of the Proportion	0.006172597
12	Interval Half Width	0.012098068
13		
14	Confidence Interval	
15	Interval Lower Limit	0.027742569
16	Interval Upper Limit	0.051938706

◀

▶ Exercise 3 (pg. 327)	Finding a 95% Confidence Interval for p

*If the PHStat2 add-in has not been loaded, you will need to load it before continuing.
Follow the instructions in Section GS 8.2.*

© 2006 Pearson Education, Inc., Upper Saddle River, NJ. All rights reserved. This material is protected under all copyright laws as they currently exist.
No portion of this material may be reproduced, in any form or by any means, without permission in writing from the publisher.

1. Open a new, blank Excel worksheet. At the top of the screen, select **PHStat** →
    Confidence Intervals → **Estimate for the Proportion**.

2. Seven percent of the sample size, 1004, is 70. Use this number to complete the
    Estimate for the Proportion dialog box as shown below. Click **OK**.

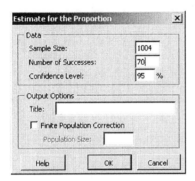

Your output should look the same as the output displayed below. The upper limit of the
95% confidence interval is 0.054 and the upper limit is 0.085.

	A	B
1	**Confidence Interval Estimate for the Mean**	
2		
3	**Data**	
4	**Sample Size**	1004
5	**Number of Successes**	70
6	**Confidence Level**	95%
7		
8	Intermediate Calculations	
9	Sample Proportion	0.069721116
10	Z Value	-1.95996398
11	Standard Error of the Proportion	0.008037517
12	Interval Half Width	0.015753243
13		
14	Confidence Interval	
15	**Interval Lower Limit**	0.053967872
16	**Interval Upper Limit**	0.085474359

◀

▶ **Exercise 4 (pg. 327)**   Simulating a Most Admired Poll

1. Open a new, blank Excel worksheet. Enter the labels shown below for displaying
    the output of five simulations.

© 2006 Pearson Education, Inc., Upper Saddle River, NJ. All rights reserved. This material is protected under all copyright laws as they currently exist.
No portion of this material may be reproduced, in any form or by any means, without permission in writing from the publisher.

	A
1	Time 1
2	Time 2
3	Time 3
4	Time 4
5	Time 5

2.   At the top of the screen, select **Tools → Data Analysis**. Select **Random Number Generation**. Click **OK**.

If Data Analysis does not appear as a choice in the Tools menu, you will need to load the Microsoft Excel Analysis ToolPak add-in. Follow the procedure in Section GS 8.1 before continuing.

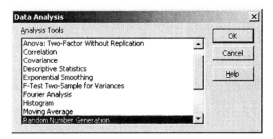

3.   Complete the Random Number Generation dialog box as shown below. Click **OK**.

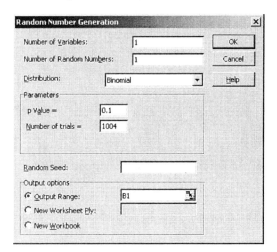

© 2006 Pearson Education, Inc., Upper Saddle River, NJ. All rights reserved. This material is protected under all copyright laws as they currently exist. No portion of this material may be reproduced, in any form or by any means, without permission in writing from the publisher.

For Time 1, the number of persons (out of 1001) selecting Oprah Winfrey is 110. Because this number was generated randomly, it is unlikely that your number is exactly the same.

	A	B
1	Time 1	110
2	Time 2	
3	Time 3	
4	Time 4	
5	Time 5	

4. Begin Time 2 the same way that you did Time 1. At the top of the screen, click **Tools** → **Data Analysis**. Select **Random Number Generation**. Click **OK**.

5. Complete the Random Number Generation dialog box in the same way as you did for Time 1 except change the location of the output to cell B2 as shown below. Click **OK**.

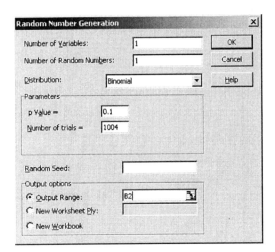

6. Repeat this procedure until you have carried out the simulation five times. The output I generated is displayed below.

	A	B
1	Time 1	110
2	Time 2	113
3	Time 3	94
4	Time 4	109
5	Time 5	99

© 2006 Pearson Education, Inc., Upper Saddle River, NJ. All rights reserved. This material is protected under all copyright laws as they currently exist. No portion of this material may be reproduced, in any form or by any means, without permission in writing from the publisher.

Hypothesis Testing with One Sample

CHAPTER 7

Section 7.2 Hypothesis Testing for the Mean (Large Samples)

| ► Example 6 (pg. 352) | Using a Technology Tool to Find a P-value |

If the PHStat add-in has not been loaded, you will need to load it before continuing. Follow the instructions in Section GS 8.2.

1. First open a new Excel worksheet. Then, at the top of the screen, select **PHStat→ One-Sample Tests→Z Test for the Mean, sigma known**.

2. Complete the Z Test for the Mean dialog box as shown at the top of the next page. Click **OK**.

© 2006 Pearson Education, Inc., Upper Saddle River, NJ. All rights reserved. This material is protected under all copyright laws as they currently exist. No portion of this material may be reproduced, in any form or by any means, without permission in writing from the publisher.

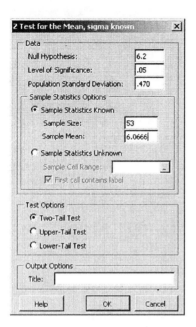

Your output should look like the output displayed below.

	A	B
1	Z Test of Hypothesis for the Mean	
2		
3	Data	
4	Null Hypothesis $\mu=$	6.2
5	Level of Significance	0.05
6	Population Standard Deviation	0.47
7	Sample Size	53
8	Sample Mean	6.0666
9		
10	Intermediate Calculations	
11	Standard Error of the Mean	0.064559465
12	Z Test Statistic	-2.066312041
13		
14	Two-Tail Test	
15	Lower Critical Value	-1.959963985
16	Upper Critical Value	1.959963985
17	p-Value	0.038799025
18	Reject the null hypothesis	

© 2006 Pearson Education, Inc., Upper Saddle River, NJ. All rights reserved. This material is protected under all copyright laws as they currently exist.
No portion of this material may be reproduced, in any form or by any means, without permission in writing from the publisher.

▶ Example 9 (pg. 355) | Testing μ with a Large Sample

If the PHStat add-in has not been loaded, you will need to load it before continuing. Follow the instructions in Section GS 8.2.

3. First open a new Excel worksheet. Then, at the top of the screen, select **PHStat→ One-Sample Tests→Z Test for the Mean, sigma known**.

4. Complete the Z Test for the Mean dialog box as shown below.   Be sure to select **Lower-Tail Test**. Click **OK**.

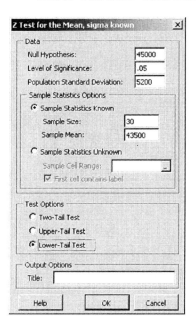

© 2006 Pearson Education, Inc., Upper Saddle River, NJ. All rights reserved. This material is protected under all copyright laws as they currently exist. No portion of this material may be reproduced, in any form or by any means, without permission in writing from the publisher.

Your output should look like the output displayed below.

	A	B
1	Z Test of Hypothesis for the Mean	
2		
3	Data	
4	Null Hypothesis $\mu=$	45000
5	Level of Significance	0.05
6	Population Standard Deviation	5200
7	Sample Size	30
8	Sample Mean	43500
9		
10	Intermediate Calculations	
11	Standard Error of the Mean	949.3857663
12	Z Test Statistic	-1.579968916
13		
14	Lower-Tail Test	
15	Lower Critical Value	-1.644853627
16	p-Value	0.057056993
17	Do not reject the null hypothesis	

► Exercise 37 (pg. 360)	Testing That the Mean Time to Quit Smoking Is 15 Years

If the PHStat add-in has not been loaded, you will need to load it before continuing. Follow the instructions in Section GS 8.2.

1. Open the "Ex7_2-37" worksheet in the Chapter 7 folder.

2. Your textbook indicates that the standard deviation of a sample may be used in the z-test formula instead of a known population standard deviation if the sample size is 30 or greater. You will use Excel's Descriptive Statistics tool to obtain the sample standard deviation. At the top of the screen, click **Tools→Data Analysis**. Select **Descriptive Statistics**. Click **OK**.

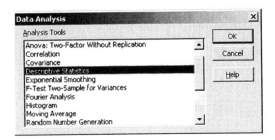

© 2006 Pearson Education, Inc., Upper Saddle River, NJ. All rights reserved. This material is protected under all copyright laws as they currently exist.
No portion of this material may be reproduced, in any form or by any means, without permission in writing from the publisher.

3. Complete the Descriptive Statistics dialog box as shown below. Be sure to select **Summary statistics**. Click **OK**.

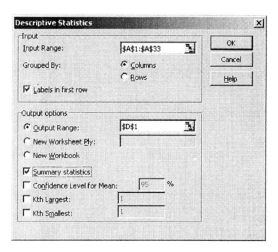

4. You will want to adjust the width of column D so that you can read all the labels. The standard deviation of the sample is 4.2876, the mean is 14.8344, and the count is 32. You will use this information when you carry out the statistical test. At the top of the screen, select **PHStat→One-Sample Tests→Z Test for the Mean, sigma known**.

	A	B	C	D	E
1	years to quit smoking			years to quit smoking	
2	15.7				
3	13.2			Mean	14.83438
4	22.6			Standard Error	0.75795
5	13			Median	14.65
6	10.7			Mode	13.2
7	18.1			Standard Deviation	4.287612
8	14.7			Sample Variance	18.38362
9	7			Kurtosis	-0.57155
10	17.3			Skewness	0.042962
11	7.5			Range	15.6
12	21.8			Minimum	7
13	12.3			Maximum	22.6
14	19.8			Sum	474.7
15	13.8			Count	32

© 2006 Pearson Education, Inc., Upper Saddle River, NJ. All rights reserved. This material is protected under all copyright laws as they currently exist. No portion of this material may be reproduced, in any form or by any means, without permission in writing from the publisher.

5.   Complete the Z Test for the Mean dialog box as shown below. Click **OK**.

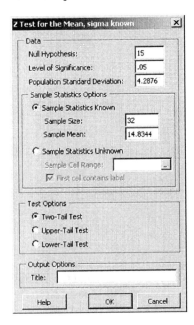

Your output should look like the output displayed below.

	A	B
1	Z Test of Hypothesis for the Mean	
2		
3	Data	
4	Null Hypothesis μ=	15
5	Level of Significance	0.05
6	Population Standard Deviation	4.2876
7	Sample Size	32
8	Sample Mean	14.8344
9		
10	Intermediate Calculations	
11	Standard Error of the Mean	0.757947759
12	Z Test Statistic	-0.218484715
13		
14	Two-Tail Test	
15	Lower Critical Value	-1.959963985
16	Upper Critical Value	1.959963985
17	p-Value	0.827051466
18	Do not reject the null hypothesis	

© 2006 Pearson Education, Inc., Upper Saddle River, NJ. All rights reserved. This material is protected under all copyright laws as they currently exist.
No portion of this material may be reproduced, in any form or by any means, without permission in writing from the publisher.

Section 7.3 Hypothesis Testing for the Mean (Small Samples)

> ▶ Example 4 (pg. 367)   Testing μ with a Small Sample

If the PHStat add-in has not been loaded, you will need to load it before continuing. Follow the instructions in Section GS 8.2

1. First open a new Excel worksheet. Then, at the top of the screen, select **PHStat→One-Sample Tests→t Test for the Mean, sigma unknown**.

2. Complete the t Test for the Mean dialog box as shown below. Click **OK**.

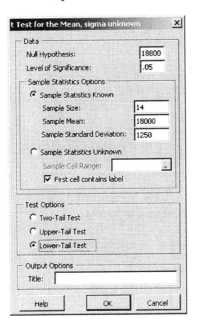

© 2006 Pearson Education, Inc., Upper Saddle River, NJ. All rights reserved. This material is protected under all copyright laws as they currently exist. No portion of this material may be reproduced, in any form or by any means, without permission in writing from the publisher.

Your output should look like the output shown below.

	A	B	C	D	E
1	t Test for Hypothesis of the Mean				
2					
3	Data				
4	Null Hypothesis μ=	18800			
5	Level of Significance	0.05			
6	Sample Size	14			
7	Sample Mean	18000			
8	Sample Standard Deviation	1250			
9					
10	Intermediate Calculations				
11	Standard Error of the Mean	334.0765524			
12	Degrees of Freedom	13			
13	t Test Statistic	-2.394660728			
14					
15	Lower-Tail Test			Calculations Area	
16	Lower Critical Value	-1.770933383		For one-tailed tests:	
17	p-Value	0.016203608		TDIST value	0.016204
18	Reject the null hypothesis			1-TDIST value	0.983796

◄

▶ Example 6 (pg. 369)   **Using P-Values with a t-Test**

If the PHStat add-in has not been loaded, you will need to load it before continuing.
Follow the instructions in Section GS 8.2.

---

1. First open a new Excel worksheet. Then, at the top of the screen, select
   PHStat→One-Sample Tests→t Test for the Mean, sigma unknown.

2. Complete the t Test for the Mean dialog box as shown at the top of the next page.
   Click **OK**.

© 2006 Pearson Education, Inc., Upper Saddle River, NJ. All rights reserved. This material is protected under all copyright laws as they currently exist. No portion of this material may be reproduced, in any form or by any means, without permission in writing from the publisher.

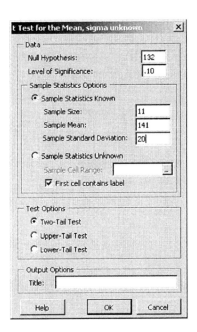

Your output should look like the output displayed below.

	A	B
1	t Test for Hypothesis of the Mean	
2		
3	Data	
4	Null Hypothesis μ=	132
5	Level of Significance	0.1
6	Sample Size	11
7	Sample Mean	141
8	Sample Standard Deviation	20
9		
10	Intermediate Calculations	
11	Standard Error of the Mean	6.030226892
12	Degrees of Freedom	10
13	t Test Statistic	1.492481156
14		
15	Two-Tail Test	
16	Lower Critical Value	-1.812461102
17	Upper Critical Value	1.812461102
18	p-Value	0.166433529
19	Do not reject the null hypothesis	

© 2006 Pearson Education, Inc., Upper Saddle River, NJ. All rights reserved. This material is protected under all copyright laws as they currently exist. No portion of this material may be reproduced, in any form or by any means, without permission in writing from the publisher.

▶ Exercise 25 (pg. 371) | Testing the Claim That the Mean Recycled Waste Is More Than 1 Lb. Per Day

If the PHStat add-in has not been loaded, you will need to load it before continuing. Follow the instructions in Section GS 8.2.

1. First open a new Excel worksheet. Then, at the top of the screen, select **PHStat→One-Sample Tests→t Test for the Mean, sigma unknown**.

2. Complete the t Test for the Mean dialog box as shown below. Be sure to select **Upper-Tail Test**. Click **OK**.

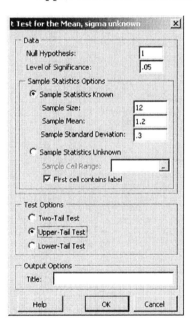

© 2006 Pearson Education, Inc., Upper Saddle River, NJ. All rights reserved. This material is protected under all copyright laws as they currently exist. No portion of this material may be reproduced, in any form or by any means, without permission in writing from the publisher.

Your output should be the same as the output displayed below.

	A	B	C	D	E
1	t Test for Hypothesis of the Mean				
2					
3	Data				
4	Null Hypothesis μ=	1			
5	Level of Significance	0.05			
6	Sample Size	12			
7	Sample Mean	1.2			
8	Sample Standard Deviation	0.3			
9					
10	Intermediate Calculations				
11	Standard Error of the Mean	0.08660254			
12	Degrees of Freedom	11			
13	t Test Statistic	2.309401077			
14					
15	Upper-Tail Test			Calculations Area	
16	Upper Critical Value	1.795884814		For one-tailed tests:	
17	p-Value	0.020671133		TDIST value	0.020671
18	Reject the null hypothesis			1-TDIST value	0.979329

◀

▶ **Exercise 30 (pg. 372)**   **Testing the Claim That Teachers Spend a Mean of More Than $580**

If the PHStat add-in has not been loaded, you will need to load it before continuing. Follow the instructions in Section GS 8.2.

1. Open the "Ex7_3-30" worksheet in the Chapter 7 folder.

2. At the top of the screen, select **PHStat→ One-Sample Tests→t Test for the Mean, sigma unknown**.

© 2006 Pearson Education, Inc., Upper Saddle River, NJ. All rights reserved. This material is protected under all copyright laws as they currently exist. No portion of this material may be reproduced, in any form or by any means, without permission in writing from the publisher.

3.   Complete the t Test for the Mean dialog box as shown below. Click **OK**.

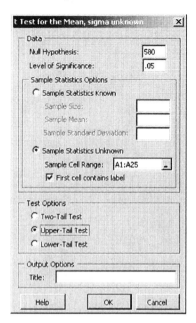

Your output should look like the output displayed below.

	A	B	C	D	E
1	t Test for Hypothesis of the Mean				
2					
3	Data				
4	Null Hypothesis $\mu=$	580			
5	Level of Significance	0.05			
6	Sample Size	24			
7	Sample Mean	635.75			
8	Sample Standard Deviation	146.7841509			
9					
10	Intermediate Calculations				
11	Standard Error of the Mean	29.96218934			
12	Degrees of Freedom	23			
13	*t* Test Statistic	1.86067845			
14					
15	Upper-Tail Test			Calculations Area	
16	Upper Critical Value	1.713871517		For one-tailed tests:	
17	*p*-Value	0.037811391		TDIST value	0.037811
18	Reject the null hypothesis			1-TDIST value	0.962189

© 2006 Pearson Education, Inc., Upper Saddle River, NJ. All rights reserved. This material is protected under all copyright laws as they currently exist.
No portion of this material may be reproduced, in any form or by any means, without permission in writing from the publisher.

Section 7.4 Hypothesis Testing for Proportions

▶ Example 1 (pg. 375)	Hypothesis Test for a Proportion

If the PHStat add-in has not been loaded, you will need to load it before continuing. Follow the instructions in Section GS 8.2.

1. First open a new Excel worksheet. Then, at the top of the screen, select **PHStat**→ **One-Sample Tests**→**Z Test for the Proportion**.

2. Complete the Z Test for the Proportion dialog box as shown at the top of the next page. Click **OK**.

© 2006 Pearson Education, Inc., Upper Saddle River, NJ. All rights reserved. This material is protected under all copyright laws as they currently exist. No portion of this material may be reproduced, in any form or by any means, without permission in writing from the publisher.

Your output should be the same as the output displayed below.

	A	B	C
1	Z Test of Hypothesis for the Proportion		
2			
3	Data		
4	Null Hypothesis p=	0.2	
5	Level of Significance	0.01	
6	Number of Successes	15	
7	Sample Size	100	
8			
9	Intermediate Calculations		
10	Sample Proportion	0.15	
11	Standard Error	0.04	
12	Z Test Statistic	-1.25	
13			
14	Lower-Tail Test		
15	Lower Critical Value	-2.326347874	
16	p-Value	0.105649774	
17	Do not reject the null hypothesis		

◄

► Exercise 11 (pg. 378)	Testing the Claim That More Than 30% of Consumers Stopped Buying a Product

If the PHStat add-in has not been loaded, you will need to load it before continuing. Follow the instructions in Section GS 8.2.

1. First open a new Excel worksheet. Then, at the top of the screen, select **PHStat→ One-Sample Tests→Z Test for the Proportion**.

2. Complete the Z Test for the Proportion dialog box as shown below. Click **OK**.

Note that 32% of 1050 is 336.

© 2006 Pearson Education, Inc., Upper Saddle River, NJ. All rights reserved. This material is protected under all copyright laws as they currently exist. No portion of this material may be reproduced, in any form or by any means, without permission in writing from the publisher.

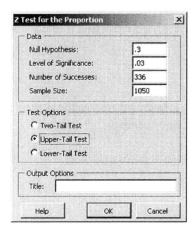

Your output should be the same as the output displayed below.

	A	B	C
1	Z Test of Hypothesis for the Proportion		
2			
3	Data		
4	Null Hypothesis $p=$	0.3	
5	Level of Significance	0.03	
6	Number of Successes	336	
7	Sample Size	1050	
8			
9	Intermediate Calculations		
10	Sample Proportion	0.32	
11	Standard Error	0.014142136	
12	Z Test Statistic	1.414213562	
13			
14	Upper-Tail Test		
15	Upper Critical Value	1.880793608	
16	p-Value	0.078649604	
17	Do not reject the null hypothesis		

© 2006 Pearson Education, Inc., Upper Saddle River, NJ. All rights reserved. This material is protected under all copyright laws as they currently exist.
No portion of this material may be reproduced, in any form or by any means, without permission in writing from the publisher.

Section 7.5 Hypothesis Testing for Variance and Standard Deviation

► Exercise 25 (pg. 388)	Using the P-Value Method to Perform the Hypothesis Test for Exercise 21

1.   Open a new Excel worksheet and click in cell **A1** to place the output there.

2.   At the top of the screen, select **Insert→Function**.

3.   Select the **Statistical** category. Select the **CHIDIST** function. Click **OK**.

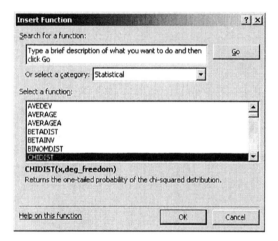

4.   Complete the CHIDIST dialog box as shown below. Click **OK**.

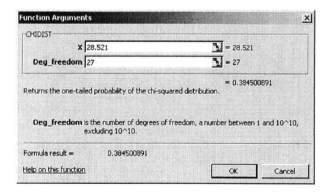

© 2006 Pearson Education, Inc., Upper Saddle River, NJ. All rights reserved. This material is protected under all copyright laws as they currently exist. No portion of this material may be reproduced, in any form or by any means, without permission in writing from the publisher.

With df=27, the one-tailed probability of X^2 is 0.3845.

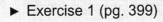

Technology

▶ Exercise 1 (pg. 399)	Testing the Claim That the Proportion Is Equal to 0.53

If the PHStat add-in has not been loaded, you will need to load it before continuing. Follow the instructions in Section GS 8.2.

1. First open a new Excel worksheet. Then, at the top of the screen, select **PHStat→ One-Sample Tests→Z Test for the Proportion**.

2. Complete the Z Test for the Proportion dialog box as shown below. Click **OK**.

© 2006 Pearson Education, Inc., Upper Saddle River, NJ. All rights reserved. This material is protected under all copyright laws as they currently exist. No portion of this material may be reproduced, in any form or by any means, without permission in writing from the publisher.

Your output should appear the same as the output shown below.

	A	B	C
1	Z Test of Hypothesis for the Proportion		
2			
3	Data		
4	Null Hypothesis $p=$	0.53	
5	Level of Significance	0.01	
6	Number of Successes	102	
7	Sample Size	350	
8			
9	Intermediate Calculations		
10	Sample Proportion	0.291428571	
11	Standard Error	0.026677974	
12	Z Test Statistic	-8.942636739	
13			
14	Two-Tail Test		
15	Lower Critical Value	-2.575829304	
16	Upper Critical value	2.575829304	
17	p-Value	0	
18	Reject the null hypothesis		

◄

© 2006 Pearson Education, Inc., Upper Saddle River, NJ. All rights reserved. This material is protected under all copyright laws as they currently exist. No portion of this material may be reproduced, in any form or by any means, without permission in writing from the publisher.

Hypothesis Testing with Two Samples

Section 8.1 Testing the Difference Between Means (Large Independent Samples)

▶ Exercise 19 (pg. 411)	Testing the Claim That Children Ages 3-12 Watched TV More in 1981 Than Today

1. Open worksheet "Ex8_1-19" in the Chapter 8 folder.

2. Your textbook indicates that the variance of a sample may be used in the z-test formula instead of a known population variance if the sample size is sufficiently large. You will use Excel's Descriptive Statistics tool to obtain the sample variance. At the top of the screen, click **Tools→Data Analysis**. Select **Descriptive Statistics**. Click **OK**.

If Data Analysis does not appear as a choice in the Tools menu, you will need to load the Microsoft Excel ToolPak add-in. Follow the procedure in Section GS 8.1 before continuing.

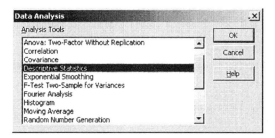

© 2006 Pearson Education, Inc., Upper Saddle River, NJ. All rights reserved. This material is protected under all copyright laws as they currently exist. No portion of this material may be reproduced, in any form or by any means, without permission in writing from the publisher.

3. Complete the Descriptive Statistics dialog box as shown below. Click **OK**.

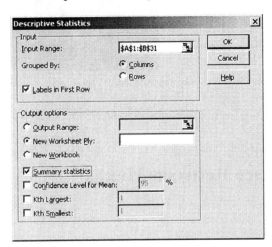

4. You will want to make column A and column C wider so that the labels are easier to read. The variance of Time A is 0.2401 and the variance of Time B is 0.1075. Return to the worksheet that contains the data. To do this, click on the **Sheet1** tab near the bottom of the screen.

	A	B	C	D
1	Time A		Time B	
2				
3	Mean	2.13	Mean	1.593333
4	Standard Error	0.089462	Standard Error	0.059872
5	Median	2.1	Median	1.6
6	Mode	2.1	Mode	1.6
7	Standard Deviation	0.490004	Standard Deviation	0.327933
8	Sample Variance	0.240103	Sample Variance	0.10754
9	Kurtosis	0.863836	Kurtosis	-0.57822
10	Skewness	-0.00957	Skewness	-0.25732
11	Range	2.3	Range	1.3
12	Minimum	1	Minimum	0.9
13	Maximum	3.3	Maximum	2.2
14	Sum	63.9	Sum	47.8
15	Count	30	Count	30

5. At the top of the screen, click **Tools→Data Analysis**. Select **z-Test: Two Sample for Means** and click **OK**.

© 2006 Pearson Education, Inc., Upper Saddle River, NJ. All rights reserved. This material is protected under all copyright laws as they currently exist. No portion of this material may be reproduced, in any form or by any means, without permission in writing from the publisher.

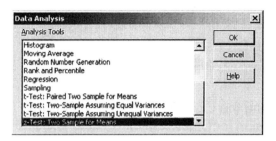

6. Complete the z-Test: Two Sample for Means dialog box as shown below. Click **OK**.

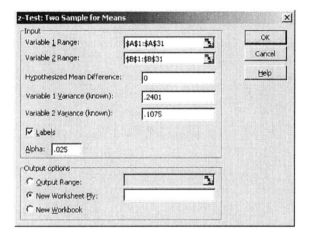

The output is displayed in a new worksheet. You will want to adjust the width of column A so that you can read the labels. Your output should look similar to the output displayed below.

	A	B	C
1	z-Test: Two Sample for Means		
2			
3		Time A	Time B
4	Mean	2.13	1.593333
5	Known Variance	0.2401	0.1075
6	Observations	30	30
7	Hypothesized Mean Difference	0	
8	z	4.985691	
9	P(Z<=z) one-tail	3.09E-07	
10	z Critical one-tail	1.959964	
11	P(Z<=z) two-tail	6.17E-07	
12	z Critical two-tail	2.241403	

◀

© 2006 Pearson Education, Inc., Upper Saddle River, NJ. All rights reserved. This material is protected under all copyright laws as they currently exist. No portion of this material may be reproduced, in any form or by any means, without permission in writing from the publisher.

Section 8.2 Testing the Difference Between Means (Small Independent Samples)

▶ Exercise 15 (pg. 421)	Testing the Claim That the Mean Footwell Intrusion for Small & Midsize Cars Is Equal

If the PHStat add-in has not been loaded, you will need to load it before continuing. Follow the instructions in Section GS 8.2.

1. First open a new Excel worksheet.   Then, at the top of the screen, select **PHStat→Two-Sample Tests→t Test for Differences in Two Means**.

2. Complete the t Test for Differences in Two Means dialog box as shown at the top of the next page. Click **OK**.

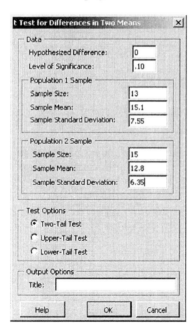

The output is displayed in a new worksheet named "Hypothesis." You may need to scroll down a couple rows to see all of it.

© 2006 Pearson Education, Inc., Upper Saddle River, NJ. All rights reserved. This material is protected under all copyright laws as they currently exist. No portion of this material may be reproduced, in any form or by any means, without permission in writing from the publisher.

	A	B
1	t Test for Differences in Two Means	
2		
3	Data	
4	Hypothesized Difference	0
5	Level of Significance	0.1
6	Population 1 Sample	
7	Sample Size	13
8	Sample Mean	15.1
9	Sample Standard Deviation	7.55
10	Population 2 Sample	
11	Sample Size	15
12	Sample Mean	12.8
13	Sample Standard Deviation	6.35
14		
15	Intermediate Calculations	
16	Population 1 Sample Degrees of Freedom	12
17	Population 2 Sample Degrees of Freedom	14
18	Total Degrees of Freedom	26
19	Pooled Variance	48.02096
20	Difference in Sample Means	2.3
21	t Test Statistic	0.875892
22		
23	Two-Tail Test	
24	Lower Critical Value	-1.70562

Ɪꞩ ◀ ▶ ▶Ɩ \\Hypothesis / Sheet1 / Sheet2 / Sheet3 /

◀

Section 8.3 Testing the Difference Between Means (Dependent Samples)

▶ Example 2 (pg. 428)

The t-Test for the Difference Between Means

1. Open a new Excel worksheet and enter the golfers' scores as shown below.

	A	B
1	Old	New
2	89	83
3	84	83
4	96	92
5	82	84
6	74	76
7	92	91
8	85	80
9	91	91

2. At the top of the screen, click **Tools→Data Analysis**. Select **t-Test: Paired Two Sample for Means**. Click **OK**.

© 2006 Pearson Education, Inc., Upper Saddle River, NJ. All rights reserved. This material is protected under all copyright laws as they currently exist. No portion of this material may be reproduced, in any form or by any means, without permission in writing from the publisher.

If Data Analysis does not appear as a choice in the Tools menu, you will need to load the Microsoft Excel ToolPak add-in. Follow the procedure in Section GS 8.1 before continuing.

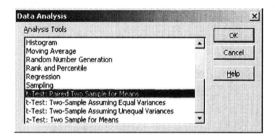

3. Complete the t-Test: Paired Two Sample for Means dialog box as shown below. Click **OK**.

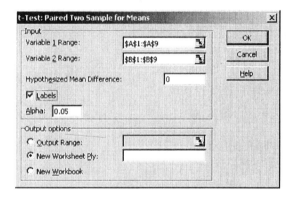

© 2006 Pearson Education, Inc., Upper Saddle River, NJ. All rights reserved. This material is protected under all copyright laws as they currently exist. No portion of this material may be reproduced, in any form or by any means, without permission in writing from the publisher.

The output is displayed in a new worksheet. You will want to adjust the width of the columns so that you can read all the labels. Your output should look similar to the output displayed below.

	A	B	C
1	t-Test: Paired Two Sample for Means		
2			
3		Old	New
4	Mean	86.625	85
5	Variance	47.41071	33.71429
6	Observations	8	8
7	Pearson Correlation	0.896872	
8	Hypothesized Mean Difference	0	
9	df	7	
10	t Stat	1.49826	
11	P(T<=t) one-tail	0.088869	
12	t Critical one-tail	1.894579	
13	P(T<=t) two-tail	0.177738	
14	t Critical two-tail	2.364624	

◀

► Exercise 17 (pg. 432)	Testing the Hypothesis That Verbal SAT Scores Improved the Second Time

1. Open worksheet "Ex8_3-17" in the Chapter 8 folder.

2. At the top of the screen, click **Tools→Data Analysis**. Select **t-Test: Paired Two Sample for Means**. Click **OK**.

If Data Analysis does not appear as a choice in the Tools menu, you will need to load the Microsoft Excel ToolPak add-in. Follow the procedure in Section GS 8.1 before continuing.

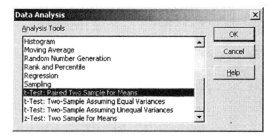

© 2006 Pearson Education, Inc., Upper Saddle River, NJ. All rights reserved. This material is protected under all copyright laws as they currently exist. No portion of this material may be reproduced, in any form or by any means, without permission in writing from the publisher.

3.   Complete the t-Test: Paired Two Sample for Means dialog box as shown below.
     Click **OK**.

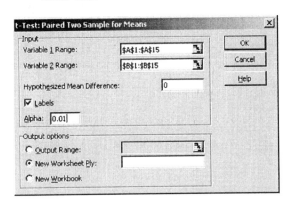

The output is displayed in a new worksheet. You will want to make the columns wider
so that you can read all the labels. Your output should appear similar to the output shown
below.

	A	B	C
1	t-Test: Paired Two Sample for Means		
2			
3		First SAT	Second SAT
4	Mean	483.6428571	517.3571429
5	Variance	8372.554945	5060.093407
6	Observations	14	14
7	Pearson Correlation	0.896141834	
8	Hypothesized Mean Difference	0	
9	df	13	
10	t Stat	-3.001096523	
11	P(T<=t) one-tail	0.005108665	
12	t Critical one-tail	2.650308836	
13	P(T<=t) two-tail	0.01021733	
14	t Critical two-tail	3.012275833	

◀

▶ **Exercise 29 (pg. 436)**   Constructing a 90% Confidence Interval for
μ_D, the Mean Increase in Hours of Sleep

1.   Open worksheet "Ex8_3-29" in the Chapter 8 folder.

2.   Use Excel to calculate a difference score for each of the 16 patients. First, click in
     cell C2 and key in the label **Difference**.

© 2006 Pearson Education, Inc., Upper Saddle River, NJ. All rights reserved. This material is protected under all copyright laws as they currently exist.
No portion of this material may be reproduced, in any form or by any means, without permission in writing from the publisher.

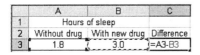

	A	B	C
1		Hours of sleep	
2	Without drug	With new drug	Difference
3	1.8	3.0	
4	2.0	3.6	

3. Click in cell C3 and enter the formula **=A3-B3** as shown below. Press [**Enter**].

	A	B	C
1		Hours of sleep	
2	Without drug	With new drug	Difference
3	1.8	3.0	=A3-B3

4. Click in cell **C3** (where –1.2 now appears) and copy the contents of that cell to cells C4 through C18.

	A	B	C
1		Hours of sleep	
2	Without drug	With new drug	Difference
3	1.8	3.0	-1.2
4	2.0	3.6	-1.6
5	3.4	4.0	-0.6
6	3.5	4.4	-0.9
7	3.7	4.5	-0.8
8	3.8	5.2	-1.4
9	3.9	5.5	-1.6
10	3.9	5.7	-1.8
11	4.0	6.2	-2.2
12	4.9	6.3	-1.4
13	5.1	6.6	-1.5
14	5.2	7.8	-2.6
15	5.0	7.2	-2.2
16	4.5	6.5	-2.0
17	4.2	5.6	-1.4
18	4.7	5.9	-1.2

5. You will now obtain descriptive statistics for Difference. At the top of the screen, click **Tools→Data Analysis**. Select **Descriptive Statistics**. Click **OK**.

If Data Analysis does not appear as a choice in the Tools menu, you will need to load the Microsoft Excel ToolPak add-in. Follow the procedure in Section GS 8.1 before continuing.

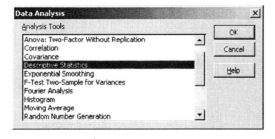

© 2006 Pearson Education, Inc., Upper Saddle River, NJ. All rights reserved. This material is protected under all copyright laws as they currently exist. No portion of this material may be reproduced, in any form or by any means, without permission in writing from the publisher.

6. Complete the Descriptive Statistics dialog box as shown below. Click **OK**.

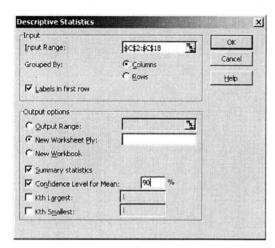

The output is displayed in a new worksheet. The mean is printed at the top and the confidence level is printed at the bottom. To calculate the lower limit of the 90% confidence interval, subtract 0.2376 from –1.525. To calculate the upper limit, add 0.2376 to –1.525.

	A	B
1	Difference	
2		
3	Mean	-1.525
4	Standard Error	0.135554
5	Median	-1.45
6	Mode	-1.6
7	Standard Deviation	0.542218
8	Sample Variance	0.294
9	Kurtosis	-0.26069
10	Skewness	-0.23658
11	Range	2
12	Minimum	-2.6
13	Maximum	-0.6
14	Sum	-24.4
15	Count	16
16	Confidence Level(90.0%)	0.237634

© 2006 Pearson Education, Inc., Upper Saddle River, NJ. All rights reserved. This material is protected under all copyright laws as they currently exist. No portion of this material may be reproduced, in any form or by any means, without permission in writing from the publisher.

Section 8.4 Testing the Difference Between Proportions

▶ Example 1 (pg. 439)	A Two-Sample z-Test for the Difference Between Proportions

If the PHStat add-in has not been loaded, you will need to load it before continuing. Follow the instructions in Section GS 8.2.

1. First open a new Excel worksheet. Then, at the top of the screen, select **PHStat→Two-Sample Tests→Z Test for Differences in Two Proportions**.

2. Complete the Z Test for Differences in Two Proportions dialog box as shown below. Click **OK**.

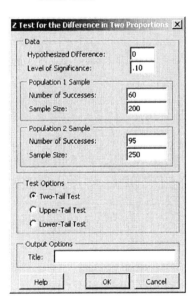

© 2006 Pearson Education, Inc., Upper Saddle River, NJ. All rights reserved. This material is protected under all copyright laws as they currently exist. No portion of this material may be reproduced, in any form or by any means, without permission in writing from the publisher.

The output is displayed in a worksheet named "Hypothesis."

	A	B
1	Z Test for Differences in Two Proportions	
2		
3	Data	
4	Hypothesized Difference	0
5	Level of Significance	0.1
6	Group 1	
7	Number of Successes	60
8	Sample Size	200
9	Group 2	
10	Number of Successes	95
11	Sample Size	250
12		
13	Intermediate Calculations	
14	Group 1 Proportion	0.3
15	Group 2 Proportion	0.38
16	Difference in Two Proportions	-0.08
17	Average Proportion	0.344444444
18	Z Test Statistic	-1.774615984
19		
20	Two-Tail Test	
21	Lower Critical Value	-1.644853627
22	Upper Critical Value	1.644853627
23	p-Value	0.075961316
24	Reject the null hypothesis	

◀

▶ **Exercise 7 (pg. 441)**   **Testing the Claim That the Use of Alternative Medicines Has Not Changed**

If the PHStat add-in has not been loaded, you will need to load it before continuing. Follow the instructions in Section GS 8.2.

---

1. First open a new Excel worksheet. Then, at the top of the screen, select **PHStat→Two-Sample Tests→Z Test for Differences in Two Proportions**.

2. Complete the Z Test for Differences in Two Proportions dialog box as shown at the top of the next page. Click **OK**.

© 2006 Pearson Education, Inc., Upper Saddle River, NJ. All rights reserved. This material is protected under all copyright laws as they currently exist.
No portion of this material may be reproduced, in any form or by any means, without permission in writing from the publisher.

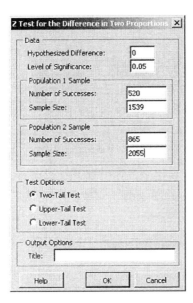

The output is displayed in a worksheet named "Hypothesis."

	A	B
1	Z Test for Differences in Two Proportions	
2		
3	Data	
4	Hypothesized Difference	0
5	Level of Significance	0.05
6	Group 1	
7	Number of Successes	520
8	Sample Size	1539
9	Group 2	
10	Number of Successes	865
11	Sample Size	2055
12		
13	Intermediate Calculations	
14	Group 1 Proportion	0.337881741
15	Group 2 Proportion	0.420924574
16	Difference in Two Proportions	-0.083042833
17	Average Proportion	0.385364496
18	Z Test Statistic	-5.06166817
19		
20	Two-Tail Test	
21	Lower Critical Value	-1.959963985
22	Upper Critical Value	1.959963985
23	p-Value	4.15604E-07
24	Reject the null hypothesis	

© 2006 Pearson Education, Inc., Upper Saddle River, NJ. All rights reserved. This material is protected under all copyright laws as they currently exist. No portion of this material may be reproduced, in any form or by any means, without permission in writing from the publisher.

Technology

▶ Exercise 1 (pg. 453) Testing the Hypothesis That the Probability of a "Found Coin" Lying Heads Up Is 0.5

If the PHStat add-in has not been loaded, you will need to load it before continuing. Follow the instructions in Section GS 8.2.

1. First open a new Excel worksheet. Then, at the top of the screen, select **PHStat→One-Sample Tests→Z Test for the Proportion**.

2. Complete the Z Test for the Proportion dialog box as shown below. Click **OK**.

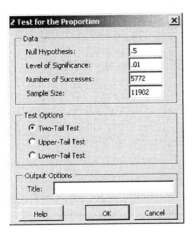

© 2006 Pearson Education, Inc., Upper Saddle River, NJ. All rights reserved. This material is protected under all copyright laws as they currently exist. No portion of this material may be reproduced, in any form or by any means, without permission in writing from the publisher.

Your output should look similar to the output displayed below.

	A	B	C
1	Z Test of Hypothesis for the Proportion		
2			
3	Data		
4	Null Hypothesis $p=$	0.5	
5	Level of Significance	0.01	
6	Number of Successes	5772	
7	Sample Size	11902	
8			
9	Intermediate Calculations		
10	Sample Proportion	0.484960511	
11	Standard Error	0.004583107	
12	Z Test Statistic	-3.281504874	
13			
14	Two-Tail Test		
15	Lower Critical Value	-2.575829304	
16	Upper Critical value	2.575829304	
17	p-Value	0.001032547	
18	Reject the null hypothesis		

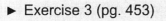

▶ Exercise 3 (pg. 453)   Simulating "Tails Over Heads"

---

1. Open a new Excel worksheet.

2. At the top of the screen, select **Tools→Data Analysis**. Select **Random Number Generation**. Click **OK**.

If Data Analysis does not appear as a choice in the Tools menu, you will need to load the Microsoft Excel ToolPak add-in. Follow the procedure in Section GS 8.1 before continuing.

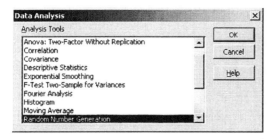

© 2006 Pearson Education, Inc., Upper Saddle River, NJ. All rights reserved. This material is protected under all copyright laws as they currently exist. No portion of this material may be reproduced, in any form or by any means, without permission in writing from the publisher.

Complete the Random Number Generation dialog box as shown below. The output will be placed in cell A1. Click **OK**.

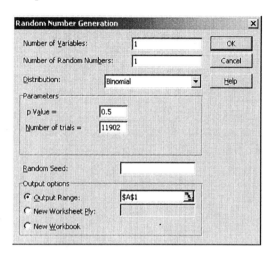

The output for this simulation indicates that 5,955 of the 11,902 coins were found heads up. Because this output was generated randomly, it is unlikely that your output will be exactly the same.

© 2006 Pearson Education, Inc., Upper Saddle River, NJ. All rights reserved. This material is protected under all copyright laws as they currently exist. No portion of this material may be reproduced, in any form or by any means, without permission in writing from the publisher.

Correlation and Regression

Section 9.1 Correlation

| ▶ Example 3 (pg. 460) | Constructing a Scatter Plot Using Technology |

1. Open worksheet "Oldfaithful" in the Chapter 9 folder.

2. Click on any cell within the table of data. At the top of the screen, click **Insert** and select **Chart** from the menu that appears.

3. In the Chart Type dialog box, select the **XY (Scatter)** chart type by clicking on it. Then click on the topmost chart sub-type. Click **Next**.

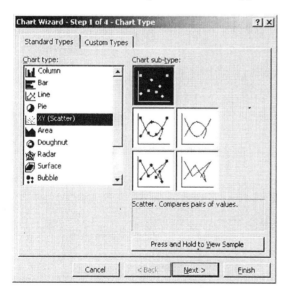

© 2006 Pearson Education, Inc., Upper Saddle River, NJ. All rights reserved. This material is protected under all copyright laws as they currently exist. No portion of this material may be reproduced, in any form or by any means, without permission in writing from the publisher.

4. In the Chart Source Data dialog box, the entry in the data range field should be **=Sheet1!$A$2:$B$37**. You will need to change $A$1 to $A$2. Click **Next**.

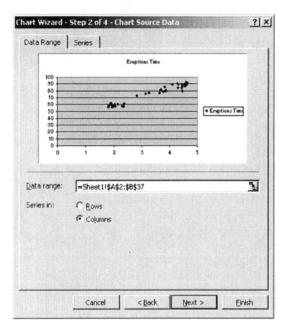

5. Click the **Titles** tab at the top of the Chart Options dialog box. In the Chart title field, change the title to **Duration of Old Faithful's Eruptions by Time Until the Next Eruption**. In the Value (X) axis field, enter **Duration (in minutes)**. In the Value (Y) axis field, enter **Time Until the Next Eruption (in minutes)**.

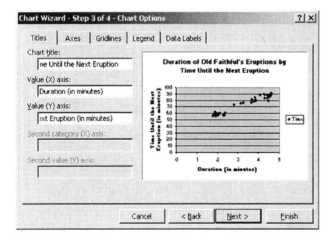

© 2006 Pearson Education, Inc., Upper Saddle River, NJ. All rights reserved. This material is protected under all copyright laws as they currently exist.
No portion of this material may be reproduced, in any form or by any means, without permission in writing from the publisher.

6. Click the **Legend** tab at the top of the Chart Options dialog box. Click in the box to the left of **Show Legend** so that a checkmark does not appear there. This removes the Time legend from the right side of the scatter plot. Click **Next**.

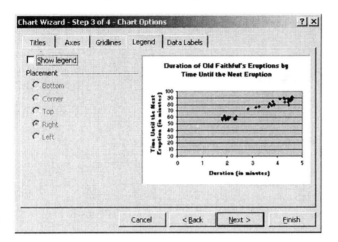

7. The Chart Location dialog box presents two options for placement of the scatter plot. For this example, select **As new sheet**. Click **Finish**.

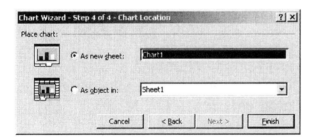

© 2006 Pearson Education, Inc., Upper Saddle River, NJ. All rights reserved. This material is protected under all copyright laws as they currently exist. No portion of this material may be reproduced, in any form or by any means, without permission in writing from the publisher.

Your scatter plot should look similar to the one shown below.

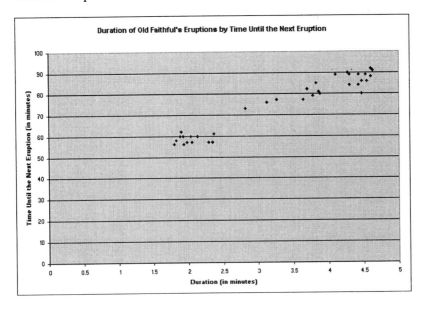

Duration of Old Faithful's Eruptions by Time Until the Next Eruption

▶ Example 5 (pg. 463)   Using Technology to Find a Correlation Coefficient

1. Open worksheet "Oldfaithful" in the Chapter 9 folder and click in cell **C1** to place the output there.

	A	B	C
1	Eruptions		
2	Duration	Time	
3	1.8	56	

2. At the top of the screen, click **Insert→Function**.

© 2006 Pearson Education, Inc., Upper Saddle River, NJ. All rights reserved. This material is protected under all copyright laws as they currently exist. No portion of this material may be reproduced, in any form or by any means, without permission in writing from the publisher.

3. Select the **Statistical** category. Select the **CORREL** function. Click **OK**.

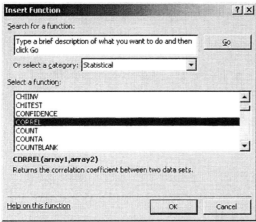

4. Complete the CORREL dialog box as shown below. Click **OK**.

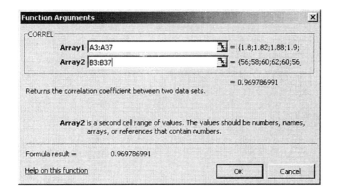

Your output should look like the output shown below.

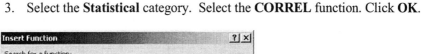

© 2006 Pearson Education, Inc., Upper Saddle River, NJ. All rights reserved. This material is protected under all copyright laws as they currently exist. No portion of this material may be reproduced, in any form or by any means, without permission in writing from the publisher.

| ► Exercise 17 (pg. 470) | Scatter Plot and Correlation for Hours Studying and Test Scores |

1. Open worksheet "Ex9_1-17" in the Chapter 9 folder.

2. Click on any cell within the table of data. At the top of the screen, click **Insert** and select **Chart** from the menu that appears.

3. In the Chart Type dialog box, select the **XY (Scatter)** chart type by clicking on it. Then click on the topmost chart sub-type. Click **Next**.

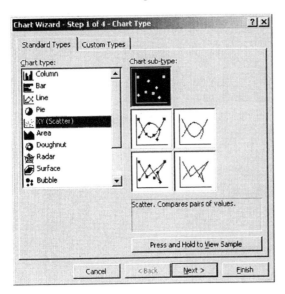

© 2006 Pearson Education, Inc., Upper Saddle River, NJ. All rights reserved. This material is protected under all copyright laws as they currently exist. No portion of this material may be reproduced, in any form or by any means, without permission in writing from the publisher.

4. In the Chart Source Data dialog box, the entry in the data range field should be **=Sheet1!$A$1:$B$14**. Make any necessary corrections. Then click **Next**.

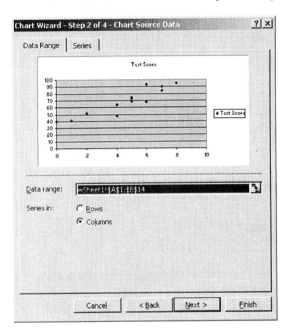

5. Click the **Titles** tab at the top of the Chart Options dialog box. In the Chart title field, change the title to **Hours Spent Studying for a Test by Test Score**. In the Value (X) axis field, enter **Hours**. In the Value (Y) axis field, enter **Test Score**.

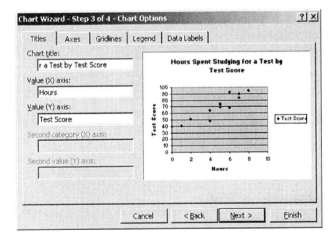

© 2006 Pearson Education, Inc., Upper Saddle River, NJ. All rights reserved. This material is protected under all copyright laws as they currently exist. No portion of this material may be reproduced, in any form or by any means, without permission in writing from the publisher.

6. Click the **Legend** tab at the top of the Chart Options dialog box. Click in the box to the left of **Show Legend** so that a checkmark does not appear there. This removes the Test Score legend from the right side of the scatter plot. Click **Next**.

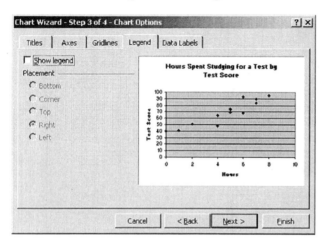

7. The Chart Location dialog box presents two options for placement of the scatter plot. For this example, select **As object in** the same worksheet as the data. To do this, click the button to the left of **As object in** so that a black dot appears there. Click **Finish**.

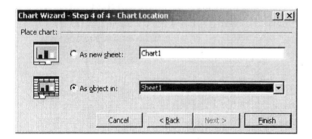

© 2006 Pearson Education, Inc., Upper Saddle River, NJ. All rights reserved. This material is protected under all copyright laws as they currently exist.
No portion of this material may be reproduced, in any form or by any means, without permission in writing from the publisher.

8. Make the chart taller so that it is easier to read. To do this, first click within the figure near a border. Black square handles appear. Then click on the center handle on the bottom border of the figure and drag it down a few rows.

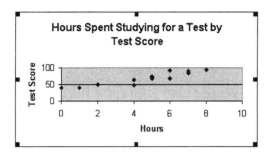

Your scatter plot should now look similar to the one shown below.

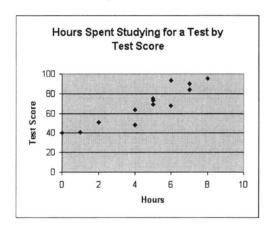

9. You will now use Excel to find the correlation between hours and test score. Click in cell **C1** of the worksheet to place the output there.

	A	B	C
1	Hours studying	Test Score	
2	0	40	

10. At the top of the screen, click **Insert→Function**.

© 2006 Pearson Education, Inc., Upper Saddle River, NJ. All rights reserved. This material is protected under all copyright laws as they currently exist. No portion of this material may be reproduced, in any form or by any means, without permission in writing from the publisher.

11. Select the **Statistical** category. Select the **CORREL** function. Click **OK**.

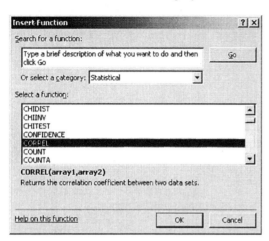

12. Complete the CORREL dialog box as shown below. Click **OK**.

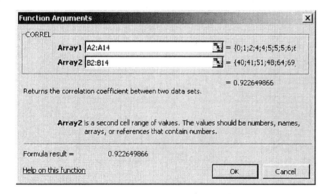

Your output should look like the output shown below.

	A	B	C
1	Hours studying	Test Score	0.92265
2	0	40	

© 2006 Pearson Education, Inc., Upper Saddle River, NJ. All rights reserved. This material is protected under all copyright laws as they currently exist. No portion of this material may be reproduced, in any form or by any means, without permission in writing from the publisher.

Section 9.2 Linear Regression Case Study

| ▶ Example 2 (pg. 476) | Using Technology to Find a Regression Equation |

1. Open worksheet "Oldfaithful" in the Chapter 9 folder.

2. You will be using Excel's functions to obtain the slope and intercept. Type the labels **Slope** and **Intercept** in the worksheet as shown below. Then click in cell **D2** where the slope will be placed.

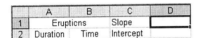

	A	B	C	D
1	Eruptions		Slope	
2	Duration	Time	Intercept	

3. At the top of the screen click **Insert→Function**.

4. Select the **Statistical** category. Select the **SLOPE** function. Click **OK**.

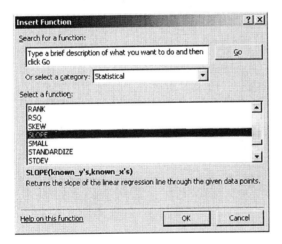

© 2006 Pearson Education, Inc., Upper Saddle River, NJ. All rights reserved. This material is protected under all copyright laws as they currently exist. No portion of this material may be reproduced, in any form or by any means, without permission in writing from the publisher.

5. Complete the SLOPE dialog box as shown below. Click **OK**.

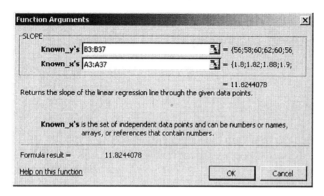

6. A slope of 11.82 is returned and placed in cell D1 of the worksheet. Click in cell **D2** where the intercept will be placed.

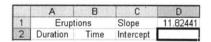

7. At the top of the screen click **Insert→Function**.

8. Select the **Statistical** category. Select the **INTERCEPT** function. Click **OK**.

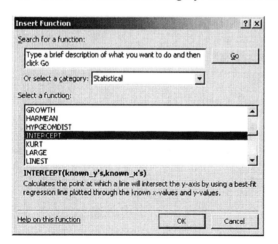

© 2006 Pearson Education, Inc., Upper Saddle River, NJ. All rights reserved. This material is protected under all copyright laws as they currently exist. No portion of this material may be reproduced, in any form or by any means, without permission in writing from the publisher.

9.   Complete the INTERCEPT dialog box as shown below. Click **OK**.

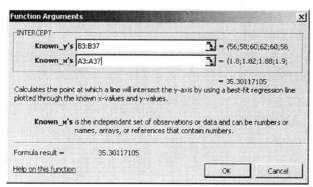

An intercept of 35.30 is returned and placed in cell D2 of the worksheet.

	A	B	C	D
1	Eruptions		Slope	11.82441
2	Duration	Time	Intercept	35.30117

◀

▶ Exercise 16 (pg. 479)	Finding the Equation of a Regression Line for TV and Test Scores

1.   Open worksheet "Ex9_2-16" in the Chapter 9 folder.

	A	B	C	D	E	F	G
1	Age	Blood Pressure					
2	16	109					
3	25	122					
4	39	143					
5	45	132					
6	49	199					
7	64	185					
8	70	199					

2.   At the top of the screen, click **Tools→Data Analysis**. Select **Regression** and click **OK**.

If Data Analysis does not appear as a choice in the Tools menu, you will need to load the Microsoft Excel Analysis ToolPak add-in. Follow the procedure in Section GS 8.1 before continuing.

© 2006 Pearson Education, Inc., Upper Saddle River, NJ. All rights reserved. This material is protected under all copyright laws as they currently exist.
No portion of this material may be reproduced, in any form or by any means, without permission in writing from the publisher.

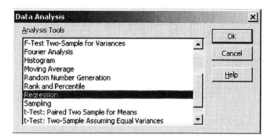

3. Complete the Regression dialog box as shown below. Click **OK**.

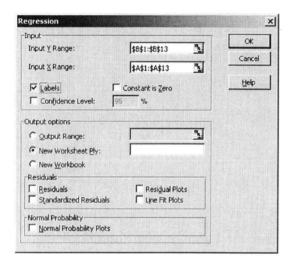

The intercept and slope of the regression equation are shown in the bottom two lines of the output under the label "Coefficients." The intercept is 93.97 and the slope is – 4.07.

16		Coefficients	Standard Error	t Stat	P-value	Lower 95%	Upper 95%
17	Intercept	93.97003745	4.523586141	20.77334984	1.48057E-09	83.890859	104.0492154
18	Hours TV	-4.06741573	0.860011871	-4.729487891	0.0008048	-5.983642	-2.151189876

© 2006 Pearson Education, Inc., Upper Saddle River, NJ. All rights reserved. This material is protected under all copyright laws as they currently exist. No portion of this material may be reproduced, in any form or by any means, without permission in writing from the publisher.

Section 9.3 Measures of Regression and Prediction Intervals

▶ Example 2 (pg. 487)	Finding the Standard Error of Estimate

1. Open a new Excel worksheet and enter the expenses and sales data as shown below.

	A	B
1	Expenses	Sales
2	2.4	225
3	1.6	184
4	2	220
5	2.6	240
6	1.4	180
7	1.6	184
8	2	186
9	2.2	215

2. At the top of the screen, click **Tools→Data Analysis**. Select **Regression** and click **OK**.

If Data Analysis does not appear as a choice in the Tools menu, you will need to load the Microsoft Excel Analysis ToolPak add-in. Follow the procedure in Section GS 8.1 before continuing.

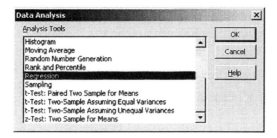

© 2006 Pearson Education, Inc., Upper Saddle River, NJ. All rights reserved. This material is protected under all copyright laws as they currently exist. No portion of this material may be reproduced, in any form or by any means, without permission in writing from the publisher.

3. Complete the Regression dialog box as shown below. If you select **Residuals**, the output will include $y - \hat{y}$ for each observation in the data set. Click **OK**.

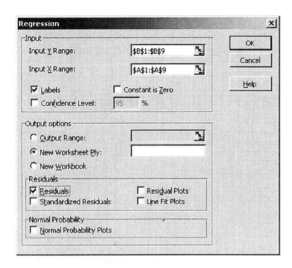

The standard error of estimate is displayed in the top part of the output. You will want to widen column A so that you can read all the labels. The standard error of estimate is equal to 10.29.

	A	B
1	SUMMARY OUTPUT	
2		
3	*Regression Statistics*	
4	Multiple R	0.912905285
5	R Square	0.833396059
6	Adjusted R Square	0.805628735
7	Standard Error	10.29032012
8	Observations	8

The residuals are displayed in the lower part of the output.

22	RESIDUAL OUTPUT		
23			
24	*Observation*	*Predicted Sales*	*Residuals*
25	1	225.8097166	-0.809716599
26	2	185.2267206	-1.226720648
27	3	205.5182186	14.48178138
28	4	235.9554656	4.044534413
29	5	175.0809717	4.91902834
30	6	185.2267206	-1.226720648
31	7	205.5182186	-19.51821862
32	8	215.6639676	-0.663967611

© 2006 Pearson Education, Inc., Upper Saddle River, NJ. All rights reserved. This material is protected under all copyright laws as they currently exist. No portion of this material may be reproduced, in any form or by any means, without permission in writing from the publisher.

Section 9.4 Multiple Regression Uses and Abuses

▶ Example 1 (pg. 494)   Finding a Multiple Regression Equation

1. Open worksheet "Salary" in the Chapter 9 folder.

2. At the top of the screen, click **Tools→Data Analysis**. Select **Regression** and click **OK**.

If Data Analysis does not appear as a choice in the Tools menu, you will need to load the Microsoft Excel Analysis ToolPak add-in. Follow the procedure in Section GS 8.1 before continuing.

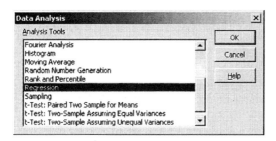

3. Complete the Regression dialog box as shown below. Click **OK**.

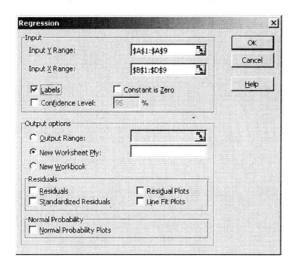

© 2006 Pearson Education, Inc., Upper Saddle River, NJ. All rights reserved. This material is protected under all copyright laws as they currently exist. No portion of this material may be reproduced, in any form or by any means, without permission in writing from the publisher.

The coefficients for the multiple regression equation are displayed in the lower portion of the output under the label "Coefficients."

16		Coefficients	Standard Error	t Stat	P-value	Lower 95%	Upper 95%
17	Intercept	29764.446	1981.346465	15.02233281	0.000114414	24263.34631	35265.54569
18	Employme	364.4120281	48.31750816	7.542028592	0.001655537	230.261119	498.5629371
19	Experienc	227.6188106	123.8361513	1.838064315	0.139912203	-116.2054654	571.4430866
20	Education	266.9350412	147.3556227	1.811502245	0.144295055	-142.189756	676.0598385

► Exercise 5 (pg. 498) | Finding a Multiple Regression Equation, the Standard Error of Estimate, and R^2

1. Open worksheet "Ex9_4-5" in the Chapter 9 folder.

2. At the top of the screen, select **Tools→Data Analysis**. Selection **Regression** and click **OK**.

If Data Analysis does not appear as a choice in the Tools menu, you will need to load the Microsoft Excel Analysis ToolPak add-in. Follow the procedure in Section GS 8.1 before continuing.

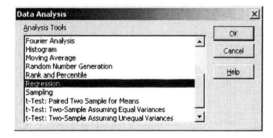

3. Complete the Regression dialog box as shown at the top of the next page. Click **OK**.

© 2006 Pearson Education, Inc., Upper Saddle River, NJ. All rights reserved. This material is protected under all copyright laws as they currently exist. No portion of this material may be reproduced, in any form or by any means, without permission in writing from the publisher.

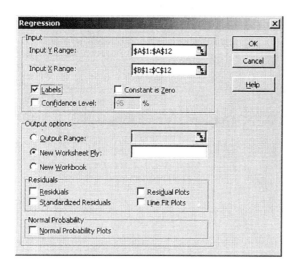

R^2 is equal to 0.9881. The standard error of estimate is equal to 34.1597. The coefficients for the multiple regression equation are displayed in the lower portion of the output under the label "Coefficients."

	A	B
1	SUMMARY OUTPUT	
2		
3	*Regression Statistics*	
4	Multiple R	0.99402309
5	R Square	0.988081903
6	Adjusted R Square	0.985102378
7	Standard Error	34.15972608
8	Observations	11

		Coefficients
16		
17	Intercept	-256.2925925
18	sq footage	103.5018943
19	Shopping centers	14.64887954

Technology

▶ Exercise 1 (pg. 507)	Constructing a Scatter Plot

If the PHStat add-in has not been loaded, you will need to load it before continuing. Follow the instructions in Section GS 8.2.

© 2006 Pearson Education, Inc., Upper Saddle River, NJ. All rights reserved. This material is protected under all copyright laws as they currently exist. No portion of this material may be reproduced, in any form or by any means, without permission in writing from the publisher.

Directions are given here for constructing a scatter plot of the calories and sugar variables. You can follow these instructions for constructing scatter plots of the other pairs of variables, but you will need to change the data ranges.

1.   Open worksheet "Tech9" in the Chapter 9 folder.

2.   At the top of the screen, select **PHStat→Regression→Simple Linear Regression**.

3.   Complete the Simple Linear Regression dialog box as shown below. Click **OK**.

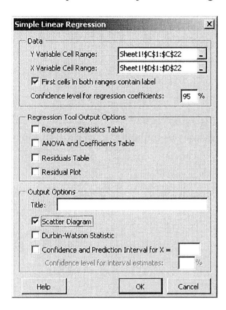

4.   To see the scatter plot, click the **Scatter** sheet tab near the bottom of the screen. There is a great deal of blank space in the lower half of the scatter plot. You will adjust this by changing the Y-axis scale. **Right-click** on any number on the Y-axis scale. I clicked on 60.

© 2006 Pearson Education, Inc., Upper Saddle River, NJ. All rights reserved. This material is protected under all copyright laws as they currently exist.
No portion of this material may be reproduced, in any form or by any means, without permission in writing from the publisher.

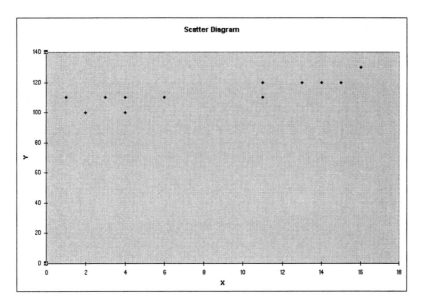

5. Select **Format Axis** from the shortcut menu that appears.

6. Click the **Scale** tab at the top. Change Minimum to **90**. Click **OK**.

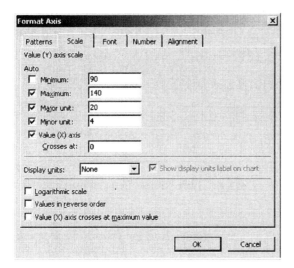

© 2006 Pearson Education, Inc., Upper Saddle River, NJ. All rights reserved. This material is protected under all copyright laws as they currently exist. No portion of this material may be reproduced, in any form or by any means, without permission in writing from the publisher.

The completed scatter plot is shown below.

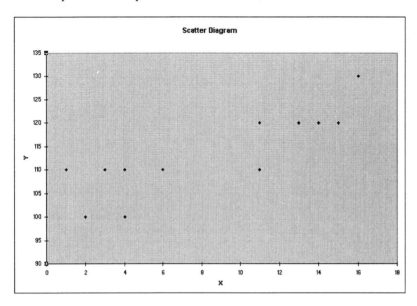

| ► Exercise 3 (pg. 507) | Find the Correlation Coefficient for Each Pair of Variables |

1. Open worksheet "Tech9" in the Chapter 9 folder.

   *If you have just completed Exercise 1 on page 507 and have not closed the Excel worksheet, return to the sheet containing the data by clicking on the **Sheet1** tab at the bottom of the screen.*

2. At the top of the screen, click **Tools→Data Analysis**. Select **Correlation** and click **OK**.

   If Data Analysis does not appear as a choice in the Tools menu, you will need to load the Microsoft Excel Analysis ToolPak add-in. Follow the procedure in Section GS 8.1 before continuing.

© 2006 Pearson Education, Inc., Upper Saddle River, NJ. All rights reserved. This material is protected under all copyright laws as they currently exist. No portion of this material may be reproduced, in any form or by any means, without permission in writing from the publisher.

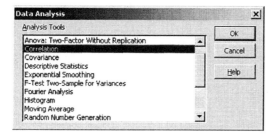

3.   Complete the Correlation dialog box as shown below. Click **OK**.

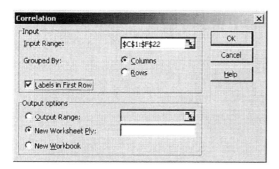

The output is a correlation matrix that displays the correlation coefficients for all pairs of variables.

	A	B	C	D	E
1		C	S	F	R
2	C	1			
3	S	0.872964	1		
4	F	0.327181	0.284779	1	
5	R	0.688963	0.754569	-0.1561	1

◀

► Exercise 4 (pg. 507)   Finding the Regression Line

Directions are given here for finding the equation for calories (X) and sugar (Y).

1.   Complete Exercise 1 on page 507 following the instructions given in this manual.
      Your output is a scatter plot of the calories and sugar variables.

2.   **Right-click** on one of the dots and select **Add Trendline**.

© 2006 Pearson Education, Inc., Upper Saddle River, NJ. All rights reserved. This material is protected under all copyright laws as they currently exist.
No portion of this material may be reproduced, in any form or by any means, without permission in writing from the publisher.

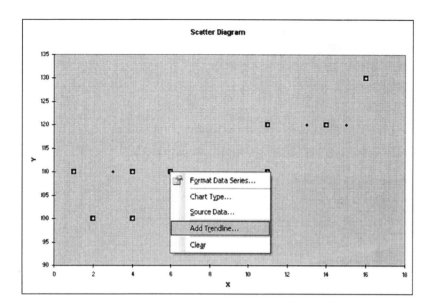

3. Select the **Linear** type by clicking on it.

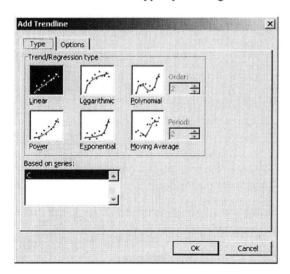

© 2006 Pearson Education, Inc., Upper Saddle River, NJ. All rights reserved. This material is protected under all copyright laws as they currently exist. No portion of this material may be reproduced, in any form or by any means, without permission in writing from the publisher.

4. Click the **Options** tab. Select **Display equation on chart**. Click **OK**.

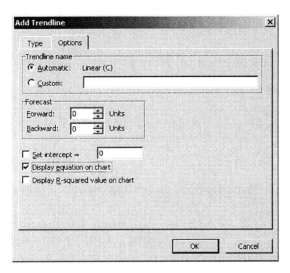

5. Move the equation to a location on the scatter plot where it can be easily read. The slope is 1.2559, and the intercept is 103.16.

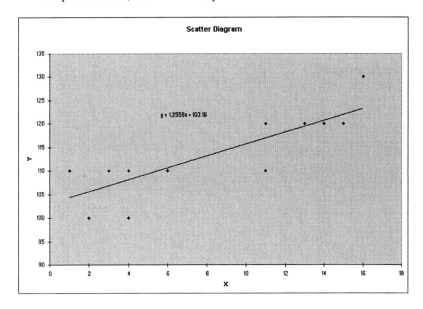

© 2006 Pearson Education, Inc., Upper Saddle River, NJ. All rights reserved. This material is protected under all copyright laws as they currently exist.
No portion of this material may be reproduced, in any form or by any means, without permission in writing from the publisher.

► Exercise 6 (pg. 507) | Finding Multiple Regression Equations

---

Directions are given here for Exercise 6 (a) $C = b + m_1S + m_2F + m_3R$.

1. Open worksheet "Tech9" in the Chapter 9 folder.

---

*If you have just completed Exercise 1, Exercise 3, or Exercise 4 on page 507 and have not closed the Excel worksheet, return to the sheet containing the data by clicking on the **Sheet1** tab at the bottom of the screen.*

---

2. At the top of the screen, click **Tools→Data Analysis**. Select **Regression** and click **OK**.

If Data Analysis does not appear as a choice in the Tools menu, you will need to load the Microsoft Excel Analysis ToolPak add-in. Follow the procedure in Section GS 8.1 before continuing.

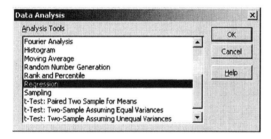

© 2006 Pearson Education, Inc., Upper Saddle River, NJ. All rights reserved. This material is protected under all copyright laws as they currently exist. No portion of this material may be reproduced, in any form or by any means, without permission in writing from the publisher.

3. Complete the Regression dialog box as shown below. Click **OK**.

The predictor variables must be located in adjacent columns in the Excel worksheet.

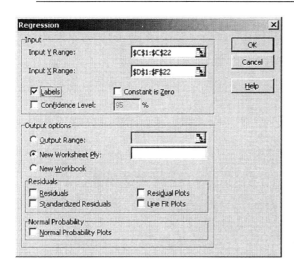

The coefficients for the equation are given in the lower part of the output.

16		Coefficients
17	Intercept	82.96688226
18	S	0.944825404
19	F	2.247001063
20	R	0.842256973

© 2006 Pearson Education, Inc., Upper Saddle River, NJ. All rights reserved. This material is protected under all copyright laws as they currently exist. No portion of this material may be reproduced, in any form or by any means, without permission in writing from the publisher.

Chi-Square Tests and the F-Distribution

CHAPTER
10

Section 10.2 Independence Case Study

> ▶ Example 3 (pg. 526) — Using Technology for a Chi-Square Independence Test

If the PHStat add-in has not been loaded, you will need to load it before continuing. Follow the instructions in Section GS 8.2.

1. First, open a new Excel worksheet. Then, at the top of the screen, select **PHStat→Multiple-Sample Tests→Chi-Square Test**.

2. Complete the Chi-Square Test dialog box as shown below. Click **OK**.

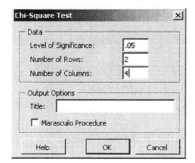

3. A Chi-Square Test worksheet will appear. Delete the user note, then complete the Observed Frequencies table in this worksheet as shown at the top of the next page. You will notice that values in other locations of the worksheet change as you enter the observed frequencies.

© 2006 Pearson Education, Inc., Upper Saddle River, NJ. All rights reserved. This material is protected under all copyright laws as they currently exist. No portion of this material may be reproduced, in any form or by any means, without permission in writing from the publisher.

	A	B	C	D	E	F
1	Chi-Square Test					
2						
3		Observed Frequencies				
4		Column variable				
5	Row variable	C1	C2	C3	C4	Total
6	R1	40	53	26	6	125
7	R2	34	68	37	11	150
8	Total	74	121	63	17	275

The critical value, the obtained chi-square test statistic, and the p-value are displayed in rows 24 through 26. The statistical decision is displayed in row 27.

17	Data	
18	Level of Significance	0.05
19	Number of Rows	2
20	Number of Columns	4
21	Degrees of Freedom	3
22		
23	Results	
24	Critical Value	7.814728
25	Chi-Square Test Statistic	3.493357
26	p-Value	0.321625
27	Do not reject the null hypothesis	
28		
29	Expected frequency assumption	
30	is met.	

◀

▶ Exercise 5 (pg. 529)	Testing the Drug for Treatment of Obsessive-Compulsive Disorder

If the PHStat add-in has not been loaded, you will need to load it before continuing. Follow the instructions in Section GS 8.2.

1. Open a new Excel worksheet. At the top of the screen, select **PHStat→Multiple-Sample Tests→Chi-Square Test**.

2. Complete the Chi-Square Test dialog box as shown at the top of the next page. Click **OK**.

© 2006 Pearson Education, Inc., Upper Saddle River, NJ. All rights reserved. This material is protected under all copyright laws as they currently exist. No portion of this material may be reproduced, in any form or by any means, without permission in writing from the publisher.

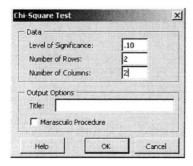

4. A Chi-Square Test worksheet will appear. Complete the Observed Frequencies table in this worksheet as shown below. Values in other locations of the worksheet change as you enter the observed frequencies.

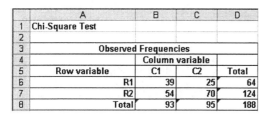

	A	B	C	D
1	Chi-Square Test			
2				
3		Observed Frequencies		
4			Column variable	
5	Row variable	C1	C2	Total
6	R1	39	25	64
7	R2	54	70	124
8	Total	93	95	188

The critical value, the obtained chi-square test statistic, and the p-value are displayed in rows 24 through 26. The statistical decision is displayed in row 27.

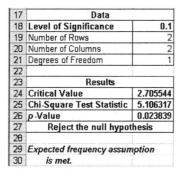

17	Data	
18	Level of Significance	0.1
19	Number of Rows	2
20	Number of Columns	2
21	Degrees of Freedom	1
22		
23	Results	
24	Critical Value	2.705544
25	Chi-Square Test Statistic	5.106317
26	p-Value	0.023839
27	Reject the null hypothesis	
28		
29	Expected frequency assumption	
30	is met.	

© 2006 Pearson Education, Inc., Upper Saddle River, NJ. All rights reserved. This material is protected under all copyright laws as they currently exist. No portion of this material may be reproduced, in any form or by any means, without permission in writing from the publisher.

Section 10.3 Comparing Two Variances

► Example 3 (pg. 537)	Performing a Two-Sample F-Test

If the PHStat add-in has not been loaded, you will need to load it before continuing. Follow the instructions in Section GS 8.2.

1. First open a new Excel worksheet. Then, at the top of the screen, select
    PHStat→Two-Sample Tests→F Test for Differences in Two Variances.

2. Complete the F Test for Differences in Two Variances dialog box as shown below. Click **OK**.

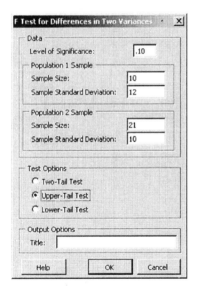

Your output should appear similar to the output displayed at the top of the next page.

© 2006 Pearson Education, Inc., Upper Saddle River, NJ. All rights reserved. This material is protected under all copyright laws as they currently exist. No portion of this material may be reproduced, in any form or by any means, without permission in writing from the publisher.

	A	B	C	D	E
1	F Test for Differences in Two Variances				
2					
3	Data				
4	Level of Significance	0.1			
5	Population 1 Sample				
6	Sample Size	10			
7	Sample Standard Deviation	12			
8	Population 2 Sample				
9	Sample Size	21			
10	Sample Standard Deviation	10			
11					
12	Intermediate Calculations				
13	F Test Statistic	1.44			
14	Population 1 Sample Degrees of Freedom	9			
15	Population 2 Sample Degrees of Freedom	20			
16				Calculations Area	
17	Upper-Tail Test			FDIST value	0.2369
18	Upper Critical Value	1.964853		1-FDIST value	0.7631
19	p-Value	0.2369			
20	Do not reject the null hypothesis				

Section 10.4 Analysis of Variance

▶ Example 2 (pg. 547) | Using Technology to Perform ANOVA Tests

1. Open worksheet "Airline" in the Chapter 10 folder.

2. At the top of the screen, click **Tools→Data Analysis**. Select **ANOVA: Single Factor** and click **OK**.

If Data Analysis does not appear as a choice in the Tools menu, you will need to load the Microsoft Excel Analysis ToolPak add-in. Follow the procedure in Section GS 8.1 before continuing.

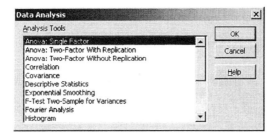

3. Complete the ANOVA: Single Factor dialog box as shown at the top of the next page. Click **OK**.

© 2006 Pearson Education, Inc., Upper Saddle River, NJ. All rights reserved. This material is protected under all copyright laws as they currently exist. No portion of this material may be reproduced, in any form or by any means, without permission in writing from the publisher.

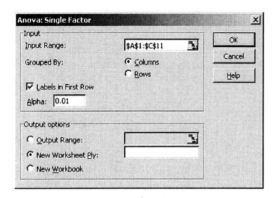

Make column A wider so that you can read all the labels. Your output should appear similar to the output displayed below.

	A	B	C	D	E	F	G
1	Anova: Single Factor						
2							
3	SUMMARY						
4	Groups	Count	Sum	Average	Variance		
5	Airline1	10	1238	123.8	106.6222		
6	Airline2	10	1315	131.5	120.2778		
7	Airline3	10	1427	142.7	215.1222		
8							
9							
10	ANOVA						
11	Source of Variation	SS	df	MS	F	P-value	F crit
12	Between Groups	1806.467	2	903.2333	6.130235	0.006383	5.488118
13	Within Groups	3978.2	27	147.3407			
14							
15	Total	5784.667	29				

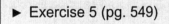

▶ Exercise 5 (pg. 549)	Testing the Claim That the Mean Toothpaste Costs Per Month Are Different

1. Open worksheet "Ex10_4-5" in the Chapter 10 folder.

2. At the top of the screen, click **Tools→Data Analysis**. Select **ANOVA: Single Factor** and click **OK**.

If Data Analysis does not appear as a choice in the Tools menu, you will need to load the Microsoft Excel Analysis ToolPak add-in. Follow the procedure in Section GS 8.1 before continuing.

© 2006 Pearson Education, Inc., Upper Saddle River, NJ. All rights reserved. This material is protected under all copyright laws as they currently exist. No portion of this material may be reproduced, in any form or by any means, without permission in writing from the publisher.

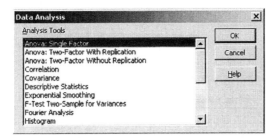

3. Complete the ANOVA: Single Factor dialog box as shown below. Click **OK**.

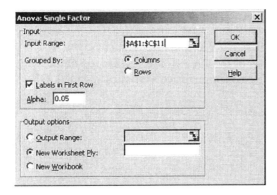

Make column A wider so that you can read all the labels. Your output should appear similar to the output displayed below.

	A	B	C	D	E	F	G
1	Anova: Single Factor						
2							
3	SUMMARY						
4	Groups	Count	Sum	Average	Variance		
5	Moderate	10	11.92	1.192	0.892129		
6	Low	10	10.26	1.026	0.160804		
7	Very Low	4	6.75	1.6875	2.530358		
8							
9							
10	ANOVA						
11	Source of Variation	SS	df	MS	F	P-value	F crit
12	Between Groups	1.253321	2	0.62666	0.77105	0.475184	3.4668
13	Within Groups	17.06748	21	0.812737			
14							
15	Total	18.3208	23				

© 2006 Pearson Education, Inc., Upper Saddle River, NJ. All rights reserved. This material is protected under all copyright laws as they currently exist.
No portion of this material may be reproduced, in any form or by any means, without permission in writing from the publisher.

Technology

| ▶ Exercise 3 (pg. 563) | Determining Whether the Populations Have Equal Variances—Teacher Salaries |

If the PHStat add-in has not been loaded, you will need to load it before continuing. Follow the instructions in Section GS 8.2.

1. Open worksheet "Tech10-a" in the Chapter 10 folder.

2. Because you are working with raw data rather than summary statistics, you first need to calculate the standard deviations of the three groups. At the top of the screen, click **Tools→Data Analysis**. Select **Descriptive Statistics** and click **OK**.

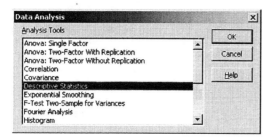

3. Complete the Descriptive Statistics dialog box as shown below. Click **OK**.

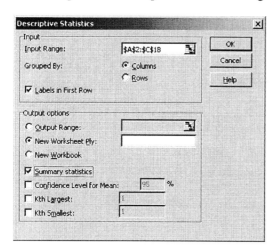

4. Make the columns wider so that you can read the labels. The standard deviations of California, Ohio, and Wyoming salaries are 7685.15, 7811.34, and 7895.52,

© 2006 Pearson Education, Inc., Upper Saddle River, NJ. All rights reserved. This material is protected under all copyright laws as they currently exist. No portion of this material may be reproduced, in any form or by any means, without permission in writing from the publisher.

respectively. For this exercise, instructions are provided only for testing the equality of the California and Ohio salaries. At the top of the screen, select **PHStat→Two-Sample Tests→F Test for Differences in Two Variances**.

	A	B	C	D	E	F
1	*California*		*Ohio*		*Wyoming*	
2						
3	Mean	54348	Mean	44266	Mean	37853
4	Standard Error	1921.288639	Standard Error	1952.834297	Standard Error	1973.88
5	Median	55986.5	Median	41650	Median	34557.5
6	Mode	59800	Mode	40500	Mode	#N/A
7	Standard Deviation	7685.154555	Standard Deviation	7811.337188	Standard Deviation	7895.52

5. Complete the F Test for Differences in Two Variances dialog box as below. Click **OK**.

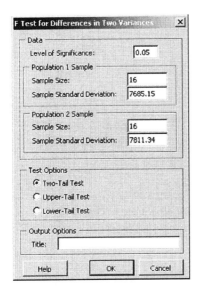

Your output should appear similar to the output displayed at the top of the next page.

© 2006 Pearson Education, Inc., Upper Saddle River, NJ. All rights reserved. This material is protected under all copyright laws as they currently exist.
No portion of this material may be reproduced, in any form or by any means, without permission in writing from the publisher.

	A	B	C	D	E
1	F Test for Differences in Two Variances				
2					
3	Data				
4	Level of Significance	0.05			
5	Population 1 Sample				
6	Sample Size	16			
7	Sample Standard Deviation	7685.15			
8	Population 2 Sample				
9	Sample Size	16			
10	Sample Standard Deviation	7811.34			
11					
12	Intermediate Calculations				
13	F Test Statistic	0.967952			
14	Population 1 Sample Degrees of Freedom	15			
15	Population 2 Sample Degrees of Freedom	15			
16				Calculations Area	
17	Two-Tail Test			FDIST value	0.524732
18	Lower Critical Value	0.349395		1-FDIST value	0.475268
19	Upper Critical Value	2.862093			
20	p-Value	0.950535			
21	Do not reject the null hypothesis				

◀

► Exercise 4 (pg. 563) **Testing the Claim That Teachers from the Three States Have the Same Mean Salary**

1. Open worksheet "Tech10-a" in the Chapter 10 folder.

*If you have just completed Exercise 3 on page 563 and have not yet closed the Excel worksheet, return to the sheet with the data by clicking on the **Sheet1** tab near the bottom of the screen.*

2. At the top of the screen, click **Tools→Data Analysis**. Select **ANOVA: Single Factor** and click **OK**.

If Data Analysis does not appear as a choice in the Tools menu, you will need to load the Microsoft Excel Analysis ToolPak add-in. Follow the procedure in Section GS 8.1 before continuing.

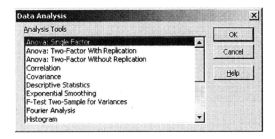

© 2006 Pearson Education, Inc., Upper Saddle River, NJ. All rights reserved. This material is protected under all copyright laws as they currently exist. No portion of this material may be reproduced, in any form or by any means, without permission in writing from the publisher.

3.   Complete the ANOVA: Single Factor dialog box as shown below.   Click **OK**.

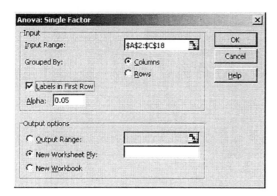

Make column A wider so that you can read all the labels. Your output should appear similar to the output shown below.

	A	B	C	D	E	F	G
1	Anova: Single Factor						
2							
3	SUMMARY						
4	*Groups*	*Count*	*Sum*	*Average*	*Variance*		
5	California	16	869568	54348	59061601		
6	Ohio	16	708256	44266	61016989		
7	Wyoming	16	605648	37853	62339239		
8							
9							
10	ANOVA						
11	*Source of Variation*	*SS*	*df*	*MS*	*F*	*P-value*	*F crit*
12	Between Groups	2.21E+09	2	1.11E+09	18.19376	1.62E-06	3.204317
13	Within Groups	2.74E+09	45	60805943			
14							
15	Total	4.95E+09	47				

© 2006 Pearson Education, Inc., Upper Saddle River, NJ. All rights reserved. This material is protected under all copyright laws as they currently exist.
No portion of this material may be reproduced, in any form or by any means, without permission in writing from the publisher.

Nonparametric Tests

Section 11.2 The Wilcoxon Tests

▶ Example 2 (pg. 581) | Performing a Wilcoxon Rank Sum Test

---

*If the PHStat add-in has not been loaded, you will need to load it before continuing.
Follow the instructions in Section GS 8.2.*

---

1. Open worksheet "Earnings." in the Chapter 11 folder.

2. At the top of the screen, select **PHStat→Two-Sample Tests→Wilcoxon Rank
   Sum Test**.

3. Complete the Wilcoxon Rank Sum Test dialog box as shown below. The
   Population 1 Sample Cell Range is A2 through A12. The Population 2 Sample Cell
   Range is B2 through B14. Click **OK**.

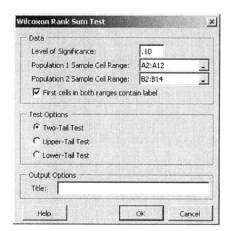

© 2006 Pearson Education, Inc., Upper Saddle River, NJ. All rights reserved. This material is protected under all copyright laws as they currently exist.
No portion of this material may be reproduced, in any form or by any means, without permission in writing from the publisher.

Your output should look similar to the output displayed below.

	A	B
1	Wilcoxon Rank Sum Test	
2		
3	Data	
4	Level of Significance	0.1
5		
6	Population 1 Sample	
7	Sample Size	10
8	Sum of Ranks	138
9	Population 2 Sample	
10	Sample Size	12
11	Sum of Ranks	115
12		
13	Intermediate Calculations	
14	Total Sample Size n	22
15	$T1$ Test Statistic	138
16	$T1$ Mean	115
17	Standard Error of $T1$	15.16575
18	Z Test Statistic	1.516575
19		
20	Two-Tail Test	
21	Lower Critical Value	-1.64485
22	Upper Critical Value	1.644854
23	p-value	0.129374
24	Do not reject the null hypothesis	

◀

Section 11.3 The Kruskal-Wallis Test

▶ Example 1 (pg. 589)   Performing a Kruskal-Wallis Rank Test

If the PHStat add-in has not been loaded, you will need to load it before continuing. Follow the instructions in Section GS 8.2.

1. Open worksheet "Payrates" in the Chapter 11 folder.

2. At the top of the screen, select **PHStat→Multiple-Sample Tests→Kruskal-Wallis Rank Test**.

© 2006 Pearson Education, Inc., Upper Saddle River, NJ. All rights reserved. This material is protected under all copyright laws as they currently exist. No portion of this material may be reproduced, in any form or by any means, without permission in writing from the publisher.

3. Complete the Kruskal-Wallis Rank Test dialog box as shown below. The Sample Data Cell Range is A1 through C11. Click **OK**.

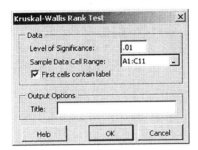

4. Your output should appear similar to the output shown below.

	A	B	C	D	E	F	G
1	**Kruskal-Wallis Rank Test for Differences in Medians**						
2							
3	**Data**						
4	**Level of Significance**	**0.01**		Group	Sample Size	Sum of Ranks	Mean Ranks
5				1	10	94.5	9.45
6	Intermediate Calculations			2	9	193	21.4444444
7	Sum of Squared Ranks/Sample Size	7207.428		3	10	147.5	14.75
8	Sum of Sample Sizes	29					
9	Number of Groups	3					
10							
11	**Test Result**						
12	**H Test Statistic**	9.412797					
13	**Critical Value**	9.21034					
14	**p-Value**	0.009037					
15	**Reject the null hypothesis**						

Technology

▶ **Exercise 3 (pg. 615)**   Performing a Wilcoxon Rank Sum Test

If the PHStat add-in has not been loaded, you will need to load it before continuing. Follow the instructions in Section GS 8.2.

1. Open worksheet "Tech11_a" in the Chapter 11 folder.

© 2006 Pearson Education, Inc., Upper Saddle River, NJ. All rights reserved. This material is protected under all copyright laws as they currently exist. No portion of this material may be reproduced, in any form or by any means, without permission in writing from the publisher.

2. At the top of the screen, select **PHStat→Two-Sample Tests→Wilcoxon Rank Sum Test**.

3. Complete the Wilcoxon Rank Sum Test dialog box as shown below. You are comparing the Northeast and the South. The Population 1 Sample Cell Range is A2 through A13, and the Population 2 Sample Cell Range is C2 through C13. Click **OK**.

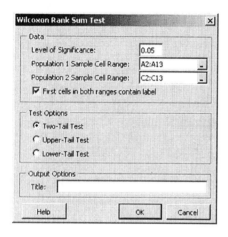

© 2006 Pearson Education, Inc., Upper Saddle River, NJ. All rights reserved. This material is protected under all copyright laws as they currently exist. No portion of this material may be reproduced, in any form or by any means, without permission in writing from the publisher.

Your output should look similar to the output shown below.

	A	B
1	**Wilcoxon Rank Sum Test**	
2		
3	**Data**	
4	Level of Significance	0.05
5		
6	Population 1 Sample	
7	Sample Size	11
8	Sum of Ranks	153
9	Population 2 Sample	
10	Sample Size	11
11	Sum of Ranks	100
12		
13	Intermediate Calculations	
14	Total Sample Size n	22
15	T1 Test Statistic	153
16	T1 Mean	126.5
17	Standard Error of T1	15.22881
18	Z Test Statistic	1.740123
19		
20	**Two-Tail Test**	
21	Lower Critical Value	-1.95996
22	Upper Critical Value	1.959964
23	p -value	0.081837
24	Do not reject the null hypothesis	

◄

► **Exercise 4 (pg. 615)**   Performing a Kruskal-Wallis Rank Test

---

If the PHStat add-in has not been loaded, you will need to load it before continuing. Follow the instructions in Section GS 8.2.

---

1. Open worksheet "Tech11_a" in the Chapter 11 folder.

---

*If you have just completed Exercise 3 on page 615 and have not yet closed the worksheet, click on the **Sheet 1** tab at the bottom of the screen to return to the worksheet containing the data.*

---

2. At the top of the screen, select **PHStat→Multiple-Sample Tests→Kruskal-Wallis Rank Test**.

© 2006 Pearson Education, Inc., Upper Saddle River, NJ. All rights reserved. This material is protected under all copyright laws as they currently exist. No portion of this material may be reproduced, in any form or by any means, without permission in writing from the publisher.

3. Complete the Kruskal-Wallis Rank Test dialog box as shown below. The Sample Data Cell Range is A2 through D13. Click **OK**.

Your output should appear similar to the output shown below. You may have to scroll down a couple rows to see the entire output.

	A	B	C	D	E	F	G
1	Kruskal-Wallis Rank Test for Differences in Medians						
2							
3	Data						
4	Level of Significance	0.05		Group	Sample Size	Sum of Ranks	Mean Ranks
5				1	11	306	27.8181818
6	Intermediate Calculations			2	11	271	24.6363636
7	Sum of Squared Ranks/Sample Size	22970.36		3	11	194	17.6363636
8	Sum of Sample Sizes	44		4	11	219	19.9090909
9	Number of Groups	4					
10							
11	Test Result						
12	H Test Statistic	4.214325					
13	Critical Value	7.814728					
14	p-Value	0.239232					
15	Do not reject the null hypothesis						

© 2006 Pearson Education, Inc., Upper Saddle River, NJ. All rights reserved. This material is protected under all copyright laws as they currently exist. No portion of this material may be reproduced, in any form or by any means, without permission in writing from the publisher.

► Exercise 5 (pg. 615)   Performing a One-Way ANOVA

1. Open worksheet "Tech11_a" in the Chapter 11 folder.

> *If you have just completed Exercise 3 or Exercise 4 on page 615 and have not yet
> closed the worksheet, click on the **Sheet 1** tab at the bottom of the screen to return to
> the worksheet containing the data.*

2. At the top of the screen, click **Tools→Data Analysis**. Select **Anova: Single Factor**
    and click **OK**.

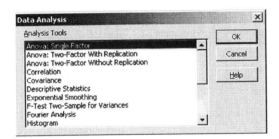

3. Complete the Anova: Single Factor dialog box as shown below. Click **OK**.

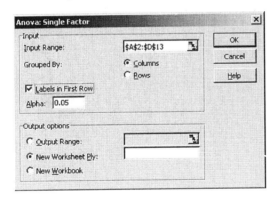

© 2006 Pearson Education, Inc., Upper Saddle River, NJ. All rights reserved. This material is protected under all copyright laws as they currently exist.
No portion of this material may be reproduced, in any form or by any means, without permission in writing from the publisher.

Adjust the column width so that you can read all the labels. Your output should appear similar to the output shown below.

	A	B	C	D	E	F	G
1	Anova: Single Factor						
2							
3	SUMMARY						
4	Groups	Count	Sum	Average	Variance		
5	Northeast	11	362071	32915.55	61697276		
6	Midwest	11	336748	30613.45	40860369		
7	South	11	284871	25897.36	37588923		
8	West	11	305445	27767.73	37447208		
9							
10							
11	ANOVA						
12	Source of Variation	SS	df	MS	F	P-value	F crit
13	Between Groups	3.16E+08	3	1.05E+08	2.372112	0.084692	2.838745
14	Within Groups	1.78E+09	40	44398444			
15							
16	Total	2.09E+09	43				

© 2006 Pearson Education, Inc., Upper Saddle River, NJ. All rights reserved. This material is protected under all copyright laws as they currently exist. No portion of this material may be reproduced, in any form or by any means, without permission in writing from the publisher.

The MINITAB Manual

▼

Elementary Statistics
Picturing the World

The MINITAB Manual

Dorothy Wakefield
Kathleen McLaughlin

▼

Elementary
Statistics

Picturing the World

Ron Larson
Betsy Farber

▶ Introduction

he *MINITAB Manual* is one of a series of companion technology manuals that provide hands-on chnology assistance to users of Larson/Farber *Elementary Statistics: Picturing the World.*

etailed instructions for working selected examples, exercises, and Technology Labs from *'ementary Statistics: Picturing the World* are provided in this manual. To make the orrelation with the text as seamless as possible, the table of contents includes page references for oth the Larson/Farber text and this manual.

ll of the data sets referenced in this manual are found on the data disk packaged in the back of 'ery new copy of Larson/Farber *Elementary Statistics: Picturing the World.* If needed, the INITAB files (.mtp) may also be downloaded from the texts' companion website at ww.prenhall.com/Larson.

▶ Contents:

Getting Started with MINITAB

▸ Using MINITAB Files

MINITAB is a Windows-based Statistical software package. It is very easy to use, and can perform many statistical analyses. When you first open MINITAB, the screen is divided into two parts. The top half is called the Session Window. The results of the statistical analyses are often displayed in the Session Window. The bottom half of the screen is the Data Window. It is called a Worksheet and will contain the data.

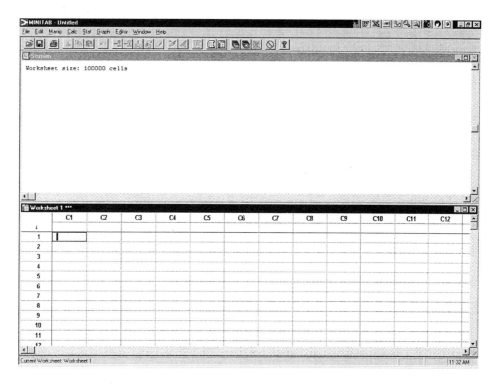

The data can either be entered directly into the Worksheet, or saved worksheets can be opened and used.

© 2006 Pearson Education, Inc., Upper Saddle River, NJ. All rights reserved. This material is protected under all copyright laws as they currently exist. No portion of this material may be reproduced, in any form or by any means, without permission in writing from the publisher.

▸ Entering Data into the Data Window

To enter the data into the Data Window, you must first click on the bottom half of the screen to make the Data Window active. You can tell which half of the screen is active by the blue bar going across the screen. In the previous picture, notice that the blue bar is in the middle of the screen, highlighting **Worksheet 1.** This indicates that the Data Window is active. The bar will be gray if the Window is not active. (Notice the Session Window bar is gray.)

In MINITAB, the columns are referred to as C1, C2, etc. Notice that there is an empty cell directly below each heading C1, C2, etc. This cell is for a column name. Column names are optional because you can refer to a column as C1 or C2, but a name helps to describe the data contained in a column. Enter the data beginning in cell 1. Notice that the cell numbers are located in the leftmost column of the worksheet.

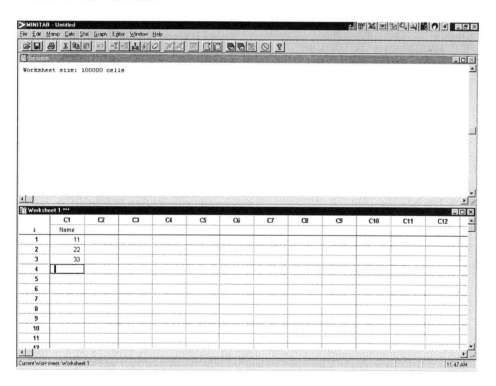

© 2006 Pearson Education, Inc., Upper Saddle River, NJ. All rights reserved. This material is protected under all copyright laws as they currently exist. No portion of this material may be reproduced, in any form or by any means, without permission in writing from the publisher.

▶ Opening Saved Worksheets

Many of the worksheets that you will be using are saved on the enclosed data disk. To open a saved worksheet, click on **File → Open Worksheet.** The following screen will appear.

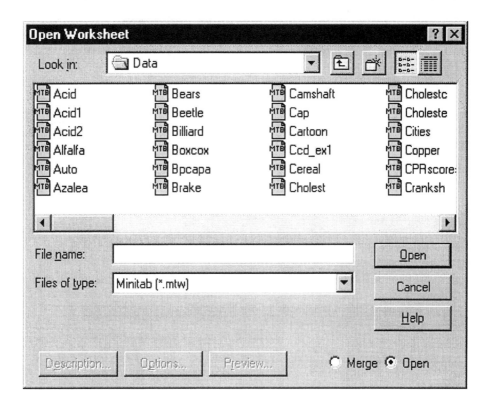

First, you must tell MINITAB where the data files are located. Since the data files are located on the data disk, you must tell MINITAB to **Look In** the **Compact Disc (D:).** To do this, click on the down arrow to the right of the top input field and select your CD drive by double-clicking on it.

© 2006 Pearson Education, Inc., Upper Saddle River, NJ. All rights reserved. This material is protected under all copyright laws as they currently exist. No portion of this material may be reproduced, in any form or by any means, without permission in writing from the publisher.

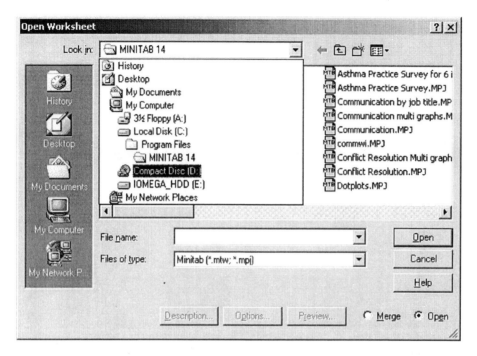

When you do this, you should see three folders listed. Select the MINITAB folder with a double-click. Now you should see a folder for each of the eleven chapters of the book.

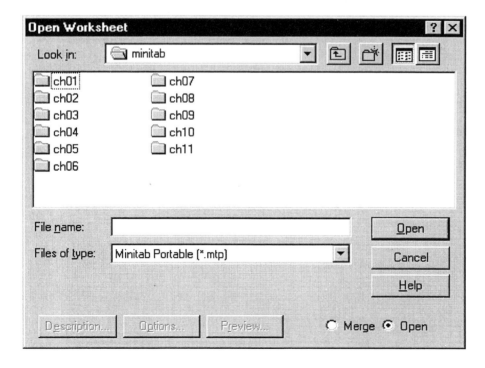

© 2006 Pearson Education, Inc., Upper Saddle River, NJ. All rights reserved. This material is protected under all copyright laws as they currently exist. No portion of this material may be reproduced, in any form or by any means, without permission in writing from the publisher.

All data files are saved as MINITAB Portable worksheets and have the extension **.mtp.** Click on the down arrow for the field called **Files of type** and select **Minitab Portable (*.mtp).**

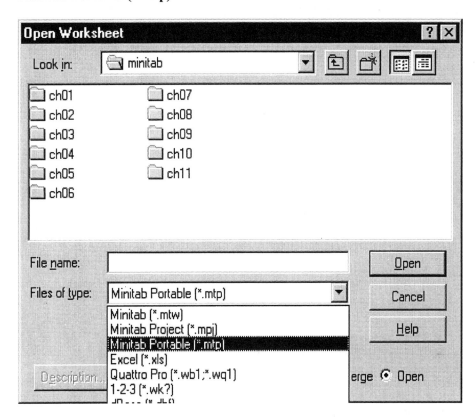

Now, select the folder called **ch01** (by double-clicking) and you should see all the MINITAB worksheets for Chapter 1.

© 2006 Pearson Education, Inc., Upper Saddle River, NJ. All rights reserved. This material is protected under all copyright laws as they currently exist. No portion of this material may be reproduced, in any form or by any means, without permission in writing from the publisher.

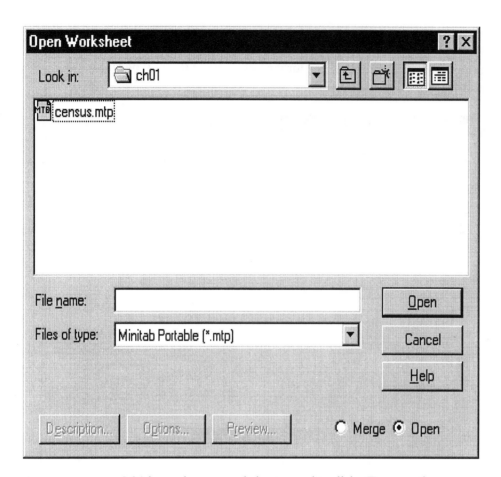

As you can see, **ch01** has only one worksheet saved to disk. To open the
worksheet **census**, double-click on it and the worksheet should appear in the Data
Window.

© 2006 Pearson Education, Inc., Upper Saddle River, NJ. All rights reserved. This material is protected under all copyright laws as they currently exist.
No portion of this material may be reproduced, in any form or by any means, without permission in writing from the publisher.

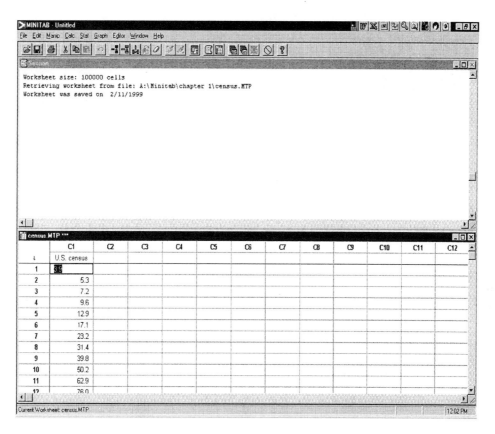

You are now ready to begin analyzing the data and learning more about MINITAB.

© 2006 Pearson Education, Inc., Upper Saddle River, NJ. All rights reserved. This material is protected under all copyright laws as they currently exist. No portion of this material may be reproduced, in any form or by any means, without permission in writing from the publisher.

Introduction to Statistics

▶ Technology Lab (pg. 31) Generating Random Numbers

1. To select 8 numbers randomly from the numbers 1 to 74, first store the
    numbers 1 to 74 in C1. Click on **Calc → Make Patterned Data → Simple
    Set of Numbers.** You should **Store patterned data in** C1. The numbers
    will begin **From the first value** 1 and go **To last value** 74 **In steps of** 1.

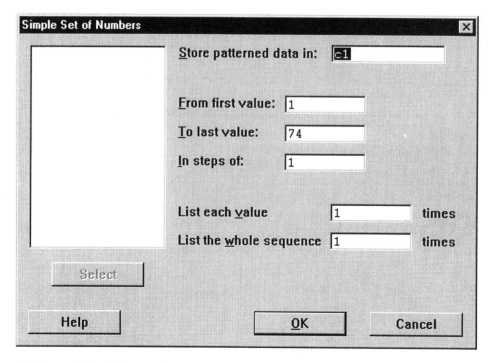

Click on **OK** and the numbers 1 to 74 should be in C1 of the Data Window.

© 2006 Pearson Education, Inc., Upper Saddle River, NJ. All rights reserved. This material is protected under all copyright laws as they currently exist.
No portion of this material may be reproduced, in any form or by any means, without permission in writing from the publisher.

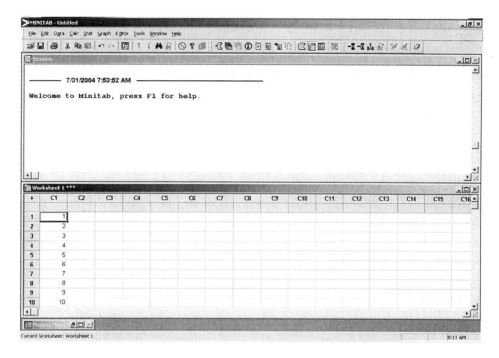

Next, you'd like to take a random sample of 8 accounts. Since you do not want repeats, you will be sampling without replacement. This is the default type of sampling in MINITAB, so you won't have to do anything special for this sample. Click on **Calc → Random Data → Sample from columns.** You need to **Sample 8 rows from column** C1 and **Store the sample in** C2.

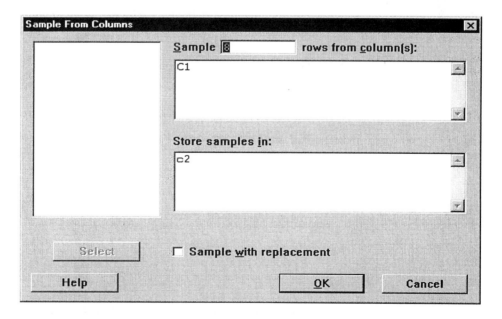

© 2006 Pearson Education, Inc., Upper Saddle River, NJ. All rights reserved. This material is protected under all copyright laws as they currently exist. No portion of this material may be reproduced, in any form or by any means, without permission in writing from the publisher.

Click on **OK** and there should be a random sample of 8 account numbers in C2.

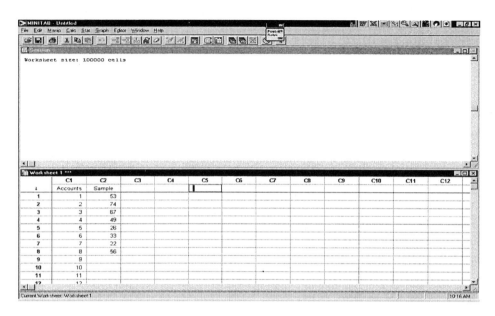

To order the sample list, click on **Data → Sort.** You should **Sort column:** C2, **By column:** C2 and **Store sorted data in Column(s) of current worksheet:** C3.

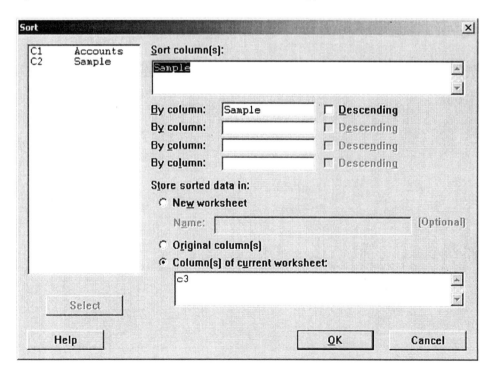

© 2006 Pearson Education, Inc., Upper Saddle River, NJ. All rights reserved. This material is protected under all copyright laws as they currently exist. No portion of this material may be reproduced, in any form or by any means, without permission in writing from the publisher.

Click on **OK** and C3 should contain the sorted sample of 8 accounts.

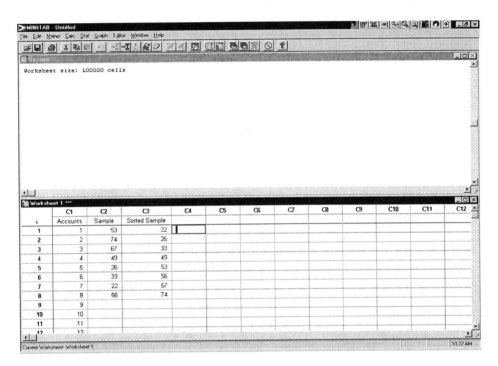

Since this is a *random* sample, each student will have different numbers in C2 and C3.

2. For this problem, use the same steps as above. Click on **Calc → Make Patterned Data → Simple Set of Numbers.** You should **Store patterned data in** C1. The numbers will begin **From the first value** 1 and go **To last value** 200 **In steps of** 1. Next, to randomly sample 20 batteries, click on **Calc → Random Data → Sample from columns.** You need to **Sample 20 rows from column** C1 and **Store the sample in** C2. Finally, to order the sample list, click on **Data → Sort.** You should **Sort column:** C2, **By column:** C2 and **Store sorted data in Column(s) of current worksheet:** C3.

3. Click on **Calc → Make Patterned Data → Simple Set of Numbers.** You should **Store patterned data in** C1. The numbers will begin **From the first value** 0 and go **To last value** 9 **In steps of** 1. Next, to randomly sample 5 digits, click on **Calc → Random Data → Sample from columns.** You need to **Sample** 5 **rows from column** C1 and **Store the sample in** C2. Repeat this two more times and **store the sample in** C3 and then in C4. Now you have generated the three samples.

© 2006 Pearson Education, Inc., Upper Saddle River, NJ. All rights reserved. This material is protected under all copyright laws as they currently exist. No portion of this material may be reproduced, in any form or by any means, without permission in writing from the publisher.

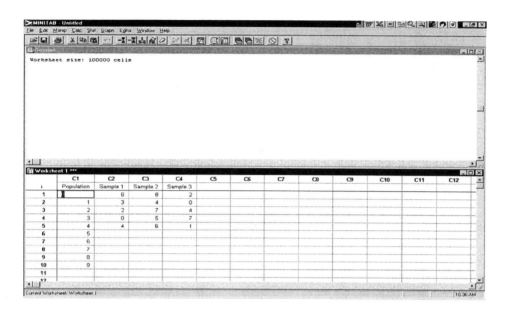

Now, to find the average of each of the four columns (C1, C2, C3, and C4), click on **Calc → Column Statistics.** The Statistic that you would like to calculate is the mean, so click on **Mean.** Enter C1 for the **Input variable** and click on **OK.**

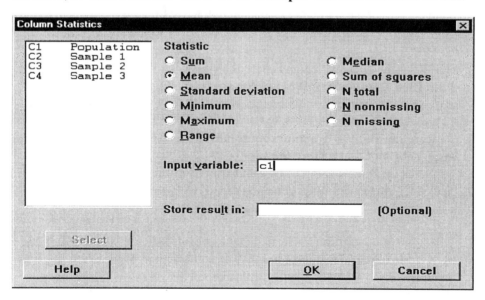

The population mean will be displayed in the Session Window. Repeat this for C2, C3, and C4.

© 2006 Pearson Education, Inc., Upper Saddle River, NJ. All rights reserved. This material is protected under all copyright laws as they currently exist. No portion of this material may be reproduced, in any form or by any means, without permission in writing from the publisher.

Since this is random data, your output will look different.

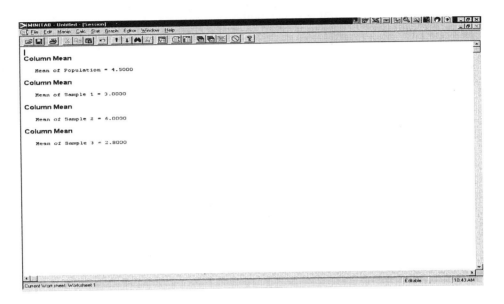

4. This problem will be very similar to the steps in problem 3. Click on **Calc →
    Make Patterned Data → Simple Set of Numbers.** You should **Store
    patterned data in** C1. The numbers will begin **From the first value** 0 and
    go **To last value** 40 **In steps of** 1. Next, to randomly sample 7 digits, click
    on **Calc → Random Data → Sample from columns.** You need to **Sample
    7 rows from column** C1 and **Store the sample in** C2. Repeat this two more
    times and **store the sample in** C3 and then in C4. Now you have generated
    the three samples. Now, to find the average of each of the four columns (C1,
    C2, C3, and C4), click on **Calc → Column Statistics.** The Statistic that you
    would like to calculate is the mean, so click on **Mean.** Enter C1 for the
    Input variable and click on **OK.** The population mean will be displayed in
    the Session Window. Repeat this for C2, C3, and C4.

5. To simulate rolling a 6-sided die, you want to sample with replacement from
    the integers 1 to 6. You could enter the numbers 1 to 6 into C1 and then
    sample with replacement. A better way to do this is to click on **Calc→
    Random Data → Integer.** You want to **Generate** 60 **rows of data** and
    Store in column C1. This represents the 60 rolls. Enter a **minimum value**
    of 1 and a **maximum value** of 6 to represent the six sides of the die.

© 2006 Pearson Education, Inc., Upper Saddle River, NJ. All rights reserved. This material is protected under all copyright laws as they currently exist.
No portion of this material may be reproduced, in any form or by any means, without permission in writing from the publisher.

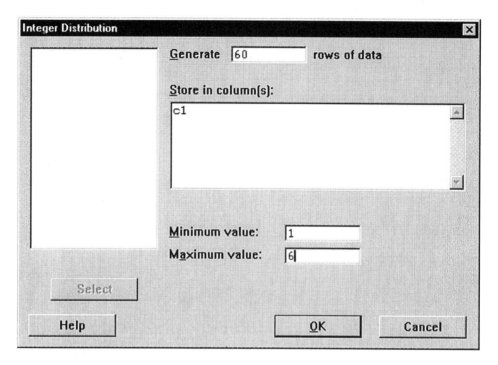

Click on **OK** and C1 should have the results of 60 rolls of a die.

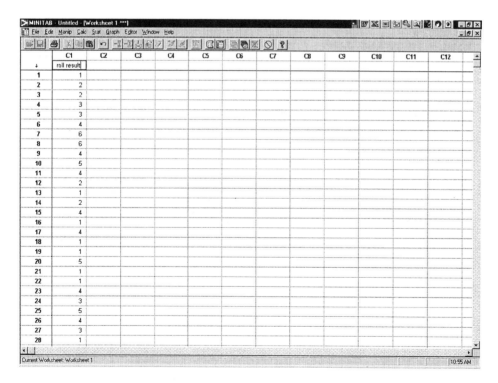

© 2006 Pearson Education, Inc., Upper Saddle River, NJ. All rights reserved. This material is protected under all copyright laws as they currently exist. No portion of this material may be reproduced, in any form or by any means, without permission in writing from the publisher.

To count how many times each number was rolled, click on **Stat → Tables → Tally Individual Variables.** Enter C1 for the **Variable** and select **Counts** by clicking on it.

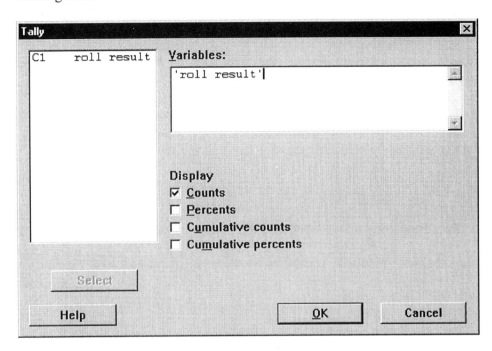

Click on **OK** and the totals will be displayed in the Session Window.

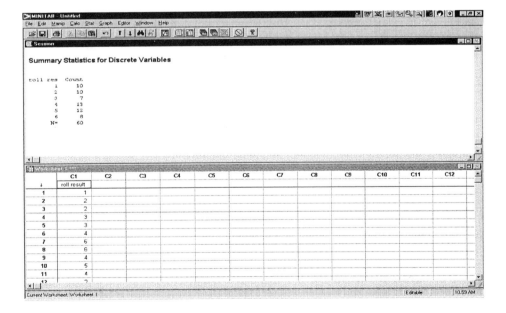

© 2006 Pearson Education, Inc., Upper Saddle River, NJ. All rights reserved. This material is protected under all copyright laws as they currently exist. No portion of this material may be reproduced, in any form or by any means, without permission in writing from the publisher.

16 Chapter 1 Introduction to Statistics

Recall that each student's results will look different because this is random data. In the results above, 10 ones, 10 twos, 7 threes, 13 fours, 12 fives, and 8 sixes were rolled.

7. To simulate tossing a coin, you can repeat the steps in problem 5. Click on **Calc → Random Data → Integer.** You want to **Generate** 100 **rows of data** and **Store in column** C1. This represents the 100 tosses. Enter a **minimum value** of 0 and a **maximum value** of 1 to represent the two sides of the coin. Click on **OK** and C1 should have the results of 100 tosses of a coin. To count how many times each side of the coined was tossed, click on **Stat → Tables → Tally Individual Variables.** Enter C1 for the **Variable** and select **Counts** by clicking on it. Click on **OK** and the counts will be displayed in the Session Window. Recall that 0 represents heads and 1 represents tails.

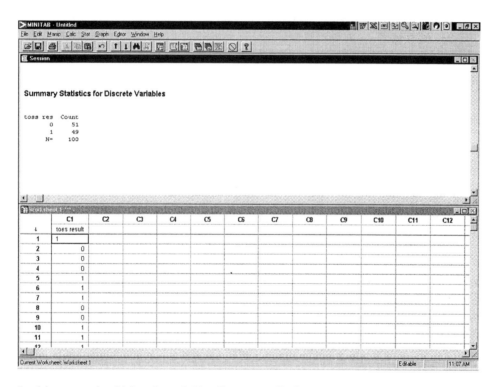

In this example, 51 heads and 49 tails were rolled.

© 2006 Pearson Education, Inc., Upper Saddle River, NJ. All rights reserved. This material is protected under all copyright laws as they currently exist. No portion of this material may be reproduced, in any form or by any means, without permission in writing from the publisher.

Descriptive Statistics

Section 2.1

> ▶ Example 3 (pg. 38): Construct a histogram using the Internet data

To create this histogram, you must open the worksheet called **internet**. When you get into MINITAB, click on: **File → Open Worksheet**. On the screen that appears, **Look In** your Compact Disc (D:) to see the list of available folders. Double-click on the Folder that is named "**Minitab**" and then select the **ch02** folder. Next click on the arrow to the right of the **Files of type** field and select **Minitab Portable (mtp).** A list of data files should now appear. Use the right arrow to scroll through the list of files until you see **internet** Click on this file, and then click on **Open.**

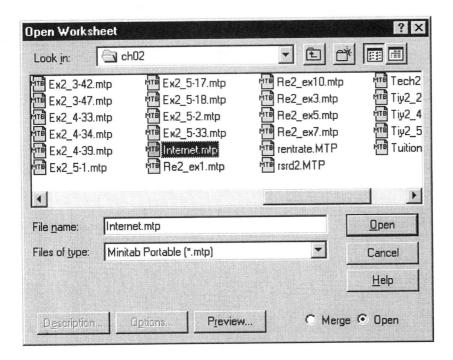

© 2006 Pearson Education, Inc., Upper Saddle River, NJ. All rights reserved. This material is protected under all copyright laws as they currently exist. No portion of this material may be reproduced, in any form or by any means, without permission in writing from the publisher.

You should now see Internet Subscriber data in Column 1.

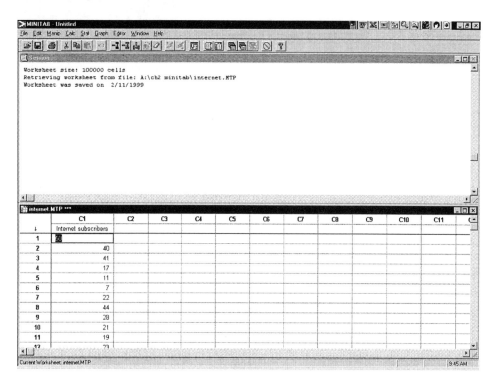

Now you are ready to make the histogram. Click on: **Graph → Histogram**.
Select a **Simple** histogram and click OK.

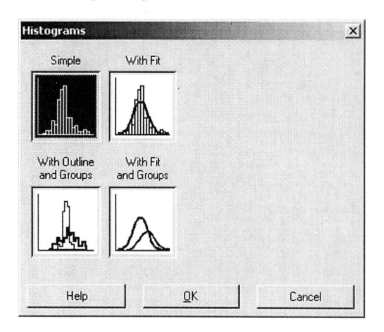

© 2006 Pearson Education, Inc., Upper Saddle River, NJ. All rights reserved. This material is protected under all copyright laws as they currently exist. No portion of this material may be reproduced, in any form or by any means, without permission in writing from the publisher.

On the main Histogram screen, double-click on C1 in the large box at the left of the screen. "Internet subscribers" should now be filled in as the **Graph variable**.

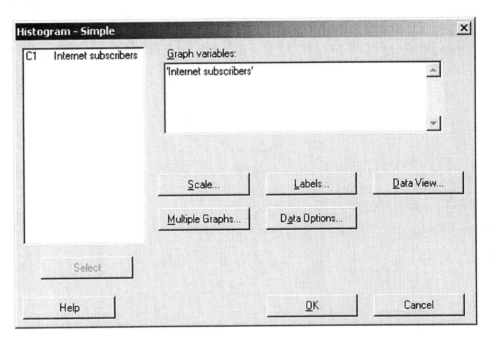

Click on the **Labels** button and enter a title for the graph. Click on **OK**.

© 2006 Pearson Education, Inc., Upper Saddle River, NJ. All rights reserved. This material is protected under all copyright laws as they currently exist.
No portion of this material may be reproduced, in any form or by any means, without permission in writing from the publisher.

At this point, if you click on **OK** again, MINITAB will draw a histogram using default settings. Your histogram will look like the one below.

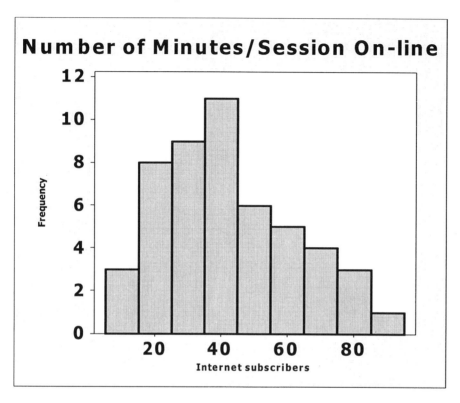

Notice the X-axis label is not "Minutes", and the numbering along the axis is not like the numbering in the textbook. We can edit the graph to fix this, however. Right-click on the X-axis and select **Edit X Scale** from the drop-down menu. Click on the **Binning** tab and check that **Midpoint** is selected. Enter "12.5 : 84.5 / 12" for **Midpoint/Cutpoint Positions**. This tells Minitab you want the numbering to go from 12.5 to 84.5 in steps of 12.

© 2006 Pearson Education, Inc., Upper Saddle River, NJ. All rights reserved. This material is protected under all copyright laws as they currently exist. No portion of this material may be reproduced, in any form or by any means, without permission in writing from the publisher.

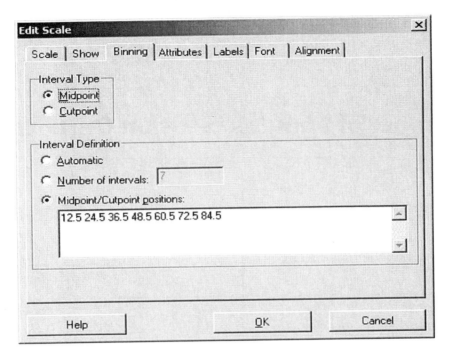

Click on **OK** and the changes should have been made to graph. Next change the
X-axis label to "Minutes". Right-click on the current axis label, and select "Edit
X axis label" from the drop-down menu. Enter "Minutes" below **Text**.

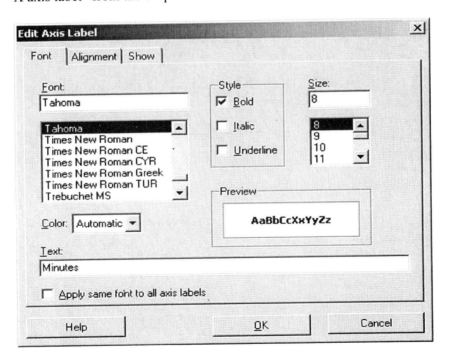

Click on **OK** to view the changes to your histogram.

© 2006 Pearson Education, Inc., Upper Saddle River, NJ. All rights reserved. This material is protected under all copyright laws as they currently exist.
No portion of this material may be reproduced, in any form or by any means, without permission in writing from the publisher.

If you would like to add the frequencies above each rectangle of the histogram
(as is shown in the text), right-click on a rectangle of the graph and select **Add→**
Data Labels. Click on **Use y-value labels** and click on **OK** to view the changes.

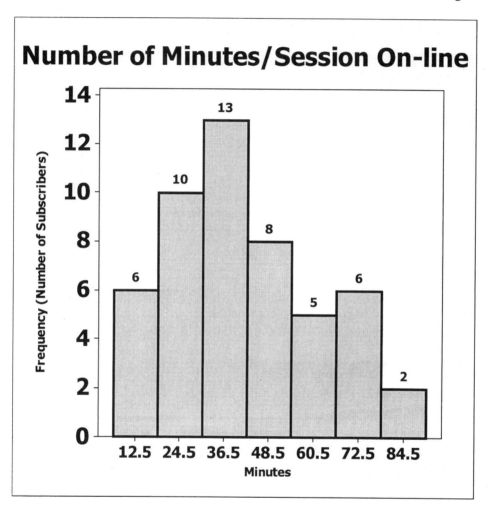

Now your histogram is exactly as in the textbook.

To print the graph, click on **File → Print Graph.** Next, click **OK** and
the graph should print.

© 2006 Pearson Education, Inc., Upper Saddle River, NJ. All rights reserved. This material is protected under all copyright laws as they currently exist.
No portion of this material may be reproduced, in any form or by any means, without permission in writing from the publisher.

▶ Exercise 25 (pg. 46) Construct a frequency histogram using 6
                        Classes

Open the worksheet **ex2_1-25** which is found in the **ch02** MINITAB folder.
Click on: **Graph → Histogram**. Select a **Simple** histogram and click OK.
On the main Histogram screen, double-click on C1 in the large box at the left of
the screen. "July Sales" should now be filled in as the **Graph variable**.

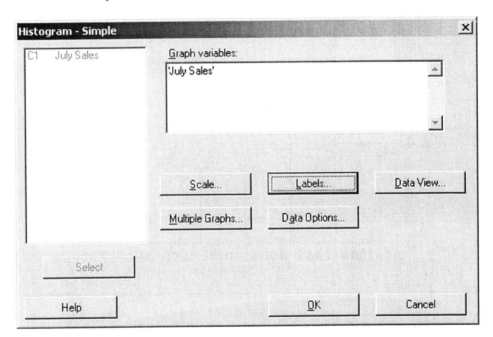

Click on the **Labels** button and enter "July Sales" for the title for the graph.
Click on **OK** twice to view the default histogram that is produced.

© 2006 Pearson Education, Inc., Upper Saddle River, NJ. All rights reserved. This material is protected under all copyright laws as they currently exist.
No portion of this material may be reproduced, in any form or by any means, without permission in writing from the publisher.

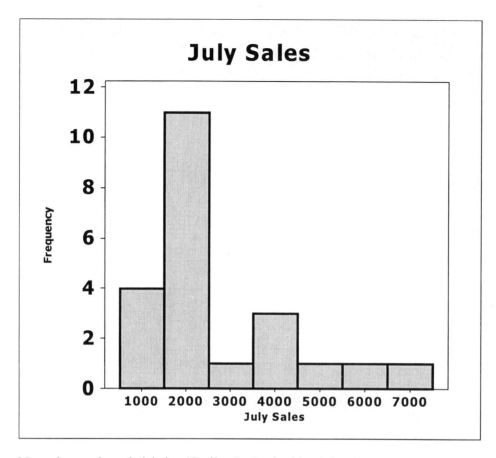

Now change the axis label to "Dollars". To do this, right-click on the axis label (July Sales), and select "Edit X axis label" from the drop-down menu. Type "Dollars" below **Text**. Click on **OK** to view the changes.

Next, decide on the numbering for the X-axis that is needed for the 6 classes. This will depend on the class limits you used in your frequency distribution. In order to use your class limits, you must tell MINITAB to use **Cutpoints.** To do this, right-click on the current X-axis numbering. Select "Edit X Scale" from the drop-down menu. Click on the **Binning** tab. Select **CutPoint** as the **Interval Type.** Next tell MINITAB what the cutpoint positions are. One solution is to use cutpoints beginning at 1000 and going up to 7600 in steps of 1100. So fill in 1000:7600/1100 for **Midpoint/cutpoint positions**.

© 2006 Pearson Education, Inc., Upper Saddle River, NJ. All rights reserved. This material is protected under all copyright laws as they currently exist. No portion of this material may be reproduced, in any form or by any means, without permission in writing from the publisher.

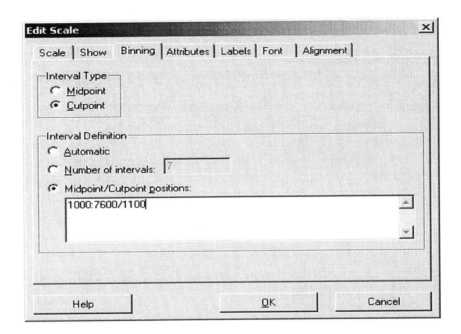

Click on **OK** to view the changes.

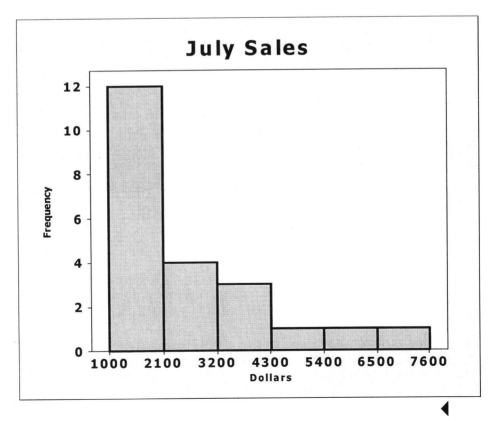

© 2006 Pearson Education, Inc., Upper Saddle River, NJ. All rights reserved. This material is protected under all copyright laws as they currently exist. No portion of this material may be reproduced, in any form or by any means, without permission in writing from the publisher.

▶ Exercise 29 (pg.46) Using the bowling scores, construct a
relative frequency histogram with 5 classes

Open worksheet **ex2_1-29** which is found in the **ch02** MINITAB folder. Click
on: **Graph → Histogram**. Select a **Simple** histogram and click OK.
On the main Histogram screen, double-click on C1 in the large box at the left of
the screen. "Bowling Score" should now be filled in as the **Graph variable**.
Click on the **Labels** button and enter "Bowling Scores" for the title for the graph.
Click on **OK** twice to view the default histogram that is produced.

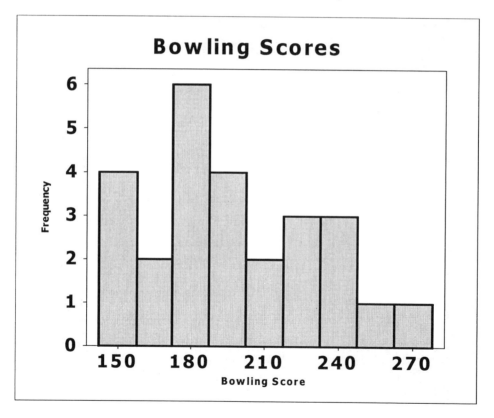

Next, change the label for the X-axis. To do this, right-click on the axis label
(Bowling Scores), and select "Edit X axis label" from the drop-down menu.
Type "Points Scored" below **Text**. Click on **OK** to view the changes.

Now, decide on the numbering for the X-axis that is needed for the 5 classes.
You can either choose the classes yourself as in the last example, or let
MINITAB do it for you. In this example, let MINITAB do it. Right-click on the
X-axis numbers and select "Edit X Scale" from the drop-down menu. Click on

© 2006 Pearson Education, Inc., Upper Saddle River, NJ. All rights reserved. This material is protected under all copyright laws as they currently exist.
No portion of this material may be reproduced, in any form or by any means, without permission in writing from the publisher.

the **Binning** tab. Select **CutPoint** as the **Interval Type.** Next tell MINITAB that the **Number of Intervals** is 5. Click on OK.

Finally, since this is a relative frequency histogram, the right-click on the Y-axis numbering, and select "Edit Y Scale" from the drop-down menu. Click on the **Type** tab and select **Percent.** Click on **OK** twice, and the histogram should have all of the changes.

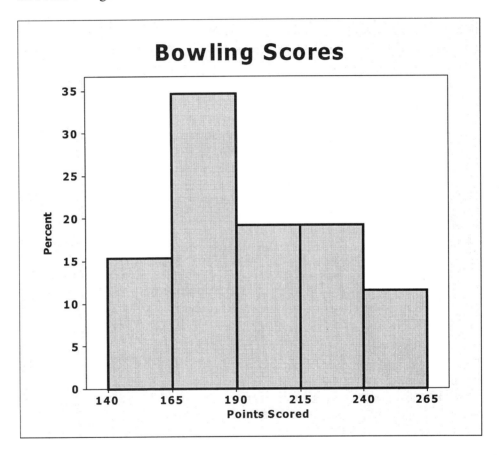

© 2006 Pearson Education, Inc., Upper Saddle River, NJ. All rights reserved. This material is protected under all copyright laws as they currently exist.
No portion of this material may be reproduced, in any form or by any means, without permission in writing from the publisher.

▶ Exercise 30 (pg. 46) Construct a relative frequency histogram
                        for the ATM data using 5 classes

Open worksheet **ex2_1-30** which is found in the **ch02** MINITAB folder. Click
on: **Graph → Histogram**. Select a **Simple** histogram and click OK.
On the main Histogram screen, double-click on C1 in the large box at the left of
the screen. "ATM withdrawals" should now be filled in as the **Graph variable**.
Click on the **Labels** button and enter "Daily Withdrawals" for the title for the
graph. Click on **OK** twice to view the default histogram that is produced.
Next, change the label for the X-axis. To do this, right-click on the axis label,
and select "Edit X axis label" from the drop-down menu. Type "Hundreds of
Dollars" below **Text**. Click on **OK** to view the changes. Now, decide on the
numbering for the X-axis that is needed for the 5 classes. You can either choose
the classes yourself as in the last example, or let MINITAB do it for you. In this
example, let MINITAB do it. Right-click on the X-axis numbers and select "Edit
X Scale" from the drop-down menu. Click on the **Binning** tab. Select **CutPoint**
as the **Interval Type.** Next tell MINITAB that the **Number of Intervals** is 5.
Click on OK. Finally, since this is a relative frequency histogram, the right-click
on the Y-axis numbering, and select "Edit Y Scale" from the drop-down menu.
Click on the **Type** tab and select **Percent.** Click on **OK** twice, and the histogram
have all of the changes.

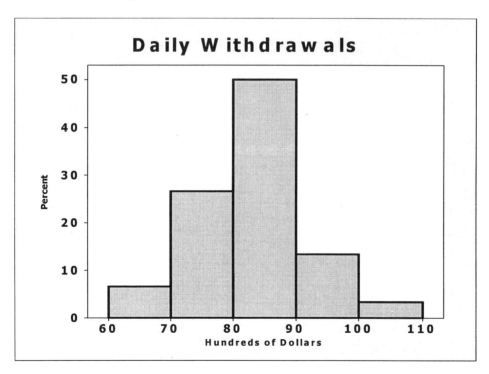

© 2006 Pearson Education, Inc., Upper Saddle River, NJ. All rights reserved. This material is protected under all copyright laws as they currently exist.
No portion of this material may be reproduced, in any form or by any means, without permission in writing from the publisher.

Section 2.2

▶ Example 2 (pg. 50) Constructing a Stem-and-Leaf Plot

Open the file **Al_rbis** which is found in the **ch02** MINITAB folder. This worksheet contains data on runs batted in (RBIs) for baseball's American League for the last 50 years. The data should appear in C1 of your worksheet.

To construct a Stem-and-leaf plot, click on **Graph → Stem-and-Leaf.**
On the screen that appears, select C1 as your **Variable** by doubling clicking on C1. Click on **OK.**

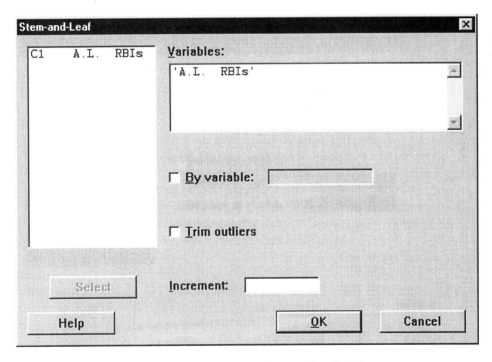

The stem and leaf plot will be displayed in the Session Window.

© 2006 Pearson Education, Inc., Upper Saddle River, NJ. All rights reserved. This material is protected under all copyright laws as they currently exist. No portion of this material may be reproduced, in any form or by any means, without permission in writing from the publisher.

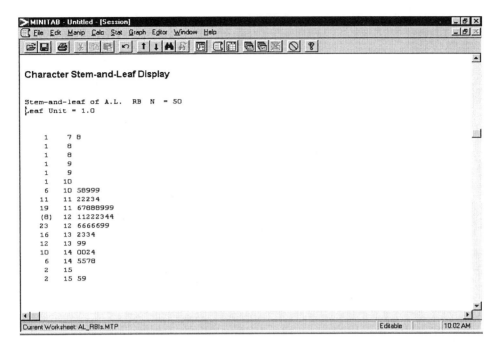

In this MINITAB display, the first column on the left is a counter. This column counts the number of data points starting from the smallest value (at the top of the plot) down to the median. It also counts from the largest data value (at the bottom of the plot) up to the median. Notice that there is only one data point in the first row of the stem and leaf. There are no data points in rows 2 through 6, so the counter on the left remains at "1". Row 7 has 5 data points so the counter increases to "6". The row that contains the median has the number "8" in parentheses. This number counts the number of data points that are in the row that contains the median.

The second column in the display is the **Stem**. In this example, the Stem values range from 7 to 15. Notice that this display contains two rows for each of the values from 8 through 15. These are called **split-stems**. For each stem value, the first row contains all data points with leaf values from 0 to 4 and the second row contains all data points with leaf values from 5 to 9. Notice that MINITAB constructs an *ordered* stem and leaf.

The leaf values are shown to the right of the stem. The leaf values may be the actual data points or they may be the rounded data points. To find the actual values of the data points in the display, use the "Leaf Unit=" statement at the top of the display. The "Leaf Unit" gives you the place value of the leaves. In this stem and leaf, the first data point has a stem value of 7 and a leaf value of 8. Since the "Leaf Unit=1.0", the 8 is the "ones" place and the 7 is in the "tens" places, thus the data point is 78.

© 2006 Pearson Education, Inc., Upper Saddle River, NJ. All rights reserved. This material is protected under all copyright laws as they currently exist. No portion of this material may be reproduced, in any form or by any means, without permission in writing from the publisher.

▶ Example 3 (pg. 51) Constructing a Dotplot

 Open the file **Al_rbis** which is found in the **ch02** MINITAB folder. To construct a dotplot, click on **Graph → Dotplot → Simple.** In the screen that appears, select C1 for **Graph Variables.** Click on the **Labels** button, enter an appropriate **Title** and click on **OK.**

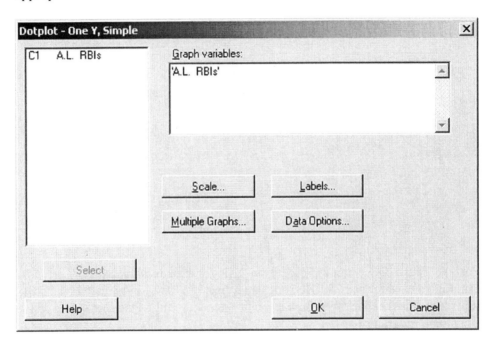

The following dotplot should appear.

© 2006 Pearson Education, Inc., Upper Saddle River, NJ. All rights reserved. This material is protected under all copyright laws as they currently exist.
No portion of this material may be reproduced, in any form or by any means, without permission in writing from the publisher.

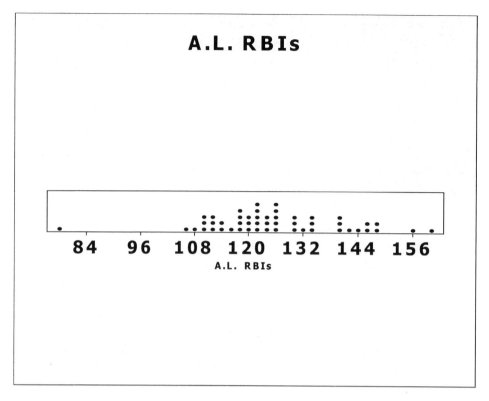

Each dot in the above plot represents the RBIs for an individual batter. For example, one batter had 78 RBIs, one batter had 108 RBIs, and 3 batters had 109 RBIs (the 3 dots above 109). You can edit the numbering along the X-axis just as in the Histograms.

© 2006 Pearson Education, Inc., Upper Saddle River, NJ. All rights reserved. This material is protected under all copyright laws as they currently exist. No portion of this material may be reproduced, in any form or by any means, without permission in writing from the publisher.

▸ Example 4 (pg. 52)   Constructing a Pie Chart

In this example, you must enter the data into the Data Window. Begin with a clean worksheet. From the table in the left margin of page 52 of the text, enter the Vehicle types into C1 and the number of occupants killed into C2. Label each column appropriately as shown below. Note: OMIT the commas in the number killed.

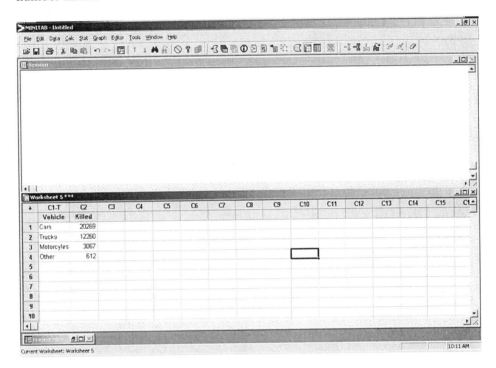

To construct the pie chart, click on **Graph → Pie Chart**. In the screen that appears, select **Chart values from a table**. Enter C1 for the **Categorical Variable** and C2 for the **Summary Variable**. Click on the **Labels** button and enter an appropriate title.

© 2006 Pearson Education, Inc., Upper Saddle River, NJ. All rights reserved. This material is protected under all copyright laws as they currently exist. No portion of this material may be reproduced, in any form or by any means, without permission in writing from the publisher.

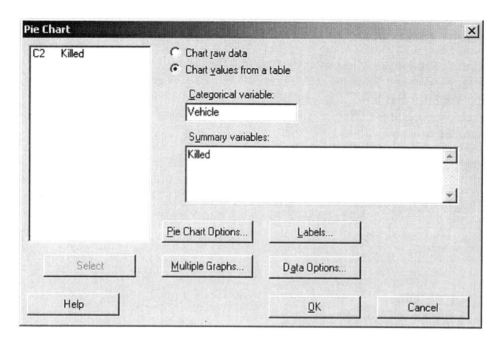

Click on **OK** to view the pie chart.

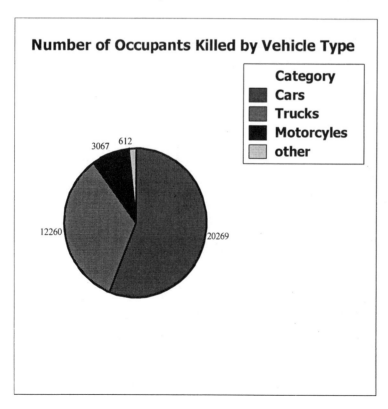

© 2006 Pearson Education, Inc., Upper Saddle River, NJ. All rights reserved. This material is protected under all copyright laws as they currently exist.
No portion of this material may be reproduced, in any form or by any means, without permission in writing from the publisher.

▶ Example 5 (pg. 53) Constructing Pareto Charts

Enter the Inventory Shrinkage data (found in the paragraph for Example 5 on page 53 of the text) into C1 and C2. Do not include the Total amount of $41.0 million. Note: Do NOT enter the $ signs into C2.

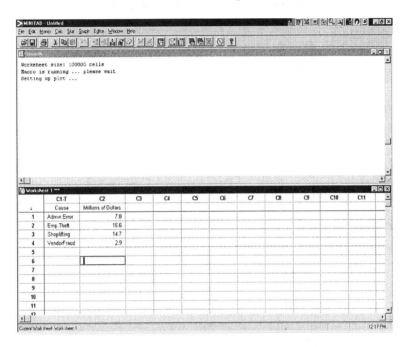

To make the Pareto chart, click on **Graph → Bar Chart**. The **Bars represent** Values from a table. Select a **Simple** chart and click on **OK**.

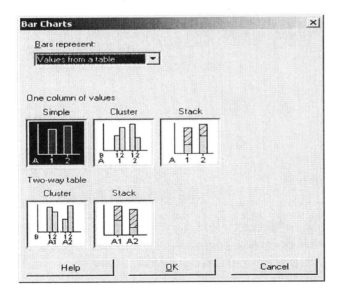

© 2006 Pearson Education, Inc., Upper Saddle River, NJ. All rights reserved. This material is protected under all copyright laws as they currently exist. No portion of this material may be reproduced, in any form or by any means, without permission in writing from the publisher.

Enter C2 for **Graph variables** and C1 for **Categorical variable.** Click on **Bar chart options** and select **Decreasing Y.** Click on the **Labels** button and enter an appropriate title. Now view the chart.

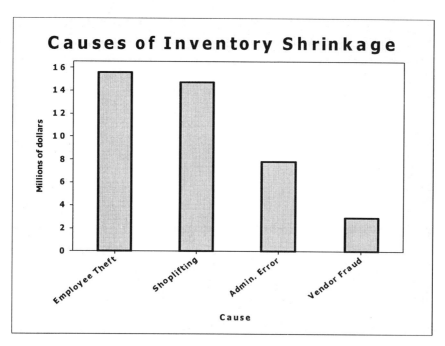

Notice that the default chart has spaces between the rectangles. To remove these spaces, just edit the graph. Right-click on the X-axis and select "Edit X Scale" from the drop-down menu. On the **Scale** tab, click on **Gap between clusters** and enter a 0. Click on **OK** to view the pareto chart.

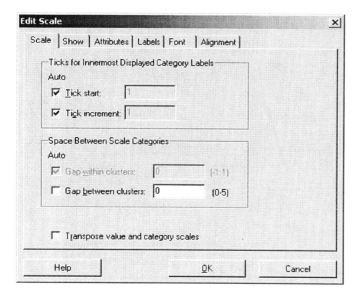

© 2006 Pearson Education, Inc., Upper Saddle River, NJ. All rights reserved. This material is protected under all copyright laws as they currently exist. No portion of this material may be reproduced, in any form or by any means, without permission in writing from the publisher.

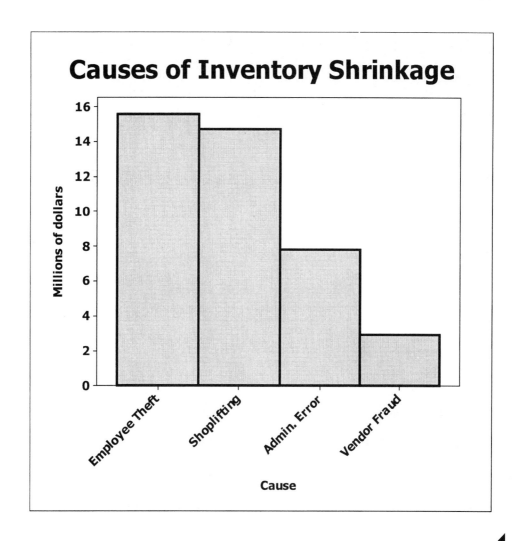

© 2006 Pearson Education, Inc., Upper Saddle River, NJ. All rights reserved. This material is protected under all copyright laws as they currently exist.
No portion of this material may be reproduced, in any form or by any means, without permission in writing from the publisher.

▸ Example 7 (pg. 55) Construct a Time Series Chart of cellular
telephone subscribers

Open worksheet **CELLPHONE** which is found in the **ch02** MINITAB folder.
Click on **Graph** → **Time Series Plot** → **Simple.** Select C2 as the **Series.** Click
on the **Time/Scale** button. Select **Stamp** and enter C1 (Year) for the **Stamp
Columns.** Click on **OK**.

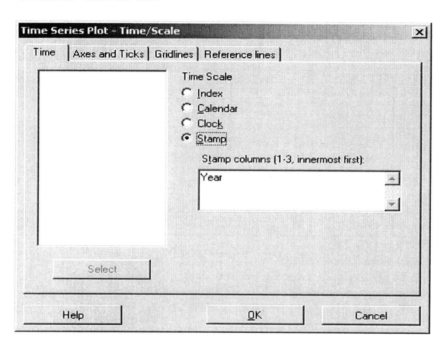

Click on the **Labels** button and enter an appropriate title for the plot.

© 2006 Pearson Education, Inc., Upper Saddle River, NJ. All rights reserved. This material is protected under all copyright laws as they currently exist.
No portion of this material may be reproduced, in any form or by any means, without permission in writing from the publisher.

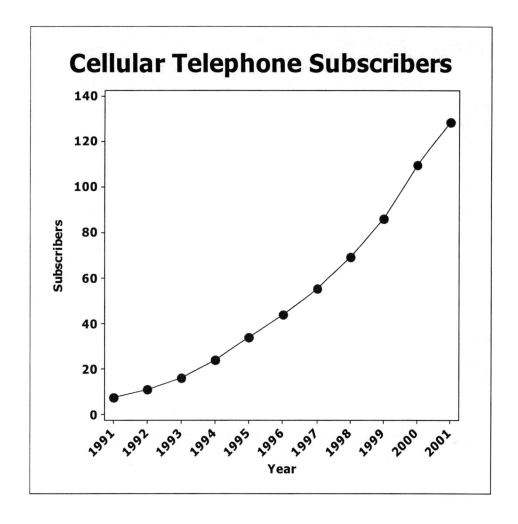

© 2006 Pearson Education, Inc., Upper Saddle River, NJ. All rights reserved. This material is protected under all copyright laws as they currently exist. No portion of this material may be reproduced, in any form or by any means, without permission in writing from the publisher.

> ▸ Exercise 15 (pg. 57) Construct a stem and leaf of the amount of
> water consumed by 24 elephants in one day

Open worksheet **ex2_2-15** which is found in the **ch02** MINITAB folder. Click
on **Graph→ Stem-and-Leaf.** Select C1 for the **Graph Variable.** Click on **OK**
and the stem and leaf plot should be in the Session Window.

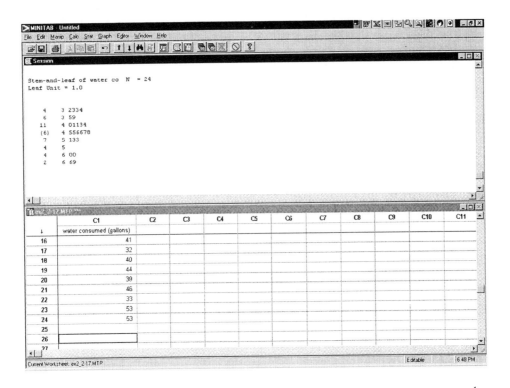

© 2006 Pearson Education, Inc., Upper Saddle River, NJ. All rights reserved. This material is protected under all copyright laws as they currently exist.
No portion of this material may be reproduced, in any form or by any means, without permission in writing from the publisher.

▶ Exercise 19 (pg. 58) Construct a dotplot of the lifespan (in days)
of houseflies

Open worksheet **ex2_2-19** which is found in the **ch02** MINITAB folder. Click
on **Graph** → **Dotplot** → **Simple**. Select C1 for the **Graph Variable.** Click on
the **Labels** button and enter an appropriate **Title.** Click on **OK** to view the
dotplot.

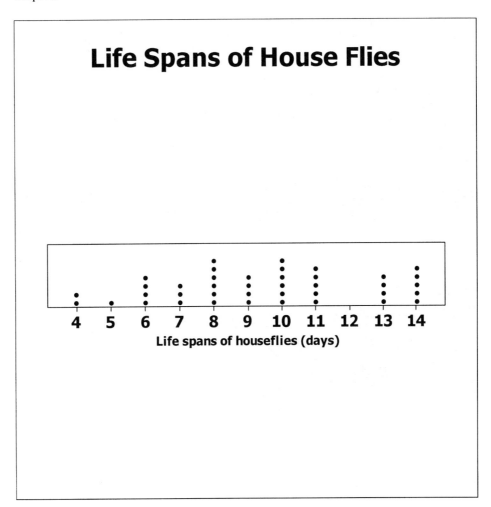

© 2006 Pearson Education, Inc., Upper Saddle River, NJ. All rights reserved. This material is protected under all copyright laws as they currently exist.
No portion of this material may be reproduced, in any form or by any means, without permission in writing from the publisher.

▶ Exercise 21 (pg. 58) Construct a Pie Chart of the data.

This data must be entered into the Data Window. Enter the categories into C1 and the Expenditures into C2. Click on **Graph → Pie Chart.** Select **Chart values from a table**. Enter C1 for the **Categorical Variable** and C2 for the **Summary Variable**. Click on the **Labels** button, enter an appropriate **Title** and click on **OK**.

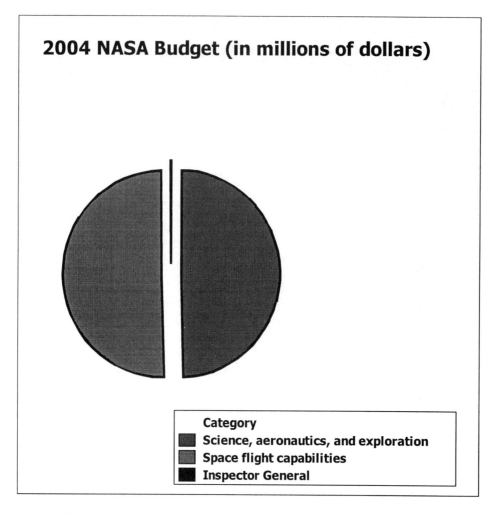

2004 NASA Budget (in millions of dollars)

Category
■ Science, aeronautics, and exploration
□ Space flight capabilities
■ Inspector General

Note: The above picture uses the option to 'explode' the slices because the slice for Inspector General was so small it did not even show up on the pie chart.

◀

© 2006 Pearson Education, Inc., Upper Saddle River, NJ. All rights reserved. This material is protected under all copyright laws as they currently exist. No portion of this material may be reproduced, in any form or by any means, without permission in writing from the publisher.

▶ Exercise 23 (pg. 58) Construct a Pareto Chart to display the data

Enter the data into the Data Window. Enter the cities into C1 and the ultraviolet index for each city into C2. To make the Pareto chart, click on **Graph → Bar Chart**. The **Bars represent** Values from a table. Select a **Simple** chart and click on **OK**. Enter C2 for **Graph variables** and C1 for **Categorical variable.** Click on **Bar chart options** and select **Decreasing Y.** Click on the **Labels** button and enter an appropriate title. Now view the default chart. Notice that the default chart has spaces between the rectangles. To remove these spaces, just edit the graph. Right-click on the X-axis and select "Edit X Scale" from the drop-down menu. On the **Scale** tab, click on **Gap between clusters** and enter a 0. Click on **OK** to view the pareto chart.

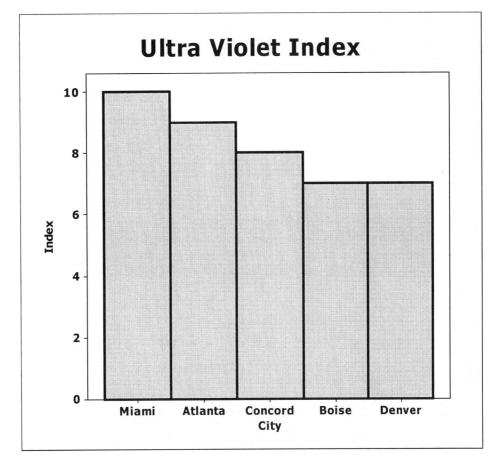

© 2006 Pearson Education, Inc., Upper Saddle River, NJ. All rights reserved. This material is protected under all copyright laws as they currently exist. No portion of this material may be reproduced, in any form or by any means, without permission in writing from the publisher.

▶ Exercise 25 (pg. 59) Construct a Scatterplot of the data.

Enter the Number of Students per Teacher into C1 and the Average Teacher's
Salary into C2 (data found to the left of exercise). Click on **Graph**→
Scatterplot → **Simple.** Select C2 for the **Y variable** and C1 for the **X variable.**
Click on the **Labels** button and enter an appropriate title. Click on **OK** twice to
view the scatterplot.

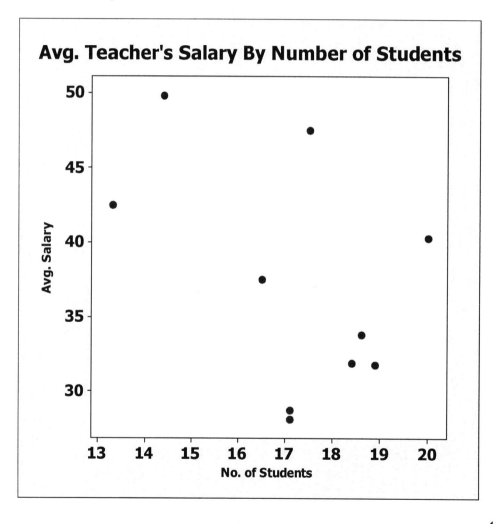

© 2006 Pearson Education, Inc., Upper Saddle River, NJ. All rights reserved. This material is protected under all copyright laws as they currently exist.
No portion of this material may be reproduced, in any form or by any means, without permission in writing from the publisher.

▶ Exercise 27 (pg. 59) Construct a Time Series Plot of the price of eggs.

Enter the data into the Data Window. Enter the Years into C1 and the Price of Eggs into C2. Click on **Graph → Time Series Plot → Simple.** Select C2 as the **Series**. Click on the **Time/Scale** button. Select **Stamp** and enter C1 (Year) for the **Stamp Columns.** Click on **OK**. Click on the **Labels** button and enter an appropriate title for the plot. Click on **OK** to view the plot.

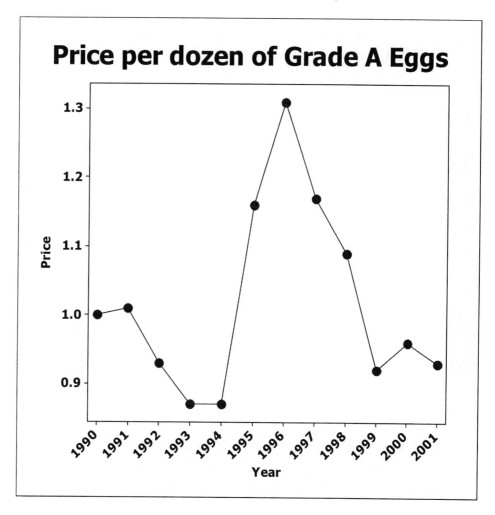

© 2006 Pearson Education, Inc., Upper Saddle River, NJ. All rights reserved. This material is protected under all copyright laws as they currently exist.
No portion of this material may be reproduced, in any form or by any means, without permission in writing from the publisher.

Section 2.3

▸ Example 6 (pg. 63) Find the mean and standard deviation of the age of students

Finding the mean and standard deviation of a dataset is very easy using MINITAB. Open the worksheet **ages** which is found in the **ch02** MINITAB folder. Click on **Stat → Basic Statistics → Display Descriptive Statistics.** You should see the input screen below.

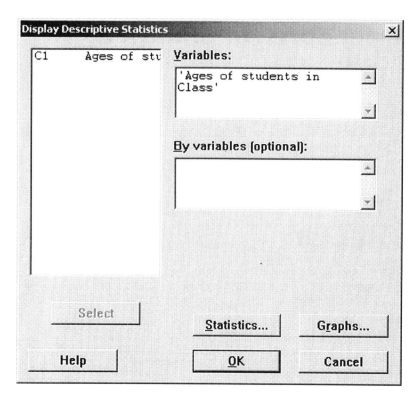

Double click on C1 to select the age data that is entered in C1. Click on **OK** and the descriptive statistics should appear in the Session Window.

© 2006 Pearson Education, Inc., Upper Saddle River, NJ. All rights reserved. This material is protected under all copyright laws as they currently exist. No portion of this material may be reproduced, in any form or by any means, without permission in writing from the publisher.

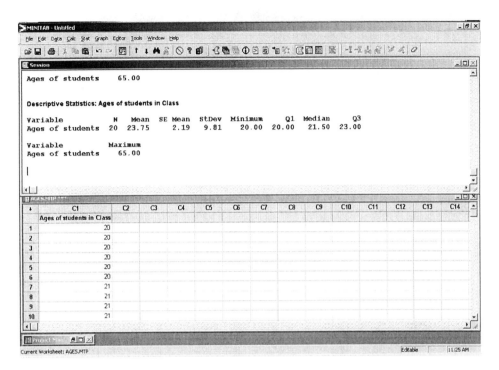

Notice that MINITAB displays several descriptive statistics: sample size, mean, standard error of the mean, standard deviation, standard error of the mean, minimum value, maximum value, median, and the first and third quartiles.

The mode is NOT produced by the above procedure, however, it is quite simple to have MINITAB tally up the data values for you, and then you can select the one with the highest count. Click on **Stat**→ **Tables** → **Tally Individual Variables**. On the input screen, double-click on C1 to select it. Also, click on **Counts** to have MINITAB count up the frequencies for you.

© 2006 Pearson Education, Inc., Upper Saddle River, NJ. All rights reserved. This material is protected under all copyright laws as they currently exist. No portion of this material may be reproduced, in any form or by any means, without permission in writing from the publisher.

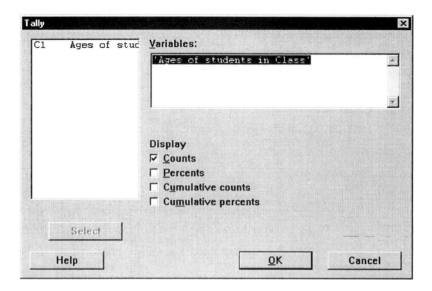

When you click on **OK**, a frequency table will appear in the Session Window.

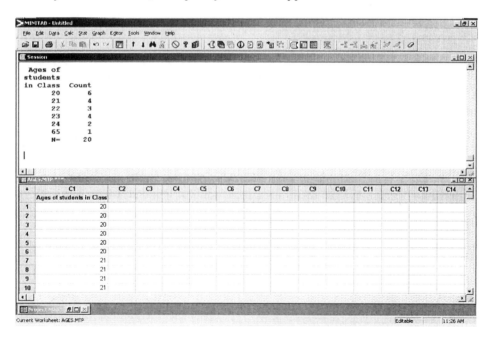

Notice that Age 20 has a count of 6. This means that 6 people in the data were age 20. Since this is the highest count, 20 is the mode.

To print the Session Window with both the descriptive statistics and the frequency table in it, click anywhere up in the Session Window to be sure that it is the active window. Next click on **File → Print Session Window**.

© 2006 Pearson Education, Inc., Upper Saddle River, NJ. All rights reserved. This material is protected under all copyright laws as they currently exist.
No portion of this material may be reproduced, in any form or by any means, without permission in writing from the publisher.

> ▶ Exercise 19 (pg. 68) Find the mean, median, mode for points per
>   game scored by each NBA team

Open worksheet **ex2_3-19** which is found in the **ch02** MINITAB folder. Click
on **Stat→ Basic Statistics → Display Descriptive Statistics.** Double-click on
C1 to select it. Click on **OK** and the results should be in the Session Window.
Next, make the frequency table to help find the mode. Click on **Stat→ Tables
→ Tally Individual Variables**. Double-click on C1, then click on **OK**. Now
both of the displays will be in the Session Window.

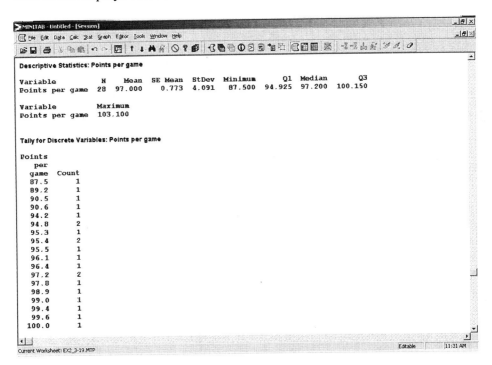

The mode is the points per game with the highest count. In this problem, there is
a 4-way tie for the mode: 94.8, 95.4, 97.2, and 103.1. Each of these has a count
of 2.

© 2006 Pearson Education, Inc., Upper Saddle River, NJ. All rights reserved. This material is protected under all copyright laws as they currently exist.
No portion of this material may be reproduced, in any form or by any means, without permission in writing from the publisher.

▸ Exercise 49 (pg. 72) Construct a frequency histogram of the
heights using 5 classes

Open worksheet **ex2_3-49** which is found in the **ch02** MINITAB folder. Click
on **Graph → Histogram → Simple.** Select C1 for the **Graph variable.** Click
on the **Labels** button and enter an appropriate title. Click on OK to view the
default histogram. Since you need 5 classes, edit the graph. Right-click on the
X-axis and select "Edit X scale" from the drop-down menu. On the **Binning** tab,
select **Cutpoints,** and enter 5 for the **Number of Intervals.** Click on **OK** to
view the changes to the graph.

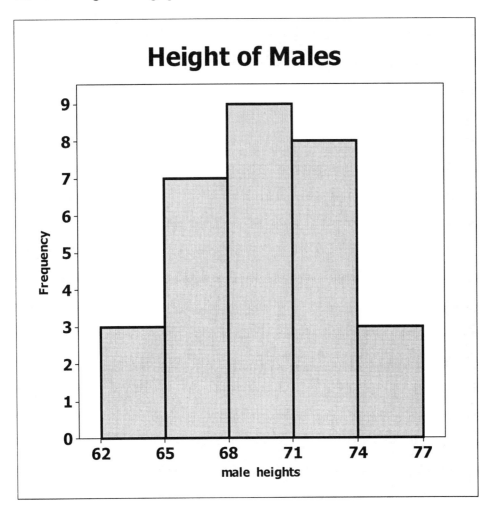

© 2006 Pearson Education, Inc., Upper Saddle River, NJ. All rights reserved. This material is protected under all copyright laws as they currently exist.
No portion of this material may be reproduced, in any form or by any means, without permission in writing from the publisher.

▶ Exercise 55 (pg. 73) Find the mean, median, and construct a
stem and leaf plot of the data

Open worksheet **ex2_3-55** which is found in the **ch02** MINITAB folder. Click
on **Stat → Basic Statistics → Display Descriptive Statistics.** Select C1 for the
Variable and click on **OK.** The descriptive statistics should be in the Session
Window. Next, click on **Graph → Stem-and-Leaf.** Select C1 for the **Variable**
and click on **OK**. The stem and leaf plot should also be in the Session Window
as shown in the next picture.

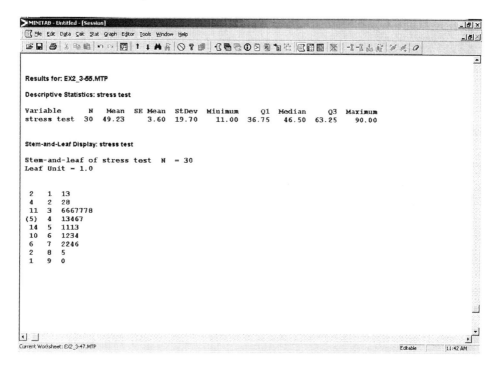

Section 2.4

▶ Example 5 (pg. 78) Calculate the mean and standard deviation for the office rental rates in Miami

Open worksheet **rentrate** which is found in the **ch02** MINITAB folder. Click on **Stat → Basic Statistics → Display Descriptive Statistics.** Select C1 for the **Variable** and click on **OK.** The descriptive statistics should be in the Session Window.

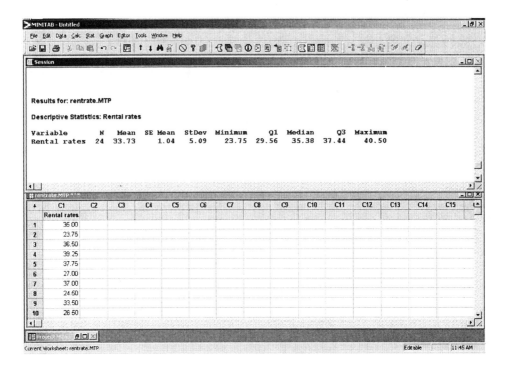

© 2006 Pearson Education, Inc., Upper Saddle River, NJ. All rights reserved. This material is protected under all copyright laws as they currently exist. No portion of this material may be reproduced, in any form or by any means, without permission in writing from the publisher.

▶ Exercise 2 (pg. 84) Find the range, mean, variance, standard
deviation of the dataset.

Enter the data into C1 of the Data Window. Click on **Stat → Basic Statistics →
Display Descriptive Statistics.** Select C1 for the **Variable** and click on **OK.**
The descriptive statistics should be in the Session Window.

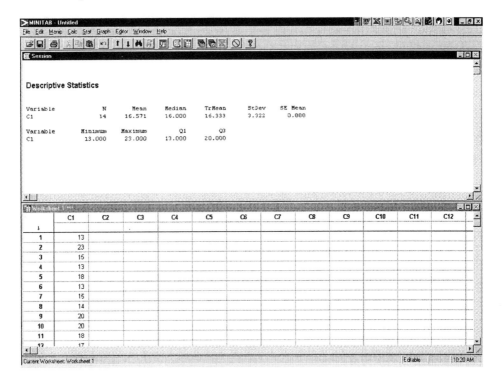

© 2006 Pearson Education, Inc., Upper Saddle River, NJ. All rights reserved. This material is protected under all copyright laws as they currently exist.
No portion of this material may be reproduced, in any form or by any means, without permission in writing from the publisher.

▶ Exercise 19 (pg. 86) Find the mean, range, standard deviation
and variance for each city

Enter the data into C1 and C2 of the Data Window. Be sure to label the columns.
Click on **Stat → Basic Statistics → Display Descriptive Statistics.** Select both
C1 and C2 for the **Variable** and click on **OK.** The descriptive statistics should
be in the Session Window.

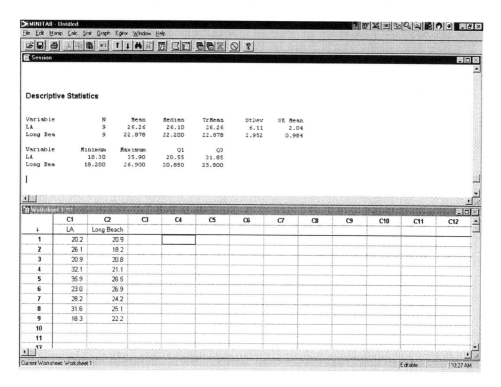

© 2006 Pearson Education, Inc., Upper Saddle River, NJ. All rights reserved. This material is protected under all copyright laws as they currently exist.
No portion of this material may be reproduced, in any form or by any means, without permission in writing from the publisher.

Section 2.5

▶ Example 2 (pg. 94) Find the first, second, and third quartiles of the tuition data.

Open worksheet **Tuition** which is found in the **ch02** MINITAB folder. Click on **Stat → Basic Statistics → Display Descriptive Statistics.** Select C1 for the **Variable** and click on **OK.** The descriptive statistics should be in the Session Window. Recall that the median is the second quartile.

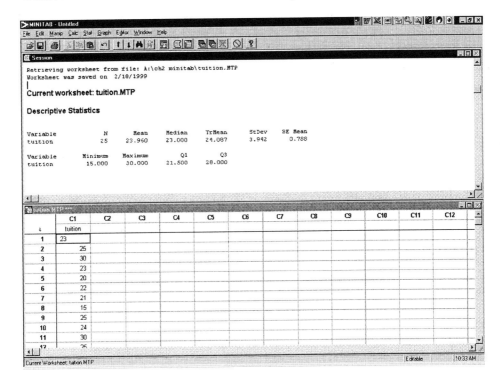

© 2006 Pearson Education, Inc., Upper Saddle River, NJ. All rights reserved. This material is protected under all copyright laws as they currently exist. No portion of this material may be reproduced, in any form or by any means, without permission in writing from the publisher.

▶ Example 4 (pg. 96) Construct a box-and-whisker plot using the
test scores given in Example 1.

Enter the data found on page 93 of the text into C1 of the Data Window. Click
on **Graph → Boxplot → Simple**. Select C1 for the **Graph variable.** Next,
since by default MINITAB plots vertically, click on the **Scale** button and select
Transpose value and category scales. This will turn the plot horizontal, as in
the textbook. Click on the **Labels** button and enter an appropriate title. Click on
OK twice to view the boxplot.

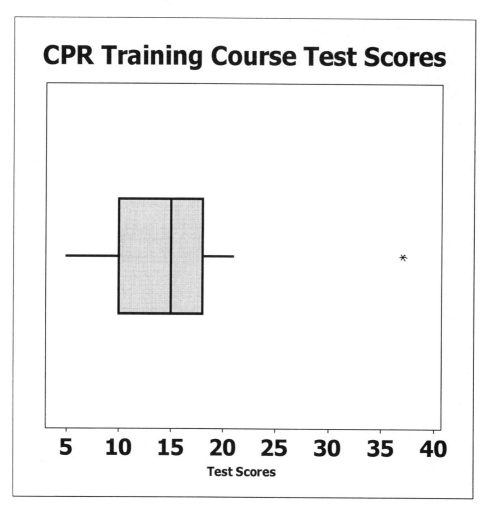

© 2006 Pearson Education, Inc., Upper Saddle River, NJ. All rights reserved. This material is protected under all copyright laws as they currently exist.
No portion of this material may be reproduced, in any form or by any means, without permission in writing from the publisher.

▶ Exercise 2 (pg. 100) Draw a boxplot of the data

Open worksheet **ex2_5-2** which is found in the **ch02** MINITAB folder. Click on **Graph → Boxplot → Simple**. Select C1 for the **Graph variable.** Next, since by default MINITAB plots vertically, click on the **Scale** button and select **Transpose value and category scales.** This will turn the plot horizontal, as in the textbook. Click on the **Labels** button and enter an appropriate title. Click on **OK** twice to view the boxplot.

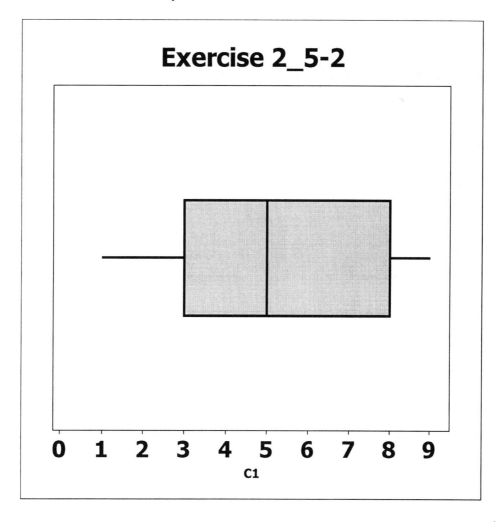

© 2006 Pearson Education, Inc., Upper Saddle River, NJ. All rights reserved. This material is protected under all copyright laws as they currently exist.
No portion of this material may be reproduced, in any form or by any means, without permission in writing from the publisher.

▸ Exercise 19 (pg. 101) Draw a boxplot of hours of TV
watched per day

Open worksheet **ex2_5-19** which is found in the **ch02** MINITAB folder. Click
on **Graph → Boxplot → Simple**. Select C1 for the **Graph variable.** Next,
since by default MINITAB plots vertically, click on the **Scale** button and select
Transpose value and category scales. This will turn the plot horizontal, as in
the textbook. Click on the **Labels** button and enter an appropriate title. Click on
OK twice to view the boxplot.

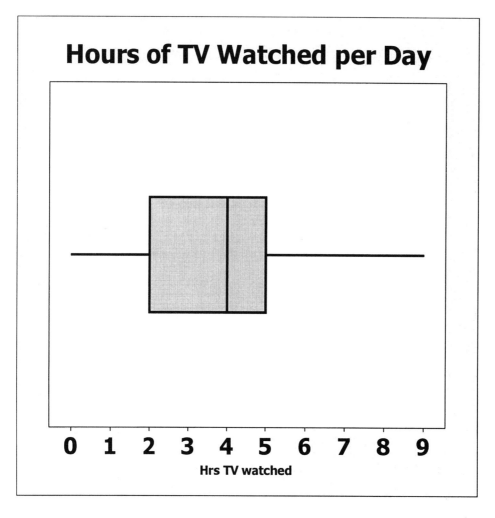

© 2006 Pearson Education, Inc., Upper Saddle River, NJ. All rights reserved. This material is protected under all copyright laws as they currently exist.
No portion of this material may be reproduced, in any form or by any means, without permission in writing from the publisher.

▶ Technology Lab (pg. 113) Use descriptive statistics and a
histogram to describe the milk data

Open worksheet **Tech2** which is found in the **ch02** MINITAB folder. Click on
Stat → Basic Statistics → Display Descriptive Statistics. Click on **OK** and the
descriptive statistics will be displayed in your Session Window.

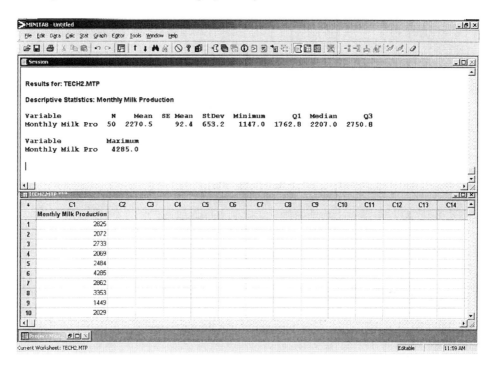

Next construct the histogram. Click on **Graph → Histogram → Simple.** Select
C1 for the **Graph variable.** Click on the **Labels** button and enter an appropriate
title. Click on OK to view the default histogram. Since you need a class width
of 500, edit the graph. Right-click on the X-axis and select "Edit X scale" from
the drop-down menu. On the **Binning** tab, select **Cutpoints.** Using the
information from the descriptive statistics, you can see that the minimum value is
1147 and the maximum is 4285. Since you want a class width of 500, use
positions beginning at 1100 and going up to 4600 in steps of 500. Thus, on the
Binning tab enter the **Midpoint/cutpoint positions** as **1100:4300/500.** Click on
OK to view the changes to the graph.

© 2006 Pearson Education, Inc., Upper Saddle River, NJ. All rights reserved. This material is protected under all copyright laws as they currently exist.
No portion of this material may be reproduced, in any form or by any means, without permission in writing from the publisher.

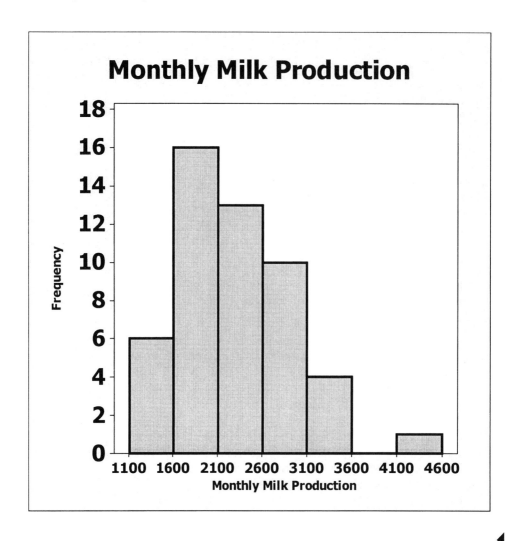

© 2006 Pearson Education, Inc., Upper Saddle River, NJ. All rights reserved. This material is protected under all copyright laws as they currently exist. No portion of this material may be reproduced, in any form or by any means, without permission in writing from the publisher.

Probability

Section 3.1

> ▶ Law of Large Numbers (pg. 122) Coin Simulation

You can use MINITAB to simulate repeatedly tossing a fair coin and then calculate the empirical probability of tossing a head. This empirical probability will more closely approximate the theoretical probability as the number of tosses gets large. To do this simulation, generate 1000 "tosses" of a fair coin. Let "0" represent a head, and "1" represent a tail. Click on **Calc → Random Data → Bernoulli**. **Generate** 1000 **rows of data** and **Store in column** C1. Use .5 for the **Probability of Success**. When you click on **OK**, you should see C1 filled with 1's and 0's. To count up the number of "0"s, click on **Stat → Tables → Tally Individual Variables.** Select C1 for **Variables** (by double clicking on C1), and choose both **counts and percents** by clicking on the box to the left of each one. When you click on **OK**, the summary statistics will appear in the Session Window. In the following example, notice that there were 511 heads and 489 tails. Thus, the empirical of tossing a head is .511 (51.1%). This is a very good approximation of the theoretical probability of .5.

© 2006 Pearson Education, Inc., Upper Saddle River, NJ. All rights reserved. This material is protected under all copyright laws as they currently exist. No portion of this material may be reproduced, in any form or by any means, without permission in writing from the publisher.

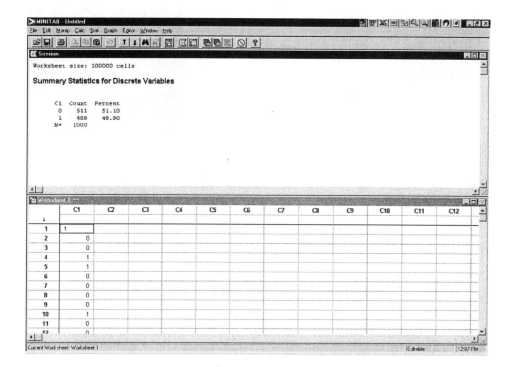

© 2006 Pearson Education, Inc., Upper Saddle River, NJ. All rights reserved. This material is protected under all copyright laws as they currently exist. No portion of this material may be reproduced, in any form or by any means, without permission in writing from the publisher.

Section 3.2

> ▶ Exercise 32 (pg. 139) Birthday Problem

Simulate the "Birthday Problem" using MINITAB. To do this simulation, the days of the year will be represented by the numbers 1 to 365. Click on **Calc→ Random Data → Integer. Generate** 24 **rows of data** (representing the 24 people in the room), **Store In** C1, **Minimum value** is 1 (representing Jan.1ˢᵗ) and **Maximum value** is 365 (representing Dec. 31ˢᵗ). When you click on **OK**, you should see C1 filled with 24 numbers ranging between 1 and 365. These numbers represent the birthdays of the 24 students in the class. The question is: Are there at least two people in the room with the same birthday? To answer this question, we must first summarize the data from this simulation. To do this, click on **Stat → Tables → Tally Individual variables.** On the screen that appears, select C1 for **Variables** and select **Counts.** Next click on **OK**, and in the Session Window, you will see a summary table of C1. This table lists each of the different birthdays that occurred in this simulation, as well as a count of the number of people who had that birthday. Notice that most counts are 1's. If you see a count of "2" or more, then you have at least two people in the room with the same birthday.

Repeat the simulation 9 more times and tally the results each time. How many of the 10 columns had at least two people with the same birthday? The empirical probability that at least two people in a room of 24 people will share a birthday can be calculated as follows: (# of columns having at least two people with the same birthday) divided by 10 (which is the total number of simulations).

◀

© 2006 Pearson Education, Inc., Upper Saddle River, NJ. All rights reserved. This material is protected under all copyright laws as they currently exist. No portion of this material may be reproduced, in any form or by any means, without permission in writing from the publisher.

▶ Technology Lab (pg. 169)   Composing Mozart Variations

3. Click on **Calc → Random Data → Integer. Generate 1 row of data, Store In Column** C1, **Minimum value** is 1 and **Maximum value** is 11. For Part B, repeat these steps but **Generate** 100 **rows of data** (instead of 1 row). To tally the results, click on **Stat → Tables → Tally Individual variables.** Select both **Counts** and **Percents.** The results will appear in the Session Window. Compare the percents to the theoretical probabilities you found in Part A.

5. Click on **Calc → Random Data → Integer. Generate** 2 **rows of data, Store In** C1, **Minimum value** is 1 and **Maximum value** is 6. Add the two numbers and subtract 1 to obtain the total. For Part B, **Generate** 100 **rows of data, Store In Columns** C1-C2, **Minimum value** is 1 and **Maximum value** is 6. The total will be calculated for each row by adding the two numbers from C1 and C2 and then subtracting 1. To do this, click on **Calc → Calculator. Store result in variable** C3. For **Expression,** type in the following: C1 + C2 - 1. Click on **OK,** and the totals should be in C3. To tally the results, click on **Stat → Tables → Tally Individual variables.** Select both **Counts** and **Percents.** The results will appear in the Session Window. Compare the percents to the theoretical probabilities you found in Part A.

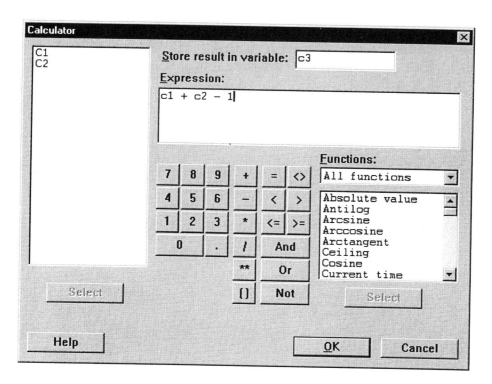

© 2006 Pearson Education, Inc., Upper Saddle River, NJ. All rights reserved. This material is protected under all copyright laws as they currently exist. No portion of this material may be reproduced, in any form or by any means, without permission in writing from the publisher.

To choose a minuet, Mozart suggested that the player toss a pair of dice 16 times. For the 8th and 16th bars, choose Option 1 if the dice total is odd, and Option 2 if the dice total is even. For each of the other 14 bars, subtract 1 from the dice total. To do this in MINITAB, first simulate rolling the dice 16 times. Click on **Calc → Random Data → Integer. Generate 16 rows of data, Store In Columns** C1-C2, **Minimum value** is 1 and **Maximum value** is 6. The total will be calculated for each row by adding the two numbers from C1 and C2 and then subtracting 1. To do this, click on **Calc → Calculator. Store result in variable** C3. For **Expression** type in: C1+C2-1. Click on **OK**, and the totals should be in C3.

	C1	C2	C3	C4	C5	C6	C7	C8	C9	C10	C11	C12
	Roll 1	Roll 2	Total-1									
1	3	6	8									
2	3	4	6									
3	1	1	1									
4	3	4	6									
5	2	4	5									
6	5	6	10									
7	6	1	6									
8	1	2	2									
9	5	4	8									
10	6	5	10									
11	3	1	3									
12	6	6	11									
13	6	4	9									
14	6	1	6									
15	5	1	5									
16	6	1	6									
17												
18												
19												
20												
21												
22												
23												
24												
25												
26												
27												
28												

The numbers in C3 will be the minuet, except for the 8th and 16th bars. To find these, add C1 + C2 for rows 8 and 16. If the total is odd, choose Option 1 and if the total is even, choose Option 2. For example, the total in row 8 is 3 and Option 1 should be chosen. The total in row 16 is 7, and Option 1 should be chosen again. Thus, the minuet for this simulation is:

8	6	1	6	5	10	6	1
8	10	3	11	9	6	5	1

Notice the 8th and 16th bars are both 1.

© 2006 Pearson Education, Inc., Upper Saddle River, NJ. All rights reserved. This material is protected under all copyright laws as they currently exist. No portion of this material may be reproduced, in any form or by any means, without permission in writing from the publisher.

Discrete Probability Distributions

CHAPTER

4

Section 4.2

▶ Example 4 (pg. 188) Find the probability that 65 out of 100 households own a gas grill

In this example, 58% of American households own a gas grill and a random sample of 100 American households is selected. Thus n = 100 and p = .58. Click on **Calc → Probability Distributions → Binomial.** To find the probability that exactly 65 of the 100 households own a gas grill, select **Probability.** This tells MINITAB what type of calculation you want to do. The **Number of Trials** is 100 and the **Probability of Success** is .58. To find the probability of 65 households owning a gas grill, click on the circle to the left of **Input Constant** and enter 65 in the box to the right of **Input Constant.** Leave all other fields blank. Click on **OK.**

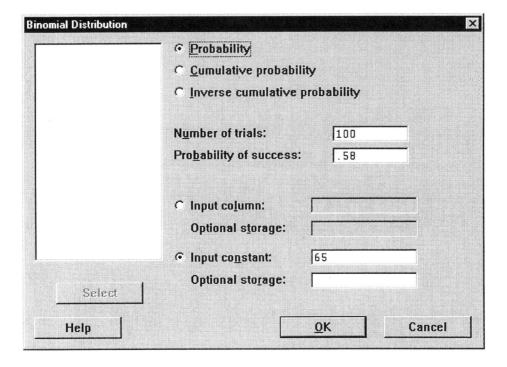

© 2006 Pearson Education, Inc., Upper Saddle River, NJ. All rights reserved. This material is protected under all copyright laws as they currently exist. No portion of this material may be reproduced, in any form or by any means, without permission in writing from the publisher.

The probability that 65 of the 100 households sampled own a gas grill will be displayed in the Session Window. Notice that the probability is .0299216.

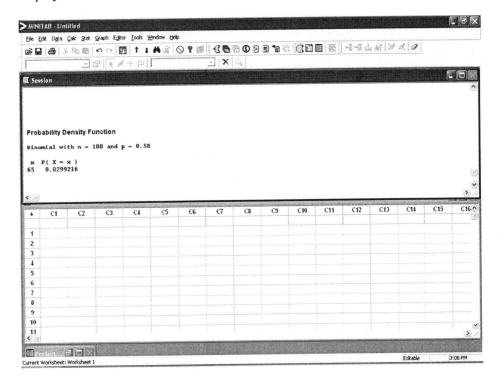

© 2006 Pearson Education, Inc., Upper Saddle River, NJ. All rights reserved. This material is protected under all copyright laws as they currently exist. No portion of this material may be reproduced, in any form or by any means, without permission in writing from the publisher.

▶ Example 7 (pg. 191)   Graphing a Binomial Distribution

In order to graph the binomial distribution, you must first create the distribution and save it in the Data Window. In C1, type in the values of X. Since n=6, the values of X are 0, 1, 2, 3, 4, 5, and 6. Next, use MINITAB to generate the binomial probabilities for n=6 and p=0.65. Click on **Calc→ Probability Distributions→ Binomial.** Select **Probability.** The **Number of Trials** is 6 and the **Probability of Success** is .65. Select **Input Column** by clicking on the circle on the left. Now, tell MINITAB that the X values are in C1 and that you want the probabilities stored in C2 by entering C1 as the **Input Column** and entering C2 for **Optional Storage.**

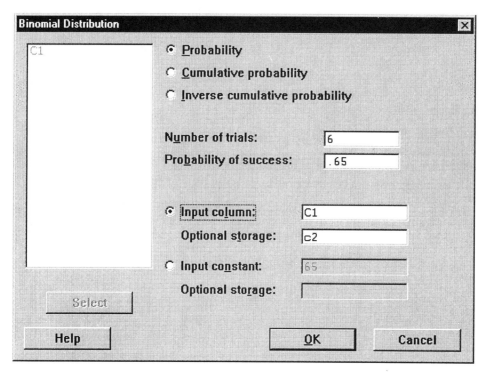

Click on **OK**. The probabilities should now be in C2. Label C1 as "X" and C2 as "P(X)". This will be helpful when you graph the distribution.

© 2006 Pearson Education, Inc., Upper Saddle River, NJ. All rights reserved. This material is protected under all copyright laws as they currently exist. No portion of this material may be reproduced, in any form or by any means, without permission in writing from the publisher.

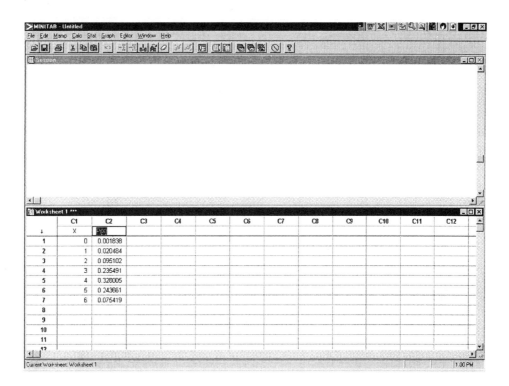

To create the graph, click on **Graph → Bar Chart.** On the screen that appears, below **Bars represent,** click on the down arrow and select **Values from a table.** In the section labeled **One column of values**, select the **Simple** Bar Chart. Click on **OK**. On the screen that appears, select 'C2 P(X)' for the **Graph variable** and select 'C1 X' for the **Categorical variable**. Click on **Labels** and enter an appropriate title. Click on **OK** twice to view the graph.

On the graph, right click on the label ('X') for the X-axis. Click on **Edit X label** and, in the box for **Text**, enter 'Households.' Next, right click on any numerical value on the X-axis (for example, right click on '1' under the first bar of the chart.) Click on **Edit X scale**. On the screen that appears, click on the check mark to the left of **Gap between clusters**. (This will remove the check mark.) In the box to the right of **Gap between clusters**, enter '0'. Click on OK and the new graph will appear.

© 2006 Pearson Education, Inc., Upper Saddle River, NJ. All rights reserved. This material is protected under all copyright laws as they currently exist. No portion of this material may be reproduced, in any form or by any means, without permission in writing from the publisher.

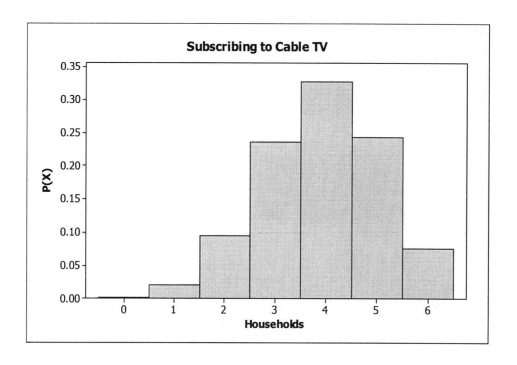

© 2006 Pearson Education, Inc., Upper Saddle River, NJ. All rights reserved. This material is protected under all copyright laws as they currently exist.
No portion of this material may be reproduced, in any form or by any means, without permission in writing from the publisher.

Section 4.3

▶ Example 3 (pg. 200) Finding Poisson Probabilities

Since there is an average of 3.6 rabbits per acre living in a field, $\mu = 3.6$ for this Poisson example. To find the probability that 2 rabbits are found on any given acre of the field, click on **Calc → Probability Distributions → Poisson.** Since you want a simple probability, select **Probability** and enter 3.6 for the **Mean.** To find the probability that X=2, select **Input constant** and enter 2 for the value.

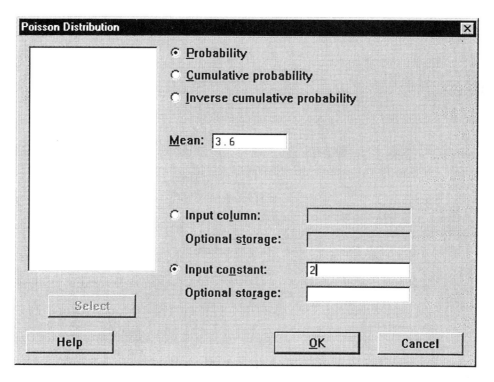

Click on **OK** and the probability will be displayed in the Session Window.

© 2006 Pearson Education, Inc., Upper Saddle River, NJ. All rights reserved. This material is protected under all copyright laws as they currently exist. No portion of this material may be reproduced, in any form or by any means, without permission in writing from the publisher.

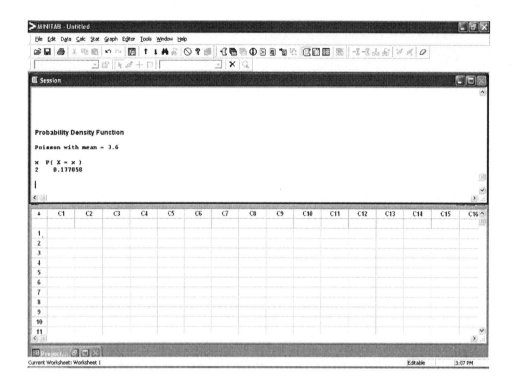

© 2006 Pearson Education, Inc., Upper Saddle River, NJ. All rights reserved. This material is protected under all copyright laws as they currently exist. No portion of this material may be reproduced, in any form or by any means, without permission in writing from the publisher.

▸ Technology Lab (pg. 213)

1. First, create the Poisson distribution and save it in the Data Window. In C1, type in the values of X. Since n=20, the values of X are 0, 1, 2, 3, 4, 5, …20. Next, use MINITAB to generate the Poisson probabilities for n=20 and μ=4. Click on **Calc → Probability Distributions → Poisson.** Select **Probability.** The **Mean** is 4. Now, tell MINITAB that the X values are in C1 and that you want the probabilities stored in C2 by entering C1 as the **Input Column** and entering C2 for **Optional Storage.** Click **OK.** The probabilities will be displayed in C2 of the Data Window. Notice, for example, that P(X=4) = .195367. This probability is the height at X=4 on the histogram that is displayed in the upper right corner of pg. 213.

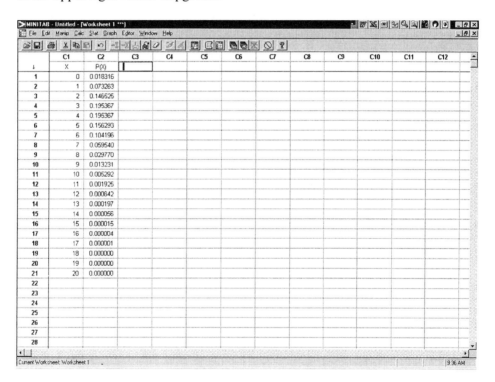

3. To generate 20 random numbers from a Poisson distribution with mean=4, click on **Calc → Random Data → Poisson. Generate** 20 **rows of data** and **Store in column** C3. Enter a **Mean** of 4 and click on **OK.**

© 2006 Pearson Education, Inc., Upper Saddle River, NJ. All rights reserved. This material is protected under all copyright laws as they currently exist. No portion of this material may be reproduced, in any form or by any means, without permission in writing from the publisher.

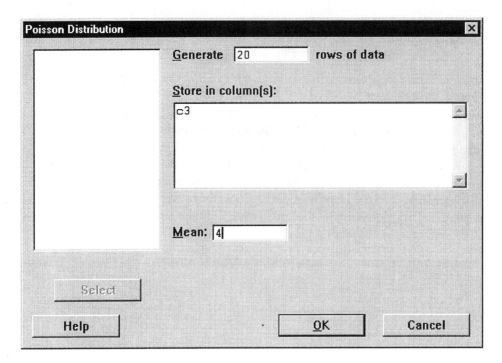

Use the random numbers that are in C3 of the Data Window to create (by hand) the table of waiting customers.

5. Repeat the steps in Exercise 3, but enter a **Mean** of 5 this time and **Store in column** C4.

6. To calculate P(X=10) for a Poisson random variable with a mean of 5, click on **Calc → Probability Distributions → Poisson.** Since you want a simple probability, select **Probability** and enter 5 for the **Mean** and 10 for the **Input constant.**

7. To find the probabilities for parts a - c, use the Poisson probability distribution that you created in C1 and C2.

© 2006 Pearson Education, Inc., Upper Saddle River, NJ. All rights reserved. This material is protected under all copyright laws as they currently exist.
No portion of this material may be reproduced, in any form or by any means, without permission in writing from the publisher.

Normal Probability Distributions

CHAPTER

5

Section 5.2

▶ Example 3 (pg. 231) Using MINITAB to find Normal
Probabilities.

Cholesterol levels of American men are normally distributed with μ=215 and
σ=25. Find the probability that a randomly selected American man has a
cholesterol level that is less than 175. To do this in MINITAB, click on **Calc→
Probability Distributions → Normal.** On the input screen, select **Cumulative
probability.** (Cumulative probability '*accumulates*' all probability to the left of
the input constant.) Enter 215 for the **Mean** and 25 for the **Standard deviation.**
Next select **Input Constant** and enter the value 175.

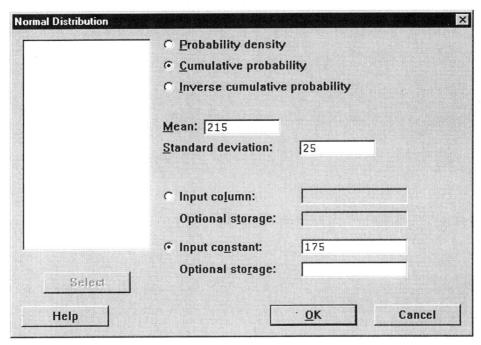

Click on **OK** and the probability should be displayed in the Session Window. As
you can see, the probability that a randomly selected American man has a
cholesterol level that is less than 175 is equal to .0547993.

© 2006 Pearson Education, Inc., Upper Saddle River, NJ. All rights reserved. This material is protected under all copyright laws as they currently exist.
No portion of this material may be reproduced, in any form or by any means, without permission in writing from the publisher.

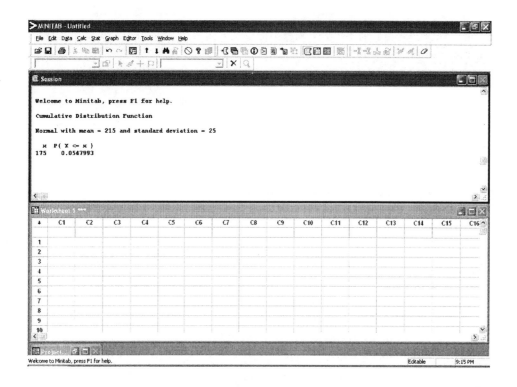

© 2006 Pearson Education, Inc., Upper Saddle River, NJ. All rights reserved. This material is protected under all copyright laws as they currently exist.
No portion of this material may be reproduced, in any form or by any means, without permission in writing from the publisher.

▶ Exercise 13 (pg. 233) Height of American Males

Heights are normally distributed with μ=69.2 inches and σ=2.9 inches. To complete parts (a) - (c), you will need MINITAB to give you two probabilities: one using X=66 and the other using X=72. Click on **Calc → Probability Distributions → Normal.** On the input screen, select **Cumulative probability.** Enter 69.2 for the **Mean** and 2.9 for the **Standard deviation.** Next select **Input Constant** and enter the value 66. Click on **OK.** Repeat the above steps using an **Input constant** of 72. Now the Session Window should contain P(X ≤ 66) and P(X ≤ 72)

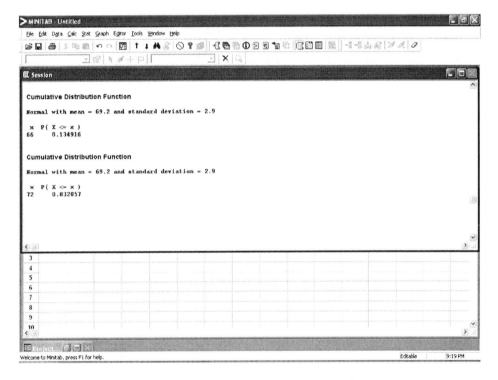

So, for Part (a), the P(X ≤ 66) = .134916. For Part (b), to find the P(66 ≤ X ≤ 72), you must subtract the two probabilities. Thus, the P(66 ≤ X ≤ 72) = .832857 - .134916 = .697941. For Part (c), to find P(X > 72), it is 1 - .832857 = .167143.

© 2006 Pearson Education, Inc., Upper Saddle River, NJ. All rights reserved. This material is protected under all copyright laws as they currently exist. No portion of this material may be reproduced, in any form or by any means, without permission in writing from the publisher.

Section 5.3

▶ Example 4 (pg. 240) Finding a specific data value

Scores for a civil service exam are normally distributed with μ=75 and σ=6.5. To be eligible for employment, you must score in the top 5%. Find the lowest score you can earn and still be eligible for employment. To do this in MINITAB, click on **Calc → Probability Distributions → Normal.** On the input screen, select **Inverse Cumulative probability.** Enter 75 for the **Mean** and 6.5 for the **Standard deviation.** For this type of problem, the **Input constant** will be the area to the left of the X-value we are looking for. This input constant will be a decimal number between 0 and 1. For this example, select **Input Constant** and enter the value .95 since 5% of the test scores are above this number and therefore, 95% are below this number. Click on **OK** and the X-value should be in the Session Window. Notice that the test score that qualifies you for employment is 85.6915.

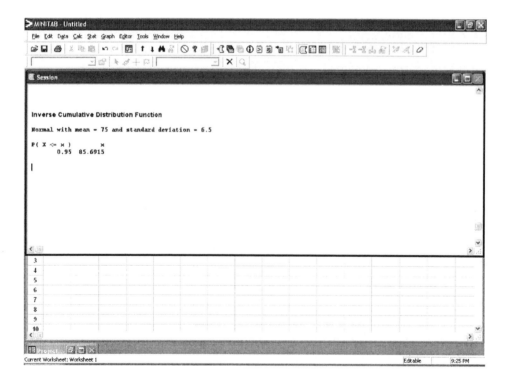

© 2006 Pearson Education, Inc., Upper Saddle River, NJ. All rights reserved. This material is protected under all copyright laws as they currently exist. No portion of this material may be reproduced, in any form or by any means, without permission in writing from the publisher.

Section 5.4

▶ Example 6 (pg. 253) Finding Probabilities for X and $\overline{X}$

Credit card balances are normally distributed, with a mean of $2870 and a standard deviation of $900.

1. To find the probability that a randomly selected card holder has a balance less than $2500, click on **Calc → Probability Distributions → Normal.** On the input screen, select **Cumulative probability.** Enter 2870 for the **Mean** and 900 for the **Standard deviation.** Next select **Input Constant** and enter the value 2500. Click on **OK** and the probability should appear in the Session Window.

2. To find the probability that the *mean* balance of 25 card holders is less than $2500, you will need to calculate the standard deviation of $\overline{x}$ which is equal to $900/\sqrt{25} = 180$. (Use a hand calculator for this calculation.) Now let MINITAB do the rest for you. Click on **Calc → Probability Distributions → Normal.** On the input screen, select **Cumulative probability.** Enter 2870 for the **Mean** and 180 for the **Standard deviation.** Next select **Input Constant** and enter the value 2500. Click on **OK** and the probability should appear in the Session Window.

◀

© 2006 Pearson Education, Inc., Upper Saddle River, NJ. All rights reserved. This material is protected under all copyright laws as they currently exist. No portion of this material may be reproduced, in any form or by any means, without permission in writing from the publisher.

▶ Technology Lab (pg. 277) Age Distribution in the United States

In this lab, you will compare the age distribution in the United States to the sampling distribution that is created by taking 36 random samples of size n=40 from the population and calculating the sample means.

Open worksheet **Tech5** which is found in the **ch05** folder. C1 should now contain the mean ages from the 36 random samples.

1. From the table on page 277 in your textbook, enter the Class Midpoints into C2. To enter the midpoints, click on **Calc → Make Patterned Data → Simple Set of Numbers.** On the input screen, you should **Store patterned data in** C2, **from the first value** of 2.5 **to the last value** of 97.5, **in steps of** 5. Click on **OK** and the midpoints should now be in C2. Next enter the relative frequencies, converted to proportions, into C3. So for a relative frequency of 6.9%, you should enter .069 into C3. The mean of this distribution is $\Sigma x\, p(x)$. To calculate the mean, you will have to multiply C2 and C3. To do this, click on **Calc → Calculator.** Type in the **Expression** C2 * C3 and **store result in variable** C4. Click on **OK** and in C4 you should now see the product of C2 and C3.

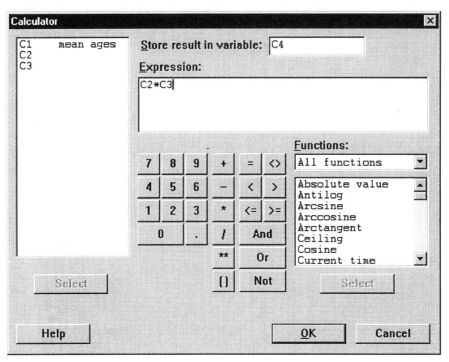

© 2006 Pearson Education, Inc., Upper Saddle River, NJ. All rights reserved. This material is protected under all copyright laws as they currently exist. No portion of this material may be reproduced, in any form or by any means, without permission in writing from the publisher.

Now find the sum of C4. Click on **Calc → Column Statistics.** On the input screen, select **Sum** and use C4 for the **Input variable.** Click on **OK** and the column sum should be in the Session Window. As you can see, the mean age in the United States is 36.565.

2. The 36 sample means are in C1. To find the mean, click on **Stat → Basic Statistics → Display Descriptive Statistics.** Select C1 for the **Variable** and click on **OK.** The descriptive statistics will be displayed in the Session Window. The mean of the set of sample means is 36.209 and the standard deviation is 3.552. (You will need the standard deviation for question 6.)

4. To draw the histogram, click on **Graph → Histogram.** Select C1 for the **Graph variable.** In order to create a *relative frequency* histogram, click on **Options** and select **Percent.** Click on **OK** twice and you should be able to view the histogram.

5. To find the standard deviation of the ages of Americans, you must use the formula for the standard deviation of a Discrete Random variable, found on page 167 in the textbook. The shortcut formula will make this calculation easier. Use the formula $\Sigma x^2 p(x) - \mu^2$ and take the square root of this value. In MINITAB, first square all the midpoints. Click on **Calc → Calculator.** Type in the **Expression** C2 * C2 and **store result in variable** C5. Click on **OK** and in C5 you should now see the midpoints squared. To calculate x^2 p(x), you must multiply C5 by C3. Click on **Calc → Calculator.** Type in the **Expression** C5 * C3 and **store result in variable** C6.

© 2006 Pearson Education, Inc., Upper Saddle River, NJ. All rights reserved. This material is protected under all copyright laws as they currently exist. No portion of this material may be reproduced, in any form or by any means, without permission in writing from the publisher.

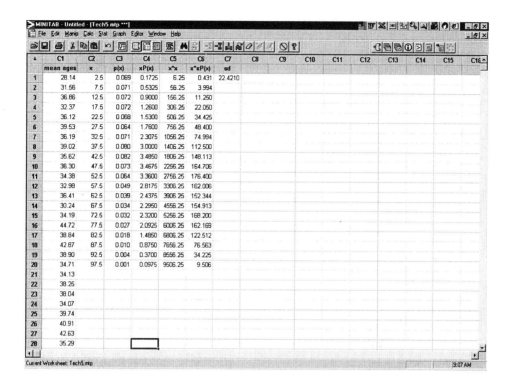

Now find the sum of C6. Click on **Calc → Column Statistics.** On the input screen, select **Sum** and use C6 for the **Input variable.** Click on **OK** and the column sum should be in the Session Window. As you can see, $\Sigma x^2 p(x)$ is 1839.7. Next, subtract μ^2 from 1839.7 and take the square root. (Recall that $\mu = 36.565$) Click on **Calc → Calculator.** Type in the **Expression** SQRT(1839.7 -36.565*36.565) and **store result in variable** C7. The standard deviation is the number now in C7, 22.4210.

6. The standard deviation of the 36 sample means can be found in the descriptive statistics that you produced for question 2.

© 2006 Pearson Education, Inc., Upper Saddle River, NJ. All rights reserved. This material is protected under all copyright laws as they currently exist. No portion of this material may be reproduced, in any form or by any means, without permission in writing from the publisher.

Confidence Intervals

Section 6.1

▸ Example 4 (pg. 284)   Construct a 99% Confidence Interval for the mean number of sentences in an ad

Open the worksheet **Sentence** which is found in the **ch06** Folder. The data will be in C1. First find the standard deviation of the data. Click on **Calc → Column Statistics.** Select **Standard deviation** and enter C1 for the **Input variable.** Click on **OK** and the standard deviation will be displayed in the Session Window. To construct the confidence interval, click on **Stat → Basic Statistics → 1-Sample Z.** Enter C1 in **Samples in columns**. For **Standard deviation,** enter the assumed standard deviation of 5.

1-Sample Z (Test and Confidence Interval)	✕

⊙ **Samples in columns:**

Sentence

○ **Summarized data**

S̲ample size: [   ]

M̲ean: [   ]

S̲tandard deviation: [5.   ]

T̲est mean: [   ]   **(required for test)**

Select   Gr̲aphs...   O̲ptions...

Help   O̲K   Cancel

© 2006 Pearson Education, Inc., Upper Saddle River, NJ. All rights reserved. This material is protected under all copyright laws as they currently exist. No portion of this material may be reproduced, in any form or by any means, without permission in writing from the publisher.

Next, click on **Options** and enter 99.0 for the **Confidence Level.**

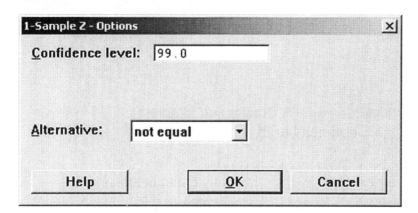

Click on **OK** twice and the results will be displayed in the Session Window. As you can see, the 99% confidence interval is (10.673, 14.179).

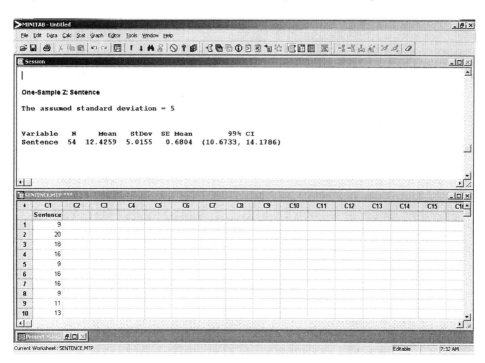

© 2006 Pearson Education, Inc., Upper Saddle River, NJ. All rights reserved. This material is protected under all copyright laws as they currently exist. No portion of this material may be reproduced, in any form or by any means, without permission in writing from the publisher.

▶ Exercise 47 (pg. 289) Construct 90% and 99% confidence
intervals for mean reading time

Enter the data into C1. To construct the confidence interval, click on **Stat→
Basic Statistics → 1-Sample Z.** Enter C1 for **Samples in columns**. Enter the
assumed value of 1.5 for the **Standard deviation**. Next, select **Options** and
enter 90.0 for the **Confidence Level.** Click on **OK** and the interval will be
displayed in the Session Window. Repeat the above steps using 99.0 for the
Confidence Level.

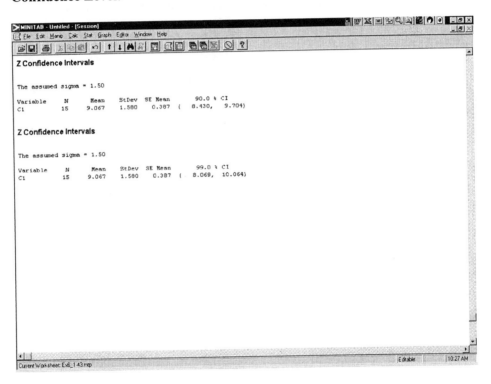

© 2006 Pearson Education, Inc., Upper Saddle River, NJ. All rights reserved. This material is protected under all copyright laws as they currently exist.
No portion of this material may be reproduced, in any form or by any means, without permission in writing from the publisher.

> ▸ Exercise 61 (pg. 292) Construct a 95% confidence interval for airfare prices

Open worksheet **Ex6_1-61.mtp** in the **ch06** Folder. The airfares are in C1. Find the standard deviation of the sample. Click on **Calc → Column Statistics.** Select **Standard deviation** and enter C1 for the **Input variable.** Click on **OK** and the standard deviation will be displayed in the Session Window. To construct the confidence interval, click on **Stat → Basic Statistics → 1-Sample Z.** Enter C1 in **Samples in columns**. For **Standard deviation,** enter the standard deviation that is displayed in the Session Window. Next, select **Options** and enter 95.0 for the **Confidence Level.** Click **OK** twice.

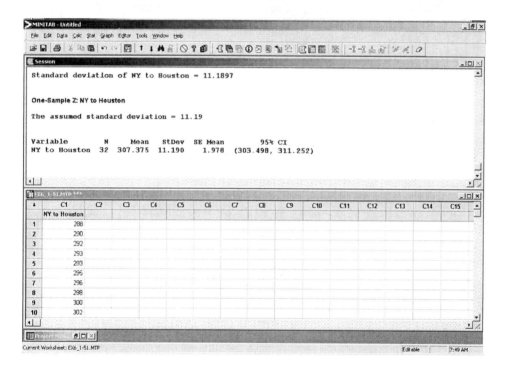

© 2006 Pearson Education, Inc., Upper Saddle River, NJ. All rights reserved. This material is protected under all copyright laws as they currently exist. No portion of this material may be reproduced, in any form or by any means, without permission in writing from the publisher.

Section 6.2

▶ **Example 2 (pg. 297)** Construct a 95% Confidence Interval for the mean temperature of coffee sold

Using the summarized data found on page 297 of the text, construct a 95% confidence interval for the temperatures of the coffee sold at 16 randomly selected restaurants.   Since n=16 and the population standard deviation is unknown, you should construct a t-interval for this problem. Click on **Stat→ Basic Statistics → 1-Sample t**. Select **Summarized data**. The **Sample size** is 16, the **Mean** is 162, and the **Standard deviation** is 10.   Next, select **Options** and enter 95.0 for the **Confidence Level.** Click on **OK** twice and the output will be displayed in the Session Window.

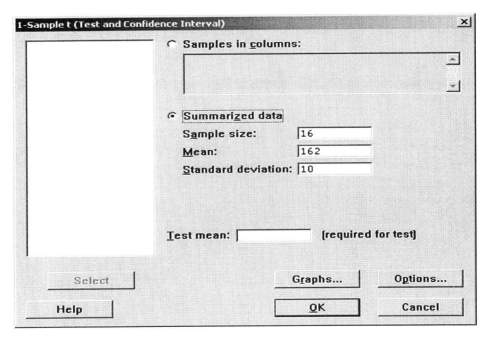

The following confidence interval will be displayed in the Session Window.

One-Sample T

N	Mean	StDev	SE Mean	95% CI
16	162.000	10.000	2.500	(156.671, 167.329)

© 2006 Pearson Education, Inc., Upper Saddle River, NJ. All rights reserved. This material is protected under all copyright laws as they currently exist.
No portion of this material may be reproduced, in any form or by any means, without permission in writing from the publisher.

▸ Exercise 19 (pg. 301)   Construct a 99% confidence interval for
the mean SAT scores

Enter the SAT scores into C1. Since n=12 and the population standard deviation
is unknown, you should construct a t-interval for this problem. Click on **Stat**→
Basic Statistics → 1-Sample t. Enter C1 in **Samples in column**. Next, select
Options and enter 99.0 for the **Confidence Level.** Click on **OK** twice and the
output will be displayed in the Session Window.

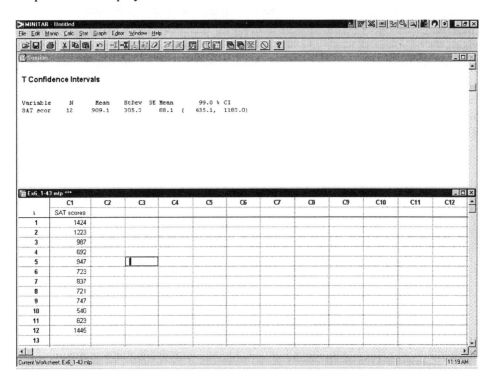

© 2006 Pearson Education, Inc., Upper Saddle River, NJ. All rights reserved. This material is protected under all copyright laws as they currently exist.
No portion of this material may be reproduced, in any form or by any means, without permission in writing from the publisher.

Section 6.3

> ▶ Example 2 (pg. 305) Construct a 95% confidence interval for p

From Example 1, on page 303 of the textbook, you know that 293 of 1011 American adults said that their favorite sport was football. To construct a 95% confidence interval, click on **Stat → Basic Statistics → 1 Proportion.** Select **Summarized Data.** The **Number of trials** is 1011 and the **Number of events** is 293.

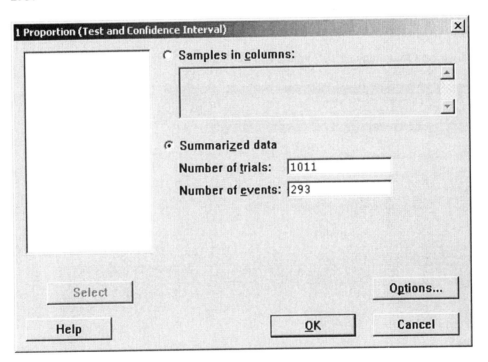

Next, to select the confidence level, click on **Options.** Enter 95.0 for the **Confidence Level.** Also, select **Use test and interval based on normal distribution.**

© 2006 Pearson Education, Inc., Upper Saddle River, NJ. All rights reserved. This material is protected under all copyright laws as they currently exist. No portion of this material may be reproduced, in any form or by any means, without permission in writing from the publisher.

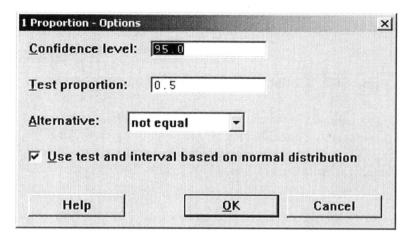

Click on **OK** twice and the output will be displayed in the Session Window.

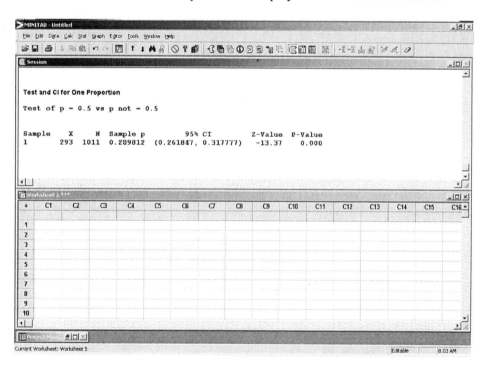

Notice the interval is (.262, .318). This means that with 95% confidence, you can say that the proportion of adults who say football is their favorite sport is between 26.2% and 31.8%.

© 2006 Pearson Education, Inc., Upper Saddle River, NJ. All rights reserved. This material is protected under all copyright laws as they currently exist. No portion of this material may be reproduced, in any form or by any means, without permission in writing from the publisher.

▶ Exercise 19 (pg. 309) Construct intervals for the proportion of children planning to join the armed forces

A study of 848 children found that 102 planned to join the armed forces in the future. Construct both 95% and 99% confidence intervals for the true proportion of children who plan to enlist. Click on **Stat** → **Basic Statistics** → **1 Proportion.** Select **Summarized Data.** The **Number of trials** is 848 and the **Number of event** is 102. Next, to select the confidence level, click on **Options.** Enter 95.0 for the **Confidence Level.** Also, select **Use test and interval based on normal distribution.** Click on **OK** twice and the results will be in the Session Window. Repeat using 99.0 for the **Confidence Level.**

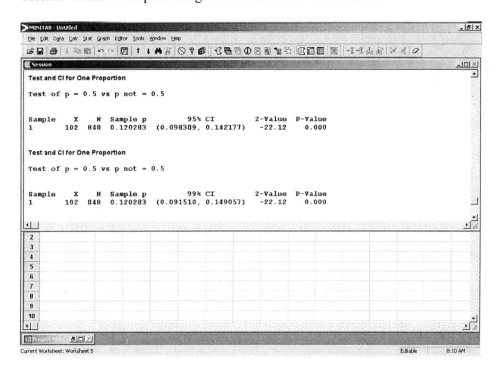

© 2006 Pearson Education, Inc., Upper Saddle River, NJ. All rights reserved. This material is protected under all copyright laws as they currently exist.
No portion of this material may be reproduced, in any form or by any means, without permission in writing from the publisher.

▸ Technology Lab (pg. 327)

1. Click on **Stat → Basic Statistics → 1 Proportion.** Select **Summarized Data.** The **Number of trials** is 1004 and the **Number of events** is 40. Next, to select the confidence level, click on **Options.** Enter 95.0 for the **Confidence Level.** Also, select **Use test and interval based on normal distribution.** Click on **OK** twice and the results will be in the Session Window.

3. Oprah Winfrey was named by 7% of the people in the sample. That means that 70 (.07 x 1004 = 70.28) of the 1004 named Oprah Winfrey. Use the steps in question 1 to construct the 95% confidence interval. This time the **Number of events** is 70.

4. To do this simulation, you will generate random binomial data with n=1004 and p=.10. The result displayed in each cell of C1 will represent the number of people who named Oprah. Click on **Calc → Random Data → Binomial.** Generate 200 **rows of data** and **Store in column** C1. The **Number of trials** is 1004 and the **Probability of success** is .10. When you click on **OK**, C1 will contain a simulation of 200 samples.

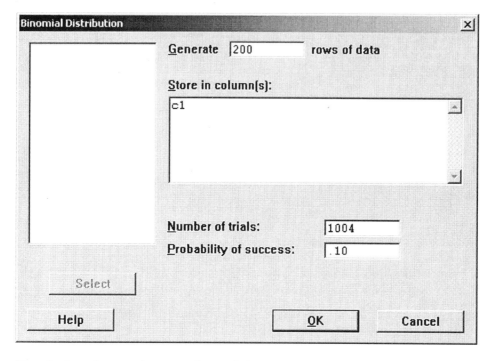

To calculate the sample proportions, click on **Calc→ Calculator.** Enter C1/1004 for the **Expression** and **Store the result in** C2. Click on **OK.** Now C2 contains 200 values of the sample proportion. Sort C2 to find the smallest and

© 2006 Pearson Education, Inc., Upper Saddle River, NJ. All rights reserved. This material is protected under all copyright laws as they currently exist. No portion of this material may be reproduced, in any form or by any means, without permission in writing from the publisher.

largest value. Click on **Data** → **Sort. Sort column** C2, **By column** C2 and
Store sorted data in column of current worksheet C3.

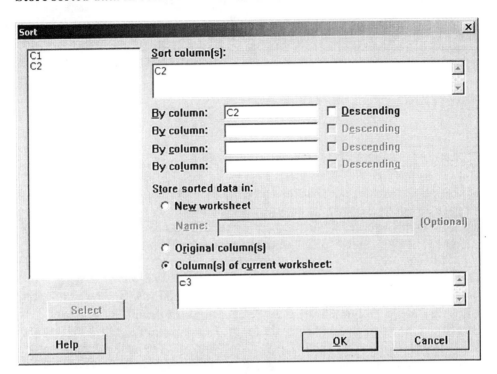

Click on **OK** and C3 should contain the sample proportions sorted from smallest
to largest. Thus, the smallest value should be in Row 1 and the largest value
should be in Row 200. Since this is random data, results will vary each time this
is repeated.

© 2006 Pearson Education, Inc., Upper Saddle River, NJ. All rights reserved. This material is protected under all copyright laws as they currently exist.
No portion of this material may be reproduced, in any form or by any means, without permission in writing from the publisher.

Hypothesis Testing with One Sample

CHAPTER

7

Section 7.2

▶ | Example 5 (pg. 351) | Hypothesis Testing Using P-values

You think that the average franchise investment information given in the graph on page 351 of the textbook is incorrect, so you randomly select 30 franchises and determine the necessary investment for each. Is there enough evidence to support your claim at $\alpha = .05$? Use the P-value to interpret.

Open worksheet **Franchise,** which is found in the **ch07** MINITAB folder. The data should be in C1. To do a 1-Sample Z-test in MINITAB, you must know σ. Click on **Calc → Column Statistics.** Select **Standard deviation** for the **Statistic** to be calculated and enter C1 for the **Input Variable.** Click on **OK** and the standard deviation will be in the Session Window. You will enter this value in the input screen for the 1-Sample Z-test. Click on **Stat → Basic Statistics → 1-Sample Z.** Enter C1 for **Samples in columns,** 30000 for **Standard deviation,** and 143260 for **Test mean.**

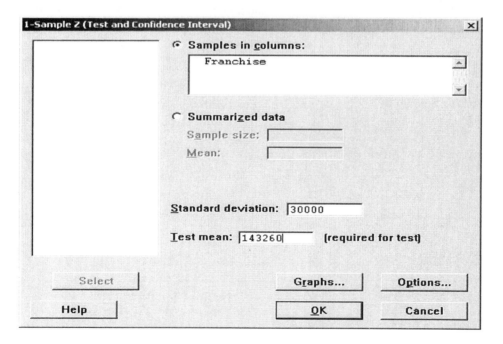

© 2006 Pearson Education, Inc., Upper Saddle River, NJ. All rights reserved. This material is protected under all copyright laws as they currently exist. No portion of this material may be reproduced, in any form or by any means, without permission in writing from the publisher.

Since the claim is "the mean is different from $143,260", you will perform a two-tailed test. Click on **Options**, and set **Alternative** to "not equal".

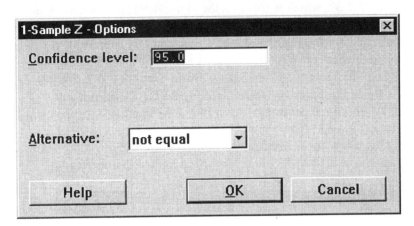

Click on **OK** twice and the results should be displayed in the Session Window.

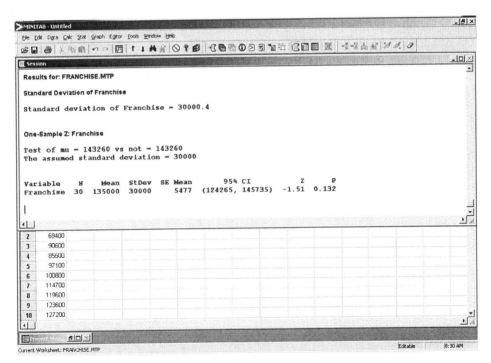

Notice that both the test statistic and the P-value are given. From the output, note that z = -1.51 and P = .132. Since the P-value is larger than α, you should Fail to Reject the null hypothesis.

© 2006 Pearson Education, Inc., Upper Saddle River, NJ. All rights reserved. This material is protected under all copyright laws as they currently exist. No portion of this material may be reproduced, in any form or by any means, without permission in writing from the publisher.

▸ Exercise 37 (pg. 360) Years taken to quit smoking permanently

Open worksheet **Ex7_2-37,** which is found in the **ch07** MINITAB folder.   Click
on **Calc → Column Statistics.** Select **Standard deviation** for the **Statistic** to be
calculated and enter C1 for the **Input Variable.** Click on **OK** and the standard
deviation will be in the Session Window. You will enter this value in the input
screen for the 1-Sample Z test. Click on **Stat → Basic Statistics → 1-Sample Z.**
Click on **Stat → Basic Statistics → 1-Sample Z.** Enter C1 for **Samples in
columns,** 4.288 for **Standard deviation,** and 15 for **Test mean.** Since the claim
is "the mean time is 15 years", you will perform a two-tailed test. Click on
Options and use the down arrow beside **Alternative** to select "not equal". Click
on **OK** and the results of the test should be displayed in the Session Window.

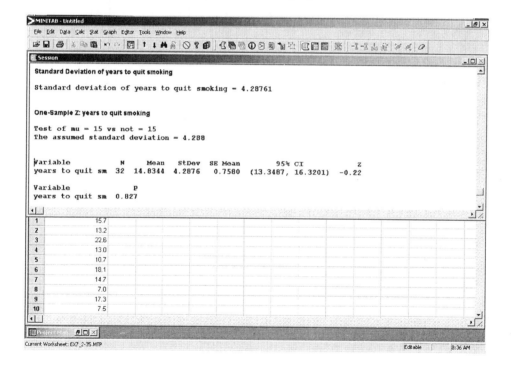

© 2006 Pearson Education, Inc., Upper Saddle River, NJ. All rights reserved. This material is protected under all copyright laws as they currently exist.
No portion of this material may be reproduced, in any form or by any means, without permission in writing from the publisher.

> ▸ Exercise 43 (pg. 361) Nitrogen Dioxide Level in West London

Open worksheet **Ex7_2-43,** which is found in the **ch07** MINITAB folder.   Click
on **Calc → Column Statistics.** Select **Standard deviation** for the **Statistic** to be
calculated and enter C1 for the **Input Variable.** Click on **OK** and the standard
deviation will be in the Session Window. You will enter this value in the input
screen for the 1-Sample Z test. Click on **Stat → Basic Statistics → 1-Sample Z.**
Enter C1 for **Samples in columns,** 22.128 for **Standard deviation,** and 28 for
Test mean. Since the claim is "the mean is greater than 28 parts per billion", you
will perform a right-tailed test. Click **Options** and then on the down arrow
beside **Alternative** and select "greater than". Click on **OK** twice and the results
of the test should be displayed in the Session Window.

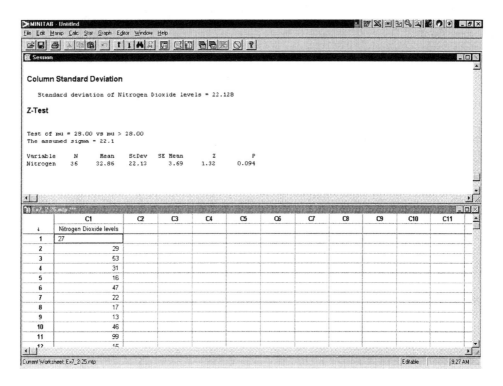

Use the P-value (.094) to draw a conclusion about the scientist's estimate at the
level of significance α = .05.

© 2006 Pearson Education, Inc., Upper Saddle River, NJ. All rights reserved. This material is protected under all copyright laws as they currently exist.
No portion of this material may be reproduced, in any form or by any means, without permission in writing from the publisher.

Section 7.3

> ▸ Example 4 (pg. 367) Testing μ with a Small Sample

A used car dealer says that the mean price of a 2002 Ford F-150 Super Cab is at least $18,800. You suspect this claim is incorrect. At $\alpha = .05$, is there enough evidence to reject the dealer's claim?

Based on a random sample of 14 similar vehicles, you found that the mean price is $18,000 with a standard deviation of $1250. Be sure to enter the data in numeric form. So enter the amount $18,000 as 18000. Since this is a small sample problem, you will be performing a 1-Sample t-test. Click on **Stat→ Basic Statistics → 1-Sample t.** Click on **Summarized data,** and enter a **Sample size** of 14, a **Mean** of 18000, and a **Standard deviation** of 1250. Since you suspect that the used car dealer's claim is too high, you will perform a left-tailed test. Click on **Options** and then on the down arrow beside **Alternative** to select "less than". Click on **OK** and the results of the test should be displayed in the Session Window.

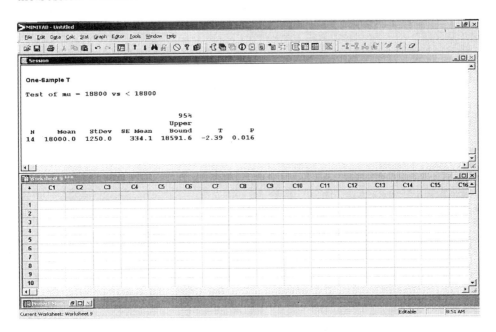

Notice that MINITAB gives the test statistic and the P-value, so that you can make your conclusion using either value. Since the P-value is smaller than α, you should Reject the null hypothesis.

© 2006 Pearson Education, Inc., Upper Saddle River, NJ. All rights reserved. This material is protected under all copyright laws as they currently exist.
No portion of this material may be reproduced, in any form or by any means, without permission in writing from the publisher.

▶ Exercise 29 (pg. 372) Soda consumed by teen-age males

Open worksheet **Ex7_3-29,** which is found in the **ch07** MINITAB folder. Click
on **Stat** → **Basic Statistics** →**1-Sample t.** Enter C1 for **Samples in columns,**
and **Test mean** is 3. Since the claim is "teenage males drink less than 3 servings",
you will perform a left-tailed test. Click on **Options** and then on the down arrow
beside **Alternative** to select "less than". Click on **OK** twice and the results of the
test should be displayed in the Session Window.

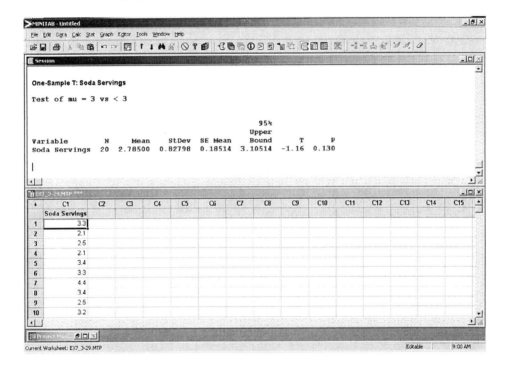

© 2006 Pearson Education, Inc., Upper Saddle River, NJ. All rights reserved. This material is protected under all copyright laws as they currently exist.
No portion of this material may be reproduced, in any form or by any means, without permission in writing from the publisher.

> ▶ **Exercise 30 (pg. 372)** Water consumed by American adults

Open worksheet **Ex7_3-30,** which is found in the **ch07** MINITAB folder. Click on **Stat → Basic Statistics →1-Sample t.** Enter C1 for **Samples in columns,** and **Test mean** is 5. Since the claim is "teachers spend more than $580 of their own money on school supplies per year", you will perform a right-tailed test. Click on **Options** and then on the down arrow beside **Alternative** to select "greater than". Click on **OK** and the results of the test should be displayed in the Session Window.

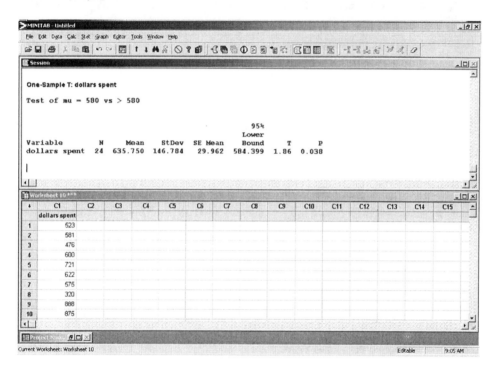

© 2006 Pearson Education, Inc., Upper Saddle River, NJ. All rights reserved. This material is protected under all copyright laws as they currently exist. No portion of this material may be reproduced, in any form or by any means, without permission in writing from the publisher.

Section 7.4

> ▸ Example 2 (pg. 376) Hypothesis Test for a Proportion

Of 200 Americans, 27% are in favor of outlawing cigarettes. At $\alpha = .05$, is there enough evidence to reject the claim that 23% of Americans favor outlawing cigarettes?

Click on **Stat → Basic Statistics → 1-Proportion.** The data is given in a summarized form, so select **Summarized data**. Enter 200 for the **Number of trials.** Since 27% of the sample were in favor, the **Number of events** is 54 (.27 * 200).

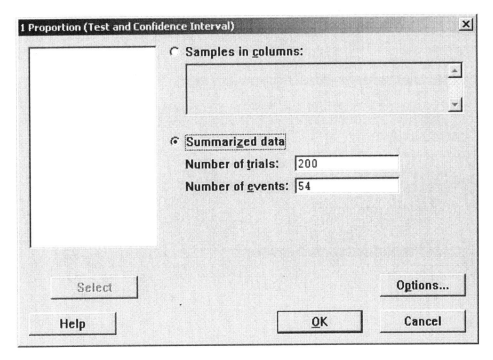

Click on **Options**. Enter .23 for the **Test Proportion** because it is claimed that 23% are in favor, and select "not equal" for the **Alternative**. Since np and nq are both larger than 5, click on **Use test and interval based on normal distribution,** and then click on **OK** twice.

© 2006 Pearson Education, Inc., Upper Saddle River, NJ. All rights reserved. This material is protected under all copyright laws as they currently exist. No portion of this material may be reproduced, in any form or by any means, without permission in writing from the publisher.

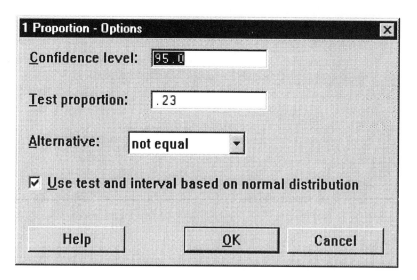

The results should be displayed in the Session Window.

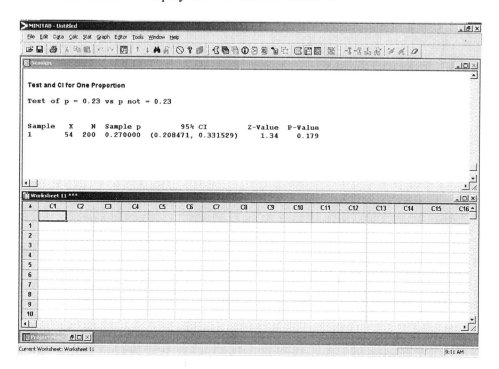

Notice that the test statistic (z = 1.34), the P-value (P = .179) and a 95% confidence interval for the true proportion of Americans in favor of outlawing cigarettes are all displayed in the output. With such a large P-value, you should Fail to Reject the null hypothesis.

© 2006 Pearson Education, Inc., Upper Saddle River, NJ. All rights reserved. This material is protected under all copyright laws as they currently exist. No portion of this material may be reproduced, in any form or by any means, without permission in writing from the publisher.

▶ Exercise 11 (pg. 378) Consumer Pollution Concerns

Click on **Stat → Basic Statistics → 1-Proportion.** The data is given in a summarized form, so select **Summarized data.** Enter 1050 for the **Number of trials.** Since 32% of the sample have stopped buying this product because of pollution concerns, the **Number of events** is 336 (.32 * 1050 = 336). Click on **Options** and enter .30 for the **Test Proportion** because it is claimed that more than 30% have stopped buying the product, and select "greater than" for the **Alternative.** Click on **Use test and interval based on normal distribution,** and then click on **OK** twice.

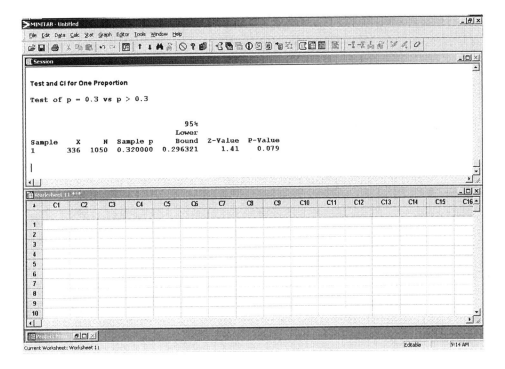

© 2006 Pearson Education, Inc., Upper Saddle River, NJ. All rights reserved. This material is protected under all copyright laws as they currently exist. No portion of this material may be reproduced, in any form or by any means, without permission in writing from the publisher.

▸ Exercise 13 (pg. 379) Finding a Real Estate Agent

Click on **Stat → Basic Statistics → 1-Proportion.** The data is given in a summarized form, so select **Summarized data.** Enter 1762 for the **Number of trials.** Since 722 home buyers in the sample found their real estate agent through a friend, the **Number of events** is 722. Click on **Options.** Enter .44 for the **Test Proportion** because it is claimed that 44% have found their agent through friends, and select "not equal" for the **Alternative.** Click on **Use test and interval based on normal distribution,** and then click on **OK** twice.

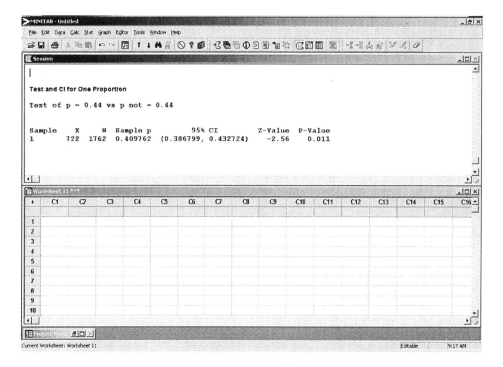

© 2006 Pearson Education, Inc., Upper Saddle River, NJ. All rights reserved. This material is protected under all copyright laws as they currently exist. No portion of this material may be reproduced, in any form or by any means, without permission in writing from the publisher.

Section 7.5

> **Example 4 (pg. 383)** Finding P-values for a Chi-Square Test

Once you have calculated the test statistic, χ^2, MINITAB can calculate the exact
P-value of the test for you. For Example 4 on page 383 of the text, $\chi^2 = 43.2$ and
there are 40 degrees of freedom. Click on **Calc → Probability distributions →
Chi-square.** Select **Cumulative Probability** with a **Noncentrality parameter**
of 0. Enter 40 **Degrees of Freedom.** Next, click on **Input Constant** and enter
the test statistic, 43.2. Click on **OK** and the output will be displayed in the
Session Window. Since you have found $P(\chi^2 < 43.2) = .6638$, you need to
subtract the probability from 1 to find the P-value. So, the P-value is 1 - .6638 =
.3362.

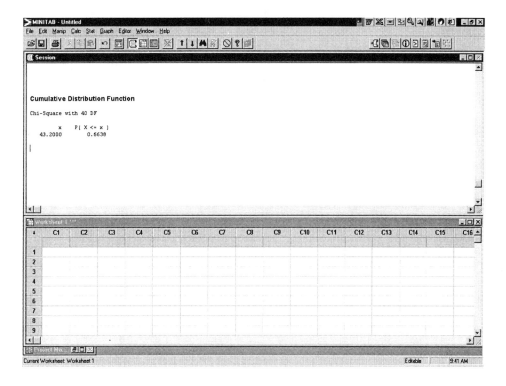

© 2006 Pearson Education, Inc., Upper Saddle River, NJ. All rights reserved. This material is protected under all copyright laws as they currently exist.
No portion of this material may be reproduced, in any form or by any means, without permission in writing from the publisher.

> **Technology Lab (pg. 399)** The Case of the Vanishing Women

4. Click on **Stat → Basic Statistics → 1-Proportion.** The data is given in a summarized form, so select **Summarized data.** Enter 100 for the **Number of trials.** Since 9 women were selected, the **Number of events** is 9. Click on **Options.** Enter .2914 for the **Test Proportion** because 29.14% of the original sample were women, and select "not equal" for the **Alternative.** Click on **Use test and interval based on normal distribution,** and then click on **OK** twice.

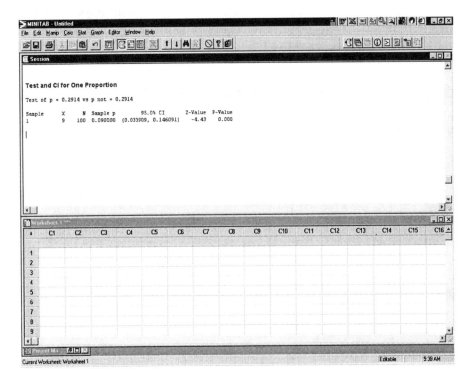

© 2006 Pearson Education, Inc., Upper Saddle River, NJ. All rights reserved. This material is protected under all copyright laws as they currently exist. No portion of this material may be reproduced, in any form or by any means, without permission in writing from the publisher.

Hypothesis Testing with Two Samples

CHAPTER

8

Section 8.1

▸ Exercise 19 (pg. 411) Time spent watching TV

Open worksheet **Ex8_1-19.mtp**, which is found in the **ch08** MINITAB folder. The 1981 data (Time A) is in C1 and the new data (Time B) is in C2. Notice that for both samples, n = 30. MINITAB does not have a 2-sample Z-test, but you can use a 2-sample t-test instead since the t distribution becomes very similar to the normal distribution as the sample size approaches 30. Click on **Stat→ Basic Statistics → 2-Sample t.** Select **Samples in different columns** and enter C1 for the **First** and C2 for the **Second** column.

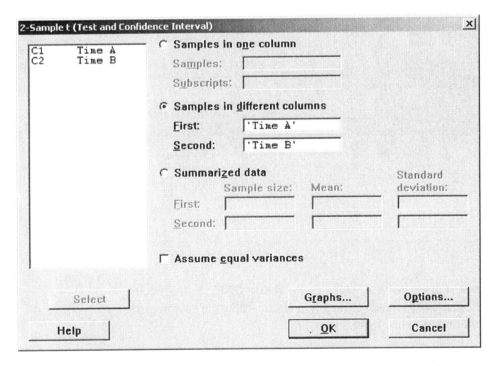

Click on **Options**, and then on the down arrow beside **Alternative** and select **greater than** since the sociologist claims that children spent more time watching TV in 1981 than they do today. Be sure that **Test difference** is 0.

© 2006 Pearson Education, Inc., Upper Saddle River, NJ. All rights reserved. This material is protected under all copyright laws as they currently exist. No portion of this material may be reproduced, in any form or by any means, without permission in writing from the publisher.

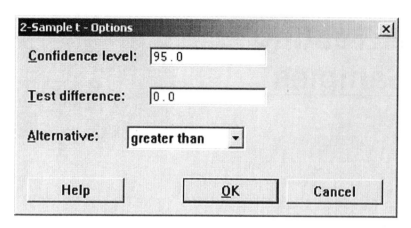

Click on **OK** twice and the results of the test should be displayed in the Session Window.

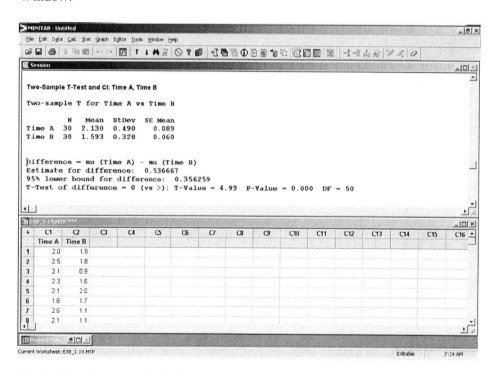

Notice that the test statistic is T = 4.99 with a P-value = .0000. Since this P-value is so small, you would Reject H_0 at any α level. Thus, the sociologist's claim is true – children watched more TV in 1981.

© 2006 Pearson Education, Inc., Upper Saddle River, NJ. All rights reserved. This material is protected under all copyright laws as they currently exist. No portion of this material may be reproduced, in any form or by any means, without permission in writing from the publisher.

▶ Exercise 21 (pg. 412) Difference between Washer Diameters

Open worksheet **Ex8_1-21.mtp**, which is found in the **ch08** MINITAB folder.
The diameters from the first method are in C1 and the diameters from the second
method are in C2. Notice that for both samples, n = 35. MINITAB does not
have a 2-sample Z-test, but you can use a 2-sample t-test instead since the t
distribution becomes very similar to the normal distribution as the sample size
gets larger than 30. Click on **Stat** → **Basic Statistics** → **2-Sample t.** Select
Samples in different columns and enter C1 for the **First** and C2 for the **Second**
column. Click on **Options**, and then on the down arrow beside **Alternative** and
select **not equal** since the production engineer claims there is no difference
between the two methods. Click on **OK** twice and the results of the test should be
displayed in the Session Window.

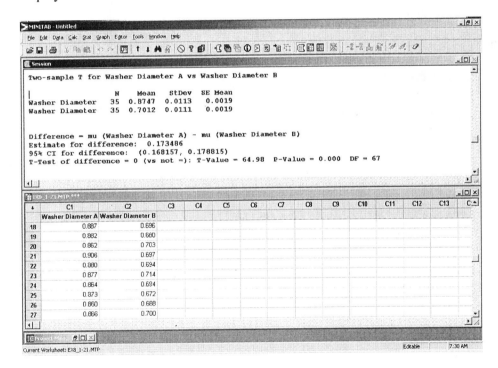

Since the P-value is so small, you would Reject H_0 at any α level.

© 2006 Pearson Education, Inc., Upper Saddle River, NJ. All rights reserved. This material is protected under all copyright laws as they currently exist.
No portion of this material may be reproduced, in any form or by any means, without permission in writing from the publisher.

> ▸ Exercise 22 (pg. 412)   Difference between Nut Diameters

Open worksheet **Ex8_1-22.mtp**, which is found in the **ch08** MINITAB folder. The diameters from the first method are in C1 and the diameters from the second method are in C2. Notice that for both samples, n = 40. MINITAB does not have a 2-sample Z-test, but you can use a 2-sample t-test instead since the t distribution becomes very similar to the normal distribution as the sample size gets larger than 30. Click on **Stat → Basic Statistics → 2-Sample t.** Select **Samples in different columns** and enter C1 for the **First** and C2 for the **Second** column. Click on **Options**, and then on the down arrow beside **Alternative** and select **not equal** since the production engineer claims there is no difference between the two methods. Click on **OK** twice and the results of the test should be displayed in the Session Window.

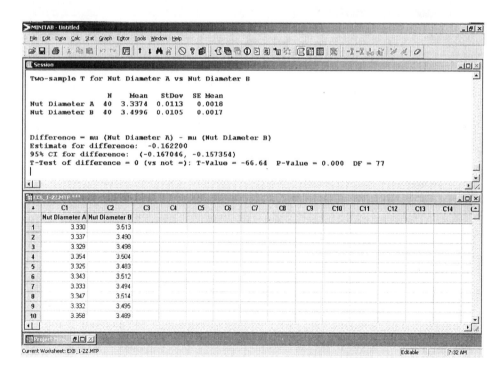

Since the P-value is so small, you would Reject H_0 at any α level.

© 2006 Pearson Education, Inc., Upper Saddle River, NJ. All rights reserved. This material is protected under all copyright laws as they currently exist. No portion of this material may be reproduced, in any form or by any means, without permission in writing from the publisher.

Section 8.2

> ▸ Example 1 (pg. 418) Snow Tire Performance

Consumer Reports tested stopping distances of 10 Firestone Winterfire tires and 12 Michelin Alpin tires when traveling on ice at 15 mph. The summarized data is shown on the left of page 418 in the text. Click on **Stat→ Basic Statistics → 2-Sample t.** Select **Summarized data** and enter the Winterfire data for the **First** sample and the Alpin data for the **Second** sample. Click on **Options**, and then on the down arrow beside **Alternative** and select **not equal** since you want to test whether the mean stopping distances are different.

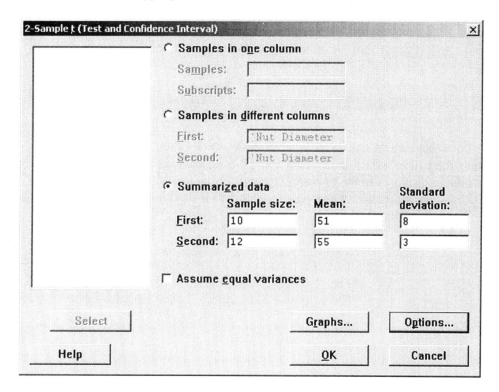

Click on **OK** twice and the results of the test should be displayed in the Session Window.

© 2006 Pearson Education, Inc., Upper Saddle River, NJ. All rights reserved. This material is protected under all copyright laws as they currently exist. No portion of this material may be reproduced, in any form or by any means, without permission in writing from the publisher.

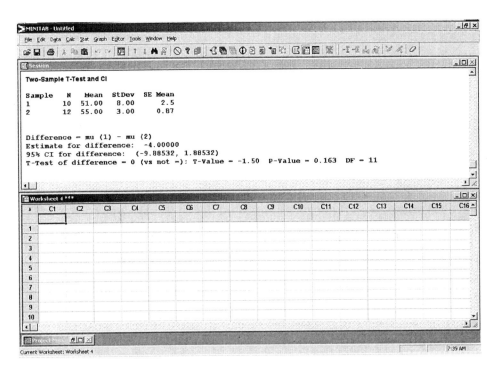

Notice that the test statistic is T= -1.5. Since the P-value = .163 and is greater than the α-level of .01, there is not enough evidence to conclude that the mean stopping distances of the tires are different. (Note that Minitab uses 11 degrees of freedom, rather than 9 degrees of freedom as is used in the textbook. The p-value will be slightly different.)

© 2006 Pearson Education, Inc., Upper Saddle River, NJ. All rights reserved. This material is protected under all copyright laws as they currently exist.
No portion of this material may be reproduced, in any form or by any means, without permission in writing from the publisher.

▸ Exercise 21 (pg. 422) Tensile Strength of Steel Bars

Open worksheet **Ex8_2-21.mtp**, which is found in the **ch08** MINITAB folder.
The New method data is in C1 and the Old method data is in C2. Click on **Stat
→ Basic Statistics → 2-Sample t.** Select **Samples in different columns** and
enter C1 for the **First** and C2 for the **Second** column. Select **Assume Equal
Variances,** since the problem tells you to assume the population variances are
equal. Click on **Options**, and then on the down arrow beside **Alternative** and
select **not equal** since you want to test if the new treatment makes a difference in
the tensile strength of steel bars. Click on **OK** twice and the results of the test
should be displayed in the Session Window.

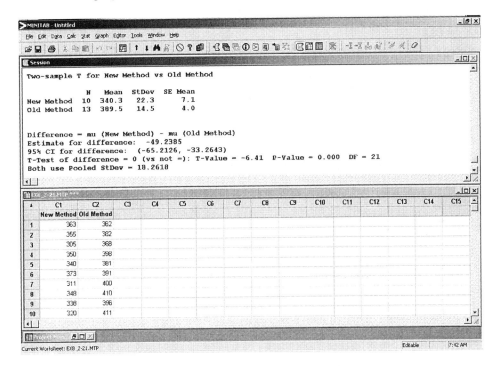

© 2006 Pearson Education, Inc., Upper Saddle River, NJ. All rights reserved. This material is protected under all copyright laws as they currently exist.
No portion of this material may be reproduced, in any form or by any means, without permission in writing from the publisher.

| ▸ Exercise 24 (pg. 423) | Comparing Teaching Methods

Open worksheet **Ex8_2-24.mtp**, which is found in the **ch08** MINITAB folder.
The Traditional Lab data is in C1 and the Interactive data is in C2. Click on **Stat**
→ **Basic Statistics** → **2-Sample t.** Select **Samples in different columns** and
enter C1 for the **First** and C2 for the **Second** column. Select **Assume Equal
Variances,** since the problem tells you to assume the population variances are
equal. Click on **Options**, and then on the down arrow beside **Alternative** and
select **less than** since you want to test if the students taught in a traditional lab
had lower science test scores than students taught with the interactive simulation
software. Click on **OK** twice and the results of the test should be displayed in the
Session Window.

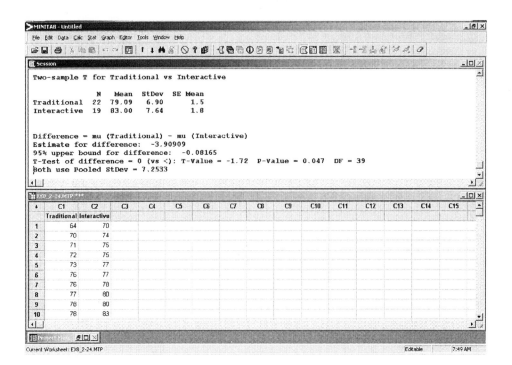

© 2006 Pearson Education, Inc., Upper Saddle River, NJ. All rights reserved. This material is protected under all copyright laws as they currently exist.
No portion of this material may be reproduced, in any form or by any means, without permission in writing from the publisher.

Section 8.3

▶ Example 2 (pg. 428) Golf Scores

Enter the data, found on page 428 of the textbook, into the MINITAB Data
Window. Put the Old Design data in C1 and the New Design data in C2. Click
on **Stat → Basic Statistics → Paired t.** Enter C1 for the **First Sample** and C2
for the **Second Sample.**

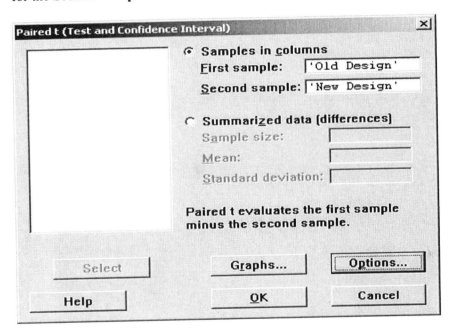

Click on **Options.** Enter 0 for **Test Mean** and select **greater than** as the
Alternative. Click on **OK** twice to display the results.

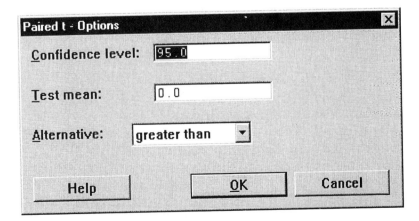

© 2006 Pearson Education, Inc., Upper Saddle River, NJ. All rights reserved. This material is protected under all copyright laws as they currently exist.
No portion of this material may be reproduced, in any form or by any means, without permission in writing from the publisher.

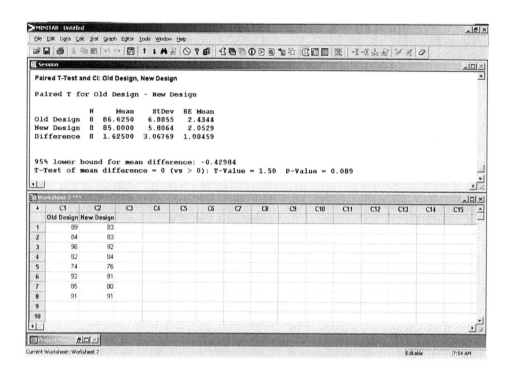

© 2006 Pearson Education, Inc., Upper Saddle River, NJ. All rights reserved. This material is protected under all copyright laws as they currently exist. No portion of this material may be reproduced, in any form or by any means, without permission in writing from the publisher.

▶ **Exercise 17 (pg. 432)** Verbal SAT Scores

Open worksheet **Ex8_3-17.mtp**, which is found in the **ch08** MINITAB folder. The scores on the first SAT are in C1 and the scores on the second SAT are in C2. Click on **Stat → Basic Statistics → Paired t.** Enter C1 for the **First Sample** and C2 for the **Second Sample.** Click on **Options.** Enter 0 for **Test Mean** and select **less than** as the **Alternative** because, if the scores have improved, then the difference (first SAT - second SAT) will be less than 0. Click on **OK** twice to display the results.

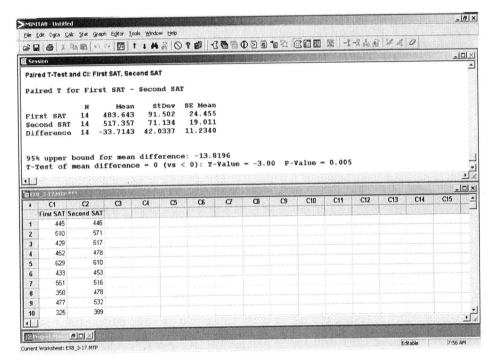

© 2006 Pearson Education, Inc., Upper Saddle River, NJ. All rights reserved. This material is protected under all copyright laws as they currently exist. No portion of this material may be reproduced, in any form or by any means, without permission in writing from the publisher.

▶ **Exercise 25 (pg. 435)** Does new drug reduce blood pressure?

Open worksheet **Ex8_3-25.mtp**, which is found in the **ch08** MINITAB folder.
The "before" blood pressures are in C1 and the "after" blood pressures are in C2.
Click on **Stat → Basic Statistics → Paired t.** Enter C1 for the **First Sample**
and C2 for the **Second Sample.** Click on **Options.** Enter 0 for **Test Mean** and
select **greater than** as the **Alternative** because if the new drug reduces blood
pressure, then the difference (before - after) will be greater than 0. Click on **OK**
twice to display the results.

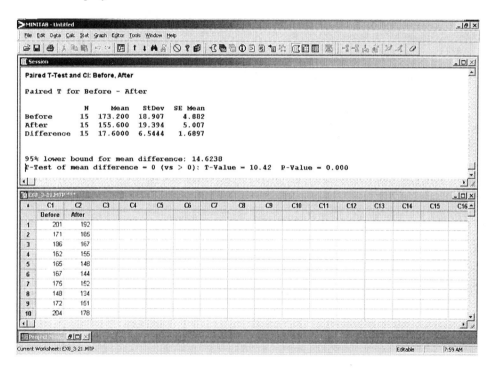

Since the P-value is so small, you should Reject the null hypothesis. Thus, the
new drug appears to reduce blood pressure.

© 2006 Pearson Education, Inc., Upper Saddle River, NJ. All rights reserved. This material is protected under all copyright laws as they currently exist.
No portion of this material may be reproduced, in any form or by any means, without permission in writing from the publisher.

Section 8.4

> ▶ **Example 1 (pg. 439)** Difference between male and female
> Internet Users

In a study of 200 female and 250 male Internet users, 30% of the females and 38% of the males plan to shop on-line. This is a summary of the results of the study. To test if there is a difference in the proportion of male and female users who plan to shop on-line, click on **Stat → Basic Statistics → 2 Proportions.** Select **Summarized Data** and use the data for Females as the **First sample.** Enter 200 **Trials** and 60 **Events** (200 x .30). Use the data for Males as the **Second sample.** Enter 250 **Trials** and 95 **Events** (250 x .38).

2 Proportions (Test and Confidence Interval) ☒

    ○ **Samples in one column**

      Samples: [ ]

      Subscripts: [ ]

    ○ **Samples in different columns**

      First: [ ]

      Second: [ ]

    ⊙ **Summarized data**

	Trials:	Events:
First:	200	60
Second:	250	95

Select   Options...

Help   OK   Cancel

Click on **Options.** Enter 0 for **Test mean**, and select **not equal** as the **Alternative** since you want to test if there is a difference between the proportion of male and female shoppers. Next click on **Use pooled estimate of p for test.**

© 2006 Pearson Education, Inc., Upper Saddle River, NJ. All rights reserved. This material is protected under all copyright laws as they currently exist. No portion of this material may be reproduced, in any form or by any means, without permission in writing from the publisher.

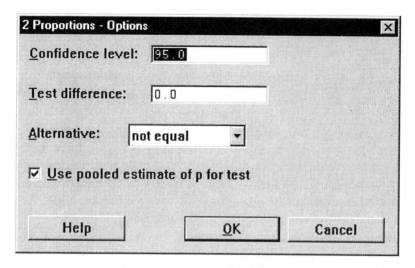

Click on **OK** twice to display the results in the Session Window.

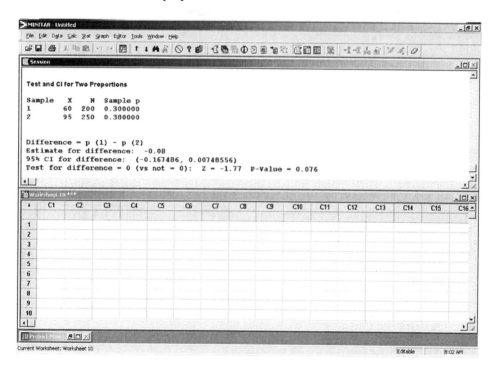

Since the P-value is smaller than α, you should Reject the null hypothesis.

© 2006 Pearson Education, Inc., Upper Saddle River, NJ. All rights reserved. This material is protected under all copyright laws as they currently exist. No portion of this material may be reproduced, in any form or by any means, without permission in writing from the publisher.

▶ **Exercise 7 (pg. 441)** Alternative Medicine Usage

To test if there is a difference in the proportion of adults who used alternative medicine in 1991 and the proportion of adults who use it now, click on **Stat→ Basic Statistics → 2 Proportions.** Select **Summarized Data** and use the data for 1991 as the **First sample.** Enter 1539 **Trials** and 520 **Events.** Use the recent study data as the **Second sample.** Enter 2055 **Trials** and 865 **Events.** Click on **Options.** Enter 0 for **Test mean**, and select **not equal** as the **Alternative** since you want to test if there is a difference between the proportion of users in 1991 and the present. Next click on **Use pooled estimate of p for test.**
Click on **OK** twice to display the results in the Session Window.

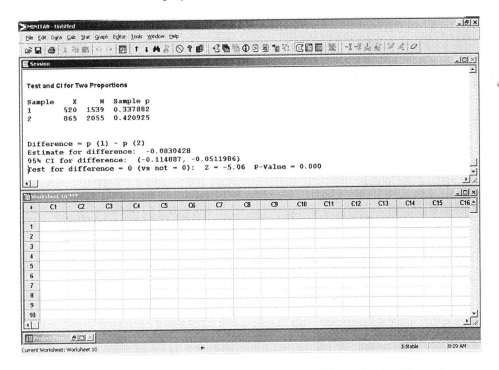

With such a small P-value, you should Reject the null hypothesis. Thus, the proportion of adults using alternative medicines has changed since 1991.

© 2006 Pearson Education, Inc., Upper Saddle River, NJ. All rights reserved. This material is protected under all copyright laws as they currently exist. No portion of this material may be reproduced, in any form or by any means, without permission in writing from the publisher.

▸ Exercise 12 (pg. 442) Fewer Smokers in California?

To test if the proportion of adult smokers in California is lower than the proportion of adult smokers in Oregon, click on **Stat → Basic Statistics → 2 Proportions.** Select **Summarized Data** and use the data for California as the **First sample**. Enter 1500 **Trials** and 246 **Events** (1500 x .164). Use the Oregon data as the **Second sample**. Enter 1000 **Trials** and 266 **Events** (1000 x .266). Click on **Options**. Enter 0 for **Test mean**, and select **less than** as the **Alternative** since you want to test if the proportion of smokers in California is lower than the proportion in Oregon. Next click on **Use pooled estimate of p for test.**
Click on **OK** twice to display the results in the Session Window.

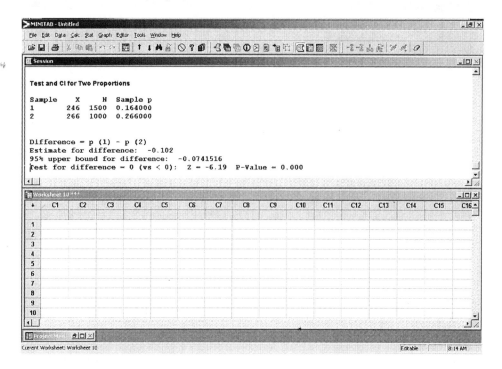

© 2006 Pearson Education, Inc., Upper Saddle River, NJ. All rights reserved. This material is protected under all copyright laws as they currently exist. No portion of this material may be reproduced, in any form or by any means, without permission in writing from the publisher.

▶ Technology Lab (pg. 453) Tails Over Heads

1. Click on **Stat → Basic Statistics → 1 Proportion.** Select **Summarized Data** and enter 11902 **Trials** and 5772 **Events**. Click on **Options.** Enter .5 for **Test proportion**, and select **not equal** as the **Alternative** since you want to test if the probability is .5 or not. Next click on **Use test and interval based on normal distribution.** Click on **OK** twice to display the results in the Session Window.

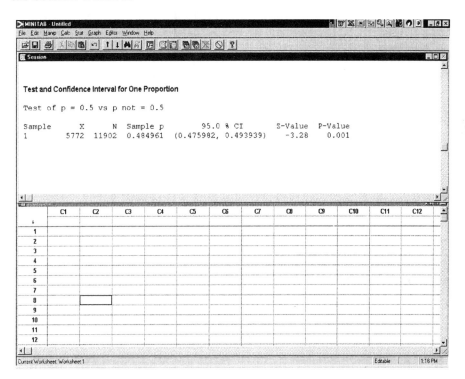

3. To repeat the simulation, click on **Calc → Random data → Binomial.** You want to **Generate** 500 **rows of data** and **Store In Column** C1. The **Number of trials** is 11902 and the **Probability of success** is .5. Click on **OK** and C1 should have 500 rows of data in it. To draw the histogram, click on **Graph → Histogram → Simple.** Enter C1 for the **Graph variable.** Click on **OK** to view the histogram.

© 2006 Pearson Education, Inc., Upper Saddle River, NJ. All rights reserved. This material is protected under all copyright laws as they currently exist.
No portion of this material may be reproduced, in any form or by any means, without permission in writing from the publisher.

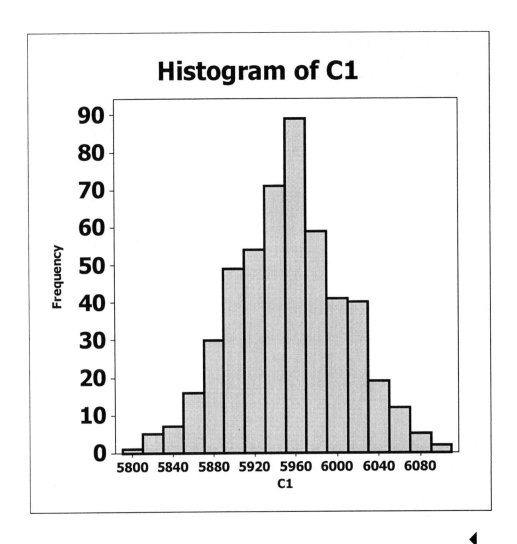

© 2006 Pearson Education, Inc., Upper Saddle River, NJ. All rights reserved. This material is protected under all copyright laws as they currently exist.
No portion of this material may be reproduced, in any form or by any means, without permission in writing from the publisher.

Correlation and Regression

Section 9.1

▶ | Example 3 (pg. 460) | Constructing a Scatter Plot

Open worksheet **OldFaithful,** which is found in the **ch09** MINITAB folder. The duration (in minutes) of several of Old Faithful's eruptions should be in C1, and the time (in minutes) until the next eruption should be in C2. Notice that Duration is the x-variable and Time is the y-variable. To plot the data, click on **Graph → Scatterplot → Simple.** On the input screen, enter C2 for the **Y variable** and C1 for the **X variable.**

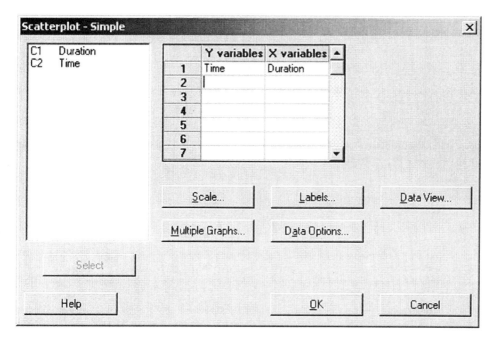

Next, click on **Labels** and enter a title for the plot. Click on OK to view the plot produced using Minitab default settings.

© 2006 Pearson Education, Inc., Upper Saddle River, NJ. All rights reserved. This material is protected under all copyright laws as they currently exist. No portion of this material may be reproduced, in any form or by any means, without permission in writing from the publisher.

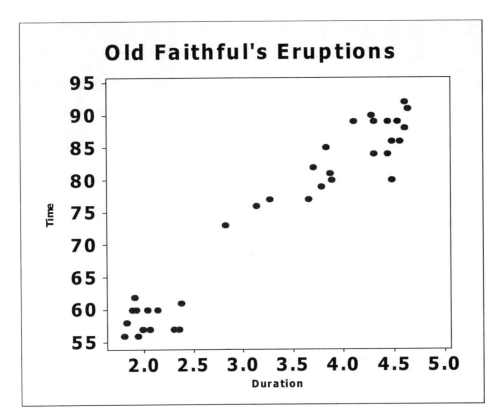

Click on **OK** twice to view the scatter plot. This plot would be better if both axes
started at 0. To make this change, right-click on the X-axis scale and select "Edit
X-scale". Enter 0 : 5 / .5 for **Position of ticks**. Click on **OK**. Next right-click
on the Y-axis scale and select "Edit Y-scale". Enter 0 : 100 / 10 for **Position of
ticks**. Click on **OK** to view the completed plot.

© 2006 Pearson Education, Inc., Upper Saddle River, NJ. All rights reserved. This material is protected under all copyright laws as they currently exist.
No portion of this material may be reproduced, in any form or by any means, without permission in writing from the publisher.

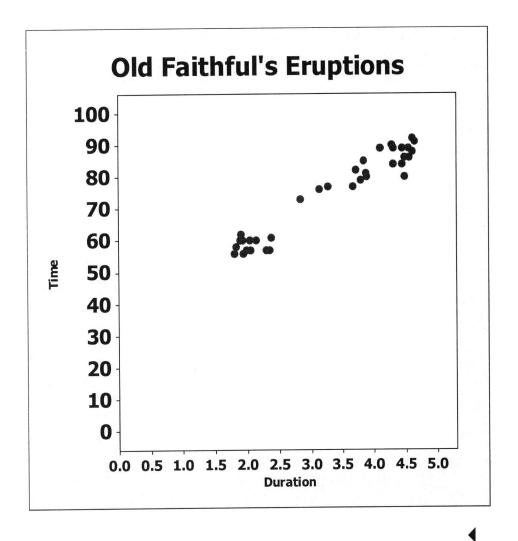

© 2006 Pearson Education, Inc., Upper Saddle River, NJ. All rights reserved. This material is protected under all copyright laws as they currently exist. No portion of this material may be reproduced, in any form or by any means, without permission in writing from the publisher.

▶ Example 5 (pg. 463) Finding the Correlation Coefficient

Open worksheet **OldFaithful,** which is found in the **ch09** MINITAB folder. The
duration (in minutes) of several of Old Faithful's eruptions should be in C1, and
the time (in minutes) until the next eruption should be in C2. Notice that
Duration is the x-variable and Time is the y-variable. To find the correlation
coefficient, click on **Stat → Basics Statistics → Correlation.** On the input
screen, select both C1 and C2 for **Variables**, by double-clicking on each one.

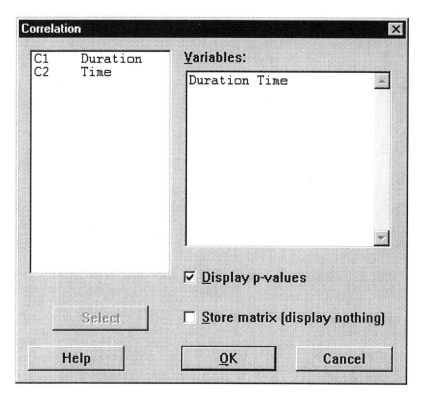

Click on **OK** and the Correlation Coefficient will be displayed in the Session
Window.

© 2006 Pearson Education, Inc., Upper Saddle River, NJ. All rights reserved. This material is protected under all copyright laws as they currently exist.
No portion of this material may be reproduced, in any form or by any means, without permission in writing from the publisher.

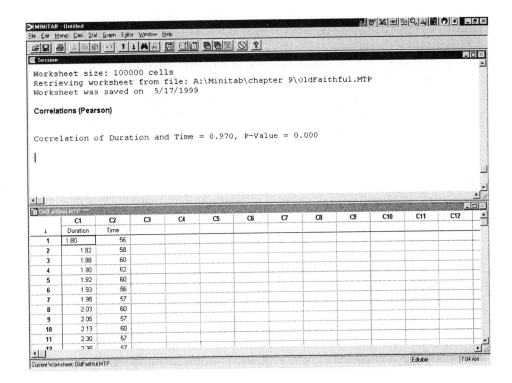

© 2006 Pearson Education, Inc., Upper Saddle River, NJ. All rights reserved. This material is protected under all copyright laws as they currently exist.
No portion of this material may be reproduced, in any form or by any means, without permission in writing from the publisher.

> ▸ **Exercise 17 (pg. 470)** Plot of Study Hours vs. Test Scores

Open worksheet **Ex9_1-17,** which is found in the **ch09** MINITAB folder. The
hours spent studying should be in C1, and the test scores should be in C2. Notice
that "Hours study" is the x-variable and "Test Scores" is the y-variable. To plot
the data, click on **Graph → Scatterplot → Simple.** On the input screen, enter
C2 for the **Y variable** and C1 for the **X variable.** Next, click on **Labels** and
enter a title for the plot. Click on OK to view the plot produced using Minitab
default settings. Edit the plot to set the tick mark positions so that both axes
begin at zero. One possibility is to enter the tick positions for the **X variable** as
0:8/1 (0 to 8 in steps of 1) and for the **Y variable** as 0:100/10 (0 to 100 in steps
of 10). Click on **OK** twice to view the scatter plot.

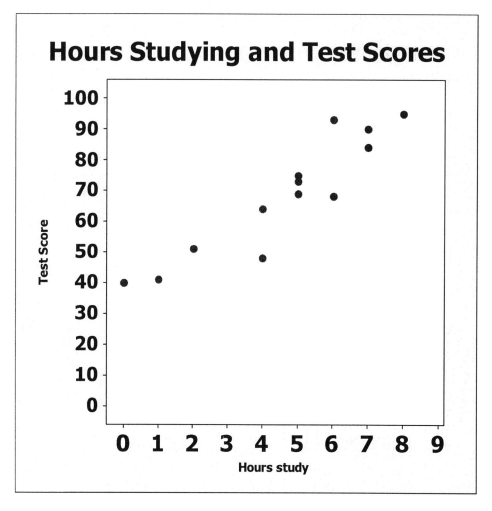

Now, to find the correlation coefficient, click on **Stat→ Basics Statistics →
Correlation.** On the input screen, select both C1 and C2 for **Variables**, by

© 2006 Pearson Education, Inc., Upper Saddle River, NJ. All rights reserved. This material is protected under all copyright laws as they currently exist.
No portion of this material may be reproduced, in any form or by any means, without permission in writing from the publisher.

double-clicking on each one. Click on **OK** and the output should be in the
Session Window.

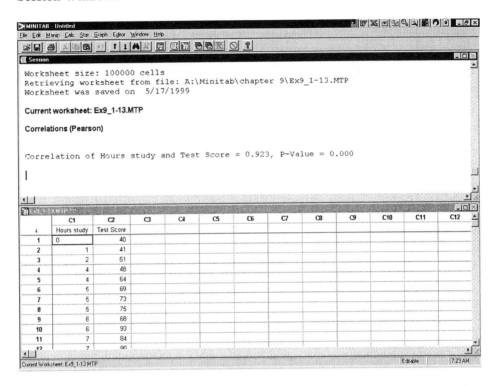

© 2006 Pearson Education, Inc., Upper Saddle River, NJ. All rights reserved. This material is protected under all copyright laws as they currently exist.
No portion of this material may be reproduced, in any form or by any means, without permission in writing from the publisher.

Section 9.2

▶ Example 2 (pg. 476) Finding a Regression Equation

Open worksheet **OldFaithful,** which is found in the **ch09** MINITAB folder. The
duration (in minutes) of several of Old Faithful's eruptions should be in C1, and
the time (in minutes) until the next eruption should be in C2. Notice that
Duration is the x-variable and Time is the y-variable. To find the regression
equation, click on **Stat → Regression → Regression.** Enter C2 for the
Response variable, and C1 as the **Predictor.**

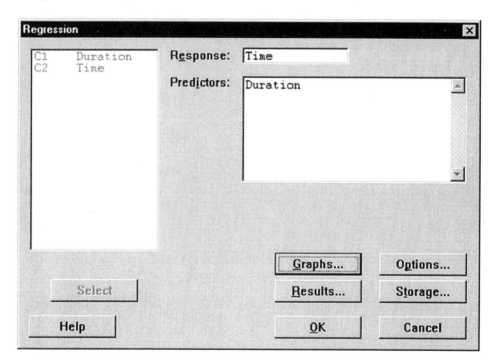

Click on **Results.** Select **Regression equation, table of coefficients, s, R-squared, and basic analysis of variance.**

© 2006 Pearson Education, Inc., Upper Saddle River, NJ. All rights reserved. This material is protected under all copyright laws as they currently exist.
No portion of this material may be reproduced, in any form or by any means, without permission in writing from the publisher.

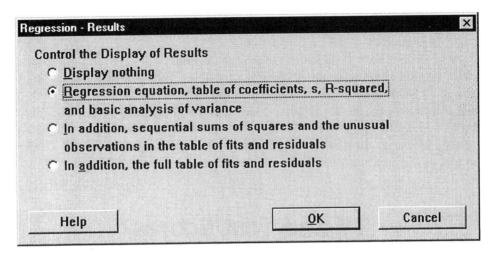

Click on **OK** twice to view the output in the Session Window.

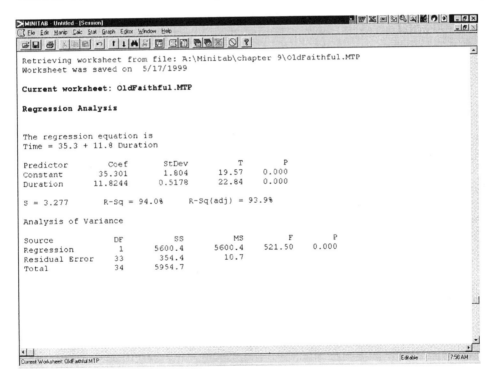

Notice that the regression equation is Time = 35.3 + 11.8 * Duration.

© 2006 Pearson Education, Inc., Upper Saddle River, NJ. All rights reserved. This material is protected under all copyright laws as they currently exist. No portion of this material may be reproduced, in any form or by any means, without permission in writing from the publisher.

▸ Exercise 16 (pg. 479)   TV vs. Test scores

Open worksheet **Ex9_2-16,** which is found in the **ch09** MINITAB folder. Hours
of TV is in C1 and Test is in C2. First plot the data. To plot the data, click on
Graph → Scatterplot → Simple. On the input screen, enter C2 for the **Y
variable** and C1 for the **X variable.** Next, click on **Labels** and enter a title for
the plot. Click on OK to view the plot produced using Minitab default settings.
Edit the plot to set the tick mark positions so that both axes begin at zero. Click
on **OK** to view the scatter plot.

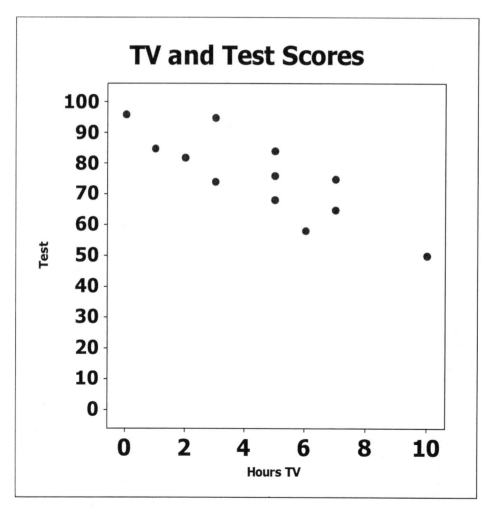

To find the regression equation, click on **Stat → Regression → Regression.**
Enter C2 for the **Response** variable, and C1 as the **Predictor.** Click on **Results.**
Select **Regression equation, table of coefficients, s, R-squared, and basic
analysis of variance.** Click on **OK** twice.

© 2006 Pearson Education, Inc., Upper Saddle River, NJ. All rights reserved. This material is protected under all copyright laws as they currently exist.
No portion of this material may be reproduced, in any form or by any means, without permission in writing from the publisher.

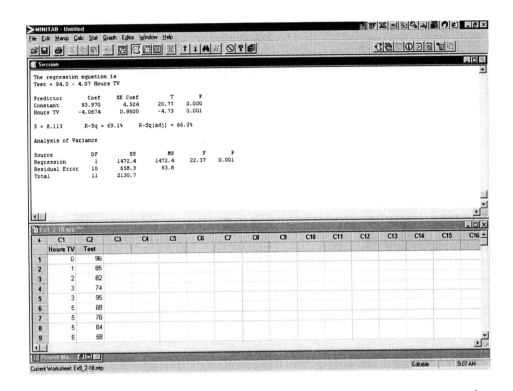

© 2006 Pearson Education, Inc., Upper Saddle River, NJ. All rights reserved. This material is protected under all copyright laws as they currently exist. No portion of this material may be reproduced, in any form or by any means, without permission in writing from the publisher.

Section 9.3

> ▸ Example 2 (pg. 487) Finding the Standard Error and the Coefficient of Determination

Enter the first two columns of data (found on page 487 of the textbook) into the MINITAB Data Window. Enter the x's into C1 and name it Expenses. Enter the y's into C2 and name it Sales. Both the coefficient of determination and the standard error of the estimate are part of the regression output. To find the regression equation, click on **Stat → Regression → Regression.** Enter C2 for the **Response** variable, and C1 as the **Predictor.** Click on **Results.** Select **Regression equation, table of coefficients, s, R-squared, and basic analysis of variance.** Click on **OK** twice.

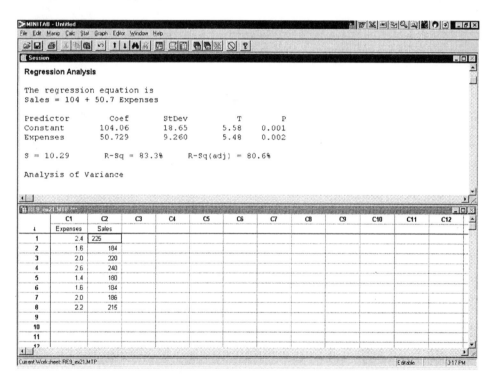

Notice that the standard error of the estimate is S = 10.29 and the coefficient of determination is R-Sq = 83.3%.

◀

© 2006 Pearson Education, Inc., Upper Saddle River, NJ. All rights reserved. This material is protected under all copyright laws as they currently exist. No portion of this material may be reproduced, in any form or by any means, without permission in writing from the publisher.

> **Example 3 (pg. 489)**   Constructing a Prediction Interval

Enter the first two columns of data (found on page 487 of the textbook) into the MINITAB Data Window. Enter the x's into C1 and name it Expenses. Enter the y's into C2 and name it Sales. To find the regression equation, click on **Stat→ Regression → Regression.** Enter C2 for the **Response** variable, and C1 as the **Predictor.** Now, to find both the point estimate and the prediction interval, click on **Options. (Fit Intercept** is selected by default.) Next enter the advertising expenditure. Although the amount given in this problem is $2100, the data is stored in thousands of dollars. So enter 2.1 for **Prediction interval for new observations.** Enter 95 for the **Confidence level** and select **Prediction limits.**

Click on **OK.** Click on **Results.** If you would like to see the other regression output, then select **Regression equation, table of coefficients, s, R-squared, and basic analysis of variance.** If you only want to see the prediction interval, then select **Display nothing.** Click on **OK** twice and view the output in the Session Window.

© 2006 Pearson Education, Inc., Upper Saddle River, NJ. All rights reserved. This material is protected under all copyright laws as they currently exist. No portion of this material may be reproduced, in any form or by any means, without permission in writing from the publisher.

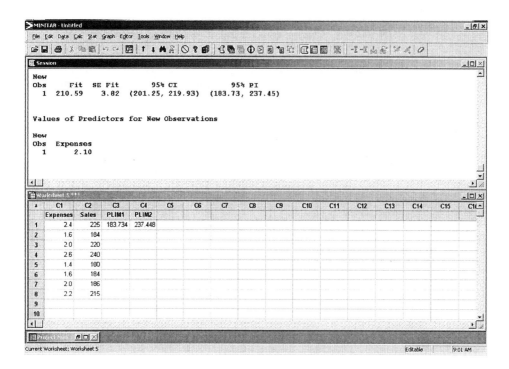

Notice that the predicted value, 210.59, is listed below **Fit** and the prediction interval, (183.73, 237.45), is listed below **95% PI.**

© 2006 Pearson Education, Inc., Upper Saddle River, NJ. All rights reserved. This material is protected under all copyright laws as they currently exist. No portion of this material may be reproduced, in any form or by any means, without permission in writing from the publisher.

> ▸ Exercise 11 (pg. 491) and Exercise 19 (pg. 492) Retail space
> vs. Sales

Open worksheet **Ex9_3-11,** which is found in the **ch09** MINITAB folder. Square
footage is in C1 and Sales is in C2. For these two problems, you need to find the
coefficient of determination, the standard error of the estimate, and a 90%
prediction interval when square footage is 4.5 billion. This can be accomplished
all at once in MINITAB. Click on **Stat → Regression → Regression.** Enter C2
for the **Response** variable, and C1 as the **Predictor.** Now, to find both the point
estimate and the prediction interval, click on **Options.** Select **Fit Intercept** by
clicking on it. Next enter the square footage. So enter 4.5 for **Prediction
interval for new observations.** Enter 90 for the **Confidence level** and select
Prediction limits. Click on **OK.** Click on **Results.** Since you would like to see
the other regression output, then select **Regression equation, table of
coefficients, s, R-squared, and basic analysis of variance.** Click on **OK** twice
and view the output in the Session Window.

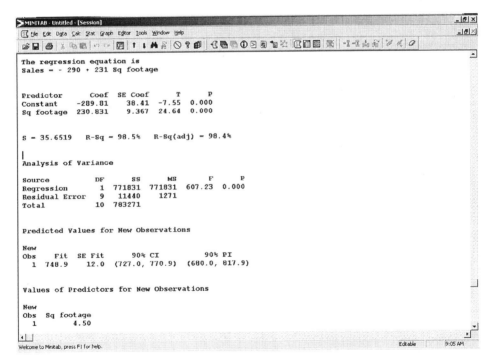

© 2006 Pearson Education, Inc., Upper Saddle River, NJ. All rights reserved. This material is protected under all copyright laws as they currently exist.
No portion of this material may be reproduced, in any form or by any means, without permission in writing from the publisher.

Section 9.4

> ▸ Example 1 (pg. 494) Finding a Multiple Regression Equation

Open worksheet **Salary,** which is found in the **ch09** MINITAB folder.
Salary should be in C1, Employment in C2, Experience in C3, and Education in
C4. Click on **Stat** → **Regression** → **Regression.** Enter C1 for the **Response**
variable, and enter C2, C3, and C4 as the **Predictors.** Click on **Results.** Since
you would like to see the other regression output, then select **Regression
equation, table of coefficients, s, R-squared, and basic analysis of variance.**
Click on **OK** twice and view the output in the Session Window.

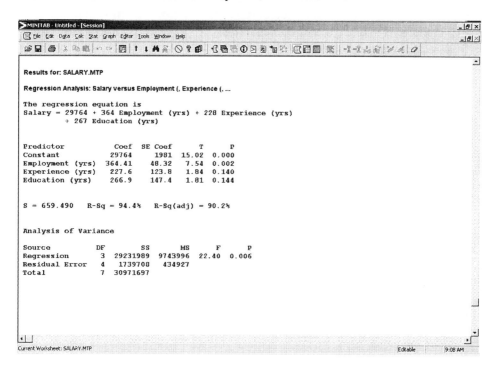

The regression equation is listed at the beginning of the output. Notice that the
regression equation uses the values listed below **Coef.** These values are the
coefficients of the multiple regression equation.

© 2006 Pearson Education, Inc., Upper Saddle River, NJ. All rights reserved. This material is protected under all copyright laws as they currently exist.
No portion of this material may be reproduced, in any form or by any means, without permission in writing from the publisher.

▶ Exercise 5 (pg. 498) Finding a Multiple Regression Equation

Open worksheet **Ex9_4-5,** which is found in the **ch09** MINITAB folder.
Sales should be in C1, Square footage in C2, and Number of shopping centers in
C3. Click on **Stat → Regression → Regression.** Enter C1 for the **Response**
variable, and enter C2 and C3 as the **Predictors.** Click on **Results.** Since you
would like to see the other regression output, then select **Regression equation,
table of coefficients, s, R-squared, and basic analysis of variance.** Click on
OK twice and view the output in the Session Window.

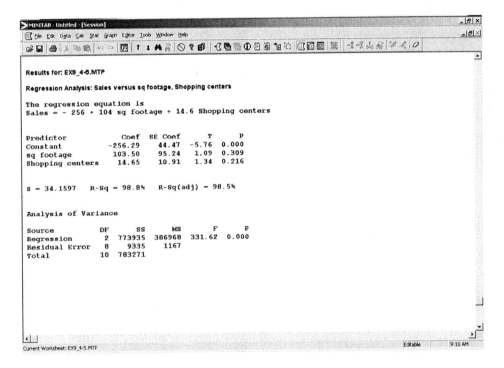

© 2006 Pearson Education, Inc., Upper Saddle River, NJ. All rights reserved. This material is protected under all copyright laws as they currently exist.
No portion of this material may be reproduced, in any form or by any means, without permission in writing from the publisher.

> ▶ Technology Lab (pg. 507) Sugar, Fat, and Carbohydrates

Open worksheet **Tech9,** which is found in the **ch09** MINITAB folder. Cereal Name is in C1, Calories is in C2, Sugar is in C3, Fat is in C4, and Carbohydrates is in C5.

1.   Click on **Graph → Scatterplot → Simple.** On the input screen, enter C2 for the **X variable** and C3 for the **Y variable.** Click on **Labels** and enter a title. Click on **OK.** Repeat these steps for parts b - f, changing the variables as directed in each part.

3.   Click on **Stat → Basics Statistics → Correlation.** On the input screen, select both C2 and C3 for **Variables**, by double-clicking on each one. Click on **OK** and the output should be in the Session Window. Repeat these steps for each pair of variables listed in question 1, parts b - f.

4.   (Do both 4 & 5 at one time here). Click on **Stat → Regression → Regression.** Enter C3 for the **Response** variable, and enter C2 as the **Predictor.** Next, to predict the sugar content of 1 cup of cereal with a calorie content of 120 kcal, click on **Options.** Select **Fit Intercept** by clicking on it. Next enter the calorie content. So enter 120 for **Prediction interval for new observations.** Enter 95 for the **Confidence level** and select **Prediction limits.** Click on **OK.** Next, click on **Results.** Since you would like to see the other regression output, select **Regression equation, table of coefficients, s, R-squared, and basic analysis of variance.** Click on **OK** twice and view the output in the Session Window. Repeat these steps using C5 for the **Response** variable.

5.   (Do both 6 & 7 at one time here). Click on **Stat → Regression → Regression.** Enter C2 for the **Response** variable, and enter C3, C4, and C5 as the **Predictors.** Next, click on **Results.** Since you would like to see the other regression output, then select **Regression equation, table of coefficients, s, R-squared, and basic analysis of variance.** Click on **OK** twice and view the output in the Session Window. For part b, repeat these steps using C3 and C5 for the **Predictors**. Next, to predict the calorie content of 1 cup of cereal with 10g of sugar and 25g of carbohydrates, click on **Options.** Select **Fit Intercept** by clicking on it. Next enter the sugar and carbohydrate contents. To enter both of these, type in a 10 (for the sugar), leave a space, and then type in a 25 (for the carbohydrate) for **Prediction interval for new observations.** Click on **OK.** Next, click on **Results.** Since you would like to see the other regression output, then select **Regression equation, table of coefficients, s, R-squared, and basic analysis of variance.** Click on **OK** twice and view the output in the Session Window.

◀

© 2006 Pearson Education, Inc., Upper Saddle River, NJ. All rights reserved. This material is protected under all copyright laws as they currently exist.
No portion of this material may be reproduced, in any form or by any means, without permission in writing from the publisher.

Chi-Square Tests and the F-Distribution

CHAPTER 10

Section 10.1

▶ Example 3 (pg. 514)   The Chi-Square Goodness-of-Fit Test

Enter the data into the MINITAB Data Window. Enter the Responses into C1 and name it Response. Enter the frequencies into C2 and name it Observed. Enter the distribution (from the null hypothesis) into C3 and name it Distribution. These values should be proportions, not percentages. Thus, 61% should be entered as .61.

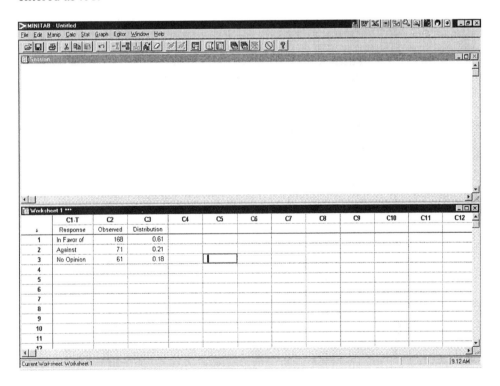

To calculate the expected frequencies, you will multiply the distribution times the sample size, which is 300 in this example. Click on **Calc→ Calculator.** You will **Store the result in** C4, and calculate the **Expression** C3*300. Click on **OK.** Name C4 Expected since it now contains the expected frequencies.

© 2006 Pearson Education, Inc., Upper Saddle River, NJ. All rights reserved. This material is protected under all copyright laws as they currently exist.
No portion of this material may be reproduced, in any form or by any means, without permission in writing from the publisher.

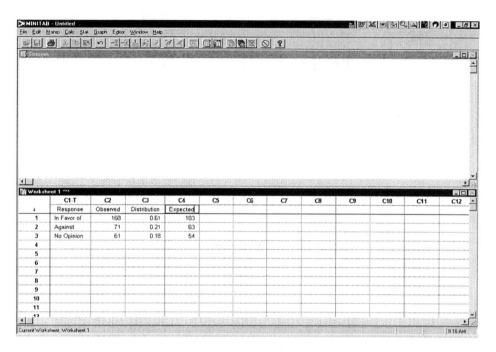

Next, calculate the chi-square test statistic, $(O - E)^2 / E$. Click on **Calc → Calculator.** You will **Store the result in** C5, and calculate the **Expression** (C2 - C4)**2 / C4. Click on **OK** and C5 should contain the calculated values.

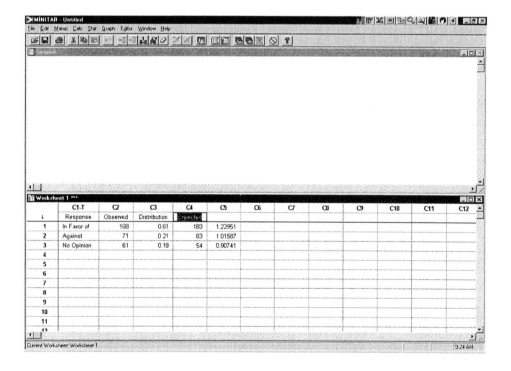

© 2006 Pearson Education, Inc., Upper Saddle River, NJ. All rights reserved. This material is protected under all copyright laws as they currently exist. No portion of this material may be reproduced, in any form or by any means, without permission in writing from the publisher.

Now, just add up the values in C5 and the sum is the test statistic. Click on **Calc** → **Column Statistics.** Select **Sum** and enter C5 for the **Input Variable.** Click on **OK** and the Chi-Square test statistic will be displayed in the Session Window. In this example, the test statistic is 3.1528. Next, calculate the P-value to help you decide if you should reject the null hypothesis. Click on **Calc** → **Probability Distributions** → **Chi-square.** Select **Cumulative Probability** and enter 2 **Degrees of Freedom.** Enter the value of the test statistic, 3.1528, for the **Input Constant.** Click on **OK** and P(X ≤ 3.1528) will be in the Session Window.

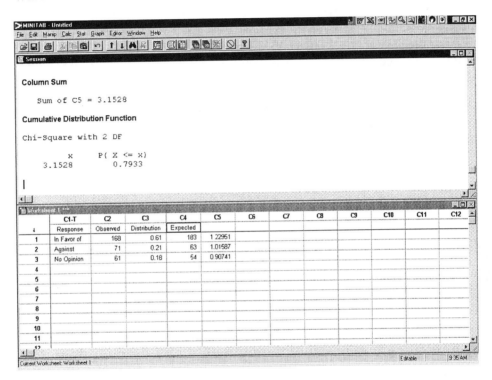

The P(X ≤ 3.1528) is .7933. The P-value is P(X ≥ 3.1528), which is 1 - P(X ≤ 3.1528). This value is 1 - .7933 = .2067. Since this P-value is larger than α = .05, you should not reject the null hypothesis.

© 2006 Pearson Education, Inc., Upper Saddle River, NJ. All rights reserved. This material is protected under all copyright laws as they currently exist. No portion of this material may be reproduced, in any form or by any means, without permission in writing from the publisher.

> ▶ Exercise 13 (pg. 518)   Roadside Hazard Crash Deaths

Enter the data into the MINITAB Data Window. Enter the Objects into C1 and name it Object. Enter the frequencies into C2 and name it Observed. Enter the distribution into C3 and name it Distribution. (These values should be entered as proportions, and not percentages.) To calculate the expected frequencies, you will multiply the distribution times the sample size, which is 691 in this example. The sample size can be found by adding up the frequencies. (To do this in MINITAB, click on **Calc → Column Statistics.** Select **Sum** and enter C2 for the **Input Variable.**) Click on **Calc → Calculator.** You will **Store the result in** C4, and calculate the **Expression** C3*691. Click on **OK.** Name C4 Expected since it now contains the expected frequencies. Next, calculate the chi-square test statistic, $(O - E)^2 / E$. Click on **Calc → Calculator.** You will **Store the result in** C5, and calculate the **Expression** (C2 - C4)**2 / C4. Click on **OK** and C5 should contain the calculated values.

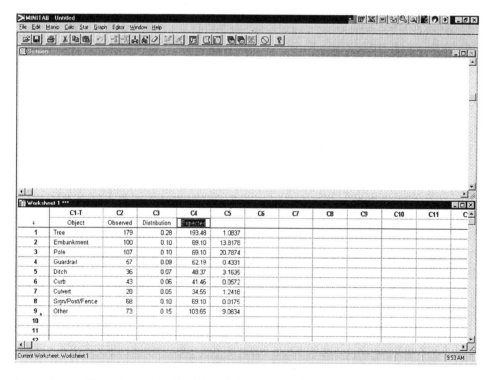

Now, just add up the values in C5 and the sum is the test statistic. Click on **Calc → Column Statistics.** Select **Sum** and enter C5 for the **Input Variable**. Click on **OK** and the Chi-Square test statistic will be displayed in the Session Window. In this example, the test statistic is 49.665.

© 2006 Pearson Education, Inc., Upper Saddle River, NJ. All rights reserved. This material is protected under all copyright laws as they currently exist. No portion of this material may be reproduced, in any form or by any means, without permission in writing from the publisher.

Next, calculate the P-value to help you decide if you should reject the null hypothesis. Click on **Calc → Probability Distributions → Chi-square.** Select **Cumulative Probability** and enter 8 **Degrees of Freedom.** Enter the value of the test statistic, 49.665, for the **Input Constant.** When you click on **OK** , the $P(X \leq 49.665)$ will be in the Session Window. The P-value is $P(X \geq 49.665) = 1 - P(X \leq 49.665) = 1 - 1 = 0$. Since this P-value is so small, you would reject the null hypothesis at any α-level.

◀

© 2006 Pearson Education, Inc., Upper Saddle River, NJ. All rights reserved. This material is protected under all copyright laws as they currently exist. No portion of this material may be reproduced, in any form or by any means, without permission in writing from the publisher.

Section 10.2

> ▸ **Example 3 (pg. 526)**   Chi-Square Independence Test

Enter the data into the MINITAB Data Window. First label the columns: use Gender for C1, "0-1" for C2, … "6-7" for C5. Now enter the data into the appropriate columns. Do not enter any totals.

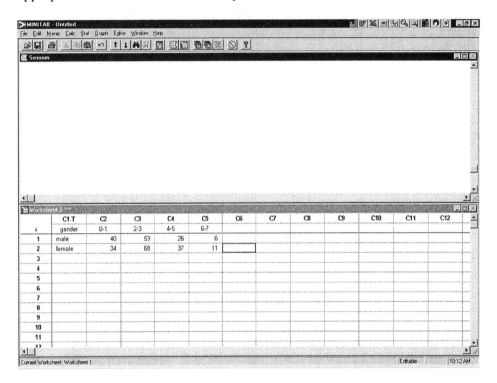

To perform the chi-square independence test, click on **Stat → Tables → Chi-square Test.** On the input screen, select C2 - C5 for the **Columns containing the table.** Click on **OK** and the test results will be displayed in the Session Window.

© 2006 Pearson Education, Inc., Upper Saddle River, NJ. All rights reserved. This material is protected under all copyright laws as they currently exist.
No portion of this material may be reproduced, in any form or by any means, without permission in writing from the publisher.

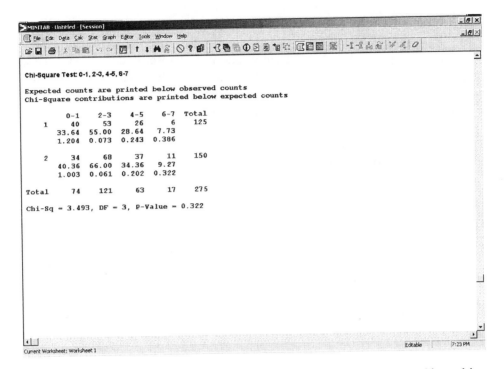

Notice that the test statistic is Chi-Sq = 3.493 and the P-value = .322. Since this
P-value is larger than α = .05, you should not reject the null hypothesis. Thus,
there is not enough evidence to conclude that the number of days per week spent
exercising is related to gender.

© 2006 Pearson Education, Inc., Upper Saddle River, NJ. All rights reserved. This material is protected under all copyright laws as they currently exist.
No portion of this material may be reproduced, in any form or by any means, without permission in writing from the publisher.

▸ Exercise 13 (pg. 529) Should the drug be used as treatment?

Enter the data into the MINITAB Data Window. Enter Result data into C1, Drug
data into C2 and Placebo data into C3. To perform the chi-square independence
test, click on **Stat → Tables → Chi-square Test.** On the input screen, select C2
- C3 for the **Columns containing the table.** Click on **OK** and the test results
will be displayed in the Session Window.

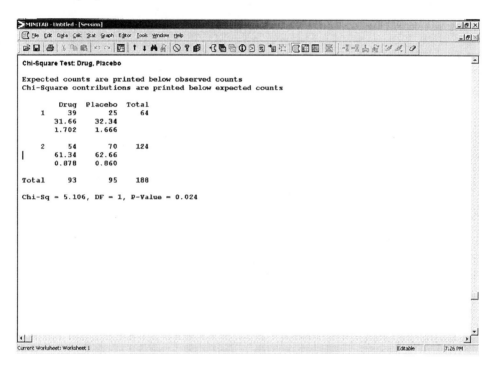

Notice that the test statistic is Chi-Sq = 5.106 and the P-value = .024. Since this
P-value is smaller than α = .10, you should reject the null hypothesis. Thus,
there is evidence to conclude that the drug should be used as part of the
treatment.

© 2006 Pearson Education, Inc., Upper Saddle River, NJ. All rights reserved. This material is protected under all copyright laws as they currently exist.
No portion of this material may be reproduced, in any form or by any means, without permission in writing from the publisher.

Section 10.3

▶ **Picturing the World (pg. 537)** Performing a Two-Sample F-Test

MINITAB requires the raw data values in order to perform a two-sample F-test, so you will use the data "Picturing the World" found in the margin of page 537. Enter the data for the Northeast section into C1 and for the Other sections into C2. To perform a two-sample F-test, MINITAB requires that the data be stacked into one column with a second column identifying which sample each data value came from. To do this, click on **Data → Stack → Columns.** Select both columns to be stacked on top of each other. **Column of current worksheet** should be C3 and **Store subscripts in** C4. The subscripts will be numbers 1 or 2 to indicate which column the data value came from, or if you select **Use variable names in subscript column** then the column names will be your subscripts.

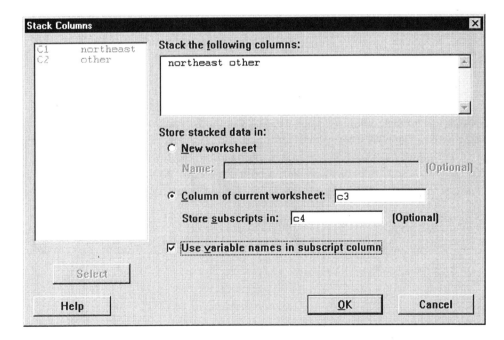

Click on **OK** and look in the Data Window. C3 should have all of the data stored in it and C4 should have the section the data represents. If you didn't use the variable names, then C4 will have numbers 1 (this tells you that the data value came from C1) or 2 (this tells you that the data value came from C2) in it.

© 2006 Pearson Education, Inc., Upper Saddle River, NJ. All rights reserved. This material is protected under all copyright laws as they currently exist.
No portion of this material may be reproduced, in any form or by any means, without permission in writing from the publisher.

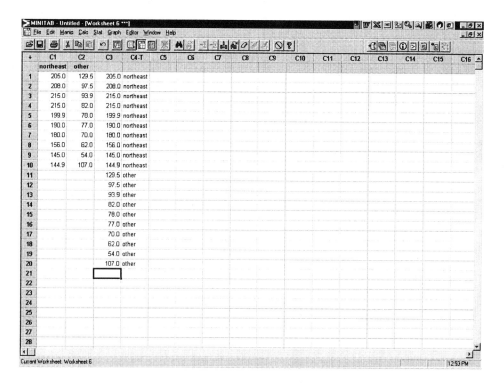

Now, to perform the two-sample F-test, click on **Stat→ ANOVA → Test for Equal Variances.** On the input screen, C3 is the **Response** variable and C4 is the **Factor.** Enter an appropriate **Title** and click on **OK.** This test produces quite a lot of output. However, you are only interested in the results of the F-test. You can see the results of the F-test in both the Graph Window and in the Session Window. Below are the results in the Graph Window.

© 2006 Pearson Education, Inc., Upper Saddle River, NJ. All rights reserved. This material is protected under all copyright laws as they currently exist. No portion of this material may be reproduced, in any form or by any means, without permission in writing from the publisher.

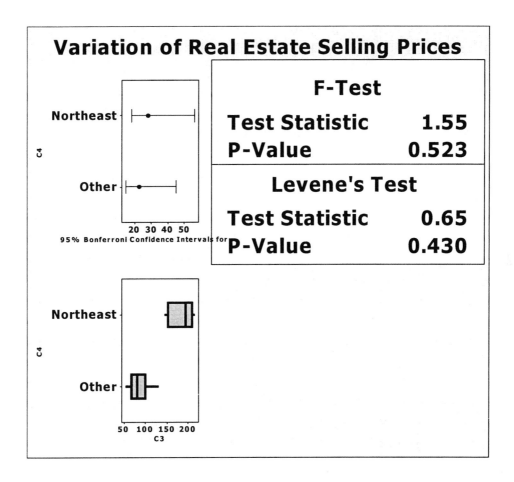

The F-test results show that the test statistic = 1.55 and the P-value = .523. Since this is a large P-value, you would fail to reject the null hypothesis. Thus, the two variances are approximately equal.

© 2006 Pearson Education, Inc., Upper Saddle River, NJ. All rights reserved. This material is protected under all copyright laws as they currently exist. No portion of this material may be reproduced, in any form or by any means, without permission in writing from the publisher.

Section 10.4

> ▶ Example 2 (pg. 547) ANOVA Tests

Open worksheet **Airline** found in the MINITAB folder **ch10.** The data for the three airlines should be in C1, C2, and C3. To perform a one-way analysis of variance, click on **Stat → ANOVA → One Way (Unstacked).** Select all three columns and click on **OK.** The results of the test will be in the Session Window.

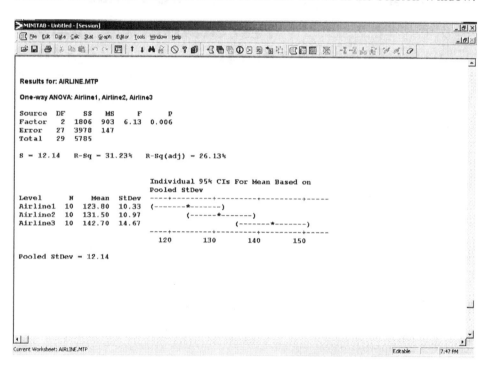

Notice that the test statistic is listed (F = 6.13), as well as the P-value (.006). Since the P-value = .006, and this is smaller than α = .01, you should reject the null hypothesis. Thus, there is a difference in the average flight times.

© 2006 Pearson Education, Inc., Upper Saddle River, NJ. All rights reserved. This material is protected under all copyright laws as they currently exist.
No portion of this material may be reproduced, in any form or by any means, without permission in writing from the publisher.

> ▶ Exercise 5 (pg. 549)   Costs per month of different toothpastes

Open worksheet **Ex10_4-5** found in the MINITAB folder **ch10.** The data for the three different degrees of abrasiveness should be in C1, C2, and C3. To perform a one-way analysis of variance, click on **Stat → ANOVA → One Way (Unstacked).** Select all three columns and click on **OK.** The results of the test will be in the Session Window.

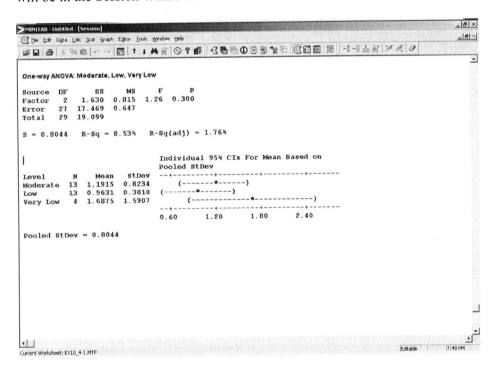

Since the P-value = .300 and is larger than α, you should not reject the null hypothesis. Thus, the average cost per month is the same for all three types of toothpaste.

© 2006 Pearson Education, Inc., Upper Saddle River, NJ. All rights reserved. This material is protected under all copyright laws as they currently exist. No portion of this material may be reproduced, in any form or by any means, without permission in writing from the publisher.

▸ **Exercise 9 (pg. 550)** Days spent in a Hospital

Open worksheet **Ex10_4-9** found in the MINITAB folder **ch10.** The data for the four different regions of the United States should be in C1 - C4. To perform a one-way analysis of variance, click on **Stat → ANOVA → One-Way (Unstacked).** Select all four columns and click on **OK.** The results of the test will be in the Session Window.

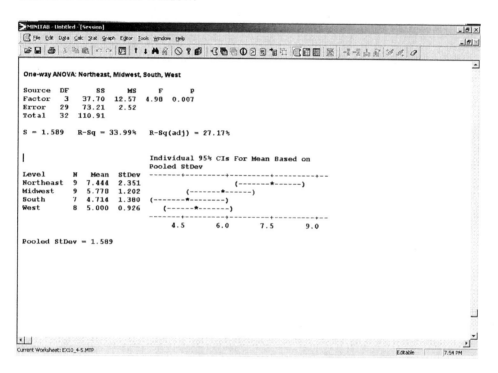

Since the P-value = .007 and is smaller than α, you should reject the null hypothesis. Thus, the average number of days spent in a hospital is not the same for all four regions of the United States.

◀

© 2006 Pearson Education, Inc., Upper Saddle River, NJ. All rights reserved. This material is protected under all copyright laws as they currently exist. No portion of this material may be reproduced, in any form or by any means, without permission in writing from the publisher.

▶ Technology Lab (pg. 563)   Teacher Salaries

Open worksheet **Tech10_a** found in the MINITAB folder **ch10.** The data for the three types of vehicles should be in C1 - C3.

1. Since the three states represent different populations and the three samples were randomly chosen, the samples are independent.

2. MINITAB has a test for normality. Click on **Stat**→ **Basic Statistics** → **Normality Test.** Select C1 for the **Variable** and **Kolmogorov-Smirnov** for the **Test of Normality.** Click on **OK** and a normal plot will be displayed.

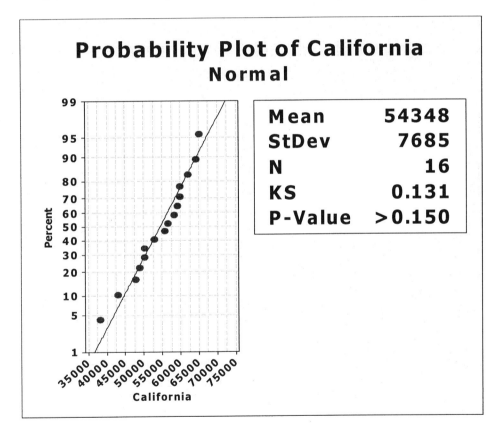

Notice the P-value is listed with results. Since this P-value is larger than .10 (our α), then you can assume that the data is approximately normal. Repeat this test for the other two columns of data.

© 2006 Pearson Education, Inc., Upper Saddle River, NJ. All rights reserved. This material is protected under all copyright laws as they currently exist. No portion of this material may be reproduced, in any form or by any means, without permission in writing from the publisher.

3. For each pair of datasets, perform the Test for Equal Variances. To do this, click on **Manip → Stack → Stack Columns.** Select both columns to be stacked on top of each other. **Column of current worksheet** is C4 and **Store subscripts in** C5. Notice that the subscripts will the vehicle type as long as you selected **Use variable names in subscript column**. Click on **OK** and look in the Data Window. C4 should have all of the data stored in it and C5 should have the vehicle type in it. Now, to perform the two-sample F-test, click on **Stat → ANOVA → Test for Equal Variances.** On the input screen, C4 is the **Response** variable and C5 is the **Factor.** Enter an appropriate **Title** and click on **OK.** This test produces quite a lot of output. However, you are only interested in the results of the F-test.

4. To do a one-way ANOVA, click on **Stat → ANOVA → One-Way (Unstacked).** Select all three columns and click on **OK.** The results of the test will be in the Session Window. Look at the P-value. If it is smaller than α, you should reject the null hypothesis.

5. Repeat Exercises 1 - 4 using worksheet **Tech10_b** found in the MINITAB folder **ch10.**

© 2006 Pearson Education, Inc., Upper Saddle River, NJ. All rights reserved. This material is protected under all copyright laws as they currently exist. No portion of this material may be reproduced, in any form or by any means, without permission in writing from the publisher.

Nonparametric Tests

CHAPTER

11

Section 11.1

▸ Example 3 (pg. 571) Using the Paired-Sample Sign Test

Open worksheet **Prison** which is found in the **ch11** MINITAB folder. The 'Before' data is in C1 and the 'After' data is in C2. Since we are interested in the difference between C1 and C2, we will create a new column that is C1 - C2. Click on **Calc → Calculator. Store result in variable** C3 and calculate the **Expression** C1 - C2. Click on **OK** and C3 should contain the differences. Now perform a 1-sample Sign test on C3. Click on **Stat → Nonparametrics → 1-sample Sign.** Select C3 as the **Variable.** Since you would like to test if the number of repeat offenders has decreased after the special course, you would expect that the differences in C3 would be greater than 0. Thus, enter 0 for **Test median** and select **greater than** for the **Alternative.**

1-Sample Sign	
C1 Before C2 After C3 Difference	**Variables:** Difference
	○ **Confidence interval** Level: 95.0
	⊙ **Test median:** 0 **Alternative:** greater than ▾
Select	
Help	OK Cancel

© 2006 Pearson Education, Inc., Upper Saddle River, NJ. All rights reserved. This material is protected under all copyright laws as they currently exist.
No portion of this material may be reproduced, in any form or by any means, without permission in writing from the publisher.

Click on **OK** and the results will be in the Session Window.

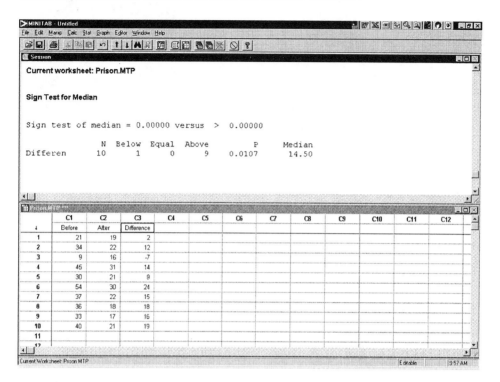

Notice that the P-value = .0107. Since this value is smaller than α=.025, you would reject the null hypothesis. Thus, there is sufficient evidence to conclude that the number of repeat offenders decreases after taking the special course.

© 2006 Pearson Education, Inc., Upper Saddle River, NJ. All rights reserved. This material is protected under all copyright laws as they currently exist. No portion of this material may be reproduced, in any form or by any means, without permission in writing from the publisher.

> ▸ Exercise 3 (pg. 572)   Credit Card Charges

Enter the data into C1 in the MINITAB Data Window. (Do not type in the $ sign.) To perform the Sign Test, click on **Stat → Nonparametrics → 1-sample Sign.** Select C1 as the **Variable.** Since you would like to test if the median amount of new credit card charges was more than $200, enter 200 for **Test median** and select **greater than** for the **Alternative.**

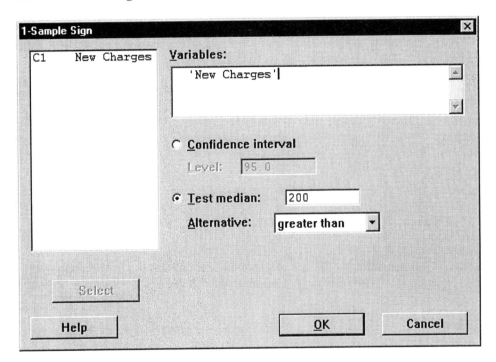

Click on **OK** and the results will be displayed in the Session Window.

© 2006 Pearson Education, Inc., Upper Saddle River, NJ. All rights reserved. This material is protected under all copyright laws as they currently exist.
No portion of this material may be reproduced, in any form or by any means, without permission in writing from the publisher.

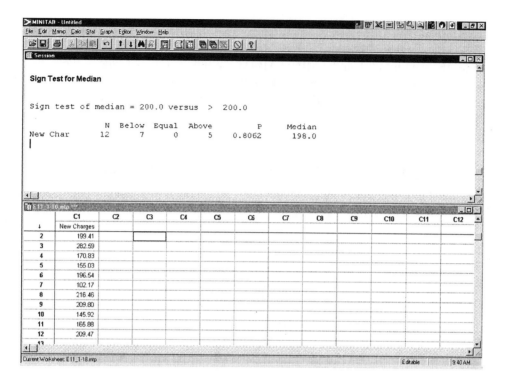

Notice that the P-value = .8062. Since this is such a large P-value, you would fail to reject the null hypothesis. Thus, the accountant can **not** conclude that the median amount of new charges was more than $200.

© 2006 Pearson Education, Inc., Upper Saddle River, NJ. All rights reserved. This material is protected under all copyright laws as they currently exist.
No portion of this material may be reproduced, in any form or by any means, without permission in writing from the publisher.

▶ Exercise 16 (pg. 574) Does therapy reduce headache hours?

Open worksheet **Ex11_1-16** which is found in the **ch11** MINITAB folder.
Headache hours before therapy is in C1 of the MINITAB Data Window and
Headache hours after therapy is in C2. Calculate the differences. Click on **Calc**
→ **Calculator.** Next **Store result in variable** C3 and calculate the **Expression**
C1-C2. Click on **OK** and C3 should contain the differences. Now perform a 1-
sample Sign test on C3. Click on **Stat** → **Nonparametrics** → **1-sample Sign.**
Select C3 as the **Variable.** Since you would like to test if the number of
headache hours has decreased after the special therapy, you would expect that the
differences in C3 would be greater than 0. Thus, enter 0 for **Test median** and
select **greater than** for the **Alternative.** Click on **OK.**

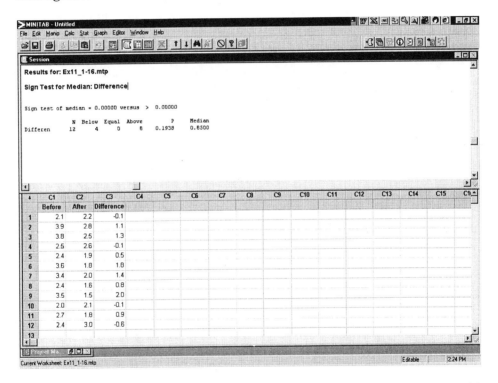

Notice that the P-value = .1938. Since this value is larger than α=.05, you would
fail to reject the null hypothesis. Thus, there is not enough evidence to conclude
that the number of headache hours decreases with this special therapy.

◀

© 2006 Pearson Education, Inc., Upper Saddle River, NJ. All rights reserved. This material is protected under all copyright laws as they currently exist.
No portion of this material may be reproduced, in any form or by any means, without permission in writing from the publisher.

Section 11.2

▶ **Example 1 (pg. 578)** Performing a Wilcoxon Signed-Rank Test

Open worksheet **music** which is found in the **ch11** MINITAB folder. Notice that 'With Music' data is in C1 and 'Without Music' data is in C2. To calculate the differences, click **Calc → Calculator. Store the result in variable** C3 and calculate the **Expression** C1-C2. Click on **OK** and C3 should contain the differences. To perform the Wilcoxon Signed Rank Test, click on **Stat →
Nonparametrics → 1-sample Wilcoxon.** You should use C3 for the **Variable.** Since you are using the differences in this example, you want to compare the median difference to 0. So, enter 0 for **Test Median** and choose **not equal** as the **Alternative.**

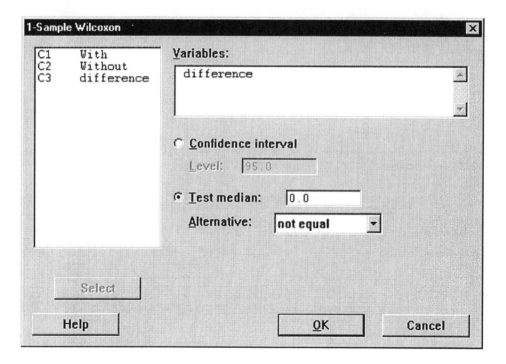

Click on **OK** to view the results of the test in the Session Window.

© 2006 Pearson Education, Inc., Upper Saddle River, NJ. All rights reserved. This material is protected under all copyright laws as they currently exist.
No portion of this material may be reproduced, in any form or by any means, without permission in writing from the publisher.

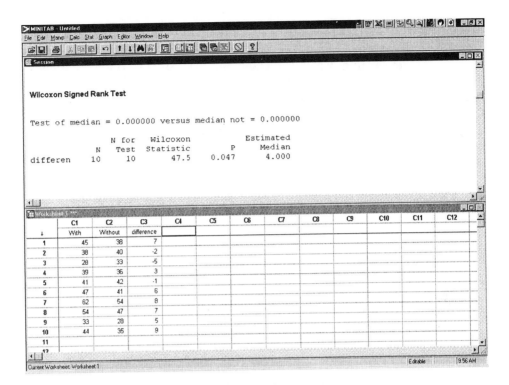

The MINITAB output tells you that the Wilcoxon Statistic is 47.5 and the P-value is .047. Although the textbook tells you to select the smaller of the absolute value of the two sums of the ranks, MINITAB simply uses the sum of the positive ranks. This makes no difference in interpreting the results. The important thing to notice is that the P-value = .047. Since this is smaller than α = .05, you would reject the null hypothesis. Thus, there is sufficient evidence to say that music affects the length of the workout sessions.

© 2006 Pearson Education, Inc., Upper Saddle River, NJ. All rights reserved. This material is protected under all copyright laws as they currently exist. No portion of this material may be reproduced, in any form or by any means, without permission in writing from the publisher.

> ▶ Example 2 (pg. 581) Performing a Wilcoxon Rank Sum Test

Open worksheet **earnings** which is found in the **ch11** MINITAB folder. Male
earnings are in C1 and Female earnings are in C2. In MINITAB, the Wilcoxon
Rank Sum Test is called the Mann-Whitney test. Click on **Stat→**
Nonparametrics → Mann-Whitney. Enter C1 for the **First Sample,** C2 for the
Second Sample, and select n**ot equal** as the **Alternative** since you want to see if
there is a difference between the earnings.

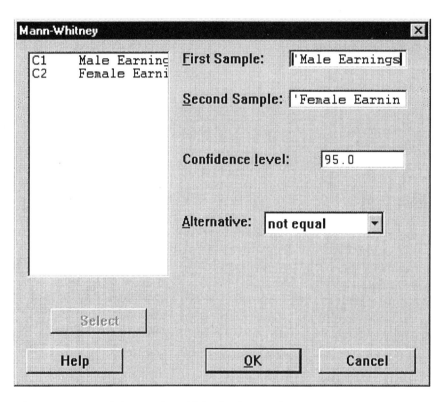

Click on **OK** and the results will be in the Session Window.

© 2006 Pearson Education, Inc., Upper Saddle River, NJ. All rights reserved. This material is protected under all copyright laws as they currently exist.
No portion of this material may be reproduced, in any form or by any means, without permission in writing from the publisher.

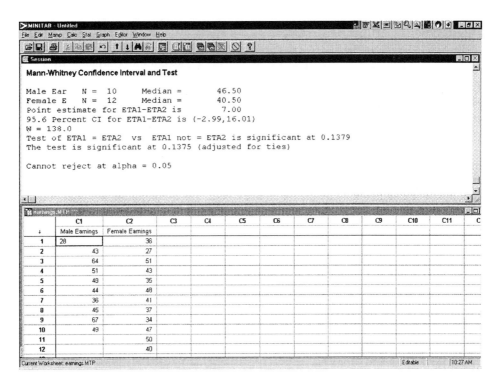

Look at the results carefully. The P-value is .1379. The rank sum for male earnings is also listed, W = 138. In this example, since the P-value is larger than α=.10, you would fail to reject the null hypothesis. Thus, there is no difference between male and female earnings.

© 2006 Pearson Education, Inc., Upper Saddle River, NJ. All rights reserved. This material is protected under all copyright laws as they currently exist. No portion of this material may be reproduced, in any form or by any means, without permission in writing from the publisher.

> ▸ Exercise 7 (pg. 584) Teacher salaries

Open worksheet **Ex11_2-7** which is found in the **Chapter 11** MINITAB folder.
Click on **Stat → Nonparametrics → Mann-Whitney.** Enter C1 for the **First
Sample,** C2 for the **Second Sample**, and select n**ot equal** as the **Alternative**
since you want to see if there is a difference between the salaries in Ohio and
Pennsylvania. Click on **OK**. The results should be in the Session Window.

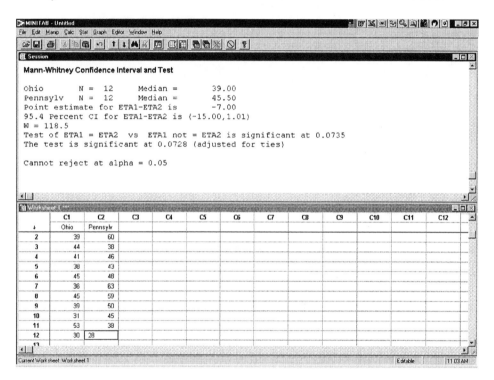

Since the P-value = .0735 and is larger than α=.05, you would fail to reject the
null hypothesis. There is not enough evidence to conclude there is a difference in
teacher salaries in Ohio and Pennsylvania.

◀

© 2006 Pearson Education, Inc., Upper Saddle River, NJ. All rights reserved. This material is protected under all copyright laws as they currently exist.
No portion of this material may be reproduced, in any form or by any means, without permission in writing from the publisher.

Section 11.3

▶ Example 1 (pg. 589) Performing a Kruskal-Wallis Test

Open worksheet **payrates** which is found in the **ch11** MINITAB folder. To perform a Kruskal-Wallis test, MINITAB requires that the data be stacked into one column with a second column identifying which sample each data value came from. To do this, click on **Data → Stack → Columns.** Select all three columns to be stacked on top of each other. Select **Column of current worksheet** and enter C4 and **Store subscripts in** C5. The subscripts will be numbers 1, 2, or 3 to indicate which column the data value came from. Be sure that **Use variable names in subscript column** is NOT selected.

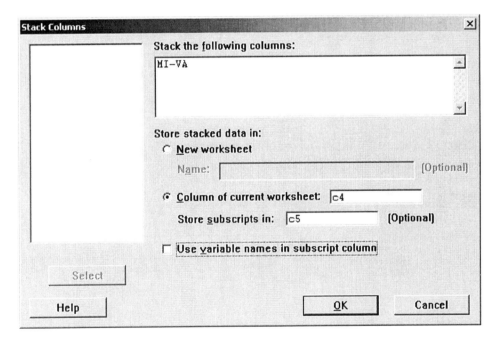

Click on **OK.** Name C4 Payrates and C5 State. Notice that in C5, 1 represents Michigan, 2 represents New York, and 3 represents Virginia.

© 2006 Pearson Education, Inc., Upper Saddle River, NJ. All rights reserved. This material is protected under all copyright laws as they currently exist.
No portion of this material may be reproduced, in any form or by any means, without permission in writing from the publisher.

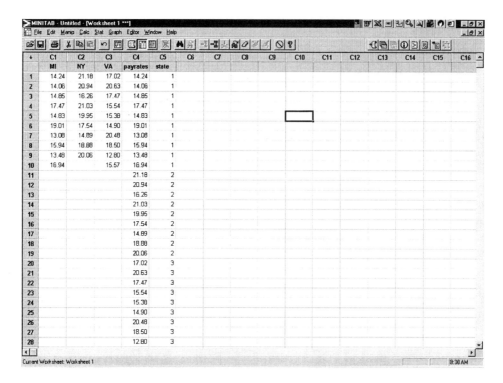

Now, to do the Kruskal-Wallis test, click on **Stat → Nonparametrics → Kruskal-Wallis.** The **Response** variable is Payrates (C4) and the **Factor** is State (C5).

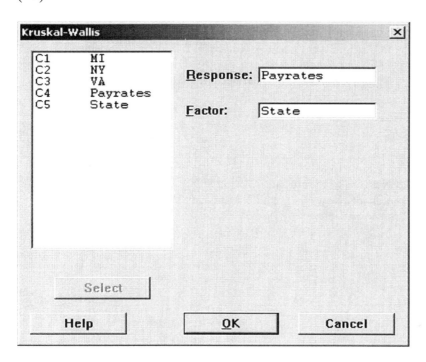

© 2006 Pearson Education, Inc., Upper Saddle River, NJ. All rights reserved. This material is protected under all copyright laws as they currently exist.
No portion of this material may be reproduced, in any form or by any means, without permission in writing from the publisher.

Click on **OK** and the results will be displayed in the Session Window.

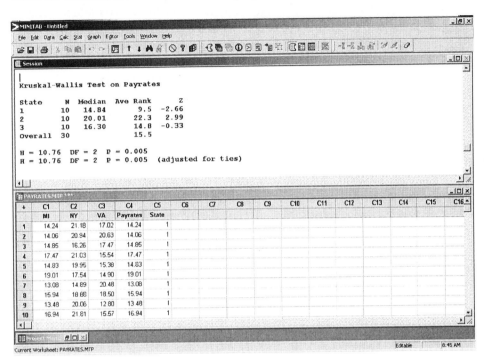

Notice that the test statistic is H=10.76 and the P-value=.005. With such a small P-value, you should reject the null hypothesis. So, there is a difference in the payrates of the three states.

© 2006 Pearson Education, Inc., Upper Saddle River, NJ. All rights reserved. This material is protected under all copyright laws as they currently exist. No portion of this material may be reproduced, in any form or by any means, without permission in writing from the publisher.

▶ ☐ Exercise 3 (pg. 591) ☐ Are the insurance premiums different?

Open worksheet **Ex11_3-3** which is found in the **ch11** MINITAB folder. The
data should be in C1, C2, and C3. To perform a Kruskal-Wallis test, MINITAB
requires that the data be stacked into one column with a second column
identifying which sample each data value came from. To do this, click on **Data**
→ **Stack** → **Columns.** Select all three columns to be stacked on top of each
other. Select **Column of current worksheet** and enter C4 and **Store subscripts
in** C5. The subscripts will be numbers 1, 2, or 3 to indicate which column the
data value came from. Be sure that **Use variable names in subscript column** is
NOT selected. Click on **OK.** Name C4 Premiums and C5 State. Notice that in
C5, 1 represents California, 2 represents Florida, and 3 represents Illinois. Now,
to do the Kruskal-Wallis test, click on **Stat** → **Nonparametrics** → **Kruskal-
Wallis.** The **Response** variable is Premiums (C4) and the **Factor** is State (C5).
Click on **OK** and the results will be displayed in the Session Window.

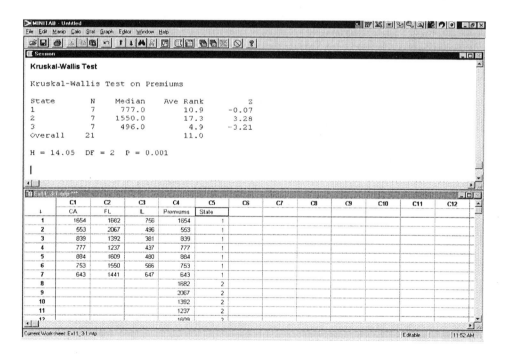

Notice that the test statistic is H=14.05 and the P-value=.001. With such a small
P-value, you should reject the null hypothesis. So, there is a difference in the
premiums of the three states.

◀

© 2006 Pearson Education, Inc., Upper Saddle River, NJ. All rights reserved. This material is protected under all copyright laws as they currently exist.
No portion of this material may be reproduced, in any form or by any means, without permission in writing from the publisher.

Section 11.4

> ▶ Example 1 (pg. 594) The Spearman Rank Correlation
> Coefficient

Enter the data into the MINITAB Data Window. Enter the Beef prices into C1 and the Lamb prices into C2. To rank the data values, click on **Data → Rank.** On the input screen, you should **Rank data in** C1 and **Store ranks in** C3. When you click on **OK**, the ranks of the Beef prices should be in C3.

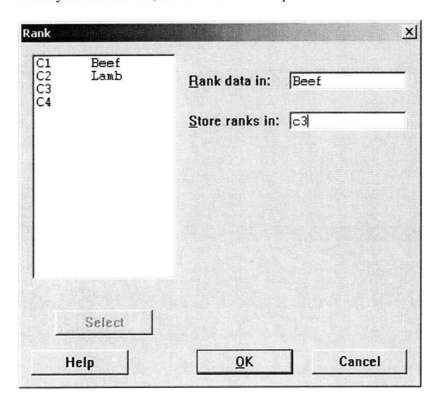

Repeat this using the Lamb prices and storing the ranks in C4. Now you should have the ranks of the data in C3 and C4.

© 2006 Pearson Education, Inc., Upper Saddle River, NJ. All rights reserved. This material is protected under all copyright laws as they currently exist. No portion of this material may be reproduced, in any form or by any means, without permission in writing from the publisher.

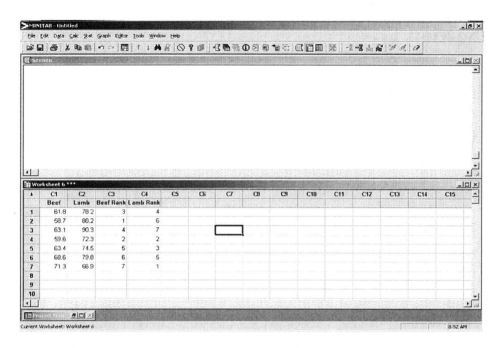

To calculate Spearman's Rank Correlation Coefficient, simply use Pearson's correlation on the ranks of the data. Click on **Stat** → **Basic Statistics** → **Correlation.** Enter C3 and C4 for the **Variables** and select **Display p-values.**

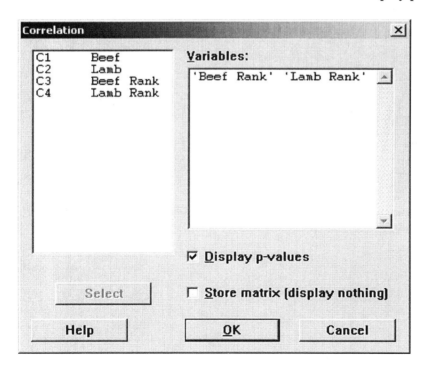

© 2006 Pearson Education, Inc., Upper Saddle River, NJ. All rights reserved. This material is protected under all copyright laws as they currently exist.
No portion of this material may be reproduced, in any form or by any means, without permission in writing from the publisher.

When you click on **OK**, the results will be displayed in the Session Window.

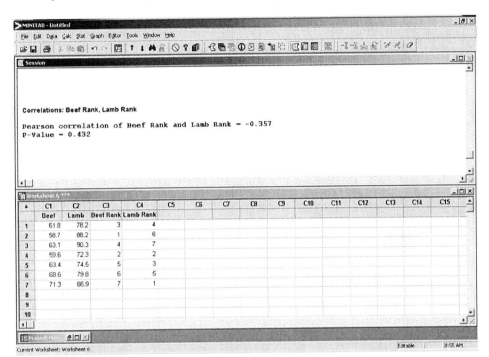

In this example, notice that the Spearman's Rank Correlation Coefficient is -.357 and the P-value is .432. Since this P-value is larger than $\alpha = .05$, you would fail to reject the null hypothesis. Thus, you can NOT conclude that there is a significant correlation between beef and lamb prices from 1995 to 2001.

© 2006 Pearson Education, Inc., Upper Saddle River, NJ. All rights reserved. This material is protected under all copyright laws as they currently exist. No portion of this material may be reproduced, in any form or by any means, without permission in writing from the publisher.

> **Exercise 6 (pg. 597)**   Is Air Conditioner Performance related to Price?

Open worksheet **Ex11_4-6** which is found in the **ch11** MINITAB folder. The overall score is in C1 and the price is in C2. First, rank the data. Click on **Data → Rank.** On the input screen, you should **Rank data in** C1 and **Store ranks in** C3. When you click on **OK**, the ranks of the Overall Scores should be in C3. Repeat this for the Prices and **store ranks in** C4. Now, calculate the correlation coefficient of the ranks. Click on **Stat → Basic Statistics → Correlation.** Enter C3 and C4 for the **Variables** and select **Display p-values.**

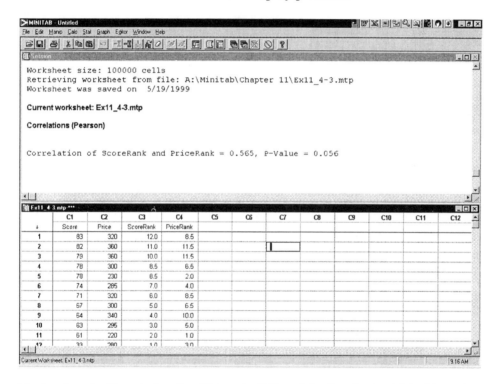

Notice that the Correlation Coefficient is .565 and the P-value is .056. Since the P-value is smaller than $\alpha=.10$, you would reject the null hypothesis. Thus, there is a significant correlation between Overall Score and Price.

© 2006 Pearson Education, Inc., Upper Saddle River, NJ. All rights reserved. This material is protected under all copyright laws as they currently exist. No portion of this material may be reproduced, in any form or by any means, without permission in writing from the publisher.

Section 11.5

▶ **Example 3 (pg. 603)** The Runs Test

Enter the data into C1 of the MINITAB Data Window. MINITAB requires
numeric data for the Runs Test, so you will have to code the data. Click on
Data → Code → Text to Numeric. On the input screen, you should **Code data
from columns** C1 and **into** C2. Code **Original values** "M" as a **New** value of 1
and "F" as 2.

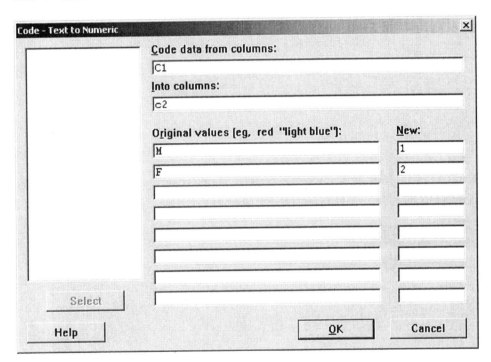

When you click on **OK**, the coded data should be in C2.

© 2006 Pearson Education, Inc., Upper Saddle River, NJ. All rights reserved. This material is protected under all copyright laws as they currently exist.
No portion of this material may be reproduced, in any form or by any means, without permission in writing from the publisher.

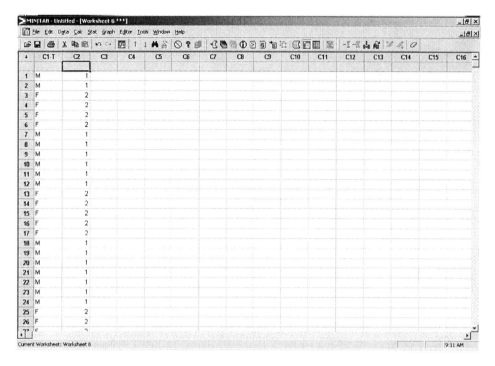

Next, click on **Stat → Nonparametrics → Runs Test.** Select C2 for the
Variable, and select **Above and below mean.**

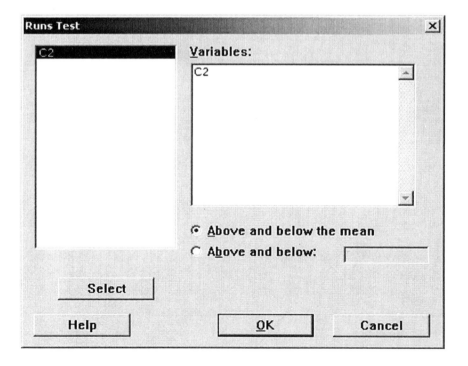

© 2006 Pearson Education, Inc., Upper Saddle River, NJ. All rights reserved. This material is protected under all copyright laws as they currently exist.
No portion of this material may be reproduced, in any form or by any means, without permission in writing from the publisher.

Click on **OK** and the results will be displayed in the Session Window.

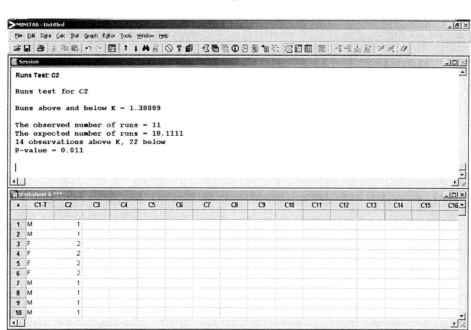

Notice that the test statistic is 18.11 and the p-value is 0.011. Since the p-value is less than .05, you can conclude that the selection of employees with respect to gender is not random.

© 2006 Pearson Education, Inc., Upper Saddle River, NJ. All rights reserved. This material is protected under all copyright laws as they currently exist. No portion of this material may be reproduced, in any form or by any means, without permission in writing from the publisher.

> ▶ **Technology Lab (pg. 615)** Annual Income

Open worksheet **Tech11_a** which is found in the **ch11** MINITAB folder. The
data should be in C1 - C4.

1.   Construct a boxplot for all four regions. Click on **Graph → Boxplot →
     Multiple Y's Simple.** Select C1, C2, C3, and C4 for the **Graph variables.**
     Click on the **Labels** button and enter an appropriate title. Click on **OK** twice
     to view the boxplots.

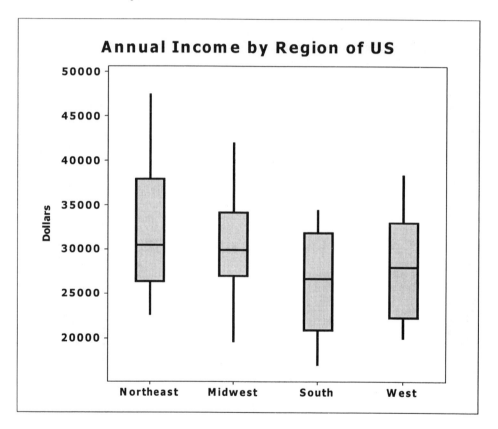

Annual Income by Region of US

2.   To perform a sign test on the data from the Midwest, click on **Stat →
     Nonparametrics → 1-Sample Sign.** Select South (C2) for the **Variable,**
     and enter 25000 for the **Test Median.** The **Alternative** should be **greater
     than** since the claim is that the median income in the Midwest is at least
     $25,000. Click on **OK** and the results will be displayed in the Session
     Window.

3.   Recall that the Wilcoxon rank sum test is the same as the Mann-Whitney test
     in MINITAB. Click on **Stat → Nonparametrics → Mann-Whitney.** Enter

© 2006 Pearson Education, Inc., Upper Saddle River, NJ. All rights reserved. This material is protected under all copyright laws as they currently exist.
No portion of this material may be reproduced, in any form or by any means, without permission in writing from the publisher.

Northeast (C1) for the **First sample** and South (C3) for the **Second sample.** The **Alternative** should be **not equal** since you are testing whether or not the median annual incomes are the same. Click on **OK** and the results will be displayed in the Session Window.

4. To perform a Kruskal-Wallis test in MINITAB, the data must be stacked in one column. To do this, click on **Data → Stack → Columns.** Choose all four columns to stack. Select **Column of current worksheet** and enter C5 and **Store subscripts in** C6. The subscripts will be numbers 1, 2, 3, or 4 to indicate which column the data value came from. Be sure that **Use variable names in subscript column** is NOT selected. When you click on **OK**, C5 and C6 should be filled in. Click on **Stat → Nonparametrics → Kruskal-Wallis.** The **Response** variable is C5 and the **Factor** is C6. Click on **OK** and the results will be displayed in the Session Window.

5. Using the stacked data in C5 and C6, perform a one-way ANOVA. Click on **Stat → ANOVA → One Way.** The **Response** variable is C5 and the **Factor** is C6. Click on **OK** and the results will be displayed in the Session Window.

6. Open worksheet **Tech11_b** which is found in the **ch11** MINITAB folder. Repeat Exercises 1, 3, 4, and 5 using the data in this worksheet.

◀

© 2006 Pearson Education, Inc., Upper Saddle River, NJ. All rights reserved. This material is protected under all copyright laws as they currently exist. No portion of this material may be reproduced, in any form or by any means, without permission in writing from the publisher.

The TI-83 and TI-83 Plus Graphing Calculator Manual

▼

Elementary Statistics
Picturing the World

The TI-83 and TI-83 Plus Graphing Calculator Manual

Kathleen McLaughlin
Dorothy Wakefield

▼

Elementary Statistics
Picturing the World

Ron Larson
Betsy Farber

▶ Introduction

The TI-83 and TI-83 Plus Graphing Calculator Manual is one of a series of companion technology manuals that provide hands-on technology assistance to users of Larson/Farber *Elementary Statistics: Picturing the World, 3rd Edition.*

Detailed instructions for working selected examples, exercises, and Technology sections from *Elementary Statistics: Picturing the World, 3rd Ed.* are provided in this manual. To make the correlation with the text as seamless as possible, the table of contents includes page references for both the Larson/Farber text and this manual.

▸ Contents:

Getting Started with the TI-83 and TI-83 Plus Graphing Calculators

▸ Overview

This manual is designed to be used with the TI-83, the TI-83 Plus and the TI-83 Silver Edition Graphing Calculators. These calculators have a variety of useful functions for doing statistical calculations and for creating statistical plots. The commands for using the statistical functions are the same for all three calculators. The main difference among the three calculators is that the TI-83 Plus and the TI-83 Silver Edition have the capability of downloading a variety of software applications that are available through the TI website (www.ti.com). TI also will provide downloadable updates to the TI-83 Plus and the TI-83 Silver Edition operating systems. These features are not available on the TI-83.

Your textbook comes with data files on the CD data disk that can be loaded onto all three of the TI-83 calculators. In order to transfer data from a computer (IBM compatible) to the TI-83 or TI-83 Plus, you must purchase a Graph Link from Texas Instruments which connects the calculator to the computer. The TI-83 Silver Edition comes with the TI-Graph Link.

Throughout this manual all references to the TI-83 are actually references to the TI-83, TI-83 Plus and the TI-83 Silver Edition calculators.

Before you begin using the TI-83, spend a few minutes becoming familiar with its basic operations. First, notice the different colored keys on the calculator. The gray keys are the number keys. The blue keys along the right side of the keyboard are the common math functions. The blue keys across the top are used to set up and display graphs. The primary function of each key is printed in white on the key. For example, when you press **STAT**, the STAT MENU is displayed.

© 2006 Pearson Education, Inc., Upper Saddle River, NJ. All rights reserved. This material is protected under all copyright laws as they currently exist. No portion of this material may be reproduced, in any form or by any means, without permission in writing from the publisher.

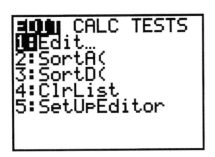

The secondary function of each key is printed in yellow above the key. When you press the 2nd key, the function printed in yellow above the key becomes active and the cursor changes from a solid rectangle to an ↑ (up-arrow). For example, when you press 2nd and the $\boxed{x^2}$ key, the $\sqrt{}$ function is activated. The notation used in this manual to indicate a secondary function is 2nd followed by the name of the secondary function. For example, to use the LIST function, found above the STAT key, the notation used in this manual is 2nd [LIST]. The LIST MENU will then be activated and displayed on the screen.

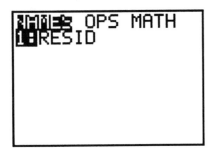

The alpha function of each key is printed in green above the key. When you press the green ALPHA key, the function printed in green above the key is activated and the cursor changes from a solid rectangle to A.

In this manual you will find detailed explanations of the different statistical functions that are programmed into the TI-83. These explanations will accompany selected examples from your textbook. This will give you the opportunity to learn the various calculator functions as they apply to the specific statistical material in each chapter.

▸ Getting Started

To operate the calculator, press ON in the lower left corner of the calculator. Begin each example with a blank screen, with a rectangular cursor flashing in the upper left corner. If you turn on your calculator and you do not have a blank screen, press the CLEAR key. You may have to press CLEAR a second time in

© 2006 Pearson Education, Inc., Upper Saddle River, NJ. All rights reserved. This material is protected under all copyright laws as they currently exist. No portion of this material may be reproduced, in any form or by any means, without permission in writing from the publisher.

order to clear the screen. If using the CLEAR key does not clear the screen, you can push 2nd [QUIT] (Note: QUIT is found above the MODE key.)

▶ Helpful Hints

To adjust the display contrast, push and release the 2nd key. Then push and hold the blue up arrow ▲ to darken or the blue down arrow ▼ to lighten.

The calculator has an automatic turn off that will turn the calculator off if it has been idle for several minutes. To restart, simply press the ON key.

There are several different graphing techniques available on the TI-83. If you inadvertently leave a graph on and attempt to use a different graphing function, your graph display may be cluttered with extraneous graphs, or you may get an ERROR message on the screen.

There are several items that you should check before graphing anything. First, press the Y= key and clear all the Y-variables. The screen should look like the following display:

```
Plot1  Plot2  Plot3
\Y1=
\Y2=
\Y3=
\Y4=
\Y5=
\Y6=
\Y7=
```

If there are any functions stored in the Y-variables, simply move the cursor to the line that isn't clear and press CLEAR ENTER.

Next, press 2nd [STAT PLOT] and check to make sure that all the STAT PLOTS are turned **OFF**.

© 2006 Pearson Education, Inc., Upper Saddle River, NJ. All rights reserved. This material is protected under all copyright laws as they currently exist. No portion of this material may be reproduced, in any form or by any means, without permission in writing from the publisher.

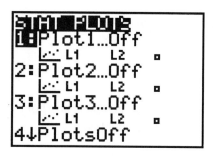

If you notice that a Plot is turned **ON**, select the Plot, press ENTER and move the cursor to **OFF** and press ENTER. Press 2nd [QUIT] to return to the home screen.

© 2006 Pearson Education, Inc., Upper Saddle River, NJ. All rights reserved. This material is protected under all copyright laws as they currently exist.
No portion of this material may be reproduced, in any form or by any means, without permission in writing from the publisher.

Introduction to Statistics

CHAPTER

1

▶ Technology (pg. 30-31)   Generating Random Numbers

To generate a random sample of integers, press **MATH** and the Math Menu will appear.

```
MATH NUM CPX PRB
1▸▸Frac
2:▸Dec
3:3
4:3√(
5:x√
6:fMin(
7↓fMax(
```

Use the blue right arrow key, ▶ , to move the cursor to highlight **PRB**. The Probability Menu will appear.

```
MATH NUM CPX PRB
1▸rand
2:nPr
3:nCr
4:!
5:randInt(
6:randNorm(
7:randBin(
```

Select **5:RandInt(** by using the blue down arrow key, ▼ , to highlight it and pressing **ENTER** or by pressing the 5 key. **RandInt(** should appear on the screen. This function requires three values: the starting integer, followed by a comma (the comma is found on the black key above the 7 key), the ending integer, followed by a comma and the number of values you want to generate. Close the parentheses and press **ENTER**. (Note: It is optional to close the parenthesis at the end of the command.)

© 2006 Pearson Education, Inc., Upper Saddle River, NJ. All rights reserved. This material is protected under all copyright laws as they currently exist. No portion of this material may be reproduced, in any form or by any means, without permission in writing from the publisher.

For an example, suppose you want to generate 15 values from the integers ranging from 1 to 50. The command is **randInt(1,50,15)**.

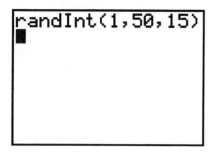

Press **ENTER** and a partial display of the 15 random integers should appear on your screen. (Note: your numbers will be different from the ones you see here.)

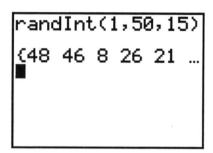

Use the right arrow to scroll through your 15 items. You might find that you have some duplicate values. The TI-83 uses a method called "sampling with replacement" to generate random numbers. This means that it is possible to select the same integer twice.

In the example in the text, you are asked to select a random sample of 15 cars from the 167 cars that are assembled at an auto plant. One way to choose the sample is to number the cars from 1 to 167 and randomly select 15 different cars. This sampling process is to be "without replacement." Since the TI-83 samples "with replacement", the best way to obtain 15 different cars is to generate more than 15 random integers, and to discard any duplicates. To be safe, you should generate 20 random integers.

© 2006 Pearson Education, Inc., Upper Saddle River, NJ. All rights reserved. This material is protected under all copyright laws as they currently exist.
No portion of this material may be reproduced, in any form or by any means, without permission in writing from the publisher.

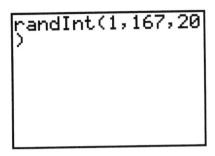

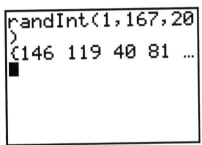

Use the right arrow to scroll to the right to see the rest of the list and write down the first 15 distinct values.

Exercises

1. You would like to sample 8 distinct accounts. The TI-83 samples "with replacement" so you may have duplicates in your sample. To obtain 8 distinct values, try selecting 10 items. Press **MATH**, highlight **PRB** and select **5:RandInt(**. Press **ENTER** and type in **1,74,10).** Press **ENTER** and the random integers will appear on the screen. Use the right arrow to scroll through the output and choose the first eight distinct integers. (Note: If you don't have 8 distinct integers, generate 10 more integers and pick as many new integers as you need from this group to complete your sample of 8).

2. Because you want 20 distinct batteries, generate 25 random integers using **randInt(1,200,25).** Use the right arrow to scroll through the list and select the first 20 distinct integers.

3. This example does not require distinct digits, so duplicates are allowed. You can select three random samples of size n=5 by using **randInt** to create each sample. To generate the first sample, press **MATH**, highlight **PRB** and select **5:RandInt(** by scrolling down through the list and highlighting **5:RandInt(** and pressing **ENTER** or by highlighting **PRB** and pressing **5**. Type in the starting digit: 0; the ending digit: 9, and the number of selections: 5.

© 2006 Pearson Education, Inc., Upper Saddle River, NJ. All rights reserved. This material is protected under all copyright laws as they currently exist. No portion of this material may be reproduced, in any form or by any means, without permission in writing from the publisher.

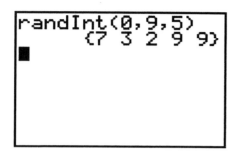

Add the digits and divide by 5 to get the average for the sample.

To generate the second and third samples, repeat this process two more times. Calculate the sample average for the 2nd and 3rd sample.

To calculate the population average, add the digits 0 through 9 and divide the answer by 10.

Compare your three sample averages with your population average.

4. Use the same procedure as in Exercise 3 with a starting value of 0 and an ending value of 40 and a sample size of 7.

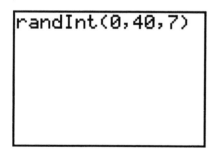

5. Use **randInt(1,6,60).** Store the results in L1 by pressing **STO** **2ⁿᵈ** **[L1]** **ENTER**. (Note: **[L1]** is found above the **1** key.) Then sort L1 by pressing **2ⁿᵈ** **[LIST]**, (**[LIST** is found above the **STAT** key), highlight **OPS** and select **1:SortA(** and press **2ⁿᵈ** **[L1]** **ENTER**. Press **2ⁿᵈ** **[L1]** **ENTER** and a partial list of the integers in L1 will appear on the screen. Use the right arrow to scroll through the list and count the number of 1's, 2's, 3's, … and 6's. Record the results in a table.

© 2006 Pearson Education, Inc., Upper Saddle River, NJ. All rights reserved. This material is protected under all copyright laws as they currently exist.
No portion of this material may be reproduced, in any form or by any means, without permission in writing from the publisher.

7. Use **randInt(0,1,100).** Store the results in L1. Press 2ⁿᵈ **[LIST]** , highlight **MATH** and select **5:sum(** and press 2ⁿᵈ **[L1]**. Close the parentheses and press **ENTER**.

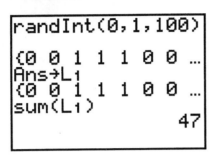

The number in your output is the sum of L1. Since L1 consists of 0's and 1's, the sum is actually the number of tails in your random sample. The (number of heads) = 100 - (no. of tails).

© 2006 Pearson Education, Inc., Upper Saddle River, NJ. All rights reserved. This material is protected under all copyright laws as they currently exist. No portion of this material may be reproduced, in any form or by any means, without permission in writing from the publisher.

Descriptive Statistics

CHAPTER

2

Section 2.1

▶ Example 7 (pg. 42) Constructing a histogram for a frequency distribution

To create this histogram, you must enter information into List1 (**L1**) and List 2 (**L2**). Refer to the frequency distribution on pg. 37 in your textbook. You will enter the midpoints into **L1** and the frequencies into **L2**. To enter the data, press **STAT** and the Statistics Menu will appear. Notice that **EDIT** is highlighted. The first selection in the **EDIT** menu, **1:Edit**, is also highlighted.

Press **ENTER** and lists **L1**, **L2** and **L3** will appear.

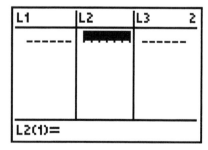

 If the lists already contain data, you should clear them before beginning this example. To clear data from a list, move your cursor so that the List name (**L1**, **L2**, or **L3**) of the list that contains data is highlighted.

© 2006 Pearson Education, Inc., Upper Saddle River, NJ. All rights reserved. This material is protected under all copyright laws as they currently exist. No portion of this material may be reproduced, in any form or by any means, without permission in writing from the publisher.

```
 ■1     |L2     |L3       1
 1      | 4     | ------
 2      | 6     |
 3      | 8     |
 10     |       |
 ------ |       |
L1 ={1,2,3,10}
```

Press **CLEAR** **ENTER**. Repeat this process until all three lists are empty.

```
L1     |L2     |L3       1
■■■■■■ | 4     | ------
       | 6     |
       | 8     |
       | ----- |
L1(1)=
```

To enter the midpoints into **L1,** move your cursor so that it is positioned in the 1st position in **L1.** Type in the first midpoint, **12.5,** and press **ENTER** or use the blue down arrow. Enter the next midpoint, **24.5.** Continue this process until all 7 midpoints are entered into **L1.** Now use the blue up-arrow to scroll to the top of **L1.** As you scroll through the data, check it. If a data point is incorrect, simply move the cursor to highlight it and type in the correct value. When you have moved to the 1st value in **L1,** use the right arrow to move to the first position in **L2.** Enter the frequencies into **L2.**

```
L1      |L2      |L3       2
12.5    | 6■■■■■ | ------
24.5    | 10     |
36.5    | 13     |
48.5    | 8      |
60.5    | 5      |
72.5    | 6      |
84.5    | 2      |
L2(1)=6
```

To graph the histogram, press **2nd** [STAT PLOT] (located above the **Y=** key).

© 2006 Pearson Education, Inc., Upper Saddle River, NJ. All rights reserved. This material is protected under all copyright laws as they currently exist. No portion of this material may be reproduced, in any form or by any means, without permission in writing from the publisher.

Select Plot1 by pressing **ENTER**.

Notice that Plot1 is highlighted. On the next line, notice that the cursor is flashing on **ON** or **OFF**. Position the cursor on **ON** and press **ENTER** to select it. The next two lines on the screen show the different types of graphs. Move your cursor to the symbol for histogram (3rd item in the 1st line of **Type**) and press **ENTER**.

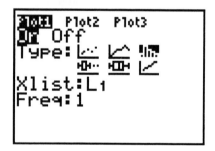

The next line is **Xlist**. Use the blue down arrow to move to this line. On this line, you tell the calculator where the data (the midpoints) are stored. In most graphing situations, the data are entered into **L1** so **L1** is the default option. Notice that the cursor is flashing on **L1**. Push **ENTER** to select **L1**. The last line is the frequency line. On this line, **1** is the default. The cursor should be flashing on **1**. Change **1** to **L2** by pressing 2nd **[L2]**.

© 2006 Pearson Education, Inc., Upper Saddle River, NJ. All rights reserved. This material is protected under all copyright laws as they currently exist. No portion of this material may be reproduced, in any form or by any means, without permission in writing from the publisher.

To view a histogram of the data, press **ZOOM**.

There are several options in the Zoom Menu. Using the blue down arrow, scroll down to option 9, **ZoomStat,** and press **ENTER**. A histogram should appear on the screen.

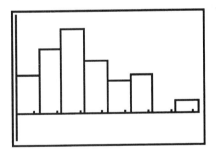

This histogram is not exactly the same as the one on pg. 42 of your textbook. You can adjust the histogram so that it does look exactly like the one in your text. Press **Window** and set **Xmin** to 12.5, **Xmax** to 96.5 (this one extra midpoint is needed to complete the picture), and **Xscl** equal to 12, which is the difference between successive midpoints in the frequency distribution. Note: It is not necessary for you to make any changes to **Ymin**, **Ymax** or **Yscl**.

© 2006 Pearson Education, Inc., Upper Saddle River, NJ. All rights reserved. This material is protected under all copyright laws as they currently exist. No portion of this material may be reproduced, in any form or by any means, without permission in writing from the publisher.

```
WINDOW
 Xmin=12.5
 Xmax=96.5
 Xscl=12
 Ymin=-3.90897
 Ymax=15.21
 Yscl=.1
 Xres=1
```

Press **GRAPH**.

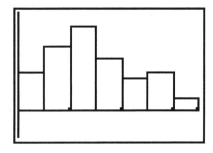

Notice the blue **TRACE** key. If you press it, a flashing cursor, *, will appear at the top of the 1st bar of the histogram.

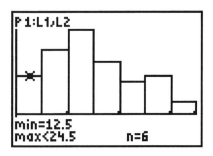

The value of the smallest midpoint is displayed as 12.5 and the number of data points in that bar is displayed as n = 6. Use the blue right arrow to move through each of the bars.

Now that you have completed this example, turn Plot1 **OFF**. Using **2nd** [STAT PLOT], select Plot1 by pressing **ENTER** and highlighting **OFF**. Press **ENTER** and **2nd** [QUIT]. (Note: Turning Plot1 **OFF** is optional. You can leave it ON but leaving it ON will effect other graphing operations of the calculator.)

◀

© 2006 Pearson Education, Inc., Upper Saddle River, NJ. All rights reserved. This material is protected under all copyright laws as they currently exist.
No portion of this material may be reproduced, in any form or by any means, without permission in writing from the publisher.

▸ Exercise 25 (pg. 46) Construct a frequency histogram using 6
classes

Push **STAT** and **ENTER** to select **1:Edit**. Highlight **L1** at the top of the first list
and press **CLEAR** and **ENTER** to clear the data in **L1**. You can also clear **L2**
although you will not be using **L2** in this example. Enter the data into **L1**. Scroll
through your completed list and verify each entry.

To set up the histogram, push **2ⁿᵈ** [STAT PLOT] and **ENTER** to select **Plot 1**.
Turn ON **Plot 1**, set **Type** to **Histogram**, set **Xlist** to **L1**. In this example, you
must set **Freq** to **1**. If the frequency is set on **L2** move the cursor so that it is
flashing on **L2** and press **CLEAR** . The cursor is now in ALPHA mode (notice
that there is an "A" flashing in the cursor). Push the **ALPHA** key and the cursor
should return to a solid flashing square. Type in the number **1.**

Press **ZOOM** and scroll down to **9:ZoomStat** and press **ENTER** and a
histogram will appear on the screen. Press **Window** to adjust the Graph
Window. Set **Xmin** equal to 1000 (the smallest data value) and **Xmax** equal to
7120 (a value, rounded to the nearest ten, that is larger than the largest data point
in the dataset). To set the scale so that you will have 6 classes, calculate (**Xmax** -
Xmin)/6: (7120 – 1000)/6 = 1020. Use this for **Xscl**. (Note: You do not need to
change the values for **Ymin**, **Ymax** or **Yscl**.)

© 2006 Pearson Education, Inc., Upper Saddle River, NJ. All rights reserved. This material is protected under all copyright laws as they currently exist.
No portion of this material may be reproduced, in any form or by any means, without permission in writing from the publisher.

```
WINDOW
 Xmin=1000
 Xmax=7120
 Xscl=1020
 Ymin=-3.90897
 Ymax=15.21
 Yscl=.1
 Xres=1
```

Press **GRAPH** and the histogram should appear.

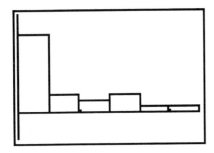

You can press **TRACE** and scroll through the bars of the histogram.
Min and Max values for each bar will appear along with the number of data
points in each class.

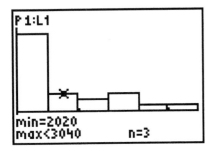

Notice, for example, with the cursor highlighting the second bar of the histogram,
you will see that **n=3** appears, indicating that there are 3 data points in the second
class which contains values from 2020 to 3039.

◀

© 2006 Pearson Education, Inc., Upper Saddle River, NJ. All rights reserved. This material is protected under all copyright laws as they currently exist.
No portion of this material may be reproduced, in any form or by any means, without permission in writing from the publisher.

Section 2.2

▸ Example 5 (pg. 53) Constructing a Pareto Chart

To construct a Pareto chart to represent the causes of inventory shrinkage, you must enter numerical labels for the specific causes into **L1** and the corresponding costs into **L2**. Since the bars are positioned in descending order in a Pareto chart, the labels in **L1** will represent the causes of inventory shrinkage from the most costly to the least costly. Press **STAT** and press **ENTER** to select **1:Edit.** Highlight the name "**L1**" and press **CLEAR** and **ENTER**. Enter the numbers 1,2,3 and 4 into **L1**. These numbers represent the four causes of inventory shrinkage: 1 = employee theft, 2 = shoplifting, 3 = administrative error and 4 = vendor fraud. Move your cursor to highlight "**L2**" and press **CLEAR** and **ENTER**. Enter the corresponding costs: 15.6, 14.7, 7.8 and 2.9.

L1	L2	L3	2
1	15.6	------	
2	14.7		
3	7.8		
4	2.9		
------	------		

L2(5) =

To draw the Pareto chart, press **2ⁿᵈ [STAT PLOT]** . Press **ENTER** and set up **Plot 1**. Highlight **On** and press **ENTER**. Highlight the histogram icon for **Type** and press **ENTER**. Set **Xlist** to **L1** and **Freq** to **L2**.

Press **ZOOM** and scroll down to **9:ZoomStat** and **ENTER**.

© 2006 Pearson Education, Inc., Upper Saddle River, NJ. All rights reserved. This material is protected under all copyright laws as they currently exist. No portion of this material may be reproduced, in any form or by any means, without permission in writing from the publisher.

To adjust the picture so that the bars are connected press **Window**. Set **Xmax** = 5 . (Note: The numbers in **L1** range from 1 to 4. To create the bars in the Pareto, **Xmax** should be set at 5, which is one value greater than the largest value in **L1**.) Set **Xscl** = 1, and press **GRAPH**.. (Note: You do not need to change the values for **Ymin**, **Ymax** or **Yscl**.)

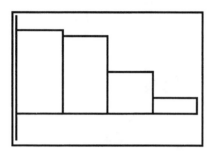

If you press **TRACE**, notice, for the first bar, min=1, max < 2 and n = 15.6. The first bar represents the No. 1 cause of inventory shrinkage. N = 15.6 is the frequency (in millions of dollars) for cause #1. You can use the right arrow key to scroll through the remaining causes.

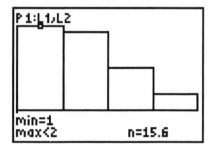

© 2006 Pearson Education, Inc., Upper Saddle River, NJ. All rights reserved. This material is protected under all copyright laws as they currently exist. No portion of this material may be reproduced, in any form or by any means, without permission in writing from the publisher.

▶ Example 7 (pg. 55)   Constructing a Time Series Chart

Press **STAT** and select **1:Edit** from the **Edit Menu**. Clear **L1** and **L2**. Enter the "years" into **L1** and the "subscribers" into **L2**.

L1	L2	L3	2
1991	7.6	------	
1992	11		
1993	16		
1994	24.1		
1995	33.8		
1996	44		
1997	55.3		

L2(1)=7.6

To construct the time series chart, press **2nd [STAT PLOT]** and select **1:Plot 1** and **ENTER**. Turn ON **Plot 1**. Set the **Type** to **Connected Scatterplot,** which is the 2nd icon in the **Type** choices. For **Xlist** select **L1** and for **Ylist** select **L2**. Next, there are three different types of **Marks** that you can select for the graph. The first choice, a small square, is the best one to use.

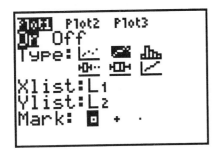

Press **ZOOM** and scroll down to **9:ZoomStat** and press **ENTER** or simply press **9** and **ZoomStat** will automatically be selected. The graph should appear on the screen.

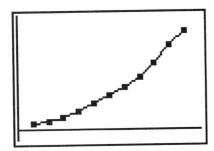

© 2006 Pearson Education, Inc., Upper Saddle River, NJ. All rights reserved. This material is protected under all copyright laws as they currently exist. No portion of this material may be reproduced, in any form or by any means, without permission in writing from the publisher.

Use **TRACE** to scroll through the data values for each year. Notice for example, the number of subscribers is 24.1 million in 1994.

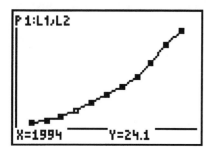

© 2006 Pearson Education, Inc., Upper Saddle River, NJ. All rights reserved. This material is protected under all copyright laws as they currently exist. No portion of this material may be reproduced, in any form or by any means, without permission in writing from the publisher.

▶ Exercise 23 (pg. 58) Pareto Chart

Press **STAT** and select **1:Edit** from the **Edit Menu**. Clear the lists and enter the numbers 1 through 5 into **L1**. These numbers are labels for the five cities. (Note: 1= Miami, the city with the highest ultraviolet index, 2 = Atlanta, the city with the second highest ultraviolet index, etc.). Enter the ultraviolet indices in descending order into **L2**. Press **2nd** [STAT PLOT] and select **Plot 1** and press **ENTER**. Set the **Type** to **Histogram**. Set **Xlist** to **L1** and Freq to **L2**. Press **ZOOM** and press 9 for **ZoomStat.** Adjust the graph by pressing **Window** and setting **Xmax** = 6 (one value higher than the largest value in **L1**) and **Xscl** = 1. (Note: You do not need to change the values for **Ymin, Ymax** or **Yscl**.) Press **GRAPH** to view the Pareto Chart.

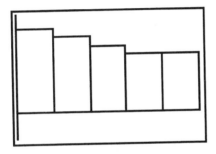

© 2006 Pearson Education, Inc., Upper Saddle River, NJ. All rights reserved. This material is protected under all copyright laws as they currently exist. No portion of this material may be reproduced, in any form or by any means, without permission in writing from the publisher.

▶ Exercise 25 (pg. 59) Scatterplot

Press **STAT** and select **1:Edit** from the **Edit menu**. Clear the lists and enter the data points for "number of students per teacher" into **L1** and the data points for "average Teacher's salary" into **L2**.

To construct the scatterplot, press 2nd [STAT PLOT] and select **1:Plot 1** and **ENTER**. Turn ON **Plot 1**. Set the **Type** to **Scatterplot** which is the 1st icon in the **Type** choices. For **Xlist** select **L1** and for **Ylist** select **L2**. For **Marks** use the first choice, the small square. Press **ZOOM** and press 9 for **ZoomStat** and view the graph.

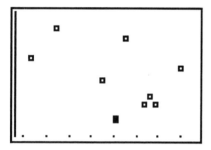

As you can see from the scatterplot, this data set has a large amount of scatter. You might notice a slight downward trend that suggests that the average teacher's salary decreases as the number of students per teacher increases.

◀

© 2006 Pearson Education, Inc., Upper Saddle River, NJ. All rights reserved. This material is protected under all copyright laws as they currently exist. No portion of this material may be reproduced, in any form or by any means, without permission in writing from the publisher.

▶ Exercise 27 (pg. 59) Time Series Chart

Press **STAT** and select **1:Edit**. Enter the "Years" into **L1** and the "prices" into **L2**. Press **2ⁿᵈ** [STAT PLOT] and select 1: **Plot 1** and press **ENTER**. Turn **ON** **Plot 1** and select the **connected scatterplot** (2ⁿᵈ icon) as **Type**. Set **Xlist** to **L1** and **Ylist** to **L2.** For **Marks** use the first choice, the small square. Press **ZOOM** and press ▓ for **ZoomStat** and view the graph.

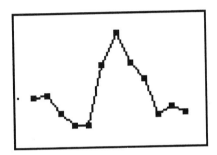

◀

© 2006 Pearson Education, Inc., Upper Saddle River, NJ. All rights reserved. This material is protected under all copyright laws as they currently exist. No portion of this material may be reproduced, in any form or by any means, without permission in writing from the publisher.

Section 2.3

▸ Example 6 (pg. 63) Comparing the mean, median, and mode

Press **STAT** and select **1:Edit**. Clear **L1** and enter the data into **L1**. Press **STAT** again and highlight **CALC** to view the Calc Menu.

Select **1:1-Var Stats** and press **ENTER**. On this line, enter the name of the column that contains the data. Since you have stored the data in **L1,** simply enter **2ⁿᵈ [L1] ENTER** and the first page of the one variable statistics will appear. (Note: If you did not enter a column name, the default column, which is **L1,** would be automatically selected.)

© 2006 Pearson Education, Inc., Upper Saddle River, NJ. All rights reserved. This material is protected under all copyright laws as they currently exist. No portion of this material may be reproduced, in any form or by any means, without permission in writing from the publisher.

The first item is the mean, $\bar{x} = 23.75$. Notice the down arrow in the bottom left corner of the screen. This indicates that more information follows this first page. Use the blue down arrow to scroll through this information. The third item you see on the second page is the median, Med = 21.5.

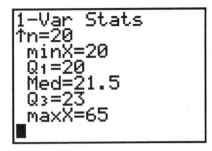

The TI-83 does not calculate the mode but, since this data set is sorted, it is easy to see from the list of data that the mode is 20.

◀

© 2006 Pearson Education, Inc., Upper Saddle River, NJ. All rights reserved. This material is protected under all copyright laws as they currently exist. No portion of this material may be reproduced, in any form or by any means, without permission in writing from the publisher.

▸ Example 7 (pg. 64) Finding a Weighted Mean

Press **STAT** and select **1:Edit**. Clear **L1** and **L2**. Enter the scores into **L1** and the weights into **L2**.

```
L1       L2      L3      2
 86      .5      ------
 96      .15
 82      .2
 98      .1
100      .05
        ▓▓▓▓

L2(6) =
```

Press **STAT** and highlight **CALC** to view the Calc Menu. Select **1:1-Var Stats**, press **ENTER** and press 2nd **[L1]** , 2nd **[L2]** . Press **ENTER**. (Note: You must place the comma between **L1** and **L2**).

```
1-Var Stats L₁,L
₂
```

Using **L1** and **L2** in the **1:1-Var Stats** calculation is necessary when calculating a weighted mean. The calculator uses the data in **L1** and the associated weights in **L2** to calculate the average. In this example, the weighted mean is 88.6.

```
1-Var Stats
 x̄=88.6
 Σx=88.6
 Σx²=7885.6
 Sx=
 σx=5.969924623
↓n=1
■
```

◀

© 2006 Pearson Education, Inc., Upper Saddle River, NJ. All rights reserved. This material is protected under all copyright laws as they currently exist. No portion of this material may be reproduced, in any form or by any means, without permission in writing from the publisher.

▶ Example 8 (pg. 65) Finding the Mean of a Frequency
Distribution

Press **STAT** and select **1:Edit**. Clear **L1** and **L2**. Enter the x-values into **L1**
and the frequencies into **L2**. Press **STAT**, highlight **CALC**, select **1:1-Var
Stats**, press **ENTER**. Next, press **2ⁿᵈ** **[L1]** **,** **2ⁿᵈ** **[L2]** **ENTER**.

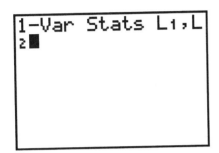

After you press **ENTER**, the sample statistics will appear on the screen. The
mean of the frequency distribution described in columns **L1** and **L2** is 41.78. In
this example you do not have the actual data. What you have is the frequency
distribution of the data summarized into categories. The mean of this frequency
distribution is an approximation of the mean of the actual data.

```
1-Var Stats
 x̄=41.78
 Σx=2089
 Σx²=107196.5
 Sx=20.16163259
 σx=19.95899797
↓n=50
```

© 2006 Pearson Education, Inc., Upper Saddle River, NJ. All rights reserved. This material is protected under all copyright laws as they currently exist.
No portion of this material may be reproduced, in any form or by any means, without permission in writing from the publisher.

> ▶ Exercise 19 (pg. 68) Finding the Mean, Median and Mode

Enter the data into **L1**. Press **STAT** and select **1:1-Var Stats** from the Calc Menu. Press **2ⁿᵈ L1 ENTER**.

```
1-Var Stats
 x̄=93.8137931
 Σx=2720.6
 Σx²=255836.06
 Sx=4.653165139
 σx=4.572234354
↓n=29
■
```

The first item in the output screen is the mean, 93.81. Scroll down through the output and find the median, Med = 92.9.

```
1-Var Stats
↑n=29
 minX=85.4
 Q₁=90.3
 Med=92.9
 Q₃=96.9
 maxX=105.2
```

Although the TI-83 does not calculate the mode, you can use the SORT feature to order the data. You can then scroll through the data to see if the data set contains a mode. To sort the data, press **2ⁿᵈ [LIST]** (Note: **List** is found above the **STAT** key). Move the cursor to highlight **OPS** and select **1:SortA(** and **ENTER**.

© 2006 Pearson Education, Inc., Upper Saddle River, NJ. All rights reserved. This material is protected under all copyright laws as they currently exist. No portion of this material may be reproduced, in any form or by any means, without permission in writing from the publisher.

```
NAMES OPS MATH
1:SortA(
2:SortD(
3:dim(
4:Fill(
5:seq(
6:cumSum(
7↓ΔList(
```

To sort **L1** in ascending order, press **2ⁿᵈ** **[L1]** , close the parentheses and press **ENTER**.

```
SortA(L1)
            Done
■
```

To view the data, press **STAT** and select **1:Edit** and press **ENTER**. Use the down arrow to scroll through **L1** to see if the data has a mode. In this example, there are two modes: 90.3 and 91.8. (Both of these values occur twice. All the other values occur only once.)

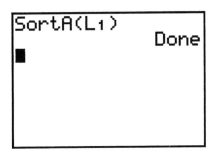

```
L1      L2     L3      2
85.4    ▬▬▬▬▬  ------
88
88.7
89.7
89.8
90.1
90.3
L2(1)=
```

© 2006 Pearson Education, Inc., Upper Saddle River, NJ. All rights reserved. This material is protected under all copyright laws as they currently exist. No portion of this material may be reproduced, in any form or by any means, without permission in writing from the publisher.

▶ Exercise 45 (pg. 71) Finding the Mean of Grouped Data

Press **STAT** and select **1:Edit**. Clear **L1** and **L2**. Enter the midpoints of each Age group into **L1** and the frequencies into **L2**.

L1	L2	L3	2
4.5	57	------	
14.5	68		
24.5	36		
34.5	55		
44.5	71		
54.5	44		
64.5	36		

L2 = {57,68,36,55...

Press **STAT** and highlight **CALC** to view the Calc Menu. Select **1:1-Var Stats**, press **ENTER** and type in **2ⁿᵈ L1** **,** **2ⁿᵈ L2.** The mean of this grouped data is 35.01.

```
1-Var Stats
 x̄=35.01413882
 Σx=13620.5
 Σx²=658407.25
 Sx=21.62813485
 σx=21.6003173
↓n=389
```

© 2006 Pearson Education, Inc., Upper Saddle River, NJ. All rights reserved. This material is protected under all copyright laws as they currently exist. No portion of this material may be reproduced, in any form or by any means, without permission in writing from the publisher.

> ▸ Exercise 49 (pg. 72) Construct a frequency histogram

Press **STAT** and select **1:Edit**. Clear **L1** and enter the data into **L1**. Press **2ⁿᵈ**
[STAT PLOT] and select **1:Plot 1** and press **ENTER**. Turn **ON** Plot 1 and set
the **Type** to **Histogram** and press **ENTER**. Move the cursor to **Xlist** and set this
to **L1**. Move the cursor to **Freq** and set it equal to **1.** (Note: The cursor may be
in **ALPHA** mode with a flashing **A** . Press **ALPHA** to return to the solid
rectangular cursor and type in **1**.)

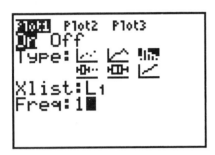

Press **ZOOM** and **9** to select **ZoomStat**. The histogram that is displayed has 7
classes. To change to 5 classes, press **Window**. Notice that **Xmin** = 62 and
Xmax = 78.33. Change **Xmax** to 79, which is the next whole number greater
than 78.33. To determine a value for **Xscl**, you must calculate (**Xmax** - **Xmin**)/5.
Press **2ⁿᵈ** [QUIT] to get out of the Window Menu. (Note: QUIT is found above
the **MODE** key). Calculate (79 - 62)/5 and round the resulting value, 3.4, to 3.
Press **Window** and set **Xscl** = 3. Press **GRAPH** and view the histogram with 5
classes. Notice that one of the bars is too tall to fit completely on the screen.
Press **Window** and set **Ymax** = 9, which is the next whole number greater than
8.19. Press **GRAPH** again. As you can see from the graph, the histogram
appears to be symmetric.

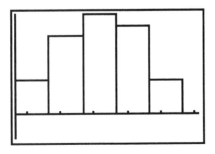

© 2006 Pearson Education, Inc., Upper Saddle River, NJ. All rights reserved. This material is protected under all copyright laws as they currently exist.
No portion of this material may be reproduced, in any form or by any means, without permission in writing from the publisher.

Exercise 55 (pg. 73) Data Analysis

Press **STAT** and select **1:Edit**. Clear **L1** and then enter the data. Press **STAT** and highlight **CALC**. Select **1:1-Var Stats** and press **2ⁿᵈ L1 ENTER** to get values for the mean and median.

Since the TI-83 does not do a stem and leaf display, you can use a histogram to get a picture of the data. Press 2ⁿᵈ [STAT PLOT] , select **1:Plot 1** and press **ENTER**. Turn ON **Plot 1**. Set **Type** to **Histogram**. The **Xlist** is **L1** and the **Freq** is **1**. Press **ZOOM** and 9 to select **ZoomStat**.

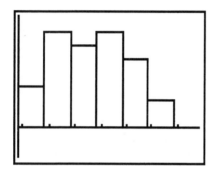

© 2006 Pearson Education, Inc., Upper Saddle River, NJ. All rights reserved. This material is protected under all copyright laws as they currently exist. No portion of this material may be reproduced, in any form or by any means, without permission in writing from the publisher.

Section 2.4

> ▶ Example 5 (pg. 78) Finding the Standard Deviation

Press **STAT** and select **1:Edit**. Clear **L1** and enter the data into **L1**. Press **STAT** and highlight **CALC** to display the Calc Menu. Select **1: 1-Var Stats** and press 2nd **L1** **ENTER**. The sample standard deviation is Sx, 5.089373342

```
1-Var Stats
 x̄=33.72916667
 Σx=809.5
 Σx²=27899.5
 Sx=5.089373342
 σx=4.982216639
↓n=24
```

◀

> ▶ Example 9 (pg. 82) Standard Deviation of Grouped Data

Press **STAT** and select **1:Edit**. Clear **L1** and **L2**. Enter the x-values into **L1** and the frequencies into **L2**. Press **STAT** and highlight **CALC** to select the Calc Menu. Select **1:1-Var Stats** and press **ENTER**. Type in 2nd **L1** , 2nd **L2** and press **ENTER**. From the statistics displayed, the mean is 1.82 and the sample standard deviation is 1.722.

```
1-Var Stats
 x̄=1.82
 Σx=91
 Σx²=311
 Sx=1.722480414
 σx=1.705168613
↓n=50
```

◀

© 2006 Pearson Education, Inc., Upper Saddle River, NJ. All rights reserved. This material is protected under all copyright laws as they currently exist.
No portion of this material may be reproduced, in any form or by any means, without permission in writing from the publisher.

▸ Exercise 19 (pg. 86) Comparing Two Datasets

Press **STAT** and select **1:Edit**. Clear **L1** and **L2**. Enter the Los Angeles Data
into **L1** and the Long Beach Data into **L2**. Press **STAT** and highlight **CALC**.
Select **1:1-Var Stats** and press **2nd** **L1** **ENTER**. The sample standard deviation
for the Los Angeles data is Sx = 6.111.

```
1-Var Stats
 x̄=26.25555556
 Σx=236.3
 Σx²=6502.97
 Sx=6.111282826
 σx=5.761772704
↓n=9
■
```

To find the range, scroll down through the display and find **minX = 18.3.**
Continue scrolling through the display and find **maxX = 35.9.** To calculate the
range, simply type in **35.9 - 18.3** and press **ENTER**. The range = 17.6.

```
minX=18.3
Q₁=20.55
Med=26.1
Q₃=31.85
maxX=35.9
35.9-18.3
          17.6
```

To find the variance, you must square the standard deviation. Type in 6.111 and
press the x^2 key. The variance is 37.344.

© 2006 Pearson Education, Inc., Upper Saddle River, NJ. All rights reserved. This material is protected under all copyright laws as they currently exist.
No portion of this material may be reproduced, in any form or by any means, without permission in writing from the publisher.

```
Med=26.1
 Q3=31.85
 maxX=35.9
35.9-18.3
                17.6
6.111²
        37.344321
```

For the Long Beach Data, press **STAT** , highlight **CALC**, select **1:1-Var Stats**, press **ENTER** and press 2nd **L2**.

```
1-Var Stats L2█
```

Press **ENTER**. The sample standard deviation for the Long Beach Data is Sx = 2.952.

```
1-Var Stats
 x̄=22.87777778
 Σx=205.9
 Σx²=4780.25
 Sx=2.952023788
 σx=2.783194718
↓n=9
█
```

Use the same procedure as you used for the Los Angeles Data, to find the range and the variance for the Long Beach Data.

◀

© 2006 Pearson Education, Inc., Upper Saddle River, NJ. All rights reserved. This material is protected under all copyright laws as they currently exist. No portion of this material may be reproduced, in any form or by any means, without permission in writing from the publisher.

Section 2.5

> ▸ Example 2 (pg. 94) Finding Quartiles

Press **STAT** and select **1:Edit**. Clear **L1** and enter the data into **L1**. Press **STAT** and highlight **CALC**. Select **1:1-Var Stats** and press **2nd L1 ENTER**. Scroll down through the descriptive statistics. You will see the first quartile, **Q1** = **21.5**, the second quartile (the median), **Med = 23** and the third quartile, **Q3 = 28**.

```
1-Var Stats
↑n=25
 minX=15
 Q₁=21.5
 Med=23
 Q₃=28
 maxX=30
```

◀

© 2006 Pearson Education, Inc., Upper Saddle River, NJ. All rights reserved. This material is protected under all copyright laws as they currently exist. No portion of this material may be reproduced, in any form or by any means, without permission in writing from the publisher.

| Example 4 (pg. 96) | Drawing a Box-and-Whisker-Plot

Press **STAT** and select **1:Edit**. Clear **L1** and enter the data from Example 1 on pg. 93 in your textbook. Press 2nd [STAT PLOT]. Select **1:Plot 1** and press **ENTER**. Turn On **Plot 1**. Using the right arrow (you can not use the down arrow to drop to the second line), scroll through the **Type** options and choose the second boxplot which is the middle entry in row 2 of the **TYPE** options. Press **ENTER**. Move to **Xlist** and type in 2nd **L1**. Press **ENTER** and move to **Freq**. Set **Freq** to **1**. If **Freq** is set on **L2**, press **ALPHA** to return the cursor to a flashing solid rectangle and type in **1**. Press **ZOOM** and **9** to select **ZoomStat**. The Boxplot will appear on your screen.

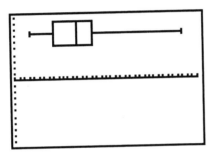

If you press **TRACE** and use the left and right arrow keys, you can display the five values that represent the five-number summary of the data.

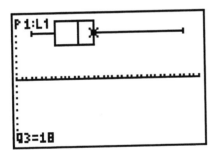

Notice in the above screen display that the trace cursor is on the right side of the box, which represents the third quartile. Also, at the bottom of the screen it is noted that Q3=18.

◀

© 2006 Pearson Education, Inc., Upper Saddle River, NJ. All rights reserved. This material is protected under all copyright laws as they currently exist. No portion of this material may be reproduced, in any form or by any means, without permission in writing from the publisher.

> **Exercise 1 (pg. 100)** Quartiles and a Box-and-Whisker-Plot

Press **STAT** and select **1:Edit**. Clear **L1** and enter the data . Press 2nd [STAT PLOT]. Select **1:Plot 1** and press **ENTER**. Turn On **Plot 1**. Using the right arrow, scroll through the **Type** options and choose the second boxplot which is the second entry in row 2 of the **TYPE** options. Press **ENTER**. Move to **Xlist** and type in 2nd **L1**. Press **ENTER** and move to **Freq**. Set **Freq** to **1**. If **Freq** is set on **L2**, press **ALPHA** to return the cursor to a flashing solid rectangle and type in **1**. Press **ZOOM** and 9 to select **ZoomStat**. The Boxplot will appear on your screen. If you press **TRACE** and use the right and left arrows, you can display **Q1, Med** and **Q3**. Notice Med=6 for this example.

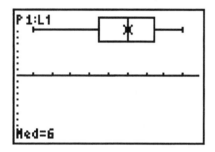

© 2006 Pearson Education, Inc., Upper Saddle River, NJ. All rights reserved. This material is protected under all copyright laws as they currently exist. No portion of this material may be reproduced, in any form or by any means, without permission in writing from the publisher.

> ▶ Exercise 19 (pg. 101) Quartiles and a Box-and-Whisker-Plot

Press **STAT** and select **1:Edit**. Clear **L1** and enter the data. Press **2ⁿᵈ** [STAT PLOT]. Select **1:Plot 1** and press **ENTER**. Turn On **Plot 1**. Using the right arrow, scroll through the **Type** options and choose the second boxplot which is the second entry in row 2 of the **TYPE** options. Press **ENTER**. Move to **Xlist** and type in **2ⁿᵈ L1**. Press **ENTER** and move to **Freq**. Set **Freq** to **1**. If **Freq** is set on **L2**, press **ALPHA** to return the cursor to a flashing solid rectangle and type in **1**. Press **ZOOM** and **9** to select **ZoomStat.** The Boxplot will appear on your screen. If you press **TRACE** and use the right and left arrows, you can display **Q1, Med** and **Q3**.

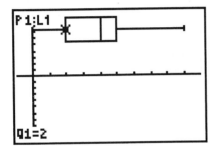

© 2006 Pearson Education, Inc., Upper Saddle River, NJ. All rights reserved. This material is protected under all copyright laws as they currently exist. No portion of this material may be reproduced, in any form or by any means, without permission in writing from the publisher.

▸ Technology (pg. 113) Monthly Milk Production

Exercises 1-2: Press **STAT** and select **1:Edit**. Clear **L1** and enter the data into **L1**. Press **STAT** and highlight **CALC**. Select **1:1-Var Stats** and press 2nd **L1 ENTER**. The sample mean and sample standard deviation can be found in the output display.

Exercises 3-4. You will use the histogram of the data to construct the frequency distribution. To construct a histogram, press 2nd [STAT PLOT]. Select **1: Plot 1** and **ENTER**. Turn ON **Plot 1** by highlighting **On** and pressing **ENTER**. Scroll through the **Type** icons, highlight the **Histogram** and press **ENTER**. Move to **Xlist** and type in 2nd **L1**. Move to the **Freq** entry and type in **1.** (Note: If the Freq entry is **L2**, Press **ALPHA** and enter **1**). To view a histogram of the data, press **ZOOM** and 9. To adjust the histogram, press **Window**. Set **Xmin = 1000** and set **Xscl = 500.** (All other entries in the Window Menu can remain unchanged). Press **GRAPH** and then press **TRACE**.

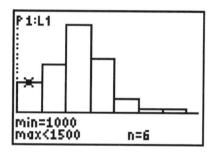

The minimum and maximum values of the first category are displayed. (**1000 and < 1500**). The midpoint of the first category is (1000+1499)/2, which is **1249.5.** The frequency for the first category is **n = 6.** Trace through the histogram and set up a frequency distribution for the data:

Category	Midpoint	Frequency
1000 – 1499	1249.5	6

Exercise 5. Using the values that you found in Exercises 1 and 2, calculate the lower and upper endpoints of the one and two standard deviation intervals: $(\bar{x} \pm 1s)$ and $(\bar{x} \pm 2s)$. Next, press 2nd [LIST]. Highlight **OPS** and select **1:SortA(** , press **ENTER**. Press 2nd [L1] and close the parentheses. Press

© 2006 Pearson Education, Inc., Upper Saddle River, NJ. All rights reserved. This material is protected under all copyright laws as they currently exist. No portion of this material may be reproduced, in any form or by any means, without permission in writing from the publisher.

ENTER. Press **STAT**, select **1:Edit** and press **ENTER**. Scroll through the data in **L1** and count the number of data points that fall in the one and two standard deviation intervals: $(\bar{x} \pm 1s)$ and $(\bar{x} \pm 2s)$. To find the percentage of data points that lie in each of these intervals, calculate: (number of data points in each interval/ 50) * 100. Compare these percentages with the percentages stated in the Empirical rule.

Exercises 6 - 7. Using the frequency distribution you created, enter the midpoints into **L2** and the frequencies into **L3**. Press **STAT** , highlight **CALC**. Select **1:1-Var Stats** and press **ENTER**. Type in **2**nd **L2** **,** **2**nd **L3** and press **ENTER**.   The mean and standard deviation for the frequency distribution will be displayed on the screen.

Exercise 8: Compare the actual values for the mean and standard deviation that you found in Exercises 1 and 2 to the estimates for the mean and standard deviation that you found in Exercises 6 and 7.

© 2006 Pearson Education, Inc., Upper Saddle River, NJ. All rights reserved. This material is protected under all copyright laws as they currently exist.
No portion of this material may be reproduced, in any form or by any means, without permission in writing from the publisher.

Probability

Section 3.1

▸ Law of Large Numbers (pg. 122)

You can use the TI-83 to simulate tossing a coin 150 times. In this simulation,
we will designate "0" as Heads and "1" as Tails.

Press **MATH**, highlight **PRB**, and select **5:randInt(** and press **ENTER**. The
randInt(command requires a minimum value, (which is 0 for this simulation), a
maximum value (which is 1), and the number of trials (150). In the **randInt(**
command type in **0** ⎸**,**⎸ **1** ⎸**,**⎸ **150.**

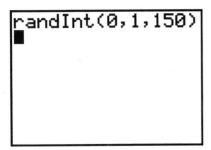

Press **ENTER**. It will take a few seconds for the calculator to generate 150
tosses. Notice, in the upper right hand corner a flashing ⎸ | ⎸, indicating that the
calculator is working. When the simulation has been completed, a string of **0's**
and **1's** will appear on the screen followed by **….,** indicating that there are more
numbers in the string that are not shown.

© 2006 Pearson Education, Inc., Upper Saddle River, NJ. All rights reserved. This material is protected under all copyright laws as they currently exist.
No portion of this material may be reproduced, in any form or by any means, without permission in writing from the publisher.

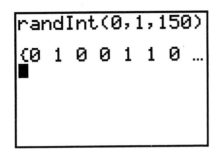

Press **STO** and 2nd **[L1]** **ENTER** . This will store the string of numbers in **L1**.
Press 2nd [LIST] and highlight **MATH**. Select **sum(** and type in **L1**.

```
randInt(0,1,150)

{0 1 0 0 1 1 0 …
Ans→L₁
{0 1 0 0 1 1 0 …
sum(L₁)
                71
```

The sum of **L1** equals the number of Tails in the list. For this particular
simulation, the sum is 71. The number of Heads is equal to (150 - no. of Tails).
The proportion of Heads is (no. of Heads / 150). How close is this proportion to
50% ?

© 2006 Pearson Education, Inc., Upper Saddle River, NJ. All rights reserved. This material is protected under all copyright laws as they currently exist.
No portion of this material may be reproduced, in any form or by any means, without permission in writing from the publisher.

Section 3.2

> ▸ Exercise 32d (pg.139) Birthday Problem

To simulate this problem, press **MATH**, highlight **PRB**, select **5:randInt(** and
enter **1** , **365** , **24.**

```
randInt(1,365,24
)
{250 364 159 26…
```

Store the data in **L1** by pressing **STO** and 2nd **[L1]** **ENTER**. To see if there are
at least two people with the same birthday, you must look for a matching pair of
numbers in **L1**. To do this, press 2nd **[LIST]**, highlight **OPS** and select **1:SortA(**
and press **ENTER**. The column you want to sort in ascending order is **L1**, so
type 2nd **[L1]** into the sort command and press **ENTER**.

```
randInt(1,365,24
)
{292 351 153 60…
Ans→L₁
{292 351 153 60…
SortA(L₁)
                 Done
```

Press **STAT** and select **1:EDIT**, press **ENTER** and scroll down through **L1** and
check for matching numbers. If you find any matching numbers, that means that
at least 2 people in your simulation have the same birthday.

© 2006 Pearson Education, Inc., Upper Saddle River, NJ. All rights reserved. This material is protected under all copyright laws as they currently exist.
No portion of this material may be reproduced, in any form or by any means, without permission in writing from the publisher.

```
L1      L2      L3      1
15      ------  ------
15
23
44
60
64
74
L1(1)=15
```

Notice in this simulation, 15 is listed twice. This represents two people with the same birthday, January 15 (the 15th day of a year). That means that for your first simulation you have found at least two people with the same birthday. Since you have found this matching pair right at the beginning of **L1**, you do not need to look further into the data in **L1**. Repeat this simulation process nine more times, each time checking to see if you have a matching pair.

How many of your simulations resulted in at least one matching pair? Suppose you found a matching pair in 5 out of your 10 simulations. That means that your estimate of the probability of finding at least 2 people with the same birthday in a room of 24 people is "5 out of 10" or 50%.

◄

© 2006 Pearson Education, Inc., Upper Saddle River, NJ. All rights reserved. This material is protected under all copyright laws as they currently exist. No portion of this material may be reproduced, in any form or by any means, without permission in writing from the publisher.

Section 3.4

▸ Example 3 (pg. 152)   Finding the Number of Permutations

You have a baseball team consisting of nine players. To find the number of different batting orders that are possible, you must calculate the number of permutations of **9** objects taken **9** at a time. The formula **nPr** is used with **n = 9** (the number of players on the team) and **r = 9** (the number of players you will be selecting). So, the formula is **9P9**.

Press 9, MATH, highlight **PRB** and select **2:nPr** and ENTER.

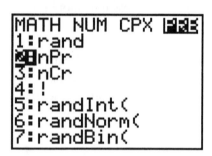

Now press 9 and ENTER. The answer, 362880, appears on the screen.

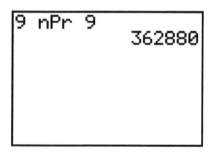

© 2006 Pearson Education, Inc., Upper Saddle River, NJ. All rights reserved. This material is protected under all copyright laws as they currently exist. No portion of this material may be reproduced, in any form or by any means, without permission in writing from the publisher.

> **Example 5 (pg. 153)** More Permutations

Use the permutation formula with **n = 43** and **r = 3.** Enter **43,** press **MATH**, highlight **PRB**, select **2:nPr** and press **ENTER**. Now enter **3** and press **ENTER**.

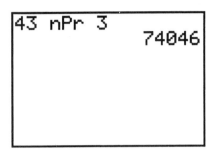

> **Example 6 (pg. 154)** Distinguishable Permutations

To calculate $\dfrac{12!}{6!4!2!}$ you will use the factorial function **(!).** Enter the first value, **12**, press **MATH**, highlight **PRB** and select **4:!** . Then press **÷** . Open the parentheses by pressing **(** . Enter the next value, **6**, press **MATH**, **PRB**, and select **4:!** . To multiply by 4!, press **x** and enter the next value, **4.** Press **MATH**, **PRB**, and select **4:!** . To multiply by 2!, press **x** and enter the next value, **2.** Press **MATH**, **PRB**, and select **4:!** . Close the parentheses **)** and press **ENTER**.

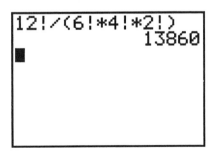

© 2006 Pearson Education, Inc., Upper Saddle River, NJ. All rights reserved. This material is protected under all copyright laws as they currently exist. No portion of this material may be reproduced, in any form or by any means, without permission in writing from the publisher.

▶ Example 7 (pg. 155) Finding the Number of Combinations

To calculate the number of different combinations of four companies that can be selected from 16 bidding companies you will use the combination formula: **nCr,** where n = the total number of items in the group and r = the number of items being selected. In this example, the formula is **16C4**. Enter the first value, **16,** press **MATH**, highlight **PRB** and select **3: nCr,** and enter the second value, **4.** Press **ENTER** and the answer will be displayed on the screen..

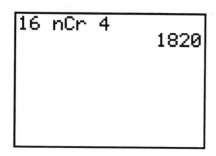

▶ Example 9 (pg. 156) Finding Probabilities

To calculate the probability of being dealt five diamonds from a standard deck of 52 playing cards, you must calculate: $\dfrac{13C5}{52C5}$.

To calculate the numerator, enter the first value, **13**, press **MATH**, highlight **PRB** and select **3:nCr** and enter the next value, **5**. Next press **÷** and enter the first value in the denominator, **52**, press **MATH**, highlight **PRB** and select **3:nCr,** enter the next value, **5.** Press **ENTER** and the answer will be displayed on your screen.

```
13 nCr 5/52 nCr
5
    4.951980792E-4
```

Notice that the answer is written in scientific notation. To convert to standard notation, move the decimal point 4 places to the left. Thus, the answer is 00495.

© 2006 Pearson Education, Inc., Upper Saddle River, NJ. All rights reserved. This material is protected under all copyright laws as they currently exist.
No portion of this material may be reproduced, in any form or by any means, without permission in writing from the publisher.

▶ Exercise 40 (pg. 159) Probability

a. To calculate **200C15**, enter the first value, **200**, press **MATH**, highlight **PRB** and select **3:nCr**, enter the next value, **15** and press **ENTER**.

b. Calculate **144C15** (follow the steps for part a.).

c. The probability that **no** minorities are selected is equal to the probability that the committee is composed completely of non-minorities. This probability can be calculated with the following formula: $\dfrac{144C15}{200C15}$.

(Use the answer from part b for the numerator and the answer from part a for the denominator.)

◀

© 2006 Pearson Education, Inc., Upper Saddle River, NJ. All rights reserved. This material is protected under all copyright laws as they currently exist. No portion of this material may be reproduced, in any form or by any means, without permission in writing from the publisher.

▶ Technology (pg. 169) Composing Mozart Variations

Exercises 3 - 4: To select one number from 1 to 11, press MATH, highlight
PRB and select **5:randInt(** and enter **1** , **11**) and press ENTER. One random
number between 1 and 11 will be displayed on the screen.

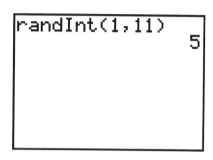

3a. Hint: Each number from 1 to 11 has an equal chance of being selected. So
each of the 11 possibilities has equal probability. What is this theoretical
probability? (Use this to answer the question in Exercise 4.)

3b. To select 100 integers between 1 and 11, press MATH, highlight **PRB** and
select **5:randInt(** and enter **1** , **11** , **100**) and press ENTER. Store the
results in **L1** by pressing STO, 2nd [L1], ENTER. Next you can create a
histogram and use it to tally your results. To create the histogram, press 2nd
[STAT PLOT], select **1:Plot 1** and press ENTER. Turn **ON** Plot 1, set **Type** to
Histogram. Set **Xlist** to **L1** and **Freq** to **1.** Press ZOOM and select 9 for
ZoomStat. Press WINDOW and set **Xscl = 1,** then press GRAPH. Use TRACE
to scroll through the bars of the histogram.

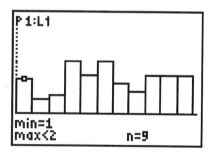

The first bar represents the number of times that a "**1**" occurred in the 100 tosses.
(Notice on the screen: min = 1and n=9). Use the right arrow to scroll through the
bars in the histogram. As the cursor moves from one bar in the histogram to the
next bar, the "min =" will indicate the current x-value and the "n=" will indicate
the corresponding frequency. Record the x-values and the corresponding
frequencies in a table. For example, using the histogram in the above diagram,
the frequency table would begin with X = 1, n = 9. Convert each frequency into

© 2006 Pearson Education, Inc., Upper Saddle River, NJ. All rights reserved. This material is protected under all copyright laws as they currently exist.
No portion of this material may be reproduced, in any form or by any means, without permission in writing from the publisher.

a relative frequency by dividing each frequency by 100, and use the relative frequencies to answer the question in Exercise 4.

Exercise 5: To select 2 random numbers from 1 to 6, press MATH, highlight **PRB** and select **5:randInt(** and enter **1** , **6** , **2**) and press ENTER. Add the two numbers in the display and subtract **1** from the total.

5a. First list all possible pairs. (There are 36 pairs: (1,1), (1,2), (1,3)....). For each pair, find the sum and subtract "1" to find a total. Make a frequency table listing all the possible totals from 1 to 11. Next to each total record the number of times that total occurred. Lastly, convert each of these frequencies to relative frequencies by dividing by 36. These relative frequencies are the theoretical probabilities. Use them to answer the question in Exercise 6.

5b. To select 100 totals, create 2 columns of 100 random numbers. Press MATH, highlight **PRB** and select **5:randInt(** and enter **1** , **6** , **100**) and press ENTER. Press STO 2nd **[L1]** and ENTER to store this first string of numbers in **L1**. Next create a second set of 100 numbers using the same procedure. Press STO 2nd **[L2]** and ENTER to store this second string of numbers in **L2**. Now you can calculate the sum of each row and subtract **1**. Press STAT and select **1:EDIT**. Move the cursor to highlight **L3**.

```
L1        L2        ▓      3
 1         4       ------
 3         2
 6         4
 2         3
 1         1
 1         2
 3         6

L3 =
```

Press ENTER and the cursor will move to the bottom of the screen. On the bottom line next to **L3 =**, type in 2nd **[L1]** + 2nd **[L2]** - 1 and press ENTER. The results should appear in **L3.**

© 2006 Pearson Education, Inc., Upper Saddle River, NJ. All rights reserved. This material is protected under all copyright laws as they currently exist. No portion of this material may be reproduced, in any form or by any means, without permission in writing from the publisher.

```
L1      L2      L3     3
1       4       4
3       2       4
6       4       9
2       3       4
1       1       1
1       2       2
3       6       8
L3(1)=4
```

Create a histogram of **L3** and use it to tally your results (follow the steps in Exercise 3 to create the histogram). Use **TRACE** to find the frequencies for each X-value and record your results in a frequency table. Convert each frequency to a relative frequency and use the relative frequencies to answer the question in Exercise 6.

◀

© 2006 Pearson Education, Inc., Upper Saddle River, NJ. All rights reserved. This material is protected under all copyright laws as they currently exist.
No portion of this material may be reproduced, in any form or by any means, without permission in writing from the publisher.

Discrete Probability Distributions

CHAPTER

4

Section 4.1

▶ Example 5 (pg. 176) Mean of a Probability Distribution

Press **STAT** and select **1:EDIT**. Clear **L1** and **L2**. Enter the X-values into **L1** and the P(x) values into **L2**. Press **STAT** and highlight **CALC**. Select **1:1-Var Stats,** press **ENTER** and press 2nd [L1] , 2nd [L2] **ENTER** to see the descriptive statistics. The mean score is 2.94.

```
1-Var Stats
 x̄=2.94
 Σx=2.94
 Σx²=10.26
 Sx=
 σx=1.271377206
↓n=1
```

© 2006 Pearson Education, Inc., Upper Saddle River, NJ. All rights reserved. This material is protected under all copyright laws as they currently exist. No portion of this material may be reproduced, in any form or by any means, without permission in writing from the publisher.

▶ Example 6 (pg. 177) The Variance and Standard Deviation

Using the data from Example 5 on pg. 176, which you stored in **L1** and **L2**, press STAT highlight **CALC**. Select **1:1-Var Stats,** press ENTER and press 2nd [L1] , 2nd **[L2]** ENTER. The population standard deviation , σx, is 1.27.

```
1-Var Stats
 x̄=2.94
 Σx=2.94
 Σx²=10.26
 Sx=
 σx=1.271377206
↓n=1
■
```

To find the variance, you must use the value of the standard deviation. Since the variance is equal to the standard deviation squared, type in **1.2714** and press the x^2 key. The population variance is **1.616**.

```
 Σx=2.94
 Σx²=10.26
 Sx=
 σx=1.271377206
↓n=1
1.2714²
        1.61645796
```

◀

© 2006 Pearson Education, Inc., Upper Saddle River, NJ. All rights reserved. This material is protected under all copyright laws as they currently exist. No portion of this material may be reproduced, in any form or by any means, without permission in writing from the publisher.

Section 4.2

▸ Example 4 (pg. 188)   Binomial Probabilities

To find a binomial probability you will use the binomial probability density function, **binompdf(n,p,x).** For this example, n = 100, p = .58 and x = 65. Press 2nd [DISTR]. Scroll down through the menu to select **0:binompdf(** and press ENTER . Type in **100** , **.58** , **65**) and press ENTER. The answer, **.0299**, will appear on the screen.

```
binompdf(100,.58
,65)
      .0299216472
■
```

© 2006 Pearson Education, Inc., Upper Saddle River, NJ. All rights reserved. This material is protected under all copyright laws as they currently exist. No portion of this material may be reproduced, in any form or by any means, without permission in writing from the publisher.

> ▸ Example 7 (pg. 191) Graphing Binomial Distributions

Construct a probability distribution for a binomial probability model with n = 6 and p = .65. Press STAT, select **1:EDIT** and clear **L1** and **L2**. Enter the values 0 through 6 into **L1**. Press 2nd [QUIT]. To calculate the probabilities for each X-value in **L1**, first change the display mode so that the probabilities displayed will be rounded to 3 decimal places. Press MODE and change from **FLOAT** to **3** and press 2nd [QUIT]. Next press 2nd [DISTR] and select **0:binompdf(** and type in **6** , **.65**) and press ENTER. Store these probabilities in **L2** by pressing STO 2nd [L2] ENTER.

```
binompdf(6,.65)
{.002 .020 .095…
Ans→L₂
{.002 .020 .095…
```

To graph the binomial distribution, press 2nd [STAT PLOT] and press ENTER. Turn **ON** Plot 1, select **Histogram** for **Type**, set **Xlist** to **L1** and set **Freq** to **L2**. Press ZOOM and select 9 for **ZoomStat**. Adjust the graph by pressing WINDOW and setting **Xmin = 0, Xmax = 7, Xscl = 1, Ymin = 0** and **Ymax = .35.** Choosing an Xmax=7, leaves some space at the right of the graph in order to complete the histogram. The Ymax value was selected by looking through the values in **L2** and then rounding the largest value UP to a convenient number. Press GRAPH to view the histogram.

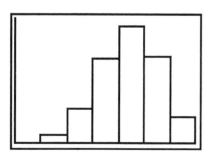

© 2006 Pearson Education, Inc., Upper Saddle River, NJ. All rights reserved. This material is protected under all copyright laws as they currently exist. No portion of this material may be reproduced, in any form or by any means, without permission in writing from the publisher.

▸ Exercise 13 (pg. 194) Binomial Probabilities

A multiple-choice quiz consists of five questions and each question has four possible answers. If you randomly guess the answer to each question, the probability of getting the correct answer is 1 in 4, so p = .25 and n = 5.

a.   To calculate P(x = 3), press 2nd [DISTR] and select **0:binompdf(** and type in **5** [,] **.25** [,] **3** [)] and press ENTER.

b-c. To calculate inequalities, such as P(X ≥ 3) or P(X < 3), you can use the cumulative probability command: **binomcdf (n,p,x)**. This command accumulates probability starting at X = 0 and ending at a specified X-value. To calculate the probability of guessing at least three answers correctly, that is P(X ≥ 3), press 2nd [DISTR] and select **A:binomcdf(** by scrolling through the options and selecting **A:binomcdf(** or by pressing ALPHA A. (Note: A is the ALPHA function on the MATH key.) Type in **5** [,] **.25** [,] **2** [)] and press ENTER. The result, P(X ≤ 2) = .896.

```
binomcdf(5,.25,2
)
                .896
```

This result is the accumulated probability that X = 0,1 or 2, since this command, **binomcdf**, accumulates probability starting at X = 0. You want P(X ≥ 3) and this is the *complement* of P(X ≤ 2). So P(X ≥ 3) = 1 - P(X ≤ 2) which is .104. The probability of guessing *less than* 3 answers correctly is P(X ≤ 2) which equals 0.896.

◀

© 2006 Pearson Education, Inc., Upper Saddle River, NJ. All rights reserved. This material is protected under all copyright laws as they currently exist. No portion of this material may be reproduced, in any form or by any means, without permission in writing from the publisher.

Section 4.3

> ▶ **Example 1 (pg. 198)** The Geometric Distribution

Suppose the probability that you will make a sale on any given telephone call is 0.23. To find the probability that your *first* sale on any given day will occur on your fourth or fifth telephone call of the day, press 2nd [DISTR] and select **D:geometpdf(** and type in **.23** , 2nd { **4** , **5** 2nd }) . This command will display 2 probabilites: $P(X = 4)$ and $P(X = 5)$. The probability that your first sale of the day will occur on your fourth or fifth sales call of the day is .105003 + .080852.

```
geometpdf(.23,{4
,5})
{.10500259 .080…
■
```

> ▶ **Example 2 (pg. 199)** The Poisson Distribution

Use the command **poissonpdf** (μ, x) with $\mu = 3$ and $x = 4$. Press 2nd [DISTR] and select **B:poissonpdf(** and type in **3** , **4**) and press ENTER. The answer will appear on the screen.

```
poissonpdf(3,4)
        .1680313557
```

© 2006 Pearson Education, Inc., Upper Saddle River, NJ. All rights reserved. This material is protected under all copyright laws as they currently exist. No portion of this material may be reproduced, in any form or by any means, without permission in writing from the publisher.

▶ Exercise 19 (pg. 203) Poisson Distribution

This is a Poisson probability problem with μ = 8.

a.   To find the probability that exactly 4 businesses will fail in any given hour, press 2nd [DISTR] and select **B:poissonpdf(** . Type in **8** , **4**) and press ENTER.

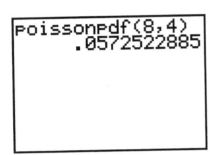

b.   Use the cumulative probability command **poissoncdf(.** This command accumulates probability starting at X = 0 and ending at the specified X-value. To calculate the probability that at least 4 businesses will fail in any given hour, that is P(X ≥ 4), you must find P(X ≤ 3) and subtract from 1. Press 2nd [DISTR] , select **C:poissoncdf(** and type in **8** , **3**) and press ENTER. The result, P(X ≤ 3), is .0424. This result is the accumulated probability that X = 0,1,2, or 3. P(X ≥ 4) is the *complement* of P(X ≤ 3). So, P(X ≥ 4) is 1 - .0424 or .9576.

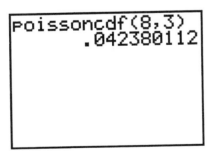

© 2006 Pearson Education, Inc., Upper Saddle River, NJ. All rights reserved. This material is protected under all copyright laws as they currently exist.
No portion of this material may be reproduced, in any form or by any means, without permission in writing from the publisher.

c. To find the probability that more than 4 businesses will fail in any given hour, find P(X > 4). So, first calculate the *complement*, P(X ≤ 4), and then subtract the answer from 1.

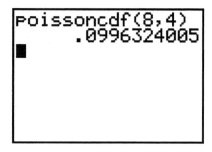

© 2006 Pearson Education, Inc., Upper Saddle River, NJ. All rights reserved. This material is protected under all copyright laws as they currently exist. No portion of this material may be reproduced, in any form or by any means, without permission in writing from the publisher.

▶ Technology (pg. 213)

Exercise 1: Create a Poisson probability distribution with $\mu = 4$ for $X = 0$ to 20. Press **STAT** and select **1:EDIT** . Clear **L1** and **L2**. Enter the integers 0,1,2,3,…20 into **L1** and press 2nd [QUIT].

For this example, it is helpful to display the probabilities with 3 decimal places. Press **MODE**. Move the cursor to the 2nd line and select **3** and press **ENTER**.

Press 2nd [DISTR] and select **B:poissonpdf(** . Type in **4** , 2nd [L1] and press **ENTER** .

```
poissonpdf(4,L1)
{.018 .073 .147…
```

A partial display of the probabilities will appear. Press **STO** and 2nd [L2] **ENTER**. Press **STAT**, and select **1:EDIT.** **L1** and **L2** will be displayed on the screen.

L1	L2	L3	1
0.0000	.018	------	
1.000	.073		
2.000	.147		
3.000	.195		
4.000	.195		
5.000	.156		
6.000	.104		

L1(1)=0

Notice that the X-values in **L1** now have 3 decimal places. This is a result of setting the **MODE** to **3.** Each value in **L2** is the poisson probability associated with the X-value in **L1**. So, for example, $P(X = 2)$ is .147. Scroll through **L2** and compare the probabilities in **L2** with the heights if the corresponding bars in the frequency histogram on page 213.

© 2006 Pearson Education, Inc., Upper Saddle River, NJ. All rights reserved. This material is protected under all copyright laws as they currently exist.
No portion of this material may be reproduced, in any form or by any means, without permission in writing from the publisher.

Exercises 3 - 5: Use another technology tool to generate the random numbers.
The TI-83 cannot generate poisson random data.

Exercise 6: For this exercise, $\mu = 5$ and $X = 10$. Press 2nd [DISTR] and select
B:poissonpdf(. Type in **5** , **10** and press ENTER .

Exercise 7: Use the probability distribution that you generated in Exercise 1.

a. Sum the probabilities in **L2** that correspond to X- values of 3, 4 and 5 in **L1**.

b. Sum the probabilities in **L2** that correspond to X- values of 0,1,2,3 and 4 in
    L1. This is $P(X \leq 4)$. Subtract this sum from **1** to get $P(X > 4)$.

c. Assuming that the number of arrivals per minute are independent events,
    raise $P(X > 4)$ to the fourth power.

© 2006 Pearson Education, Inc., Upper Saddle River, NJ. All rights reserved. This material is protected under all copyright laws as they currently exist.
No portion of this material may be reproduced, in any form or by any means, without permission in writing from the publisher.

Normal Probability Distributions

Section 5.2

▶ Example 3 (pg. 231) Normal Probabilities

Suppose that cholesterol levels of American men are normally distributed with a mean of 215 and a standard deviation of 25. If you randomly select one American male, calculate the probability that his cholesterol is less than 175, that is P(X < 175).

The TI-83 has two methods for calculating this probability.

Method 1: **Normalcdf(***lowerbound, upperbound,* μ , σ) computes probability between a *lowerbound* and an *upperbound.* In this example, you are computing the probability to the left of 175, so 175 is the *upperbound.* In examples like this, where there is no *lowerbound*, you can always use *negative infinity* as the *lowerbound.* Negative infinity is specified by ⊖ 1 2ⁿᵈ **[EE]** 9 9 (Note: **EE** is found above the comma ,). Try entering −1 EE 99 into your calculator.

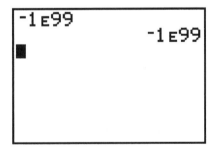

Now, to calculate P(X < 175), press 2ⁿᵈ [DISTR] and select **2:normalcdf(** and type in **-1E99** , 175 , 215 , 25) and press ENTER.

© 2006 Pearson Education, Inc., Upper Saddle River, NJ. All rights reserved. This material is protected under all copyright laws as they currently exist. No portion of this material may be reproduced, in any form or by any means, without permission in writing from the publisher.

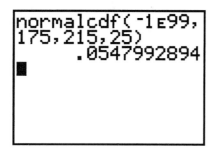

Technical note:Theoretically, the normal probability distribution (the bell-shaped curve) extends infinitely to the right and left of the mean (see Textbook pg. 216). In this particular problem, P(X < 175), you do not necessarily have to use negative infinity (-1 EE 99) as your *lowerbound*. If you look at this example in your textbook on pg. 231, the *lowerbound* is set at 0. This is a perfectly fine selection since no individual will have a cholesterol level less than 0.

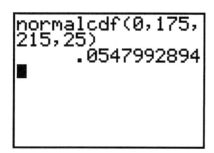

Notice that your results are the same in both of the above screens.

Method 2: This method calculates P(X < 175) and also displays a graph of the probability distribution. You must first clear the Y-registers and turn OFF all STATPLOTS. Next, set up the WINDOW so that the graph will be displayed properly. You will need to set Xmin equal to (μ - 3 σ) and Xmax equal to (μ + 3 σ). Press **WINDOW** and set **Xmin** equal to (μ - 3 σ) by entering **215 - 3 * 25.** Press **ENTER** and set **Xmax** equal to (μ + 3 σ) by entering **215 + 3 * 25.** Set **Xscl** equal to σ.

Setting the Y-range is a little more difficult to do. A good "rule - of - thumb" is to set **Ymax** equal to .5 /σ. For this example, type in **.5 / 25** for **Ymax.**

© 2006 Pearson Education, Inc., Upper Saddle River, NJ. All rights reserved. This material is protected under all copyright laws as they currently exist. No portion of this material may be reproduced, in any form or by any means, without permission in writing from the publisher.

```
WINDOW
 Xmin=140
 Xmax=290
 Xscl=25
 Ymin=-.005
 Ymax=.5/25█
 Yscl=1
 Xres=1
```

Use the blue up arrow to highlight **Ymin**. A good value for **Ymin** is **(-) Ymax /
4** so type in ⌨(-) **.02 / 4**.

```
WINDOW
 Xmin=140
 Xmax=290
 Xscl=25
 Ymin=-.02/4█
 Ymax=.02
 Yscl=1
 Xres=1
```

Press 2nd [QUIT]. Clear all the previous drawings by pressing 2nd **[DRAW]**
and selecting **1:ClrDraw** and pressing ENTER ENTER. Now you can draw the
probability distribution. Press 2nd [DISTR]. Highlight **DRAW** and select
1:ShadeNorm(and type in **-1E99** ⏎ **175** ⏎ **215** ⏎ **25** ⏎ and press ENTER. The
output displays a normal curve with the appropriate area shaded in and its value
computed.

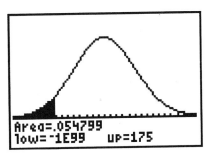

© 2006 Pearson Education, Inc., Upper Saddle River, NJ. All rights reserved. This material is protected under all copyright laws as they currently exist.
No portion of this material may be reproduced, in any form or by any means, without permission in writing from the publisher.

▶ Exercise 13 (pg. 233) Finding Probabilities

In this exercise, use a normal distribution with $\mu = 69.2$ and $\sigma = 2.9$.

Method 1:To find P(X < 66), press 2ⁿᵈ [DISTR] , select **2:normalcdf(** and type in **-1E99** ⎵ **66** ⎵ **69.2** ⎵ **2.9** ⎵ and press ENTER. (Note: Since no male will have a height less than 0 inches, you could have used "0" in place of –1 EE 99 as your lowerbound.

```
normalcdf(-1E99,
66,69.2,2.9)
         .1349163123
■
```

Method 2: To find P(X < 66) and include a graph, you must first clear the Y-registers and turn OFF all STATPLOTS. Next, set up the Graph Window. Press WINDOW and set **Xmin = 69.2 - 3 * 2.9 and Xmax = 69.2 + 3 * 2.9.** Set **Xscl = 2.9.** Set **Ymax = .5 / 2.9 and Ymin = -.172/4.**

Press 2ⁿᵈ [DRAW] and select **1:ClrDraw** and press ENTER ENTER. Press 2ⁿᵈ [DISTR], highlight **DRAW** and select **1:ShadeNorm(** and type in **-1E99** ⎵ **66** ⎵ **69.2** ⎵ **2.9** ⎵ and press ENTER.

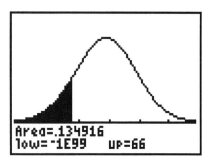

```
Area=.134916
low=-1E99    up=66
```

© 2006 Pearson Education, Inc., Upper Saddle River, NJ. All rights reserved. This material is protected under all copyright laws as they currently exist. No portion of this material may be reproduced, in any form or by any means, without permission in writing from the publisher.

To find p(66< **X** < 72), press 2ⁿᵈ [DISTR] , select **2:normalcdf(** and type in **66** [,] **72** [,] **69.2** [,] **2.9** [)] and press ENTER .

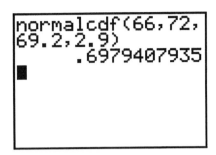

or press 2ⁿᵈ [DRAW] and select **1:ClrDraw** and press ENTER ENTER. Press 2ⁿᵈ [DISTR] , highlight **DRAW** and select **1:ShadeNorm(** and type in **66** [,] **72** [,] **69.2** [,] **2.9** [)] and press ENTER .

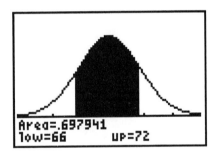

To find P(X > 72), press 2ⁿᵈ [DISTR] , select **2:normalcdf(** and type in **72** [,] **1E99** [,] **69.2** [,] **2.9** [)] and press ENTER. (Note: In this example, the lowerbound is 72 and the upperbound is positive infinity).

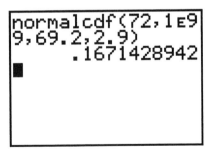

or press 2ⁿᵈ [DRAW] and select **1:ClrDraw** and press ENTER ENTER. Press 2ⁿᵈ [DISTR] , highlight **DRAW** and select **1:ShadeNorm(**and type in **72** [,] **1E99** [,] **69.2** [,] **2.9** [)] and press ENTER.

© 2006 Pearson Education, Inc., Upper Saddle River, NJ. All rights reserved. This material is protected under all copyright laws as they currently exist. No portion of this material may be reproduced, in any form or by any means, without permission in writing from the publisher.

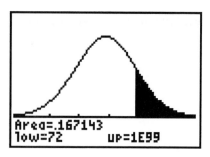

```
Area=.167143
low=72      up=1E99
```

Note: When using the TI-83 (or any other technology tool), the answers you obtain may vary slightly from the answers that you would obtain using the standard normal table. Consequently, your answers may not be exactly the same as the answers found in the answer key in your textbook. The differences are simply due to rounding.

◀

© 2006 Pearson Education, Inc., Upper Saddle River, NJ. All rights reserved. This material is protected under all copyright laws as they currently exist. No portion of this material may be reproduced, in any form or by any means, without permission in writing from the publisher.

Section 5.3

> ▸ Example 4 (pg. 240) Finding a Specific Data Value

This is called an inverse normal problem and the command **invNorm(area,** μ, σ) is used. In this type of problem, a percentage of the area under the normal curve is given and you are asked to find the corresponding X-value. In this example, the percentage given is the top 5 %. The TI-83 always calculates probability from negative infinity up to the specified X-value. To find the X-value corresponding to the top 5 %, you must accumulate the bottom 95 % of the area. Press 2nd [DISTR] and select **3:invNorm(** and type in **.95** , **75** , **6.5**) and press ENTER.

```
invNorm(.95,75,6
.5)
        85.69154857
```

In order to score in the top 5 %, you must earn a score of at least 85.69.
Assuming that scores are given as whole numbers, your score must be at least 86.

© 2006 Pearson Education, Inc., Upper Saddle River, NJ. All rights reserved. This material is protected under all copyright laws as they currently exist. No portion of this material may be reproduced, in any form or by any means, without permission in writing from the publisher.

▶ Exercise 40 (pg. 243) Heights of Males

This is a normal distribution with $\mu = 69.2$ and $\sigma = 2.9$.

a. To find the 90th percentile, press 2nd [DISTR] and select **3:invNorm(** and type in **.90** , **69.2** , **2.9**) and press ENTER.

```
invNorm(.90,69.2
,2.9)
       72.91649954
■
```

b. To find the first quartile, press 2nd [DISTR] and select **3:invNorm(** and type in **.25** , **69.2** , **2.9**) and press ENTER .

```
invNorm(.25,69.2
,2.9)
       67.24397973
■
```

◀

© 2006 Pearson Education, Inc., Upper Saddle River, NJ. All rights reserved. This material is protected under all copyright laws as they currently exist.
No portion of this material may be reproduced, in any form or by any means, without permission in writing from the publisher.

Section 5.4

▶ Example 4 (pg. 251) Probabilities for Sampling Distributions

---

In this example, data has been collected on the average daily driving time for different age groups. From the graph on pg. 251, you will find that the mean driving time for adults in the 15 to 19 age group is: $\mu = 25$ minutes. The problem states that the assumed standard deviation is $\sigma = 1.5$ minutes.

You randomly sample 50 drivers in the $15 - 19$ age group. Since n (the sample size) is greater than 30, you can conclude that the sampling distribution of the sample mean is approximately normal with $u_{\bar{x}} = 25$ and $\sigma_{\bar{x}} = 1.5/\sqrt{50}$. To calculate P($24.7 < \bar{x} < 25.5$), press 2nd [DISTR] , select **2:normalcdf(** and type in **24.7** ⎡,⎤ **25.5** ⎡,⎤ **25** ⎡,⎤ $1.5/\sqrt{50}$ ⎡)⎤ and press ENTER.

```
normalcdf(24.7,2
5.5,25,1.5/√(50)
        .9121393013
▮
```

Note: The answer in your textbook is 0.9116. This answer was calculated using the z-table. Since z-values in the table are rounded to hundredths, the answers will vary slightly from those obtained using the TI-83.

◀

© 2006 Pearson Education, Inc., Upper Saddle River, NJ. All rights reserved. This material is protected under all copyright laws as they currently exist. No portion of this material may be reproduced, in any form or by any means, without permission in writing from the publisher.

▶ Example 6 (pg. 253) Finding Probabilities for x and $\bar{x}$

The population is normally distributed with $\mu = 2870$ and $\sigma = 900$.

1. To calculate P(X <2500), press 2nd [DISTR], select **2:normalcdf(** and type in **-1E99** , **2500** , **2870** , **900**) and press ENTER. (Note: Since the minimum credit card balance is 0, the lowerbound could be set at 0, rather than negative infinity.)

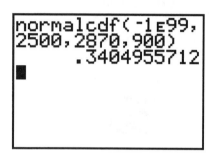

```
normalcdf(-1E99,
2500,2870,900)
        .3404955712
```

2. To calculate P($\bar{x}$ <2500), press 2nd [DISTR], select **2:normalcdf(** and type in **-1E99** , **2500** , **2870** , **900/$\sqrt{25}$**) and press ENTER.

```
normalcdf(-1E99,
2500,2870,900/√(
25))
        .0199126205
```

© 2006 Pearson Education, Inc., Upper Saddle River, NJ. All rights reserved. This material is protected under all copyright laws as they currently exist. No portion of this material may be reproduced, in any form or by any means, without permission in writing from the publisher.

▶ Exercise 29 (pg. 256) Make a Decision

To decide whether the machine needs to be reset, you must decide how unlikely it would be to find a mean of 127.9 from a sample of 40 cans if, in fact, the machine is actually operating correctly at $\mu = 128$. One method of determining the likelihood of $\bar{x} = 127.9$ is to calculate how far 127.9 is from the mean of 128. You can do this by calculating how much area there is under the normal curve to the left of 127.9. The smaller that area is, the farther 127.9 is from the mean and the more unlikely 127.9 is.

To calculate $P(\bar{x} \leq 127.9)$, press 2nd [DISTR] , select **2:normalcdf(** and type in

-1E99 ⎢,⎟ **127.9** ⎢,⎟ **128** ⎢,⎟ **0.20/$\sqrt{40}$** ⎢)⎟ and press ENTER.

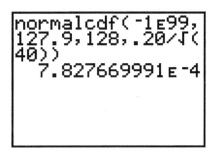

Notice that the answer is displayed in scientific notation: 7.827E-4. Convert this to standard notation, .0007827, by moving the decimal point 4 places to the left. This probability is extremely small; therefore, the event ($\bar{x} \leq 127.9$) is highly unlikely if the mean is actually 128. So, something has gone wrong with the machine and the actual mean must have shifted to a value less than 128.

© 2006 Pearson Education, Inc., Upper Saddle River, NJ. All rights reserved. This material is protected under all copyright laws as they currently exist. No portion of this material may be reproduced, in any form or by any means, without permission in writing from the publisher.

▶ Technology (pg. 277) Age Distribution in the U. S.

Exercise 1: Press STAT and select **1:EDIT**. Clear **L1**, **L2** and **L3**.
Enter the age distribution into **L1** and **L2** by putting class midpoints in **L1** and
relative frequencies (converted to decimals) into **L2**. (The first entry is 2 in **L1**
and .067 in **L2**.) To find the population mean, μ, and the population standard
deviation, σ, press STAT, highlight **CALC**, select **1:1-Var Stats**, press ENTER
and press 2nd [L1] **,** 2nd [L2] ENTER. The mean and the standard deviation
will be displayed. (Note: Use "σx" because the age data represents the entire
population distribution of ages, not a sample.)

Exercise 2: Enter the thirty-six sample means into **L3**. To find the mean
and standard deviation of these sample means, press STAT, highlight
CALC, select **1:1-Var Stats**. Press ENTER and press 2nd [L3] ENTER.
The mean and the standard deviation will be displayed. (Note: use "sx"
because the 36 sample means are a sample of 36 means, not the entire
population of all possible means of size n = 40).

Exercise 3: Construct a histogram of the age distribution. Press 2nd
[STAT PLOT] and select **1: Plot 1**. Turn **ON** Plot 1, select **Histogram**
for **Type,** set **Xlist** to **L1** and set **Freq** to **L2**. Press ZOOM and 9 for
ZoomStat. Adjust the WINDOW by pressing WINDOW and setting
Xmax = 100, Xscl = 5, Ymin = -.02 and Ymax = .09.

Exercise 4: The TI-83 will draw a frequency histogram for a set of data,
not a *relative* frequency histogram. (The shape of the data can be
determined from either type of histogram). Press 2nd **[STAT PLOT]** and
select **1: Plot 1**. **Plot 1** has already been turned **ON** and **Histogram** has
been selected for **Type**. Set **Xlist** to **L3**. On the **Freq** line, press CLEAR
and ALPHA to return to the standard rectangular cursor and enter 1. Press
ZOOM and 9 for **ZoomStat.** To adjust the histogram so that it has nine
classes, press WINDOW. Approximate the class width using (48 - 28)/9.
This value is approximately 2, so set **Xscl = 2** and press GRAPH.

Exercise 5: See the output from Exercise 1 for the population standard
deviation.

Exercise 6: See the output from Exercise 2 for the standard deviation of
the sample means.

© 2006 Pearson Education, Inc., Upper Saddle River, NJ. All rights reserved. This material is protected under all copyright laws as they currently exist.
No portion of this material may be reproduced, in any form or by any means, without permission in writing from the publisher.

Confidence Intervals

CHAPTER

6

Section 6.1

▸ Example 4 (pg. 284) Constructing a Confidence Interval

Enter the data from Example 1 on pg. 280 into **L1**. In this example, n > 30, so the sample standard deviation, Sx, is a good approximation of σ, the population standard deviation. To find Sx, press **STAT**, highlight **CALC**, select **1:1-Var Stats** and press **L1 ENTER**.

```
1-Var Stats
 x̄=12.42592593
 Σx=671
 Σx²=9671
 Sx=5.015454801
 σx=4.968798394
↓n=54
▯
```

The sample standard deviation is Sx = 5.015. Using this as an estimate of σ, you can construct a Z-Interval, a confidence interval for μ, the population mean. Press **STAT**, highlight **TESTS** and select **7:Zinterval.**

```
EDIT CALC TESTS
1:Z-Test…
2:T-Test…
3:2-SampZTest…
4:2-SampTTest…
5:1-PropZTest…
6:2-PropZTest…
7↓ZInterval…
```

On the first line of the display, you can select **Data** or **Stats.** For this example, select **Data** because you want to use the actual data which is in **L1**. Press **ENTER** . Move to the next line and enter 5.015, your estimate of σ. On the

© 2006 Pearson Education, Inc., Upper Saddle River, NJ. All rights reserved. This material is protected under all copyright laws as they currently exist. No portion of this material may be reproduced, in any form or by any means, without permission in writing from the publisher.

next line, enter **L1** for **LIST**. For **Freq**, enter **1**. For **C-Level** , enter **.99** for a 99% confidence interval. Move the cursor to **Calculate.**

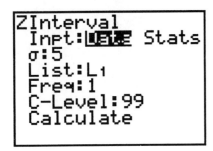

Press **ENTER** .

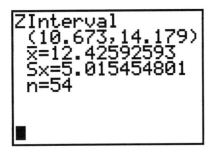

A 99% confidence interval estimate of μ , the population mean is (10.673, 14.179). The output display includes the sample mean (12.426), the sample standard deviation (5.015), and the sample size (54).

◄

© 2006 Pearson Education, Inc., Upper Saddle River, NJ. All rights reserved. This material is protected under all copyright laws as they currently exist.
No portion of this material may be reproduced, in any form or by any means, without permission in writing from the publisher.

▶ Example 5 (pg. 285) Confidence Interval for μ (σ known)

In this example, $\bar{x} = 22.9$ years, n = 20, a value for σ from previous studies is given as $\sigma = 1.5$ years, and the population is normally distributed. Construct a 90% confidence interval for μ, the mean age of all students currently enrolled at the college.

Press **STAT**, highlight **TESTS** and select **7:ZInterval**. In this example, you do not have the actual data. What you have are the summary statistics of the data, so select **Stats** and press **ENTER**. Enter the value for σ : **1.5**; enter the value for $\bar{x}$: **22.9**; enter the value for **n: 20**; and enter **.90** for **C-level**. Highlight **Calculate**.

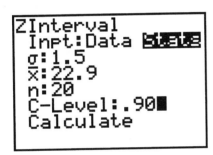

Press **ENTER** .

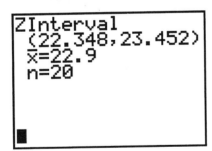

Using a 90% confidence interval, you estimate that the average age of all students is between 22.348 and 23.452.

© 2006 Pearson Education, Inc., Upper Saddle River, NJ. All rights reserved. This material is protected under all copyright laws as they currently exist. No portion of this material may be reproduced, in any form or by any means, without permission in writing from the publisher.

▸ Exercise 47 (pg. 289) Newspaper Reading Times

Enter the data into **L1**. Press **STAT**, highlight **TESTS** and select **7:ZInterval**.
Since you have entered the actual data points into **L1**, select **Data** for **Inpt** and
press **ENTER**. Enter the value for σ , **1.5**. Set **LIST = L1, Freq = 1** and **C-
level = .90**. Highlight **Calculate.**

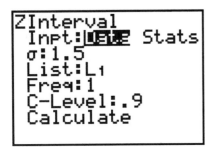

```
ZInterval
  Inpt:DATA Stats
  σ:1.5
  List:L₁
  Freq:1
  C-Level:.9
  Calculate
```

Now press **ENTER**.

```
ZInterval
  (8.4296,9.7037)
  x̄=9.066666667
  Sx=1.579632266
  n=15
  ■
```

Repeat the process and set **C-level = .99**.

```
ZInterval
  (8.0691,10.064)
  x̄=9.066666667
  Sx=1.579632266
  n=15
  ■
```

◀

© 2006 Pearson Education, Inc., Upper Saddle River, NJ. All rights reserved. This material is protected under all copyright laws as they currently exist.
No portion of this material may be reproduced, in any form or by any means, without permission in writing from the publisher.

▶ Exercise 61 (pg. 292) Using Technology

Enter the data into L1. In this example, no estimate of σ is given so you should use Sx, the sample standard deviation as a good approximation of σ since n > 30. Press **STAT**, highlight **CALC**, select **1:1-Var Stats** and press **L1 ENTER**. The sample standard deviation, Sx, is 11.19.

Press **STAT**, highlight **TESTS** and select **7:ZInterval**. For **Inpt**, select **Data**. For σ, enter **11.19**. Set **List** to **L1**, **Freq** to **1** and **C-level** to **.95**. Highlight **Calculate** and press **ENTER**.

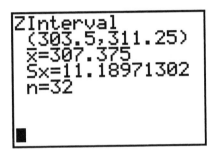

```
ZInterval
 (303.5,311.25)
 x̄=307.375
 Sx=11.18971302
 n=32
```

© 2006 Pearson Education, Inc., Upper Saddle River, NJ. All rights reserved. This material is protected under all copyright laws as they currently exist.
No portion of this material may be reproduced, in any form or by any means, without permission in writing from the publisher.

Section 6.2

▶ Example 3 (pg. 298) Constructing a Confidence Interval

In this example, n = 20, $\bar{x}$ = 6.93 and s = 0.42 and the underlying population is
assumed to be normal. Find a 99% confidence interval for μ. First, notice that
σ is unknown. The sample standard deviation, s, is not a good approximation of
σ when n < 30. To construct the confidence interval for μ, the correct
procedure under these circumstances (n < 30, σ is unknown and the population
is assumed to be normally distributed) is to use a T-Interval.

Press **STAT**, highlight **TESTS**, scroll through the options and select **8:TInterval**
and press **ENTER** . Select **Stats** for **Inpt** and press **ENTER**. Fill in $\bar{x}$, Sx, and
n with the sample statistics. Set **C-level** to **.99**. Highlight **Calculate**.

```
TInterval
 Inpt:Data Stats
 x:6.93
 Sx:.42
 n:20
 C-Level:.99█
 Calculate
```

Press **ENTER** .

```
TInterval
 (6.6613,7.1987)
 x=6.93
 Sx=.42
 n=20
```

◀

© 2006 Pearson Education, Inc., Upper Saddle River, NJ. All rights reserved. This material is protected under all copyright laws as they currently exist.
No portion of this material may be reproduced, in any form or by any means, without permission in writing from the publisher.

▶ Exercise 21 (pg. 302) Deciding on a Distribution

In this example, n = 70, $\bar{x}$ = 1.25 and s = 0.01. Notice that σ is unknown. You can use s, the sample standard deviation, as a good approximation of σ in this case because n > 30. To calculate a 95 % confidence interval for μ, press **STAT**, highlight **TESTS** and select **7:ZInterval**. Fill in the screen with the appropriate information.

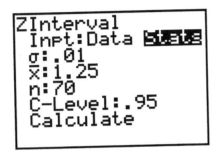

Calculate the confidence interval.

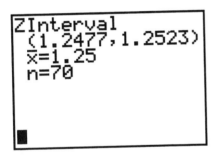

© 2006 Pearson Education, Inc., Upper Saddle River, NJ. All rights reserved. This material is protected under all copyright laws as they currently exist. No portion of this material may be reproduced, in any form or by any means, without permission in writing from the publisher.

▸ Exercise 23 (pg. 302) Deciding on a Distribution

Enter the data into **L1**. In this case, with n = 25 and σ unknown, and assuming
that the population is normally distributed, you should use a Tinterval. Press
STAT, highlight **TESTS** and select **8:TInterval**. Fill in the appropriate
information.

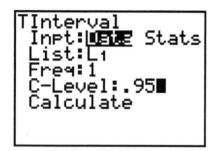

Calculate the confidence interval.

```
TInterval
 (22.762,25.238)
 x̄=24
 Sx=3
 n=25

■
```

© 2006 Pearson Education, Inc., Upper Saddle River, NJ. All rights reserved. This material is protected under all copyright laws as they currently exist.
No portion of this material may be reproduced, in any form or by any means, without permission in writing from the publisher.

Section 6.3

> ▸ Example 2 (pg. 305) Constructing a Confidence Interval for p

In this example, 1011 American adults are surveyed and 293 say that their favorite sport is football (see Example 1, pg. 303). Construct a 95 % confidence interval for p, the proportion of all Americans who say that their favorite sport is football.

Press **STAT**, highlight **TESTS**, scroll through the options and select **A:1-PropZInt**. The value for X is the number of American adults in the group of 1011 who said that football was their favorite sport, so **X = 293**. The number who were surveyed is n, so **n = 1011**. Enter **.95** for **C-level**.

```
1-PropZInt
 x:293
 n:1011
 C-Level:.95
 Calculate
```

Highlight **Calculate** and press **ENTER** .

```
1-PropZInt
 (.26185,.31778)
 p=.2898120673
 n=1011
```

In the output display the confidence interval for p is (.26185, .31778). The sample proportion, $\hat{p}$, is .28981 and the number surveyed is 1011.

◀

© 2006 Pearson Education, Inc., Upper Saddle River, NJ. All rights reserved. This material is protected under all copyright laws as they currently exist.
No portion of this material may be reproduced, in any form or by any means, without permission in writing from the publisher.

> ▸ Example 3 (pg. 306) Confidence Interval for p

From the graph, the sample proportion, $\hat{p}$, is 0.63 and n is 900. Construct a 99% confidence interval for the proportion of adults who think that teenagers are the more dangerous drivers. In order to construct this interval using the TI-83, you must have a value for X, the number of people in the study who said that teenagers were the more dangerous drivers. Multiply 0.63 by 900 to get this value. If this value is not a whole number, round to the nearest whole number. For this example, X is 567.

Press **STAT**, highlight **TESTS** and select **A:1-PropZInt** by scrolling through the options or by simply pressing **ALPHA** **A**. Enter the appropriate information from the sample.

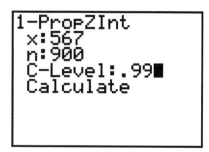

Highlight **Calculate** and press **ENTER** .

```
1-PropZInt
 (.58855,.67145)
 p=.63
 n=900
```

© 2006 Pearson Education, Inc., Upper Saddle River, NJ. All rights reserved. This material is protected under all copyright laws as they currently exist.
No portion of this material may be reproduced, in any form or by any means, without permission in writing from the publisher.

▸ Exercise 25 (pg. 310) Confidence Interval for p

a. To construct a 99% confidence interval for the proportion of men who favor
    irradiation of red meat, begin by multiplying .61 by 500 to obtain a value for
    X, the number of men in the survey who favor irradiation of red meat. Press
    STAT, highlight **TESTS** and select **A:1-PropZInt**. Fill in the appropriate
    values.

```
1-PropZInt
 x:305
 n:500
 C-Level:.99
 Calculate
```

Highlight **Calculate** and press **ENTER** .

```
1-PropZInt
 (.55381,.66619)
 p=.61
 n=500

■
```

b. To construct a 99 % confidence interval for the proportion of women who
    favor irradiation of red meat, multiply .44 by 500 to obtain a value for X, the
    number of women in the survey who favor irradiation of red meat. Press
    STAT, highlight **TESTS** and select **A:1-PropZInt**. Fill in the appropriate
    values. Highlight **Calculate** and press **ENTER** .

```
1-PropZInt
 (.38282,.49718)
 p=.44
 n=500

■
```

© 2006 Pearson Education, Inc., Upper Saddle River, NJ. All rights reserved. This material is protected under all copyright laws as they currently exist.
No portion of this material may be reproduced, in any form or by any means, without permission in writing from the publisher.

Notice that the two confidence intervals do not overlap. It is therefore unlikely that the proportion of males in the population who favor irradiation of red meat is the same as the proportion of females in the population who favor the irradiation of red meat.

◀

> **Technology (pg. 327)** "Most Admired" Polls

1. Use the survey information to construct a 95% confidence interval for the proportion of people who would have chosen Pope John Paul II as their most admired man. Press **STAT**, highlight **TESTS** and select **A:1-PropInt**. Set **X = 40** and **n = 1004**. Set **C-level** to **.95**, highlight **Calculate** and press **ENTER** .

3. To construct a 95% confidence interval for the proportion of people who would have chosen Oprah Winfrey as their most admired female, you must calculate X, the number of people in the sample who chose Oprah. Multiply .07 by 1004 and round your answer to the nearest whole number. Press **STAT**, highlight **TESTS**, select **A:1-PropZInt** and fill in the appropriate information. Press **Calculate** and press **ENTER** .

4. To do one simulation, press **MATH**, highlight **PRB**, select **7:randBin(** and type in **1004** , **.10**) . The output is the number of successes in a survey of n = 1011 people. In this case, a "success" is choosing Oprah Winfrey as your most admired female. (Note: It takes approximately one minute for the TI-83 to do the calculation).

    To run the simulation ten times use **7:randBin(1004,.10,10)**. (These simulations will take approximately 8 minutes). The output is a list of the number of successes in each of the 10 surveys. Calculate $\hat{p}$ for each of the surveys. $\hat{p}$ is equal to (number of successes)/1004. Use these 10 values of $\hat{p}$ to answer questions 4a and 4b.

◀

© 2006 Pearson Education, Inc., Upper Saddle River, NJ. All rights reserved. This material is protected under all copyright laws as they currently exist. No portion of this material may be reproduced, in any form or by any means, without permission in writing from the publisher.

Hypothesis Testing with One Sample

CHAPTER

7

Section 7.2

▸ Example 4 (pg. 350) Hypothesis Testing Using P-values

The hypothesis test, $H_o : \mu \geq 30$ vs. $H_a : \mu < 30$, is a left-tailed test. The sample statistics are $\bar{x} = 28.5$, $s = 3.5$ and $n = 36$. The sample size is greater than 30, so the **Z-Test** is the appropriate test. To run the test, press **STAT**, highlight **TESTS** and select **1:Z-Test**. Since you are using sample statistics for the analysis, select **Stats** for **Inpt** and press **ENTER**. For μ_0 enter 30, the value for μ in the null hypothesis. For σ enter **s**, the sample standard deviation. (Note: s, the sample standard deviation, is a good approximation for σ, the population standard deviation, when n is large.) Enter **28.5** for $\bar{x}$ and **36** for **n**. On the next line, choose the appropriate alternative hypothesis and press **ENTER**. For this example, it is $< \mu_0$, a left-tailed test.

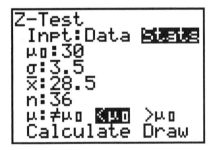

There are two choices for the output of this test. The first choice is **Calculate**. The output displays the alternative hypothesis, the calculated z-value, the P-value, $\bar{x}$ and n.

© 2006 Pearson Education, Inc., Upper Saddle River, NJ. All rights reserved. This material is protected under all copyright laws as they currently exist. No portion of this material may be reproduced, in any form or by any means, without permission in writing from the publisher.

```
Z-Test
 µ<30
 z=-2.571428571
 p=.0050640239
 x̄=28.5
 n=36
```

Since p = .005, which is less than α , the correct conclusion is to **Reject** H_o .

To view the second output option, you should start by turning **OFF** any **STATPLOT** that is turned **ON**. Press **2nd Y=** to display the **STATPLOTS**. If a **PLOT** is **ON**, select it and move the cursor to OFF and press **ENTER**. Also, clear all Y-registers.

Press **STAT**, highlight **TESTS**, and select **1:Z-Test**. All the necessary information for this example is still stored in the calculator. Scroll down to the bottom line and select **DRAW**. A normal curve is displayed with the left-tail area of .0051 shaded. This shaded area is the area to the left of the calculated Z-value. (Because the area is so small in this example, it is not actually visible in the diagram.) The Z-value and the P-value are also displayed.

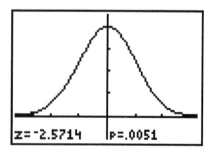

© 2006 Pearson Education, Inc., Upper Saddle River, NJ. All rights reserved. This material is protected under all copyright laws as they currently exist. No portion of this material may be reproduced, in any form or by any means, without permission in writing from the publisher.

> ▸ Example 5 (pg. 351)   Hypothesis Testing Using P-values

This test is a two-tailed test for $H_o: \mu = 143260$ vs. $H_a: \mu \neq 143260$. The sample statistics are $\bar{x} = 135000$, s = 30000 and n = 30. Press **STAT**, highlight **TESTS** and select **1:Z-Test**. Choose **Stats** for **Inpt** and press **ENTER**. For μ_0 enter 143260, the value for μ in the null hypothesis. For σ, enters **s**, the sample standard deviation. Enter **135000** for $\bar{x}$ and **30** for **n**. On the next line, choose the appropriate alternative hypothesis and press **ENTER**. For this example, it is $\neq \mu_0$, a two-tailed test.

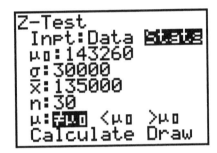

Highlight **Calculate** and press **ENTER** .

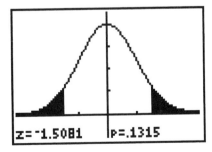

Or, highlight **Draw** and press **ENTER**.

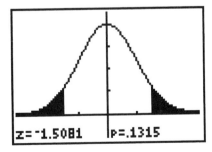

Notice the P-value is equal to .1315. In this example, α is .05. Since the P-value is greater than α, the correct conclusion is to **Fail to Reject** H_o.

© 2006 Pearson Education, Inc., Upper Saddle River, NJ. All rights reserved. This material is protected under all copyright laws as they currently exist. No portion of this material may be reproduced, in any form or by any means, without permission in writing from the publisher.

> ▶ Exercise 33(pg. 359) Testing Claims Using P-values

Test the hypotheses: $H_o: \mu \leq 260$ vs. $H_a: \mu > 260$.   The sample statistics are $\bar{x} = 265$, s = 55 and n = 85. Press **STAT**, highlight **TESTS** and select **1:Z-Test**. For **Inpt**, choose **Stats** and press **ENTER**. Fill the input screen with the appropriate information. Choose $> \mu_0$ for the alternative hypothesis and press **ENTER**. Highlight **Calculate** and press **ENTER**.

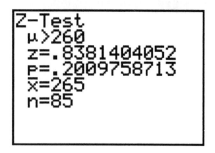

Or, highlight **Draw** and press **ENTER**.

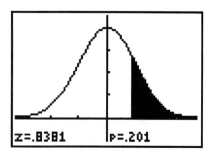

The test statistic is Z = 0.838 and the P-value is .201. Since the P-value is greater than α, the correct conclusion is to **Fail to Reject** H_o.

◀

© 2006 Pearson Education, Inc., Upper Saddle River, NJ. All rights reserved. This material is protected under all copyright laws as they currently exist. No portion of this material may be reproduced, in any form or by any means, without permission in writing from the publisher.

▶ Exercise 37(pg. 360) Testing Claims Using P-values

This is a hypothesis test for $H_o: \mu = 15$ vs. $H_a: \mu \neq 15$. Since n > 30, the appropriate test is the Z-Test. This procedure requires a value for σ. In cases with n > 30, the sample standard deviation, s, can be used to approximate σ. Begin the analysis by entering the 32 data points into **L1**. Press **STAT**, highlight **CALC** and choose **1:1-Var Stats** and press 2nd **L1** **ENTER**. The sample statistics will be displayed on the screen. The value you need for the hypothesis test is Sx, the sample standard deviation, which is 4.29.

To perform the test, press **STAT**, highlight **TESTS** and select **1:Z-Test**. Since you have the actual data points for the analysis, select **Data** for **Inpt** and press **ENTER**. Fill in the input screen with the appropriate information and select $\neq \mu_0$, as the alternative hypothesis and press **ENTER**.

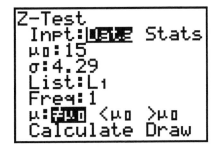

```
Z-Test
 Inpt:DATA Stats
 μ0:15
 σ:4.29
 List:L1
 Freq:1
 μ:≠μ0 <μ0 >μ0
 Calculate Draw
```

Highlight **Calculate** and press **ENTER**

```
Z-Test
 μ≠15
 z=-.2183954511
 P=.8271210783
 x̄=14.834375
 Sx=4.287612267
 n=32
■
```

Or, highlight **Draw** and press **ENTER**.

© 2006 Pearson Education, Inc., Upper Saddle River, NJ. All rights reserved. This material is protected under all copyright laws as they currently exist. No portion of this material may be reproduced, in any form or by any means, without permission in writing from the publisher.

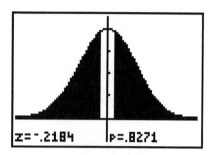

z=-.2184   P=.8271

Since the P-value is greater than α, the correct conclusion is to **Fail to Reject** H_o.

◄

© 2006 Pearson Education, Inc., Upper Saddle River, NJ. All rights reserved. This material is protected under all copyright laws as they currently exist.
No portion of this material may be reproduced, in any form or by any means, without permission in writing from the publisher.

▶ Exercise 43 (pg. 361) Testing Claims

This is a hypothesis test for $H_o : \mu \leq 28$ vs. $H_a : \mu > 28$. Since n > 30, the appropriate test is the Z-Test. This procedure requires a value for σ. In cases with n > 30, the sample standard deviation, s, can be used to approximate σ. Begin the analysis by entering the 36 data points into **L1**. Press **STAT**, highlight **CALC** and choose **1:1-Var Stats** and press 2nd **L1** **ENTER**. The sample statistics will be displayed on the screen. The value you need for the hypothesis test is Sx, the sample standard deviation, which is 22.13.

To run the hypothesis test, press **STAT**, highlight **TESTS** and select **1:Z-Test**. Since you have the actual data points for the analysis, select **Data** for **Inpt** and press **ENTER**. Enter **28** for μ_0 and enter **22.13** for σ. The data is stored in **L1** and **Freq** is **1**. The alternate hypothesis is a right-tailed test so select $> \mu_0$ and press **ENTER**.

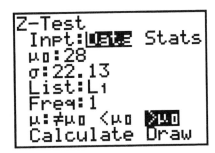

To run the test, select **Calculate** and press **ENTER**.

```
Z-Test
 μ>28
 z=1.317969574
 P=.0937569803
 x̄=32.86111111
 Sx=22.12839517
 n=36
```

Or, select **Draw** and press **ENTER**.

© 2006 Pearson Education, Inc., Upper Saddle River, NJ. All rights reserved. This material is protected under all copyright laws as they currently exist. No portion of this material may be reproduced, in any form or by any means, without permission in writing from the publisher.

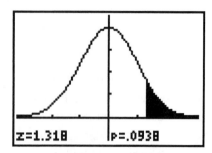

Since the P-value of .0938 is greater than α, the correct conclusion is to **Fail to Reject** H_o.

◀

© 2006 Pearson Education, Inc., Upper Saddle River, NJ. All rights reserved. This material is protected under all copyright laws as they currently exist.
No portion of this material may be reproduced, in any form or by any means, without permission in writing from the publisher.

Section 7.3

▶ Example 6 (pg. 369)   Using P-values with a T-Test

This test is a two-tailed test of $H_o: \mu = 132$ vs. $H_a: \mu \neq 132$. The sample statistics are $\bar{x} = 141$, $s = 20$ and $n = 11$. Since $n < 30$, the test is a T-Test if you assume that the underlying population is approximately normally distributed. Press **STAT**, highlight **TESTS** and select **2:T-Test**. Choose **Stats** for **Inpt** and press **ENTER**. Fill in the following information: $\mu_0 = 132$, $\bar{x} = 141$, **Sx = 20** and **n = 11**. Choose the two-tailed alternative hypothesis, $\neq \mu_0$, and press **ENTER**. Highlight **Calculate** and press **ENTER**

```
T-Test
 μ≠132
 t=1.492481156
 p=.1664335286
 x̄=141
 Sx=20
 n=11
```

Or, highlight **Draw** and press **ENTER**.

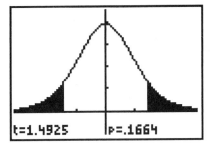

```
t=1.4925        p=.1664
```

Since the P-value is greater than α, the correct conclusion is to **Fail to Reject** H_o.

© 2006 Pearson Education, Inc., Upper Saddle River, NJ. All rights reserved. This material is protected under all copyright laws as they currently exist. No portion of this material may be reproduced, in any form or by any means, without permission in writing from the publisher.

▸ Exercise 29 (pg. 372) Testing Claims Using P-values

The correct hypothesis test is $H_o : \mu = 3$ vs. $H_a : \mu < 3$. Enter the data into L1.
Since n < 30, the appropriate test is the T-Test, if you assume that the underlying
population is approximately normal. Press **STAT**, highlight **TESTS** and select
2:T-Test. Select **Data** for **Inpt** and press **ENTER**. Fill in the screen with the
necessary information, choose **Calculate** and press **ENTER**.

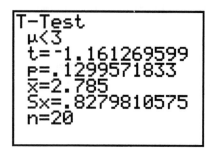

Or, choose **Draw** and press **ENTER**.

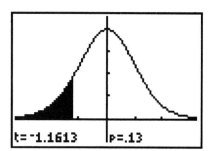

Since the P-value is greater than α, the correct conclusion is to **Fail to Reject**
H_o.

© 2006 Pearson Education, Inc., Upper Saddle River, NJ. All rights reserved. This material is protected under all copyright laws as they currently exist.
No portion of this material may be reproduced, in any form or by any means, without permission in writing from the publisher.

> ▸ Exercise 37(pg. 373) Deciding on a Distribution

This test is a left-tailed test of $H_o: \mu \geq 21$ vs. $H_a: \mu < 21$. The sample statistics are $\bar{x} = 19$, $s = 4$ and $n = 5$. Since $n < 30$ and gas mileage is normally distributed, the appropriate test is the **T-Test**. Press **STAT**, highlight **TESTS** and select **2:T-Test**. Fill in the screen with the necessary information and choose **Calculate** and press **ENTER**.

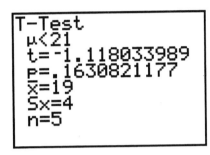

Or, choose **Draw** and press **ENTER**.

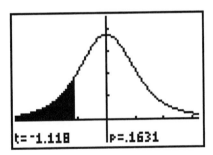

Since the P-value is greater than α, the correct conclusion is to **Fail to Reject** H_o.

© 2006 Pearson Education, Inc., Upper Saddle River, NJ. All rights reserved. This material is protected under all copyright laws as they currently exist. No portion of this material may be reproduced, in any form or by any means, without permission in writing from the publisher.

▶ Exercise 38 (pg. 373)   Deciding on a Distribution

This test is a two-tailed test of $H_o : \mu = 337$ vs. $H_a : \mu \neq 337$. The sample statistics are $\bar{x} = 332$, $s = 10$ and $n = 50$. Since $n \geq 30$, s is a good approximation of σ, so the appropriate test is the **Z-Test**. Press **STAT**, highlight **TESTS** and select **1:Z-Test**. Fill in the screen with the necessary information and choose **Calculate** and press **ENTER**.

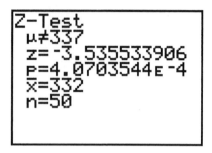

Or, choose **Draw** and press **ENTER**.

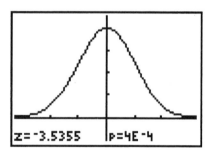

Since the P-value is smaller than α, the correct conclusion is to **Reject** H_o.

© 2006 Pearson Education, Inc., Upper Saddle River, NJ. All rights reserved. This material is protected under all copyright laws as they currently exist.
No portion of this material may be reproduced, in any form or by any means, without permission in writing from the publisher.

Section 7.4

> **Example 1 (pg. 375)**   Hypothesis Test for a Proportion

This hypothesis test is a left-tailed test of: $H_o : p \geq .20$ vs. $H_a : p < .20$. The sample statistics are $\hat{p} = .15$ and n = 100. Press **STAT**, highlight **TESTS** and select **5:1-PropZTest**. This test requires a value for p_0, which is the value for p in the null hypothesis. Enter **.20** for p_0. Next, a value for X is required. X is the number of "successes" in the sample. In this example, a success is " being allergic to medicine". Since 15% of the individuals in the sample say that they have such an allergy, **X** is equal to .15 times 100 or **15**. Next, enter the value for n. Select $< p_0$ for the alternative hypothesis and press **ENTER**.

```
1-PropZTest
 P0:.2
 x:15
 n:100
 prop≠P0  <P0  >P0
 Calculate Draw
```

Highlight **Calculate** and press **ENTER**.

```
1-PropZTest
 prop<.2
 z=-1.25
 p=.105649839
 p̂=.15
 n=100
```

Or, highlight **Draw** and press **ENTER**.

© 2006 Pearson Education, Inc., Upper Saddle River, NJ. All rights reserved. This material is protected under all copyright laws as they currently exist. No portion of this material may be reproduced, in any form or by any means, without permission in writing from the publisher.

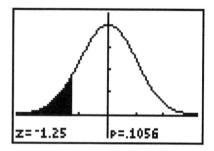

Since the P-value is greater than α, the correct conclusion is to **Fail to Reject** H_o.

◀

▶ Example 3 (pg. 377) Hypothesis Test for a Proportion

The hypothesis test is: $H_o : p \le .55$ vs. $H_a : p > .55$. The sample statistics are n = 425 and X = 255. Press **STAT**, highlight **TESTS** and select **5:1-PropZTest**. Enter the necessary information. Highlight **Calculate** and press **ENTER**.

```
1-PropZTest
  Prop>.55
  z=2.071938535
  P=.0191355209
  p=.6
  n=425
```

Or, highlight **Draw** and press **ENTER**.

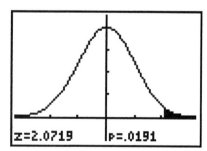

Since the P-value is less than α, the correct conclusion is to **Reject** H_o.

◀

© 2006 Pearson Education, Inc., Upper Saddle River, NJ. All rights reserved. This material is protected under all copyright laws as they currently exist. No portion of this material may be reproduced, in any form or by any means, without permission in writing from the publisher.

> ▶ Exercise 11 (pg. 378) Testing Claims

Use a right-tailed hypothesis test to test the hypotheses: $H_o : p \le .30$ vs. $H_a : p > .30$. The sample statistics are n = 1050 and $\hat{p} = .32$. Multiply n times $\hat{p}$ to find X, the number of consumers in the sample who have stopped purchasing a product because it pollutes the environment. Press **STAT**, highlight **TESTS** and select **5:1-PropZTest**. Enter the necessary information.

Highlight **Calculate** and press **ENTER**.

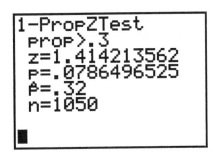

Or, highlight **Draw** and press **ENTER**.

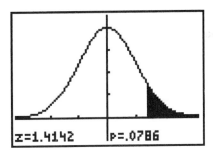

Since the P-value is .greater than α, the correct conclusion is to **Fail to Reject** H_o.

© 2006 Pearson Education, Inc., Upper Saddle River, NJ. All rights reserved. This material is protected under all copyright laws as they currently exist. No portion of this material may be reproduced, in any form or by any means, without permission in writing from the publisher.

Section 7.5

▶ Example 4 (pg. 383) Hypothesis Test for a Variance

This hypothesis test is a right-tailed test of: $H_o : \sigma^2 \leq 0.25$ vs. $H_a : \sigma^2 > 0.25$. The sample statistics are $s2 = 0.27$ and $n = 41$. First you must calculate the χ^2 value: $((41 - 1) *0.27)/0.25 = 43.2$. Next, find the p-value associated with this χ^2 value. Press 2nd **DISTR**, and scroll down to χ^2 cdf(. This function requires a *lowerbound*, an *upperbound* and the *degrees of freedom*. Since this is a right-tailed test, 43.2 is the *lowerbound* and positive infinity (1E99) is the *upperbound*. The degrees of freedom (n-1) is equal to 40.

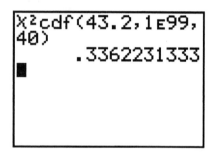

The P-value is 0.336. Since this is greater than α, the correct conclusion is to **Fail to Reject** H_o.

◀

© 2006 Pearson Education, Inc., Upper Saddle River, NJ. All rights reserved. This material is protected under all copyright laws as they currently exist. No portion of this material may be reproduced, in any form or by any means, without permission in writing from the publisher.

> **Technology (pg. 399)** The Case of the Vanishing Women

Exercise 1: Use the TI-83 to run the hypothesis test and compare your results to the MINITAB results shown in the display at the bottom of pg. 399. Use a two-tailed test to test the hypotheses: $H_o : p = 0.53$ vs. $H_a : p \neq 0.53$. The sample statistics are X = 102 women and n = 350 people selected from the Boston City Directory. Press **STAT**, highlight **TESTS** and select **5:1-PropZTest**. Fill in the appropriate information highlight **Calculate** and press **ENTER** or, highlight **Draw** and press **ENTER**.

Exercise 4: In the first stage of the jury selection process, 350 people are selected and 102 of them are women. So, at this stage, the proportion of women is 102 out of 350, or 0.2914. From this population of 350 people, a sample of 100 people is selected at random and only nine are women. Test the claim that the proportion of women in the population is 0.2914. Use a two-tailed test to test the hypotheses:
$H_o : p = 0.2914$ vs. $H_a : p \neq 0.2914$. The sample statistics are X = 9 women and n = 100 people. Press **STAT**, highlight **TESTS** and select **5:1-PropZTest**. Fill in the appropriate information, Highlight **Calculate** and press **ENTER** or highlight **Draw** and press **ENTER**.

◀

© 2006 Pearson Education, Inc., Upper Saddle River, NJ. All rights reserved. This material is protected under all copyright laws as they currently exist. No portion of this material may be reproduced, in any form or by any means, without permission in writing from the publisher.

Hypothesis Testing with Two Samples

CHAPTER

8

Section 8.1

> ▸ Example 2 (pg. 408) Two-Sample Z-Test

Test the claim that the average daily cost for meals and lodging when vacationing in Texas is less than the average costs when vacationing in Washington State. Designate Texas as population 1 and Washington as population 2. The appropriate hypothesis test is a left-tailed test of $H_o: \mu_1 \geq \mu_2$ vs $H_a: \mu_1 < \mu_2$. The sample statistics are displayed in the table at the top of pg. 408. Each sample size is greater than 30, so the correct test is a Two-sample Z-Test.

Press **STAT**, highlight **TESTS** and select **3:2-SampZTest**. Since you are using the sample statistics for your analysis, select **Stats** for **Inpt** and press **ENTER**. In order to use this test, values for σ_1 and σ_2 are required. The sample standard deviations, s_1 and s_2 can be used as approximations for σ_1 and σ_2 when both n_1 and n_2 are greater than or equal to 30. Enter 15 for σ_1. Enter 28 for σ_2. Next, enter the mean and sample size for group 1: $\bar{x}_1 = 208$ and $n_1 = 50$. Continue by entering the mean and sample size for group 2: $\bar{x}_2 = 218$ and $n_2 = 35$.

```
2-SampZTest
 Inpt:Data Stats
 σ1:15
 σ2:28
 x̄1:208
 n1:50
 x̄2:218
↓n2:35
```

Use the down arrow to display the next line. This line displays the three possible alternative hypotheses for testing: $\mu_1 \neq \mu_2$, $\mu_1 > \mu_2$, or $\mu_1 < \mu_2$. For this example, select $< \mu_2$ and press **ENTER**. Scroll down to the next line and select **Calculate** or **Draw**.

The output for **Calculate** is displayed on two pages. (Notice that the only piece of information on the second page is n_2, so that page is not displayed here.)

© 2006 Pearson Education, Inc., Upper Saddle River, NJ. All rights reserved. This material is protected under all copyright laws as they currently exist. No portion of this material may be reproduced, in any form or by any means, without permission in writing from the publisher.

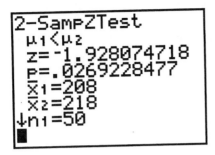

The output for **Draw** contains a graph of the normal curve with the area associated with the test statistic shaded.

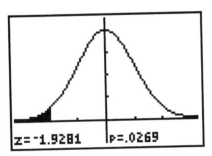

Both outputs display the P-value, which is .0269. Since the P-value is greater than α, the correct decision is to **Fail to Reject** H_o. At the 1% level of significance, there is not enough evidence to support the claim that the average cost for meals and lodging when vacationing in Texas is less than the average cost when vacationing in Washington state.

◀

© 2006 Pearson Education, Inc., Upper Saddle River, NJ. All rights reserved. This material is protected under all copyright laws as they currently exist. No portion of this material may be reproduced, in any form or by any means, without permission in writing from the publisher.

▸ Exercise 9 (pg. 410) Testing the Difference between Two Means

The appropriate hypothesis test is a two-tailed test of $H_o: \mu_1 = \mu_2$ vs $H_a: \mu_1 \neq \mu_2$. Designate Tire Type A as population 1 and Tire Type B as population 2. Press **STAT**, highlight **TESTS** and select **3:2-SampZTest**. For **Inpt,** select **Stats** and press **ENTER**. Enter the sample standard deviations as approximations of σ_1 and σ_2. Next, enter the sample statistics for each group.

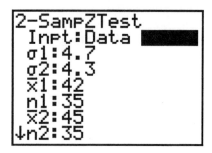

Select $\neq \mu_2$ as the alternative hypothesis and press **ENTER**. Scroll down to the next line and select **Calculate** or **Draw** and press **ENTER**.

The output for **Calculate** is:

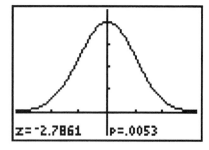

The output for **Draw** is:

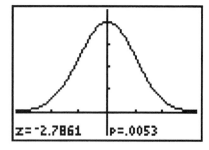

The test statistic, z, is –2.786 and the p-value is .0053. Since the P-value is less than α, the correct decision is to **Reject** H_o. ◀

© 2006 Pearson Education, Inc., Upper Saddle River, NJ. All rights reserved. This material is protected under all copyright laws as they currently exist. No portion of this material may be reproduced, in any form or by any means, without permission in writing from the publisher.

▶ Exercise 19 (pg. 411) Testing the Difference between 2 Means

Enter the data from 1981 into **L1** and enter the data from the more recent study into **L2**. The hypothesis test is: $H_o: \mu_1 \leq \mu_2$ vs $H_a: \mu_1 > \mu_2$. Since both n_1 and n_2 equal 30, the Two-Sample Z-Test can be used. In order to use this test, values for σ_1 and σ_2 are required. The sample standard deviations, s_1 and s_2 can be used as approximations for σ_1 and σ_2 when both n_1 and n_2 are greater than or equal to 30. To find the standard deviations, press **STAT**, highlight **CALC** and select **1:1-Var Stats** and press **2ⁿᵈ L1 ENTER**. The value for Sx is the sample standard deviation for the 1981 data. Next, press **STAT**, highlight **CALC** and select **1:1-Var Stats**, press **2ⁿᵈ L2 ENTER**. The value for Sx is the sample standard deviation for the more recent data.

To run the hypothesis, press **STAT**, highlight **TESTS** and select **3:2-SampZTest**. For **Inpt** select **Data** and press **ENTER**. Enter the sample standard deviations as approximations of σ_1 and σ_2. For **List1**, press **2ⁿᵈ [L1]** and for **List2** press **2ⁿᵈ [L2]** .

```
2-SampZTest
 Inpt:DATA Stats
 σ1:.49
 σ2:.33
 List1:L1
 List2:L2
 Freq1:0
↓Freq2:1
```

Select $> \mu_2$ as the alternative hypothesis and press **ENTER**. Scroll down to the next line and select **Calculate** or **Draw** and press **ENTER**.

The output for **Calculate** is:

```
2-SampZTest
 μ1>μ2
 z=4.975681069
 p=3.2559526E-7
 x̄1=2.13
 x̄2=1.593333333
↓Sx1=.490003519
```

© 2006 Pearson Education, Inc., Upper Saddle River, NJ. All rights reserved. This material is protected under all copyright laws as they currently exist. No portion of this material may be reproduced, in any form or by any means, without permission in writing from the publisher.

The output for **Draw** is:

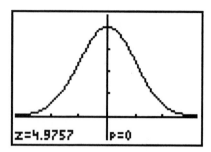

Since the P-value is smaller than α, the correct decision is to **Reject** H_o.

◀

© 2006 Pearson Education, Inc., Upper Saddle River, NJ. All rights reserved. This material is protected under all copyright laws as they currently exist. No portion of this material may be reproduced, in any form or by any means, without permission in writing from the publisher.

▶ Exercise 29 (pg. 414) Confidence Intervals for $\mu_1 - \mu_2$

Construct a confidence interval for $\mu_1 - \mu_2$, the difference between two population means. Designate the group using the herbal supplement as population 1 and the group using the placebo as population 2. The sample statistics for group 1 are: $\bar{x}_1 = 3.2$, $s_1 = 3.3$ and $n_1 = 42$. The sample statistics for group 2 are: $\bar{x}_2 = 4.1$, $s_2 = 3.9$ and $n_2 = 42$.

Press **STAT**, highlight **TESTS** and select **9:2-SampZInt**. Since you are using the sample statistics for your analysis, select **Stats** for **Inpt** and press **ENTER**. Enter the sample standard deviations as approximations for σ_1 and σ_2. Enter the sample means and sample sizes for each group.

```
2-SampZInt
 Inpt:Data Stats
 σ1:3.3
 σ2:3.9
 x̄1:3.2
 n1:42
 x̄2:4.1
↓n2:42
```

Scroll down to the next line and type in the confidence level of .95. Scroll down to the next line and press **ENTER**.

```
2-SampZInt
 (-2.445,.64505)
 x̄1=3.2
 x̄2=4.1
 n1=42
 n2=42
■
```

A 95 % confidence interval for the difference in the population means is (-2.445, .64505). Since this interval contains 0, the correct conclusion is that there is no significant difference in the means of the two groups. The herbal supplement does *not* appear to help in weight loss.

◀

© 2006 Pearson Education, Inc., Upper Saddle River, NJ. All rights reserved. This material is protected under all copyright laws as they currently exist. No portion of this material may be reproduced, in any form or by any means, without permission in writing from the publisher.

Section 8.2

▸ Example 1 (pg. 418) Two Sample t-Test

To test whether the mean stopping distances are different, use a two-tailed test: $H_o: \mu_1 = \mu_2$ vs $H_a: \mu_1 \neq \mu_2$. The sample statistics are found in the table at the top of pg. 418 in your textbook.

Press **STAT**, highlight **TESTS**, and select **4:2-SampTTest**. Since you are inputting the sample statistics, select **Stats** and press **ENTER**. Enter the sample information from the two samples. Select $\neq \mu_2$ as the alternative hypothesis and press **ENTER**. Scroll down to the next line. On this line, select **NO** because the variances are NOT assumed to be equal and therefore, you do not want a pooled estimate of the standard deviation. Press **ENTER**. Scroll down to the next line, highlight **Calculate** and press **ENTER**.

```
2-SampTTest
 μ1≠μ2
 t=-1.495915184
 p=.162535817
 df=11.10815972
 x̄1=51
↓x̄2=55
```

The output (shown above) for **Calculate** displays the alternative hypothesis, the test statistic, the P-value, the degrees of freedom and the sample statistics. Notice the degrees of freedom = 11.108. In cases, such as this one, in which the population variances are not assumed to be equal, the calculator calculates an adjusted degrees of freedom, rather than using the smaller of (n_1-1) and (n_2-1).

If you choose **Draw**, the output includes a graph with the area associated with the P-value shaded.

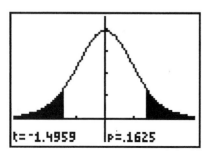

```
t=-1.4959      p=.1625
```

© 2006 Pearson Education, Inc., Upper Saddle River, NJ. All rights reserved. This material is protected under all copyright laws as they currently exist. No portion of this material may be reproduced, in any form or by any means, without permission in writing from the publisher.

> ▸ Example 2 (pg. 419) Two Sample t-Test

To test the claim that the mean range of the manufacturer's cordless phone is greater than the mean range of the competitor's phone, use a right-tailed test with $H_o: \mu_1 \leq \mu_2$ vs $H_a: \mu_1 > \mu_2$. Designate the manufacturer's data as population 1 and the competitor's data as population 2. Use the Two-Sample T-Test for the analysis, and use the pooled variance option because the population variances are assumed to be equal in this example. The sample statistics are found in the table at the top of pg. 419 in your textbook.

Press **STAT**, highlight **TESTS**, and select **4:2-SampTTest**. Fill in the input screen with the sample statistics. Select $> \mu_2$ for the alternative hypothesis and press **ENTER**. Select **YES** for **Pooled** and press **ENTER**. To do the analysis, select **Calculate** and press **ENTER**.

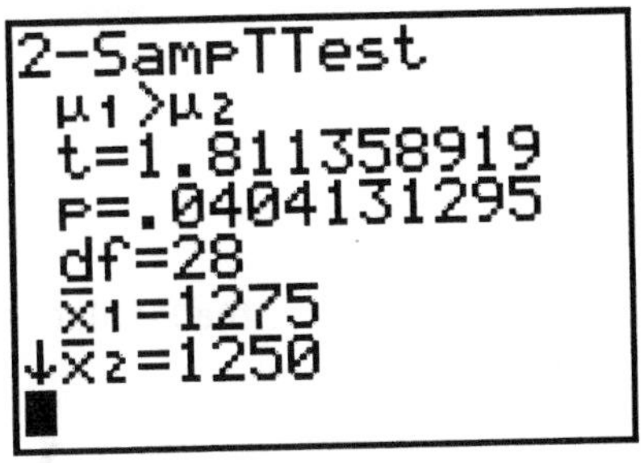

```
2-SampTTest
 μ1>μ2
 t=1.811358919
 P=.0404131295
 df=28
 x̄1=1275
↓x̄2=1250
■
```

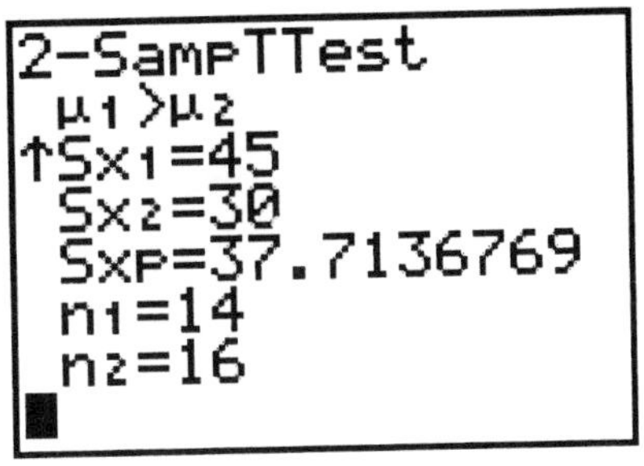

```
2-SampTTest
 μ1>μ2
↑Sx1=45
 Sx2=30
 Sxp=37.7136769
 n1=14
 n2=16
■
```

The two-page output display (shown above) includes the alternative hypothesis, the test statistic, the P-value, degrees of freedom, the sample statistics and the pooled standard deviation (Sxp = 37.7)

If you select **Draw**, the display includes a graph with the shaded area associated with the test statistic, the P-value and the test statistic.

Since the P-value is less than α, the correct decision is to **Reject** H_o.

◀

© 2006 Pearson Education, Inc., Upper Saddle River, NJ. All rights reserved. This material is protected under all copyright laws as they currently exist. No portion of this material may be reproduced, in any form or by any means, without permission in writing from the publisher.

> ▶ **Exercise 15 (pg. 421)** Testing the Difference between 2 Means

Designate the small cars as population 1 and the midsize cars as population 2. Test the hypothesis: $H_o: \mu_1 = \mu_2$ vs. $H_a: \mu_1 \neq \mu_2$. The sample statistics are: $\bar{x}_1 = 15.1$, $s_1 = 7.55$, $n_1 = 13$, $\bar{x}_2 = 12.8$, $s_2 = 6.35$ and $n_2 = 15$. Use the Two-Sample T-test with the pooled variance option. Press **STAT**, highlight **TESTS** and select **4:2-SampTTest**. Choose **Stats** for **Inpt** and press **ENTER**. Enter the sample statistics. Select $\neq \mu_2$ as the alternative hypothesis and press **ENTER**. Select **YES** for **Pooled** and press **ENTER**. Highlight **Calculate** and press **ENTER**.

```
2-SampTTest
 μ1≠μ2
 t=.8758922832
 P=.389109219
 df=26
 x̄1=15.1
↓x̄2=12.8
```

Notice that the test statistic = 0.876, and the P-value is .389. Since the P-value is greater than α, the correct decision is to **Fail to Reject** H_o.

◀

© 2006 Pearson Education, Inc., Upper Saddle River, NJ. All rights reserved. This material is protected under all copyright laws as they currently exist. No portion of this material may be reproduced, in any form or by any means, without permission in writing from the publisher.

> ▸ Exercise 23(pg. 423) Testing the difference between 2 Means

Designate the "Old curriculum" as population 1 and the "New curriculum" as population 2 and test the hypothesis: $H_o : \mu_1 \geq \mu_2$ vs. $H_a : \mu_1 < \mu_2$. Press **STAT**, select **1:Edit** and enter the data sets into **L1** (Old curriculum) and **L2** (New curriculum). Press **STAT**, highlight **TESTS** and select **4:2-SampTTest**. For this analysis, you are using the actual data so select **Data** for **Inpt** and press **ENTER**. Fill in the input screen with the appropriate information. Choose $< \mu_2$ as the alternative hypothesis and press **ENTER**. Choose **YES** for **Pooled** and press **ENTER**. Highlight **Calculate** and press **ENTER**.

```
2-SampTTest
 μ1<μ2
 t=-4.29519297
 P=5.0503069E-5
 df=42
 x̄1=56.68421053
↓x̄2=67.4
```

Since the P-value (.00005) is less than α, the correct decision is to **Reject** H_o. This means that the data supports H_a, indicating that the new method of teaching reading produces higher reading test scores than the old method. The recommendation is to change to the new method.

◀

© 2006 Pearson Education, Inc., Upper Saddle River, NJ. All rights reserved. This material is protected under all copyright laws as they currently exist. No portion of this material may be reproduced, in any form or by any means, without permission in writing from the publisher.

> ▸ Exercise 25 (pg. 424) Confidence Intervals

Compare the mean calorie content of grilled chicken sandwiches from Arby's restaurants to similar chicken sandwiches from McDonald's using a confidence interval. For this exercise, assume that the populations are normal and the variances are equal. Also, notice that the sample sizes are both less than 30. The appropriate confidence interval technique is the Two-Sample t-interval.

Press **STAT**, highlight **TESTS** and select **0:2-SampTInt**. For **Inpt**, select **Stats** and press **ENTER**. Enter the sample statistics from the two sets of data. Designate Arby's as population 1 and McDonald's as population 2. Choose **.95** for **C-level** and choose **YES** for **Pooled** and press **ENTER**. Scroll down to the next line and press **ENTER** to **Calculate** the confidence interval.

```
2-SampTInt
 (4.3375,15.663)
 df=25
 x̄1=410
 x̄2=400
 Sx1=6.2
↓Sx2=8.1
```

The output displays the 95 % confidence interval for (μ_1 - μ_2) and the sample statistics. One way to interpret the confidence interval is to state that "based on a 95% confidence interval, the difference in mean calorie content of grilled chicken sandwiches at the two restaurants is between 4.3375 and 15.663 calories." This means that the mean calorie content of the Arby's sandwiches is anywhere from 4.34 to 15.66 more than that of McDonald's.

◀

© 2006 Pearson Education, Inc., Upper Saddle River, NJ. All rights reserved. This material is protected under all copyright laws as they currently exist. No portion of this material may be reproduced, in any form or by any means, without permission in writing from the publisher.

▶ Exercise 27 (pg. 424) Confidence Intervals

Compare the mean cholesterol content of grilled sandwiches from Arby's to similar sandwiches from McDonald's using a confidence interval. For this exercise, assume the populations are normal but do NOT assume equal variances.

Press **STAT**, highlight **TESTS** and select **0:2-SampTInt**. For **Inpt**, select **Stats** and press **ENTER**. Enter the sample statistics from the table displayed in Exercise 27. Designate Arby's as population 1 and McDonald's as population 2. Choose **.90** for **C-level** and choose **NO** for **Pooled** and press **ENTER**. Scroll down to the next line and press **ENTER** to **Calculate** the confidence interval.

```
2-SampTInt
 (-11.53,-8.473)
 df=24.37225626
 x̄₁=60
 x̄₂=70
 Sx₁=3.59
↓Sx₂=2.41
■
```

The output displays the 80 % confidence interval for (μ_1 - μ_2), the adjusted degrees of freedom and the sample statistics. The confidence interval states that the mean cholesterol content for Arby's sandwiches is anywhere from 8.42 to 11.58 mgs. less than that of McDonald's.

◀

© 2006 Pearson Education, Inc., Upper Saddle River, NJ. All rights reserved. This material is protected under all copyright laws as they currently exist. No portion of this material may be reproduced, in any form or by any means, without permission in writing from the publisher.

Section 8.3

> ▶ **Example 2 (pg. 428)** The Paired t-Test

In this example, the data is paired data, with two scores for each of the 8 golfers. Enter the scores that each golfer gave as his or her most recent score using the old design clubs into L1. Enter the scores achieved after using the newly designated clubs into L2. Next, you must create a set of differences, d = (old score) - (new score). To create this set, move the cursor to highlight the label **L3,** found at the top of the third column, and press **ENTER**. Notice that the cursor is flashing on the bottom line of the display. Press **2ⁿᵈ [L1]** - **2ⁿᵈ [L2]**

L1	L2	■ 3
89	83	------
84	83	
96	92	
82	84	
74	76	
92	91	
85	80	

$L3 = L_1 - L_2$

and press **ENTER**.

L1	L2	L3	3
89	83	6	
84	83	1	
96	92	4	
82	84	-2	
74	76	-2	
92	91	1	
85	80	5	

L3(1)=6

Each value in **L3** is the difference **L1 - L2**.

To test the claim that golfers can lower their scores using the manufacturer's newly designed clubs, the hypothesis test is: $H_o : \mu_d \le 0$ vs. $H_a : \mu_d > 0$. Press **STAT**, highlight **TESTS** and select **2:T-Test**. In this example, you are using the actual data to do the analysis, so select **Data** for **Inpt** and press **ENTER**. The value for μ_o is **0**, the value in the null hypothesis. The set of differences is found in **L3**, so set **List** to **L3**. Set **Freq** equal to **1**. Choose > μ_o as the alternative hypothesis and highlight **Calculate** and press **ENTER**.

© 2006 Pearson Education, Inc., Upper Saddle River, NJ. All rights reserved. This material is protected under all copyright laws as they currently exist. No portion of this material may be reproduced, in any form or by any means, without permission in writing from the publisher.

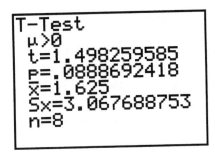

You can also highlight **DRAW** and press **ENTER**.

Since the P-value is less than α, the correct decision is to **Reject** H_o.

◀

© 2006 Pearson Education, Inc., Upper Saddle River, NJ. All rights reserved. This material is protected under all copyright laws as they currently exist. No portion of this material may be reproduced, in any form or by any means, without permission in writing from the publisher.

> ▸ Exercise 17(pg. 432) Paired Difference Test

Press **STAT** and select **1:Edit.** Enter the students' scores on the first SAT into **L1** and their scores on the second Sat into **L2**. Since this is paired data, create a column of differences, d = (first SAT) - (second SAT). To create the differences, move the cursor to highlight the label **L3,** found at the top of the third column, and press **ENTER**. Notice that the cursor is flashing on the bottom line of the display. Press **2ⁿᵈ [L1]** - **2ⁿᵈ [L2]** and press **ENTER**.

```
L1       L2       L3        3
445      446      -1
510      571      -61
429      517      -88
452      478      -26
629      610      19
433      453      -20
551      516      35

L3(1)= -1
```

Each value in **L3** is the difference **L1 - L2**.

To test the claim that students' verbal SAT scores improved the second time they took the verbal SAT, the hypotheses are:: $H_o: \mu_d \geq 0$ vs. $H_a: \mu_d < 0$. Press **STAT**, highlight **TESTS** and select **2:T-Test**. In this example, you are using the actual data to do the analysis, so select **Data** for **Inpt** and press **ENTER**. The value for μ_o is **0**, the value in the null hypothesis. The set of differences is found in **L3**, so set **List** to L3. Set **Freq** equal to **1**. Choose $< \mu_o$ as the alternative hypothesis and highlight **Calculate** and press **ENTER**.

```
T-Test
 μ<0
 t=-3.001096523
 P=.0051086649
 x̄=-33.71428571
 Sx=42.03373841
 n=14
```

Or, highlight **DRAW** and press **ENTER**.

Since the P-value is less than α, the correct decision is to **Reject** H_o.

© 2006 Pearson Education, Inc., Upper Saddle River, NJ. All rights reserved. This material is protected under all copyright laws as they currently exist. No portion of this material may be reproduced, in any form or by any means, without permission in writing from the publisher.

▶ Exercise 29(pg. 436)   Confidence Interval for μ_d

Press **STAT** and select **1:Edit**. Enter the data for "hours of sleep without the drug" into **L1** and the data for "hours of sleep using the new drug" into **L2**. Since this is paired data, create a column of differences, **d = L1 - L2**. To create the differences, move the cursor to highlight the label **L3,** found at the top of the third column, and press **ENTER**. Notice that the cursor is flashing on the bottom line of the display. Press **2nd [L1]** - **2nd [L2]** and press **ENTER**. Each value in **L3** is the difference **L1 - L2**.

To construct a confidence interval for μ_d, press **STAT**, highlight **TESTS** and select **8:Tinterval**. For **Inpt**, select **Data,** for **List**, enter **L3**. Make sure that **Freq** is equal to **1,** and the **C-level** is **90**. Highlight **Calculate** and press **ENTER**.

```
TInterval
 (-1.763,-1.287)
 x̄=-1.525
 Sx=.5422176685
 n=16
■
```

The confidence interval for μ_d is -1.763 to -1.287. This means that the average difference in hours of sleep is 1.287 hours to 1.763 hours more for patients using the new drug.

◀

© 2006 Pearson Education, Inc., Upper Saddle River, NJ. All rights reserved. This material is protected under all copyright laws as they currently exist. No portion of this material may be reproduced, in any form or by any means, without permission in writing from the publisher.

Section 8.4

> ▶ Example 1 (pg. 439) Testing the Difference Between p_1 and p_2

To test the claim that there is a difference in the proportion of female Internet users who plan to shop On-line and the proportion of male Internet users who plan to shop On-line, the correct hypothesis test is: $H_o : p_1 = p_2$ vs $H_a : p_1 \neq p_2$. Designate the females as population 1 and the males as population 2. The sample statistics are $n_1 = 200$, $\hat{p}_1 = .30$, $n_2 = 250$, and $\hat{p}_2 = .38$. To conduct this test using the TI-83, you need values for x_1, the number of females in the sample who plan to shop On-line, and x_2, he number of males who plan to shop On-line. To calculate x_1, multiply n_1 times $\hat{p}_1$. To calculate x_2, multiply n_2 times $\hat{p}_2$. (Note: These two values, x_1 and x_2, are given in the table on pg. 439.)

Press **STAT**, highlight **TESTS** and select **6:2-PropZTest** and fill in the appropriate information. Highlight **Calculate** and press **ENTER**.

```
2-PropZTest
 P1≠P2
 z=-1.774615984
 P=.0759612188
 P̂1=.3
 P̂2=.38
↓P̂=.3444444444
```

The output displays the alternative hypothesis, the test statistic, the P-value, the sample statistics and the weighted estimate of the population proportion, $\hat{p}$. Since the P-value is less than α, the correct decision is to **Reject** H_o.

◀

© 2006 Pearson Education, Inc., Upper Saddle River, NJ. All rights reserved. This material is protected under all copyright laws as they currently exist. No portion of this material may be reproduced, in any form or by any means, without permission in writing from the publisher.

> ▸ Exercise 7(pg. 441) The Difference Between Two Proportions

Designate the 1991 data as population 1 and the more recent data as population 2 and test the hypotheses: $H_o : p_1 = p_2$ vs $H_a : p_1 \neq p_2$. The sample statistics are $n_1 = 1539$, $x_1 = 520$, $n_2 = 2055$, and $x_2 = 865$.

Press **STAT**, highlight **TESTS** and select **6:2-PropZTest** and fill in the appropriate information. Highlight **Calculate** and press **ENTER**.

```
2-PropZTest
 P1≠P2
 z=-5.06166817
 P=4.1630154E-7
 P1=.3378817414
 P2=.4209245742
↓P=.3853644964
■
```

Since the P-value (.0000004163) is less than α, the correct decision is to **Reject** H_o. This indicates that the proportion of adults using alternative medicines has changed since 1991.

◀

© 2006 Pearson Education, Inc., Upper Saddle River, NJ. All rights reserved. This material is protected under all copyright laws as they currently exist. No portion of this material may be reproduced, in any form or by any means, without permission in writing from the publisher.

▶ Exercise 25 (pg. 444)   Confidence Interval for p_1 - p_2.

Construct a confidence interval to compare the proportion of students who had planned to study engineering several years ago to the proportion currently planning on studying engineering. Designate the earlier survey results as population 1 and the recent survey results as population 2. The sample statistics are $n_1 = 977000$, $\hat{p}_1 = .117$, $n_2 = 1085000$, and $\hat{p}_2 = .085$. To calculate x_1 multiply n_1 times $\hat{p}_1$. To calculate x_2, multiply n_2 times $\hat{p}_2$.

Press **STAT**, highlight **TESTS** and select **B:2-PropZInt** and fill in the appropriate information. Highlight **Calculate** and press **ENTER**.

```
2-PropZInt
 (.03117,.03283)
 p̂1=.117
 p̂2=.085
 n1=977000
 n2=1085000
```

The confidence interval (.03117, .03283) indicates that the proportion of students having chosen engineering in the past is between 3.12 % and 3.28 % higher than the proportion of students currently choosing engineering. Notice how narrow the confidence interval is. This is due to the very large sample sizes.

◀

© 2006 Pearson Education, Inc., Upper Saddle River, NJ. All rights reserved. This material is protected under all copyright laws as they currently exist. No portion of this material may be reproduced, in any form or by any means, without permission in writing from the publisher.

▶ Technology (pg. 453) Tails Over Heads

Exercise 1 - 2: Test the hypotheses: H_o: P(Heads) = .5 vs. H_a: P(Heads) ≠ .5 using the one sample test of a proportion. Press **STAT**, highlight **TESTS** and select **5:1-PropZTest.** For this example, p_o = .5. Using Casey's data, X = 5772 and n = 11902. The alternative hypothesis is ≠ . Highlight **Calculate** and press **ENTER**.

```
1-PropZTest
 prop≠.5
 z=-3.281504874
 p=.0010326665
 p̂=.4849605108
 n=11902
```

Since the P-value is less than α , the correct decision is to **Reject** H_o .

Exercise 3: The histogram at the top of the page is a graph of 500 simulations of Casey's experiment. Each simulation represents 11902 flips of a fair coin. The bars of the histogram represent frequencies. Use the histogram to estimate how often 5772 or fewer heads occurred.

To simulate this experiment, you must use an alternative technology. The TI-83 does not have the memory capacity to do this experiment.

Exercise 4: To compare the mint dates of the coins, run the hypothesis test: H_o: $\mu_1 = \mu_2$ vs. H_a: $\mu_1 \neq \mu_2$. Designate the Philadelphia data as population 1 and the Denver data as population 2.

Press **STAT**, highlight **TESTS** and select **3:2-SampZTest**. Choose **Stats** for **Inpt** and press **ENTER**. Enter the sample statistics. Use the sample standard deviations as approximations to the population standard deviations. Select ≠ μ_2 as the alternative hypothesis and press **ENTER**. Highlight **Calculate** and press **ENTER**.

© 2006 Pearson Education, Inc., Upper Saddle River, NJ. All rights reserved. This material is protected under all copyright laws as they currently exist. No portion of this material may be reproduced, in any form or by any means, without permission in writing from the publisher.

```
2-SampZTest
 μ1≠μ2
 z=8.801919011
 p=1.363493ε-18
 x̄1=1984.8
 x̄2=1983.4
↓n1=7133
```

Since the P-value is extremely small, the correct decision is to **Reject** H_o.

Exercise 5: To compare the average mint value of coins minted in Philadelphia to those minted in Denver, run the hypothesis test: $H_o : \mu_1 = \mu_2$ vs. $H_a : \mu_1 \neq \mu_2$. Designate the Philadelphia data as population 1 and the Denver data as population 2.

Press **STAT**, highlight **TESTS** and select **3:2-SampZTest**. Choose **Stats** for **Inpt** and press **ENTER**. Enter the sample statistics. Use the sample standard deviations as approximations to the population standard deviations. Select $\neq \mu_2$ as the alternative hypothesis and press **ENTER**. Highlight **Calculate** and press **ENTER**. Since the P-value is extremely small, the correct decision is to **Reject** H_o.

◀

© 2006 Pearson Education, Inc., Upper Saddle River, NJ. All rights reserved. This material is protected under all copyright laws as they currently exist. No portion of this material may be reproduced, in any form or by any means, without permission in writing from the publisher.

Correlation and Regression

CHAPTER

9

Section 9.1

▶ Example 3 (pg. 460) Constructing a Scatter plot

Press **STAT**, highlight **1:Edit** and clear **L1** and **L2**. Enter the X-values into **L1** and the Y-values into **L2**. Press **2ⁿᵈ [STAT PLOT]** , select **1:Plot1**, turn **ON** Plot 1 and press **ENTER**. For **Type** of graph, select the **scatter plot** which is the first selection. Press **ENTER**. Enter **L1** for **Xlist** and **L2** for **Ylist**. Highlight the first selection, the small square, for the type of **Mark**. Press **ENTER**. Press **ZOOM** and **9** to select **ZoomStat**.

This graph shows a positive linear correlation.

◀

© 2006 Pearson Education, Inc., Upper Saddle River, NJ. All rights reserved. This material is protected under all copyright laws as they currently exist. No portion of this material may be reproduced, in any form or by any means, without permission in writing from the publisher.

> ▸ **Example 5 (pg. 463)**   Finding a Correlation Coefficient

For this example, use the data from Example 3 on pg. 460. Enter the X-values into **L1** and the Y-values into **L2**. In order to calculate r, the correlation coefficient, you must turn **On** the **Diagnostic** command. Press **2ⁿᵈ [CATALOG]** (Note: CATALOG is found above the ⓪ key). The CATALOG of functions will appear on the screen. Use the down arrow to scroll to the **DiagnosticOn** command.

```
CATALOG          ▯
 Degree
 DelVar
 DependAsk
 DependAuto
 det(
 DiagnosticOff
▸DiagnosticOn
```

Press **ENTER ENTER**.

Press **STAT**, highlight **CALC**, scroll down to **4:LinReg(ax+b)** and press **ENTER ENTER**. (Note: This command allows you to specify which lists contain the X-values and Y-values. If you do not specify these lists, the defaults are used. The defaults are: **L1** for the X-values and **L2** for the Y-values.)

```
LinReg
 y=ax+b
 a=11.8244078
 b=35.30117105
 r²=.9404868083
 r=.9697869912
```

The correlation coefficient is r = .9697869912. This suggests a strong positive linear correlation between X and Y.

◀

© 2006 Pearson Education, Inc., Upper Saddle River, NJ. All rights reserved. This material is protected under all copyright laws as they currently exist. No portion of this material may be reproduced, in any form or by any means, without permission in writing from the publisher.

▸ Exercise 17 (pg. 470) Constructing a Scatter plot and
                       Determining r

Enter the X-values into **L1** and the Y-values into **L2**. Press **2ⁿᵈ** **[STAT PLOT]** ,
select **1:Plot1**, turn **ON** Plot 1 and press **ENTER**. For **Type** of graph, select the
scatter plot. Enter **L1** for **Xlist** and **L2** for **Ylist**. Press **ZOOM** and **9** to select
ZoomStat.

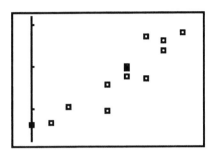

To calculate r, press **STAT**, highlight **CALC** and scroll down to
4:LinReg(ax+b) and press **ENTER ENTER**. (Note: If you have not turned **ON**
the **Diagnostics,** do that first by following the instructions for Example 5 on the
previous page.)

```
LinReg
 y=ax+b
 a=7.349665924
 b=34.6169265
 r²=.8512827753
 r=.922649866
```

The scatter plot shows a strong positive linear correlation. This is confirmed by
the r-value of 0.923.

◀

© 2006 Pearson Education, Inc., Upper Saddle River, NJ. All rights reserved. This material is protected under all copyright laws as they currently exist.
No portion of this material may be reproduced, in any form or by any means, without permission in writing from the publisher.

> ▸ Exercise 25 (pg. 472)   Testing Claims

To test the significance of the population correlation coefficient, ρ, the appropriate hypothesis test is: $\rho = 0$ vs. $\rho \neq 0$. To run the test, enter the X-values into **L1** and the Y-values into **L2**. Press **STAT**, highlight **TESTS** and select **E:LinRegTTest**. Enter **L1** for **Xlist**, **L2** for **Ylist**, and **1** for **Freq**. On the next line, β and ρ, select $\neq 0$ and press **ENTER**. Leave the next line, RegEQ, blank. Highlight **Calculate.**

```
LinRegTTest
 Xlist:L1
 Ylist:L2
 Freq:1
 β & ρ:≠0 <0 >0
 RegEQ:
 Calculate
```

Press **ENTER**.

```
LinRegTTest
 y=a+bx
 β≠0 and ρ≠0
 t=7.935104115
 p=7.0576131E-6
 df=11
↓a=34.6169265
```

The output displays several pieces of information describing the relationship between X and Y. What you are interested in for this example are the following: the test statistic (t = 7.935), the P-value (p = 7.0576131E-6) and the r value (r = .922649886). Since the P-value is less than α, the correct decision is to **Reject** the null hypothesis. This indicates that there is a significant linear relationship between X and Y.

◀

© 2006 Pearson Education, Inc., Upper Saddle River, NJ. All rights reserved. This material is protected under all copyright laws as they currently exist. No portion of this material may be reproduced, in any form or by any means, without permission in writing from the publisher.

Section 9.2

| ▸ Example 2 (pg. 476) | Finding a Regression Line

Enter the X-values into **L1** and the Y-values into **L2**. Press **STAT**, highlight
CALC and scroll down to **4:LinReg(ax+b)**. This command has several options.
One option allows you to store the regression equation into one of the Y-
variables. To use this option, with the cursor flashing on the line **LinReg(ax+b)**,
press **VARS**.

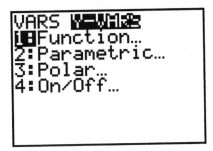

Highlight **Y-VARS.**

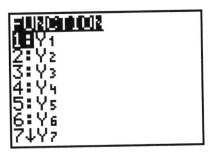

Select **1:Function** and press **ENTER**

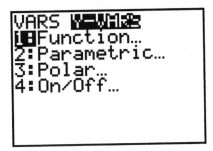

Notice that **1:Y1** is highlighted. Press **ENTER**.

© 2006 Pearson Education, Inc., Upper Saddle River, NJ. All rights reserved. This material is protected under all copyright laws as they currently exist.
No portion of this material may be reproduced, in any form or by any means, without permission in writing from the publisher.

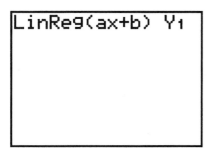

Press **ENTER**.

```
LinReg
  y=ax+b
  a=11.8244078
  b=35.30117105
  r²=.9404868083
  r=.9697869912
```

The output displays the general form of the regression equation: y = ax+b
followed by values for a and b. Next, r^2, the coefficient of determination, and r,
the correlation coefficient , are displayed. If you put the values of a and b into
the general equation, you obtain the specific linear equation for this data:
y= 11.82 x + 35.30. Press **Y=** and see that this specific equation has been pasted
to **Y1**.

```
Plot1 Plot2 Plot3
\Y1=11.824407800
243X+35.30117104
6452
\Y2=
\Y3=
\Y4=
\Y5=
```

Press **2ⁿᵈ STAT PLOT]** , select **1:Plot1**, turn **ON** Plot1, select **scatter plot**, set
Xlist to **L1** and **Ylist** to **L2**. Press **ZOOM** and **9**.

© 2006 Pearson Education, Inc., Upper Saddle River, NJ. All rights reserved. This material is protected under all copyright laws as they currently exist.
No portion of this material may be reproduced, in any form or by any means, without permission in writing from the publisher.

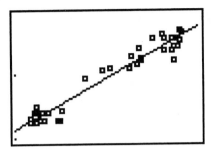

This picture displays a scatter plot of the data and the regression line. The picture indicates a strong positive linear correlation between X and Y, which is confirmed by the r-value of .970.

You can use the regression equation stored in **Y1** to predict Y-values for specific X-values. For example, suppose the duration of an eruption was equal to 1.95 minutes. Predict the time (in minutes) until the next eruption. In other words, for X = 1.95, what does the regression equation predict for Y? To find this value for Y, press **VARS**, highlight **Y-VARS**, select **1:Function**, press **ENTER**, select **1:Y1** and press **ENTER**. Press **(** 1.95 **)** and press **ENTER** .

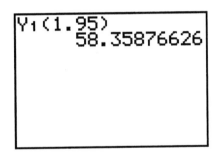

The output is a display of the predicted Y-value for X = 1.95.

© 2006 Pearson Education, Inc., Upper Saddle River, NJ. All rights reserved. This material is protected under all copyright laws as they currently exist. No portion of this material may be reproduced, in any form or by any means, without permission in writing from the publisher.

▶ Exercise 13 (pg. 479)   Finding the Equation of the Regression
Line

Enter the X-values into **L1** and the Y-values into **L2**. Press **STAT**. Highlight
CALC, select **4:LinReg(ax+b)**, press **ENTER**. Press **VARS**, highlight **Y-
VARS**, select **1:Function**, press **ENTER** and select **1:Y1** and press **ENTER**.

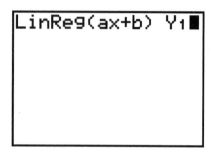

Press **ENTER**.

```
LinReg
 y=ax+b
 a=1.662361413
 b=83.33843868
 r²=.8025954185
 r=.8958768992
```

Using **a** and **b** from the output display, the resulting regression equation is y =
1.662 x + 83.338. Press **Y=** to confirm that the regression equation has been
stored in **Y1**.

To view the data and the regression line, first make sure that the scatterplot has
been selected. Press **2ⁿᵈ STAT PLOT]** , select **1:Plot1**, turn **ON** Plot1, select
scatter plot, set **Xlist** to **L1** and **Ylist** to **L2**. Press **ZOOM** and **9**
and a graph of the scatter plot with the regression line will be displayed.

© 2006 Pearson Education, Inc., Upper Saddle River, NJ. All rights reserved. This material is protected under all copyright laws as they currently exist.
No portion of this material may be reproduced, in any form or by any means, without permission in writing from the publisher.

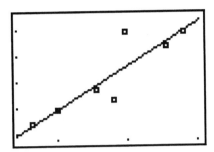

Next, you can use the regression equation to predict systolic blood pressure, Y, for various ages, X. First, check the X-values that you will be using to confirm that they are within (or close to) the range of the X-values in your data. The four X-values (18, 71, 29 and 55) meet this criteria.

Press **VARS**, highlight **Y-VARS**, select **1:Function** and press **ENTER**. Select **1:Y1** and press **ENTER**. Press (18) and **ENTER**.

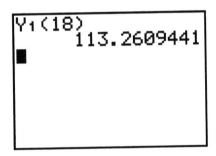

The predicted systolic blood pressure for the average 18-year-old male is 113.3.

Press **2nd** [ENTRY], (found above the ENTER key). Move the cursor so that it is flashing on '1' in the number '18' and type in 71. Press **ENTER**.

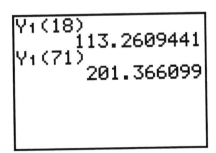

The predicted systolic blood pressure for the average 71-year-old male is 201.37.

© 2006 Pearson Education, Inc., Upper Saddle River, NJ. All rights reserved. This material is protected under all copyright laws as they currently exist.
No portion of this material may be reproduced, in any form or by any means, without permission in writing from the publisher.

Press **2**[nd] [ENTRY] . Move the cursor so that it is flashing on '**7**' in the number '71' and type in 29. Press **ENTER**.

The predicted systolic blood pressure for the average 29-year-old male is 131.55.

Press **2**[nd] [ENTRY] . Move the cursor so that it is flashing on '**2**' in the number '29' and type in 55. Press **ENTER**. The predicted systolic blood pressure for the average 55-year-old male is 174.77.

◀

© 2006 Pearson Education, Inc., Upper Saddle River, NJ. All rights reserved. This material is protected under all copyright laws as they currently exist. No portion of this material may be reproduced, in any form or by any means, without permission in writing from the publisher.

Section 9.3

> ▸ Example 2 (pg. 487)   The Standard Error of the Estimate

Enter the data into **L1** and **L2**. Press **STAT**, highlight **CALC**, select
4:LinReg(ax+b), and press **ENTER**. Press **VARS**, highlight **Y-VARS**, select
1:Function, press **ENTER**, select **1:Y1** and press **ENTER ENTER**.

The formula for s_e, the standard error of the estimate is $\sqrt{\dfrac{\sum (y_i - \hat{y}_i)^2}{n-2}}$. The

values for $(y_i - \hat{y}_i)$, called Residuals, are automatically stored to a list called
RESID. Press **2ⁿᵈ** **[LIST]**, select **7:RESID**. Press **STO**, **2ⁿᵈ** **[L3]** and **ENTER**.
This stores the residuals to **L3**.

```
LRESID→L3
{-.8097165992  -…
```

In the formula for s_e, the residuals, $(y_i - \hat{y}_i)$, are squared. To square these
values and store them in **L4**, press **STAT**, select **1:Edit** and move the cursor to
highlight the Listname **L4**. Press **ENTER**. Press **2ⁿᵈ** **[L3]** and the x^2 key.

L2	L3	**L4**	4
225	-.8097	------	
184	-1.227		
220	14.482		
240	4.0445		
180	4.919		
184	-1.227		
186	-19.52		

$L4 = L3^2$

Press **ENTER**.

© 2006 Pearson Education, Inc., Upper Saddle River, NJ. All rights reserved. This material is protected under all copyright laws as they currently exist.
No portion of this material may be reproduced, in any form or by any means, without permission in writing from the publisher.

```
L2      L3      L4      4
225     -.8097  .65564
184     -1.227  1.5048
220     14.482  209.72
240     4.0445  16.358
180     4.919   24.197
184     -1.227  1.5048
186     -19.52  380.96
L4(1)=.6556409710...
```

Press **2nd** **[QUIT]** . Next, you need to find the sum of **L4**, $\sum(y_i - \hat{y}_i)^2$. Press **2nd** **[LIST]** . Highlight **MATH**, select **5:sum(** and press **2nd** **[L4]** . Close the parentheses and press **ENTER**.

```
sum(L4)
        635.3441296
```

Divide this sum by (number of observations – 2). In this example, (n - 2) = 6. Simply press ÷ 6 and press **ENTER**.

```
sum(L4)
        635.3441296
Ans/6
        105.8906883
```

Lastly, take the square root of this answer by pressing **2nd** [$\sqrt{\ }$] **2nd** **[ANS]** . Close the parentheses and press **ENTER**.

© 2006 Pearson Education, Inc., Upper Saddle River, NJ. All rights reserved. This material is protected under all copyright laws as they currently exist. No portion of this material may be reproduced, in any form or by any means, without permission in writing from the publisher.

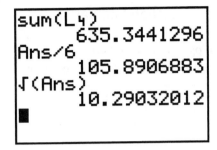

The standard error of the estimate, s_e, is 10.29.

◀

© 2006 Pearson Education, Inc., Upper Saddle River, NJ. All rights reserved. This material is protected under all copyright laws as they currently exist.
No portion of this material may be reproduced, in any form or by any means, without permission in writing from the publisher.

> ▶ **Example 3 (pg. 489)**   Constructing a Prediction Interval

This example is a continuation of Example 2 on pg. 487. To construct a prediction interval for a specific X-value, x_o, you must calculate the maximum error, E. The formula for E is: $E = t_c s_e \sqrt{(1 + \dfrac{1}{n} + \dfrac{n(x_o - \bar{x})^2}{n(\sum x^2) - (\sum x)^2}}$. The critical value for t is found in the t-table. For this example, $t_c = 2.447$. The standard error, s_e, is 10.290.

To calculate $\bar{x}$, $\sum x^2$, and $(\sum x)^2$, press **VARS**, select **5:Statistics**. Highlight **2:** $\bar{x}$ and press **ENTER ENTER**. Notice that $\bar{x} = 1.975$. Press **VARS** again, select **5:Statistics**, highlight $\sum$, select **1:** $\sum x$ and press **ENTER ENTER**. So, $\sum x = 15.8$. Press **VARS** again, select **5:Statistics**, highlight $\sum$, select **2:** $\sum x^2$, and press **ENTER ENTER**. Notice that $\sum x^2 = 32.44$.

Next, calculate the maximum error, E, when $x_o = 2.1$ using the formula for E.

```
2.447*10.29*√(1+
1/8+8(2.1-1.975)
²/(8*32.44-15.8²
)
            26.85678531
■
```

The prediction interval is $\hat{y} \pm 26.857$. To find $\hat{y}$, the predicted value for y when x = 2.1, press **VARS**, highlight **Y-VARS**, select **1:Function** and press **ENTER**. Next select **1:Y1**, press **ENTER** and press **(** 2.1 **)**. Finally, press **ENTER**.

© 2006 Pearson Education, Inc., Upper Saddle River, NJ. All rights reserved. This material is protected under all copyright laws as they currently exist. No portion of this material may be reproduced, in any form or by any means, without permission in writing from the publisher.

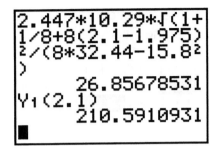

The prediction interval is 210.59 ± 26.857.

© 2006 Pearson Education, Inc., Upper Saddle River, NJ. All rights reserved. This material is protected under all copyright laws as they currently exist.
No portion of this material may be reproduced, in any form or by any means, without permission in writing from the publisher.

> ▸ Exercise 11 (pg. 491)   Coefficient of Determination and
>   Standard Error of the Estimate

Enter the data into **L1** and **L2**. Press **STAT**, highlight **CALC**, select
4:LinReg(ax+b) and press **ENTER**. Next, press **VARS**, select **Y-VARS**, select
1:Function and press **ENTER**. Lastly, select **1:Y1** and press **ENTER** **ENTER**.

```
LinReg
 y=ax+b
 a=230.8314924
 b= -289.8094201
 r²=.9853951741
 r=.9926707279
■
```

The coefficient of determination, r^2, is .9854. This means that 98.54 % of the
variation of the Y-values is explained by the X-values.

To calculate s_e, press **2ⁿᵈ** [LIST] , select **1:RESID**, press **ENTER**, **STO** , **2ⁿᵈ**
[L3] **ENTER**. This stores the residuals to **L3**. In the formula for s_e, the
residuals, $(y_i - \hat{y}_i)$, are squared. To square these values and store them in **L4**,
press **STAT**, select **1:Edit** and move the cursor to highlight the Listname **L4**.
Press **ENTER**. Press **2ⁿᵈ** [L3] and the x^2 key. Press **ENTER**.

```
L2       L3       L4      4
123.2    43.679   1907.9
211.5    -29.6    876.34
385.5    -17.19   295.33
475.1    -19.92   396.71
641.1    30.667   940.44
716.9    -55.12   3037.7
768.2    -26.9    723.53
L4(1)=1907.857859…
```

Press **2ⁿᵈ** [QUIT] . Next, you need to find the sum of **L4**, $\sum (y_i - \hat{y}_i)^2$. Press
2ⁿᵈ [LIST] . Highlight **MATH**, select **5:sum(** and press **2ⁿᵈ** [L4] . Close the
parentheses and press **ENTER**.

© 2006 Pearson Education, Inc., Upper Saddle River, NJ. All rights reserved. This material is protected under all copyright laws as they currently exist.
No portion of this material may be reproduced, in any form or by any means, without permission in writing from the publisher.

```
r²=.9853951741
r=.9926707279

LRESID→L₃
{43.67903226  -2…
sum(L₄)
        11439.53051
■
```

Divide this sum by (number of observations – 2). In this example, (n - 2) = 9.
Simply press ÷ 9 and press **ENTER**.

```
LRESID→L₃
{43.67903226  -2…
sum(L₄)
        11439.53051
Ans/9
        1271.058945
■
```

Lastly, take the square root of this answer by pressing **2ⁿᵈ** [√] **2ⁿᵈ** [ANS].
Close the parentheses and press **ENTER**.

```
{43.67903226  -2…
sum(L₄)
        11439.53051
Ans/9
        1271.058945
√(Ans)
        35.65191363
■
```

© 2006 Pearson Education, Inc., Upper Saddle River, NJ. All rights reserved. This material is protected under all copyright laws as they currently exist.
No portion of this material may be reproduced, in any form or by any means, without permission in writing from the publisher.

▸ Technology (pg. 507)   Nutrients in Breakfast Cereals

Exercises 1-2: Enter the data into **L1, L2, L3** and **L4**. To construct the scatter plots, press **2ⁿᵈ** [**STAT PLOT**], select **1:Plot1** and press **ENTER**. Turn **ON** Plot1. Select **scatter plot** for **Type**. Enter the appropriate labels for **Xlist** and **Ylist** to construct each of the scatter plots.

Exercises 3: To find the correlation coefficients, press **STAT**, highlight **CALC** and select **4:LinReg(ax+b)** and enter the labels of the columns you are using for the correlation. For example, to find the correlation coefficient for "fat" and "carbohydrates", press **2ⁿᵈ** [**L3**] , **2ⁿᵈ** [**L4**].

Press **ENTER** and notice that the correlation coefficient for fat and carbohydrates is -.156.

Exercise 4: To find the regression equations, press **STAT**, highlight **CALC** and select **4:LinReg(ax+b)** and enter the labels of the columns you are using for the regression. For example, to find the regression equation for "calories" and "carbohydrates", press **2ⁿᵈ** [**L1**] , **2ⁿᵈ** [**L4**] .

Exercise 5: Use the regression equations found in Exercise 4 to do the predictions.

Exercises 6 and 7: The TI-83 does not do multiple regression.

© 2006 Pearson Education, Inc., Upper Saddle River, NJ. All rights reserved. This material is protected under all copyright laws as they currently exist. No portion of this material may be reproduced, in any form or by any means, without permission in writing from the publisher.

Chi-Square Tests and the F-Distribution

CHAPTER

10

Section 10.2

▶ Example 3 (pg. 526) Chi-Square Independence Test

Test the hypotheses: H_o:The number of days spent exercising per week is *independent* of gender vs. H_a: The number of days spent exercising per week *depends* on gender. The first step is to enter the data in the table into **Matrix A**. On the TI-83, press **MATRX**, highlight **EDIT** and press **ENTER**. On the TI-83 Plus, press 2nd **[MATRX]**. (MATRX is found above the x^{-1} key.) Highlight **EDIT** and press **ENTER**.

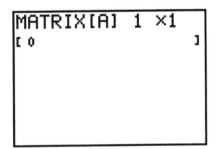

On the top row of the display, enter the size of the matrix. The matrix has 2 rows and 4 columns, so press **2** , press the right arrow key, and press **4**. Press **ENTER**. Enter the first value, 40, and press **ENTER**. Enter the second value, 53, and press **ENTER**. Continue this process and fill the matrix.

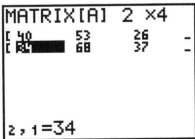

Press 2nd [Quit] . To perform the test of independence, press **STAT**, highlight **TESTS**, and select **C: χ^2-Test** and press **ENTER**.

© 2006 Pearson Education, Inc., Upper Saddle River, NJ. All rights reserved. This material is protected under all copyright laws as they currently exist. No portion of this material may be reproduced, in any form or by any means, without permission in writing from the publisher.

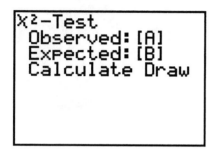

For **Observed**, **[A]** should be selected. If **[A]** is not already selected, press
MATRX, highlight **NAMES**, select **1:[A]** and press **ENTER**. For, **Expected**, **[B]**
should be selected. Move the cursor to the next line and select **Calculate** and
press **ENTER**.

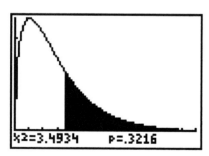

The output displays the test statistic and the P-value. Since the P-value is greater
than α, the correct decision is to **Fail to Reject** the null hypothesis. This means
that the number of days per week spent exercising is *independent* of gender.

Or, you could highlight **Draw** and press **ENTER**.

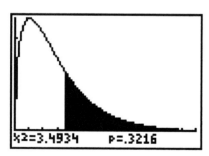

This output displays the χ^2 –**curve** with the area associated with the P-value
shaded in. The test statistic and the P-value are also displayed.

© 2006 Pearson Education, Inc., Upper Saddle River, NJ. All rights reserved. This material is protected under all copyright laws as they currently exist.
No portion of this material may be reproduced, in any form or by any means, without permission in writing from the publisher.

▶ Exercise 13 (pg. 529)   Chi-Square Test for Independence

Test the hypotheses: H_o:The Result (improvement or no change) is *independent* of Treatment (drug or placebo) vs. H_a: The Result *depends* on the Treatment.

The first step is to enter the data in the table into **Matrix A**. Press MATRX, highlight **EDIT** and press ENTER. On the top row of the display, enter the size of the matrix. The matrix has 2 rows and 2 columns, so press 2 , press the right arrow key, and press 2. Press ENTER. Enter the first value, 39, and press ENTER. Enter the second value, 25, and press ENTER. Continue this process and fill the matrix.

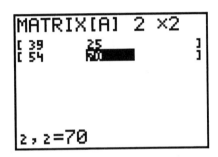

Press 2nd [Quit] . Press STAT, highlight **TESTS**, and select **C: χ^2-Test** and press ENTER. For **Observed**, **[A]** should be selected. If **[A]** is not already selected, press MATRX, highlight **NAMES**, select **1:[A]** and press ENTER. For, **Expected**, **[B]** should be selected. Move the cursor to the next line and select **Calculate** and press ENTER.

```
X²-Test
 X²=5.106317432
 P=.0238388683
 df=1
```

The output displays the test statistic and the P-value. Since the P-value is less than α, the correct decision is to **Reject** the null hypothesis. The correct recommendation is to use the drug as part of the treatment.

◀

© 2006 Pearson Education, Inc., Upper Saddle River, NJ. All rights reserved. This material is protected under all copyright laws as they currently exist. No portion of this material may be reproduced, in any form or by any means, without permission in writing from the publisher.

Section 10.3

▶ Example 3 (pg. 537)   Performing a Two-Sample F-Test

Test the hypotheses: $H_o : \sigma_1^2 \leq \sigma_2^2$ vs. $H_a : \sigma_1^2 > \sigma_2^2$. The sample statistics are: $s_1^2 = 144$, $n_1 = 10$, $s_2^2 = 100$ and $n_2 = 21$. Press **STAT**, highlight **TESTS** and select **D:2-SampFTest**. For **Inpt**, select **Stats** and press **ENTER**. On the next line, enter s_1, the standard deviation under the old system. The standard deviation is the square root of the variance, so press 2nd [$\sqrt{\ }$] and enter 144. Enter n_1 on the next line. Next, enter the standard deviation under the new system by pressing 2nd [$\sqrt{\ }$] 100. Enter n_2 on the next line. Highlight $> \sigma_2$ for the alternative hypothesis and press **ENTER**. Select **Calculate** and press **ENTER**.

```
2-SampFTest
 σ1>σ2
 F=1.44
 P=.2369000822
 Sx1=12
 Sx2=10
↓n1=10
```

The output displays the alternative hypothesis, the test statistic, the P-value and the sample statistics. Since the P-value is greater than α, the correct decision is to **Fail to Reject** the null hypothesis. There is not enough evidence to conclude that the new system decreased the variance in waiting times.

You could also select **Draw** and press **ENTER**.

© 2006 Pearson Education, Inc., Upper Saddle River, NJ. All rights reserved. This material is protected under all copyright laws as they currently exist. No portion of this material may be reproduced, in any form or by any means, without permission in writing from the publisher.

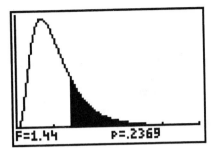

The output displays the F-distribution with the area associated with the P-value shaded in.

◀

© 2006 Pearson Education, Inc., Upper Saddle River, NJ. All rights reserved. This material is protected under all copyright laws as they currently exist.
No portion of this material may be reproduced, in any form or by any means, without permission in writing from the publisher.

▸ Exercise 19 (pg. 540)   Comparing Two Variances

Test the hypotheses: $H_o : \sigma_1^2 \leq \sigma_2^2$ vs. $H_a : \sigma_1^2 > \sigma_2^2$. The sample statistics are: $s_1 = 0.7$, $n_1 = 25$, $s_2 = 0.5$ and $n_2 = 21$. Press **STAT**, highlight **TESTS** and select **D:2-SampFTest**. For **Inpt**, select **Stats** and press **ENTER**. On the next line, enter s_1, the standard deviation under the old procedure. Enter n_1 on the next line. Next, enter the standard deviation and sample size for the new procedure and press **ENTER**. Highlight $> \sigma_2$ for the alternative hypothesis and press **ENTER**. Select **Calculate** and press **ENTER**.

```
2-SampFTest
 σ1>σ2
 F=1.96
 P=.0653066513
 Sx1=.7
 Sx2=.5
↓n1=25
```

The output displays the alternative hypothesis, the test statistic, the P-value and the sample statistics. Since the P-value is less than α, the correct decision is to **Reject** the null hypothesis. The data supports the hospital's claim that the standard deviation of the waiting times has decreased.

◀

© 2006 Pearson Education, Inc., Upper Saddle River, NJ. All rights reserved. This material is protected under all copyright laws as they currently exist. No portion of this material may be reproduced, in any form or by any means, without permission in writing from the publisher.

Section 10.4

▶ **Example 2 (pg. 547)** Performing an ANOVA Test

Test the hypotheses: $H_o : \mu_1 = \mu_2 = \mu_3$ vs. H_a :at least one mean is different from the others. Enter the data into **L1, L2,** and **L3**. Press **STAT**, highlight **TESTS** and select **F:ANOVA(** and press **ENTER**, 2nd [L1] , 2nd [L2] , 2nd [L3].

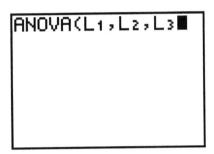

```
ANOVA(L1,L2,L3█
```

Press **ENTER** and the results will be displayed on the screen.

```
One-way ANOVA
 F=6.13023478
 p=.0063828069
 Factor
  df=2
  SS=1806.46667
↓ MS=903.233333
█
```

```
One-way ANOVA
↑ MS=903.233333
 Error
  df=27
  SS=3978.2
  MS=147.340741
 Sxp=12.1383994
█
```

The output displays the test statistic, F = 6.13, and the P-value, p = .00638. Since the P-value is less than α, the correct decision is to **Reject** the null hypothesis.

© 2006 Pearson Education, Inc., Upper Saddle River, NJ. All rights reserved. This material is protected under all copyright laws as they currently exist. No portion of this material may be reproduced, in any form or by any means, without permission in writing from the publisher.

This indicates that there is a difference in the mean flight times of the three airlines.

The output also displays all the information that is needed to set up an ANOVA table like the table on pg. 544 of your textbook.

Variation	Sum of Squares	Degrees of Freedom	Mean Squares	F
Between	1806.5	2	903.2	903.2 / 147.3
Within	3978.2	27	147.3	

Note: The TI-83 labels variation "Between" samples as variation due to the "Factor". Also, variation "Within" samples is labeled as "Error".

The final item in the output is the pooled standard deviation, Sxp = 12.14.

◀

© 2006 Pearson Education, Inc., Upper Saddle River, NJ. All rights reserved. This material is protected under all copyright laws as they currently exist. No portion of this material may be reproduced, in any form or by any means, without permission in writing from the publisher.

> ▶ Exercise 5 (pg. 549)   Performing an ANOVA Test

Test the hypotheses: $H_o : \mu_1 = \mu_2 = \mu_3$ vs. H_a :at least one mean is different from the others. Enter the data into **L1, L2,** and **L3**. Press STAT, highlight **TESTS** and select **F:ANOVA(** and press ENTER, 2nd [L1] , 2nd [L2] , 2nd [L3]. Press ENTER and the results will be displayed on the screen.

```
One-way ANOVA
 F=.7710495401
 p=.4751840735
 Factor
  df=2
  SS=1.25332083
↓ MS=.626660417
```

```
One-way ANOVA
↑ MS=.626660417
 Error
  df=21
  SS=17.067475
  MS=.812736905
 Sxp=.90151922
■
```

The output displays the test statistic, F = 0.77, and the P-value, p = 0.4752. Since the P-value is greater than α, the correct decision is to **Fail to Reject** the null hypothesis. The data does not support the claim that at least one mean cost per month is different.

◀

© 2006 Pearson Education, Inc., Upper Saddle River, NJ. All rights reserved. This material is protected under all copyright laws as they currently exist.
No portion of this material may be reproduced, in any form or by any means, without permission in writing from the publisher.

▶ Exercise 14 (pg. 552) Performing an ANOVA Test

Test the hypotheses: $H_o : \mu_1 = \mu_2 = \mu_3 = \mu_4$ vs. H_a :at least one mean is different from the others. Enter the data into **L1, L2, L3** and **L4** . Press **STAT**, highlight **TESTS** and select **F:ANOVA(** and press **ENTER**, 2nd [L1] [,] 2nd [L2] [,] 2nd [L3] [,] 2nd [L4]. Press **ENTER** and the results will be displayed on the screen.

```
One-way ANOVA
 F=8.4596944
 p=2.1962975E-4
 Factor
  df=3
  SS=61130.6776
↓ MS=20376.8925
```

```
One-way ANOVA
↑ MS=20376.8925
 Error
  df=36
  SS=86713.3134
  MS=2408.70315
 Sxp=49.0785406
■
```

The output displays the test statistic, F = 8.46, and the P-value, p = .0002196. Since the P-value is less than α, the correct decision is to **Reject** the null hypothesis. The data supports the claim that the mean energy consumption for at least one region is different.

◀

© 2006 Pearson Education, Inc., Upper Saddle River, NJ. All rights reserved. This material is protected under all copyright laws as they currently exist. No portion of this material may be reproduced, in any form or by any means, without permission in writing from the publisher.

> ▶ Technology (pg. 563)   Teacher Salaries

Exercise 2: One method of testing to see if a set of data is approximately normal is to use a Normal Probability Plot. To test the data in **L1**, press 2nd [STAT PLOT] , select Plot 1 and turn **ON** Plot1. For **Type**, select the last icon on the second line. For **Data List,** press 2nd [L1]. For **Data Axis**, select **X**. For **Mark**, select the first icon. Press ZOOM and 9 to display the normal plot.

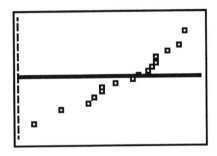

Data that is approximately normally distributed will have a plot that looks fairly linear. Although this graph is not perfectly straight, it is fairly linear and it is therefore reasonable to conclude that the data is approximately normal. Repeat this process to check the other datasets for normality.

Exercise 3: Test the hypotheses: $H_o\ \sigma_1^{\ 2} = \sigma_2^{\ 2}$ vs. $H_a : \sigma_1^{\ 2} \neq \sigma_2^2$ for each pair of samples. This test requires values for s_1 and s_2. To obtain these values, enter the data into **L1, L2** and **L3**. To find the standard deviation for **L1**, press STAT, highlight **CALC** and press **L1** ENTER. To find the standard deviation for **L2**, press STAT, highlight **CALC**, press [L2] ENTER. Repeat this process to get the standard deviation of **L3**.

For each comparison, press STAT, highlight **TESTS** and select **D:2-SampFTest**. For **Inpt**, select **Stats** and press ENTER. To compare $\sigma_1^{\ 2} and \sigma_2^{\ 2}$, enter s_1 , the sample standard deviation. Enter n_1, the corresponding sample size, on the next line. Next, enter s_2 and n_2. Highlight $\neq \sigma_2^{\ 2}$ for the alternative hypothesis and press ENTER. Select **Calculate** and press ENTER. Repeat this process to compare $\sigma_1^{\ 2} and \sigma_3^{\ 2}$. Finally compare $\sigma_2^{\ 2} and \sigma_3^{\ 2}$.

Exercise 4: Test the hypotheses: $H_o : \mu_1 = \mu_2 = \mu_3$ vs. H_a :at least one mean is different from the others. Press STAT, highlight **TESTS** and select **F:ANOVA(** and press ENTER, 2nd [L1] , 2nd [L2] , 2nd [L3] . Press ENTER and the results will be displayed on the screen.

Exercise 5: Repeat Exercises 1 - 4 using this second set of data.

© 2006 Pearson Education, Inc., Upper Saddle River, NJ. All rights reserved. This material is protected under all copyright laws as they currently exist. No portion of this material may be reproduced, in any form or by any means, without permission in writing from the publisher.